Chris Styles
15 Newton Ave
Rugby
21, 9, 09

The Jurisprudence of Lord Denning
A Study in Legal History
Volume III
Freedom under the Law
Lord Denning as Master of the Rolls 1962-1982

The Jurisprudence of Lord Denning
A Study in Legal History
Volume III
Freedom under the Law:
Lord Denning as Master of the Rolls, 1962-1982

By

Charles Stephens

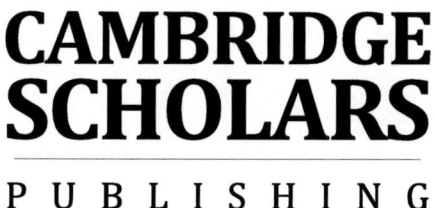

The Jurisprudence of Lord Denning
A Study in Legal History
Volume III
Freedom under the Law: Lord Denning as Master of the Rolls, 1962-1982, by Charles Stephens

This book first published 2009

Cambridge Scholars Publishing

12 Back Chapman Street, Newcastle upon Tyne, NE6 2XX, UK

British Library Cataloguing in Publication Data
A catalogue record for this book is available from the British Library

Copyright © 2009 by Charles Stephens

All rights for this book reserved. No part of this book may be reproduced, stored in a retrieval system, or transmitted, in any form or by any means, electronic, mechanical, photocopying, recording or otherwise, without the prior permission of the copyright owner.

ISBN (10): 1-4438-1246-3, ISBN (13): 978-1-4438-1246-7

As a three volume set: ISBN (10): 1-4438-1252-8, ISBN (13): 978-1-4438-1252-8

I went back to Oxford for a day or two to try for that most coveted of academic awards – a fellowship at All Souls. I could answer the legal questions all right, but we had to read Latin aloud. My pronounciation was mixed between the old and the new. That did not suit that stronghold of classicists. So I joined the distinguished company of 'Failed All Souls'! Like the more numerous company of 'Failed BA'.

—Lord Denning *The Family Story* [London 1981] pp.38-39

Yes, I could have been a judge but I never had the Latin, never had the Latin for the judging. I just never had sufficient of it to get through the rigorous judging exams. They're noted for their rigour. People came staggering out saying, 'My God, what a rigorous exam' – and so I became a miner instead. A coal miner. I managed to get through the mining exams – they're not very rigorous. They only ask one question. They say 'Who are you?' and I got 75% for that.

—Peter Cook *Sitting on the Bench* [Fortune Theatre 1961]
Tragically I Was An Only Twin – The Complete Peter Cook ed. William Cook [London 2002] p. 45

Table of Contents

Foreword ix

Acknowledgments xi

Introduction 1
The Obituaries of Lord Denning

Chapter One 12
Lord Denning as Author

Chapter Two 73
English Themes and Variations

Chapter Three 151
The History of England 1962-1982

Chapter Four 200
Someone Must be Trusted. Let it be the Judges

Conclusion 224
Lord Denning, Enoch Powell, Margaret Thatcher and The Constitution

Cases 238

Bibliography 251

Index 259

Foreword

I dedicate my work on Lord Denning, which is also a contribution to the study of English identity and the nature of English history, to three friends: Nirad C. Chaudhuri, Hamish Henderson and Michael Stenton.

In Oxford, during the winter of 1975-6 Mr Chaudhuri, or Nirad Babu as he should properly be called, the author of *The Autobiography of an Unknown Indian*, *A Passage to England* and *Thy Hand Great Anarch*, introduced me to the tragic history of the Bengali nation. In so doing, he reminded me that great nations can die, as well as be born and flourish. Like Lord Denning, Mr Chaudhuri lived to be 100.

In 1977, and over the following years until his death in 2002, Hamish Henderson shared his love of the Scottish nation with me and taught me to respect and honour that people. Hamish, a great poet, author of *Freedom Come All Ye* and the translator of Antonio Gramsci, was a 'man of the Left' but he was amused and touched by the fact that one of his poems appeared on the same double facing page as one of those written by Enoch Powell in an anthology of war poems entitled *The Terrible Rain: The War Poets 1939-1945*, edited by Brian Gardner and published by Methuen in 1966. The other poem on that double facing page was written by Frank Thompson, the brother of E.P. Thompson, author of *The Making of the English Working Class*; Frank Thompson was executed by agents of Stalin in Bulgaria in 1944. Enoch Powell retained the friendship of Michael Foot throughout his life; Tony Benn attended his memorial service. Serious students of the proper history of nations are not concerned with 'Left' or 'Right', designations emanating from the French revolutionary entity and progenitor of the 'Terror' known as the National Convention, but with piety, patriotism and loyalty; perennial virtues which were known to Herodotus and Thucydides as well at to Livy and Tacitus.

Between 1991 and 1997, in Cambridge, Michael Stenton and I taught students from the United States, Japan, Germany, France, Russia, Denmark and many other nations about the nature of English national identity. During those hot July and August days, when the Treaty of Maastricht was debated, turbulently, in Parliament, and the Conservative government slowly declined into sad incoherence and abject disgrace, Michael, a member of Peterhouse, instructed me in the continuities and complexities of English history. This work was conceived, if not completed, during that period.

The German philosopher G.W.F. Hegel observed that "wenn die Philosophie ihr Grau in Grau malt, dann ist eine Gestalt des Lebens alt geworden, und mit Grau in Grau läßt sie sich nicht verjüngen, sondern nur erkennen; die Eule der Minerva beginnt erst mit der einbrechenden Dämmerung ihren Flug" [*Grundlinien der Philosophie des Rechts* [1821] Vorrede]. It may be that the long story of England has not yet entered its *dämmerung* but, whether or whenever that eventuality may come to pass, Lord Denning will surely have an honoured place amongst the wisest of its many worthies.

ACKNOWLEDGMENTS

My wife Karin has been unfailingly supportive and optimistic. In 1998, she gave me a copy of Lord Denning's *The Family Story* for my birthday; it has proved to be an indispensable *vade mecum* and a valued *enchiridion*. I have heard it said that lawyers who use too much Latin are probably practiced deceivers and we all know that we must be on guard against Greeks bearing gifts; perhaps those who attend to the wisdom of both Rome and Greece, listening to both, but deferring to neither, are protected from the perils of fraudulent misrepresentation and sudden assault. My students at Birkbeck College, the Open University and Queen's College in Harley Street enabled me to retain a sense of proportion and to realise that my lucubrations about Lord Denning, the Law and the nature of English identity had points of contact with the quotidian world.

I am also beholden to Professor Patrick Hanafin and Dr. Piyel Haldar. Along with their colleagues at Birkbeck College's Department of Law, they guided me, with a 'kindly light', through the rebarbative thickets of 'critical legal theory'; a practice which might, by its detractors, be aptly named 'foul smelling and loathsome', as Peter Goodrich, one of its notable practitioners once described the common law. This experience provided me with a metaphorical, but indispensable, grindstone on which I sharpened the blade of my delight in the traditional patriotic verities espoused by Lord Denning whose portrait presides, in what must often be baffled perplexity, over the varied proceedings which take place in the Council Room of Birkbeck College.

Professor Gary Slapper has provided me with support and encouragement. We share a common affection for the work of the late Peter Cook. In the course of swapping favourite Peter Cook sketches by means of YouTube, I was reminded of the ways in which the lives of Peter Cook and Lord Denning were intertwined, not least in the case of *Goldsmith v Sperrings Ltd* in 1977. Like a white knight, Lord Denning came to the aid of *Private Eye* when that noble vehicle of true journalistic endeavour faced a grim nemesis in the form of Sir Jams Fishpaste. Lord Denning often joked that he possessed 'every Christian virtue, except resignation'. I recall, from the early 1980s, a cartoon in *Private Eye* which made use of this phrase to good effect. I feel that Lord Denning was the only judge of whom *Private Eye* might have approved. He was not quite

Mr Justice Cocklecarrot, once memorably played by Clive Dunn, but I feel that he could have been depicted on the stage by an actor made up from bits and pieces of all of those who entertained us in *Dad's Army*, except perhaps for the very Scottish John Laurie. H.E. Bates, like Lord Denning, a lover of Kent and of the kinder aspects of the English character, could have written the script. 'Pop' Larkin would have certainly been an attractive litigant in Lord Denning's eyes and I am quite certain that, just as Mandy Rice Davies thought him 'the nicest judge I have ever met', so Mariette and Primrose Larkin would have reminded him of the days when 'it was bluebell time in Kent'.

I owe a particular debt of gratitude to Professor Tony Lentin. We first met as trainee tutors for the Open University's pioneering foundation course in Law: *Rules, Rights and Justice: An Introduction to Law*. We were introduced to each other by Professor Gary Slapper as fellow historians. A facile comment by another trainee tutor about Lord Denning's 'racism' drew us together in shared indignation. I was already engrossed in the research on which this study of Lord Denning's jurisprudence is based. We spent the evening in pleasant discussion of Lord Denning, Lloyd-George, Lord Sumner and many other congenial matters. Professor Lentin shares my profound admiration for Lord Denning and has provided me with the support and encouragement which has enabled me to maintain the enthusiasm and determination necessary to bring my work to a successful conclusion. Unlike Professor Lentin, who corresponded with him and watched him in court, I never met Lord Denning, knowing him only from my study of the Law. On the final page of his biography of Lord Sumner, a very different, but equally great judge, Professor Lentin wrote these words:

> As an honorary Fellow of Magdalen and a frequent visitor to Oxford, Sumner often dined in College. On one such occasion in the early 1920s, a shy young law student was ushered into his presence. 'I was invited into the Senior Common Room to meet him. Even on that short occasion, I felt that he was a rather formidable character. He looked stern. He did not have an easy manner with young people like me'. The young student was the future Lord Denning, [Lentin, A. *The Last Political Law Lord: Lord Sumner [1859-1934]* Cambridge Scholars Publishing 2008 p. 258]

As I was growing up and coming to know the world, I always felt reassured by Lord Denning's presence in our national life. At the back of my mind I felt that we were all safe as long as he was Master of the Rolls. The origins of this project lie in those memories. In 1998, I started an LLB at Birkbeck College, of which Lord Denning had been President between

1953 and 1983. My first steps in the Law were taken while he was still alive and, though I never met him in person, there was not a week in which I did not look with affection at his portrait in the Council Room of Birkbeck College. Lord Denning is therefore the other person to whom I owe a debt of gratitude. It might seem a banal comment but without the particular warmth and humanity of his presence I should never have been able to spend nearly ten years of my life preparing this work which is dedicated to the preservation of his memory.

INTRODUCTION

THE OBITUARIES OF LORD DENNING

Lord Denning sat in the Court of Appeal as Master of the Rolls from 19th April 1962[1] until 29th Septermber 1982. As Master of the Rolls he was the senior judge in the Court of Appeal. In contrast with the House of Lords where, usually, five Law Lords hear a case, in the Court of Appeal, only three judges would sit. This meant that if one judge agreed with Lord Denning then his judgment would decide the case. Leave to appeal could be refused by the Court of Appeal, even though that refusal could be overruled by the House of Lords. Most cases were decided in the Court of Appeal; appeals to the House of Lords were the exception rather than the rule. During this period, for roughly every ten cases which ended in the Court of Appeal, one would be heard in the House of Lords. Furthermore, as Master of the Rolls, Lord Denning would be able to exert considerable influence in deciding which cases were heard in his court.[2] All of these factors meant that the Court of Appeal, and in particular the Master of the Rolls, could exercise a decisive effect on the shaping of the law, in particular in the development of constitutional law.[3]

Until 1966, the House of Lords were bound by its previous decisions; even after 1966, certainly before 1982, the House of Lords were sparing and cautious in their use of the power to override precedent which they had conferred on themselves in the Practice Statement of 1966. This meant that the House of Lords, although the final court of appeal, did not really act as a court in which the law was shaped and changed during the period in which Lord Denning was Master of the Rolls. While it could, and did, overrule a significant number of decisions made in the Court of Appeal, a determined Master of the Rolls could, for the reasons given above, exercise a more decisive effect on the development of the law than the House of Lords.[4] Lord Denning was such a Master of the Rolls.

When Lord Denning died at the age of 100 on the 5th of March 1999, a range of obituaries from anonymous tributes in the Daily Telegraph and Sunday Times, to the memoir of a fellow judge, Lord Goff in the Daily Telegraph, to more radical and critical, signed, appreciations in the

Guardian, by Sir Stephen Sedley and Geoffrey Robertson, acknowledged the significance of his role in developing English law.[5]

The Daily Telegraph obituary[6] described Lord Denning as 'a fearless champion of the rights of the common man' who was concerned with justice rather than law: 'Whenever 'Tom' Denning was faced with a situation that seemed to him dishonest, unjust or wrong, all his ingenuity and erudition would be directed to finding a remedy, even if the wrongdoer appeared to have law on his side. This was particularly the case when some powerful institution seemed to be oppressing a smaller body or individual......Denning was well placed to combat the insolence of office'. Lord Denning defined his concept of justice as 'the solution that the majority of right-minded people would consider fair'; the Telegraph's obituarist linked this devotion to justice with Lord Denning's religious faith, pointing out that 'he liked to have the Bible close to hand when writing judgments' and that, for many years, he was President of the Lawyer's Christian Fellowship. The fact that Lord Denning's use of language was 'simple, clear, vigorous and direct' and therefore accessible to the 'common man', in contrast with much of the language of the law, was also stressed by the obituarist. In the mind of the obituarist of the Daily Telegraph Lord Denning was a defender of a traditional conception of the English constitution which protected the rights of the 'common man' against those who abused their power in an oppressive manner. The English constitution was such that justice, of the kind defined by Lord Denning as 'the solution that the majority of right-minded people would consider fair', was accessible to all. The Daily Telegraph's obituary presented Lord Denning as an exemplar of Englishness, emphasising that he was 'fiercely patriotic'.

The association of Lord Denning's Englishness with a notion of justice which accorded with the conceptions of 'right-minded' people and which defended the rights of the 'common man' against the potential oppressions of the powerful, a justice rooted in Christian and patriotic values, was echoed in the leader in the same edition of the Daily Telegraph. The leader writer wrote of 'a deep and almost tangible Englishness' which 'shone through his many celebrated judgments. He was patriotic, sceptical and humane; intelligent without being intellectual'. However, after this eulogy, the leader writer's tone changed: 'His Englishness was sometimes a weakness. Few contemporary jurists exhibited his passion for fair play; but his sense of justice could make for remarkably bad law'. Most damning of all, in the mind of the Daily Telegraph's leader writer: 'It was in Lord Denning's time that the judiciary began to get a taste for challenging Parliament. His own forays into this field were always well-intentioned and usually harmless; but they paved the way for a generation of judges who, influenced by the practices of the Continent, saw themselves as having an explicit political role'. Lord Denning's enthusiasm for the reception of European law was also noted by the leader writer; just as he linked Lord Denning's misconceived, but 'well-intentioned' challenges to Parliament with the actions of his successors, so Lord Denning's enthusiasm for European law was associated, by the use of his own words,[7] with the enthusiastic reception of European law by the judiciary, a development profoundly distasteful to the minds of the readers of the Daily Telegraph. In notable contrast with the obituarist's judgment that Lord Denning embodied a traditional conception of the English constitution as a bulwark which protected 'right-minded' individuals from oppression, the leader writer concluded that Lord Denning's legacy was not only mixed, but detrimental in that it had encouraged the judiciary to challenge the will of Parliament and had also enabled European law, legitimised by the decisions of the judiciary, to transform the English legal order. This view of Lord Denning identified him as a radical maverick, rather than as a defender of the traditional conception of the English legal order.

The Sunday Times obituary[8] struck a decidedly equivocal note depicting Lord Denning as both 'radical', even 'revolutionary', and also 'conventional, 'square' and even 'reactionary'. On the 'reactionary' side, the obituarist noted that Lord Denning voted against the suspension of hanging in 1965, and stressed that 'in sexual matters he was firmly on the side of orthodox morality....was even more explicit in his condemnation of homosexuality....was against the supersession of the religious oath in court by a simple promise to tell the truth'. According to the Sunday Times obituarist: 'The solution of the apparent paradox of the 'revolutionary' and the 'establishment' figure was that what Denning cared for, deeply and passionately, were fundamental and traditional values - religion, the Christian orthodox morality, an ordered society and fair play. He had a romantic belief in English law as one of the supreme creations of man; if he laid what some thought were sacrilegious hands upon the sacred scrolls, it was not because he loved the law less but because he loved justice more. He felt that when the law ceased to be sensible, flexible and fair it was failing in its vital and historic mission; if it needed a shaking-up in order to ensure that it adopted a modern and relevant posture, he was ready and willing to administer the necessary and salutary shock'. The Sunday Times obituarist, like that of the Daily Telegraph, considered that Lord Denning was 'dedicated to defending the rights of the individual, the ordinary citizen, against the forces of bureaucratic government'.

Lord Goff[9] considered that Lord Denning was 'the outstanding judge of this century in the Common Law world....he reminded a whole generation of lawyers that the duty of a judge is not merely to apply the law but to do justice'. Lord Goff saw Lord Denning as a reformer of the law: 'He taught us all that, if justice was to be done, the Common Law could not stand still - it must be developed to respond to the demands of justice in a living society'. Lord Goff stressed 'the extraordinary combination of ..... tradition and modernity in his outlook'. Lord Goff concluded his appreciation by quoting the words of a document which he had read to Lord Denning, now blind, on the occasion of his 100th birthday: 'His judgments will be read by generations yet unborn. His fame will reverberate down the centuries'. This was no hyperbole. The prediction is well founded'.

The views of the obituarists of the Daily Telegraph and the Sunday Times were echoed in the eulogies of the recently deceased Lord Denning by other figures, notable in 1999, delivered in the form of easily digestible soundbites. Lord Irvine of Lairg then Lord Chancellor, said that the name of Denning was a 'byword for the law itself. His judgments were models of simple English which ordinary people understood'.[10] Tony Blair, the Labour Prime Minister, said, with characteristic banality, that 'he was prepared to use the law for its true purpose - in the interests of fairness and justice. He had a tremendous feel for ordinary people'.[11] Lord Hailsham, a former Lord Chancellor, said that Lord Denning 'would go down in history as one of the great and controversial judges of the twentieth century'.[12] Lady Thatcher, a former Prime Minister, said that Lord Denning was 'probably the greatest English judge of modern times. He combined a love of liberty with a passion for justice. His life and work will provide inspiration for generations to come'.[13] Lord Donaldson, his successor as Master of the Rolls, said that Lord Denning was 'always looking to see whether the law could be improved and had a particular regard to those whom he regarded as the underdog. He was a very great communicator, and put forward his views in words which the ordinary man in the street could fully understand, and which the tabloid reporter could report'.[14] Lord Lester of Herne Hill said that Lord Denning 'defended the vulnerable and weak and gave enlightened leadership at a time when English judicial interpretation was too often narrowly literal and too deferential to the executive'.[15]

Two, rather more considered, assessments of Lord Denning, which offered a rather different interpretation of his career, by Geoffrey Robertson and Sir Stephen Sedley, at that time a High Court judge, were published in the Guardian.[16] Geoffrey Robertson[17] argued that Lord Denning was the first English judge to 'have any notion of 'rights', albeit conceiving them as powers belonging to citizens through birth [in England], status [an unblemished and hardworking life] and loyalty, to the Crown'. Robertson continued: 'It was Denning's crusade to do 'justice' - ie to produce a result which favoured the 'good citizen' - that led him [single-handedly at first] to revolutionise the civil law to reflect the dictates of middle-class morality'. Robertson saw Lord Denning as, up to a point' a radical figure: 'His iconoclasm seemed to presage a revolution in the courts to compare with those increasingly on the streets; for the 60s law student, the Beatles, Vietnam protests, and Denning's dissenting judgments were all part of a brave new world'. Lord Denning's credo was 'I must do justice, whatever the law may be'. For Robertson, 'this revolutionary invitation - to tear up the rule book and reach a popular result - was a welcome rejection of the 'slot machine jurisprudence' theory of deciding cases by reference to precedent'. However, there were limitations to Lord Denning's radicalism: 'He always found for David against the State Goliath when David was, for example, a television license-holder unconstitutionally mulcted by the Home Office, but not when he was an alien suspected of subversion whom the Home Office wished to deport'. Robertson was referring to the case of Mark Hosenball;[18] in his opinion Lord Denning's worst decision. Robertson concluded that Lord Denning 'played Prospero to lawyers of his generation, creating the result his own opinionated mind believed 'just' through the alchemy of obscure precedents he found in old books. But it is not the role of judges to court public applause; in the end, his prejudices became his principles'.

Sir Stephen Sedley[19] described Lord Denning as 'one - perhaps the last - of a sparse succession of major judicial figures who have succeeded in shaping areas of the law into conformity with a strongly-held world view'. Sedley continued: 'Denning's most abiding and probably least deserved reputation was as a liberal. He adhered throughout his life to a conservative set of personal and public values'. Sedley emphasised Lord Denning's distaste for any interference with 'individual enterprise' and his 'paternalistic, and sometimes simplistic, views on social questions'. Sedley considered that 'his literary style, in fact, is perhaps his most underrated achievement', in that it enabled him to speak 'directly and compellingly to ordinary people in well-constructed and lucid prose. Concepts which lawyers had struggled to articulate, clashes of doctrine which seemed insoluble, would emerge in his judgments as crystalline statements of principle.....the accessibility of language was the rock on which his popularity and influence were built'.[20]

However, like Robertson, Sedley noted the limits of Lord Denning's tolerance: 'The hate-figures of the popular press - students, trade unions, squatters, prisoners - rarely won in Denning's court. His reputation was also sullied by his views on race, which were believed to have precipitated his retirement in 1982'. However, Sedley concluded that 'it would be wrong to remember Lord Denning as a judicial Alf Garnett as it would be to remember him as a beacon of judicial virtue. He was complex in his strategic views, and in many ways a vigorous modernist'. Sedley identified Lord Denning's contribution to the judicial review of executive and local government decisions and his coining of the concept of 'legitimate expectation' as notable contributions to the development of the law while criticising his 'faith in the infallibility of the Security Services' and noted that 'the peroration of his judgment in the Birmingham Six case - 'This case shows what a civilised country we are' - will remain an ironic epitaph [not on the seven other judges who shared his conclusion] but on him'.

Sedley also noted Lord Denning's 'strongly authoritarian approach to public affairs [which] marched with a rigorous view of private morality and a patrician attitude to individuals' which was clearly revealed in his 1963 report on the Profumo affair. However, Sedley also remarked that Lord Denning's response to EEC law 'suprised everybody who thought they knew his foibles. In a 1974 judgment which ranks among the great passages of English judicial prose, he avoided both grudging acquiescence and overt welcome by using as an image the great forces of nature which an island people had traditionally coped with and survived: 'The treaty is like an incoming tide. It flows into the estuaries and up the rivers. It cannot be held back'. On these great issues of political power, Lord Denning was a realist in his stewardship of the law'. Sedley's judgment was that 'if there is a label for Lord Denning's stance as a lawmaker, it is radical conservatism. The emergence of just this as the dominant mode of the political state during Lord Denning's later years is perhaps an index of his prescience and a confirmation of his status, not merely as a judge, but as a historic figure of enduring importance'.

Lord Denning's contribution to the shaping of the law was clearly controversial and complex. He can be claimed as a traditionalist, defending the ancient English constitution, or condemned as a reactionary, even a racist, who defended the secret state, was hostile to trade unions, rejected the 'permissive society', feminism and the growing tolerance of sexual minorities and was anxious about the impact of immigration from the former Commonwealth. However, he can also be seen as a reformer, a pioneer of judicial review of the executive and a major contributor to the reception of European law by the English courts. As Sedley observed, he could also be seen as a forerunner of the 'Thatcher' revolution with its insistence on the rights of the individual, Hayekian devotion to the rule of law as the basis of a market economy, rejection of the claims of Irish nationalism and hostility to the power of the organised working class. Although in some ways J.A.G. Griffith[21] criticised Lord Denning in the same way that he criticised the 'politics of the judiciary' in general as being conservative and as favouring the established order,[22] he also acknowledged Lord Denning's distinctive and constructive contribution to the development of the law: 'In practice, judges are often most reluctant to be creative in the development of the Common Law, though it is precisely there that Lord Denning had been at his most creative during his long judicial life'.[23] Hugo Young,[24] a biographer of Margaret Thatcher[25], began, but did not finish, a study of Lord Denning who fascinated him.[26] On the occasion of Lord Denning's retirement in 1982, Young wrote: 'To anyone who believes the law should liberate, not enslave, he is a beacon. He discovered that young, as a poor student, in the 1920's. He is just about the only octagenarian who has never forgotten it'.[27]

The English legal order experienced considerable stress during the period that Lord Denning was Master of the Rolls. By the time of his retirement in 1982, the outlines of a major debate about its nature and future had emerged. The English constitution is grounded on statute, moderated by judicial interpretation, and the Common Law. As Dicey emphasised,[28] the decisions of the courts were both a repository of constitutional law and also a means of developing and shaping that law. Given the relative quiescence of the House of Lords during the period in which Lord Denning was Master of the Rolls, the role of the Court of Appeal in shaping the laws of England, and the constitution itself, was decisive.[29] Although some constitutional law can be found in the statutory law of that period,[30] it is arguable, following Dicey, that the most important developments occurred in the courts and that Lord Denning's contribution was of particular signficance.

In 1962, when Lord Denning became Master of the Rolls, few doubted the superiority and stability of the English legal order. By 1982, thoughtful commentators had begun to question both the superiority and the stability of that order. The following analysis of the judgments of Lord Denning will shed light on the development of English law and the English constitution between 1962 and 1982. However, before considering Lord Denning's judgments in the Court of Appeal between 1962 and 1982, it will be necessary to examine his own writings about the law[31] in order to gain a sense of his understanding of the nature of law and the English constitution.

Notes

[1] Lord Denning was first appointed to the Court of Appeal in 1948. He was promoted to the House of Lords by Harold Macmillan on 24th April 1957. In his Romanes lecture of 1959, delivered in the University of Oxford, Lord Denning seemed to go so far as to claim that the House of Lords, in its judicial capacity, should appropriate legislative powers to itself enabling it to change the law when it needed changing, rather than having to wait on the more leisurely process of Parliamentary law making. Although the Practice Statement of 1966 was a move in this direction, in 1959 such radicalism was anathema to the senior Law Lord, Lord Simonds. Although Lord Denning often dissented from the majority decision in the Lords, his dissent could make little or no impact. Frequently he was at odds with Lord Simonds in particular who once memorably expressed his distaste for Lord Denning's preference for 'filling in the gaps' left by poor or confusing drafting as 'a naked usurpation of the legislative function under the thin disguise of interpretation'. According to the Sunday Times obituary, it was the frustration which resulted from conflict with Lord Simonds that led Lord Denning to accept the apparent demotion from the House of Lords consequent on his acceptance of the office of Master of the Rolls in April 1962. In the Court of Appeal, Lord Denning's judgments, even the dissenting ones, could have much more impact on the shaping of the law than was possible in the House of Lords. It is also worth noting that Lord Denning's appointment to the Court of Appeal on 19th April 1962 was made by Harold Macmillan. Macmillan was an unorthodox Conservative who was the author of a number of relatively radical initiatives between 1957 and 1962 ranging from the creation of Life Peerages, the setting up of the National Economic Development Council, the establishment of new Universities and, most radically of all, the application, in 1961 of the United Kingdom to join the European Economic Community. Macmillan's appointment of Lord Denning to the Court of Appeal, as Master of the Rolls, in April 1962 could be seen in this context as an unorthodox, but inherently conservative, attempt to modernise the institution of the law along similar lines to those which Macmillan adopted with regard to other institutions during the period of his premiership. Lord Denning's appointment came between the Orpington by-election, in the seat next door to that of the Prime Minister, which the Conservatives lost to the Liberals, and the so-called 'night of the long knives' on 13th July 1962 when Macmillan sacked seven Cabinet ministers, including the Lord Chancellor. It was a time of decided instability in the fortunes of the Conservative government. In this context, Macmillan's appointment of Lord Denning to conduct the inquiry into the circumstances surrounding the resignation of John Profumo in June 1963 should be considered an astute manouevre; the deployment of a conservative, but unorthodox, judge of Lord Denning's calibre was perhaps the only way in which

the gravest crisis of his premiership could have been resolved satisfactorily. In the febrile atmosphere of the summer of 1963, a judge of the stamp of Lord Simonds would not have been able to construct a report which would been credible, let alone have saved the government. Lord Denning did not disappoint; his Report saved Macmillan, perhaps even the Establishment itself. Despite his modest criticism of his conduct as Prime Minster during the affair, Lord Denning retained a substantial amount of respect for Harold Macmillan. He concluded his account of the whole business in *Landmarks in the Law* by quoting from the letter which Harold Macmillan wrote to him on his retirement on 28th July 1982 in which he praised him for his 'commonsense, fair play and justice' and concluded 'as Lord Mansfield and Lord Camden, so Lord Denning'. Lord Denning then commented that 'Macmillan was a very great man'. *Landmarks in the Law* [London 1984 p. 365].

[2] Lord Denning sat in Court Number 3 in the Royal Courts of Justice

[3] According to Dicey, Constitutional Law was made in the ordinary courts of law: 'Every man's legal rights and liberties are almost invariably determined by the ordinary courts of the realm, and each man's individual rights are far less the result of our constitution than the basis on which that constitution is founded'. Dicey, A.V. *The Law of the Constitution* 8th Edition 1915 lv

[4] Stevens, R. *The House of Lords: Law and Politics 1800-1976* [London 1979]; Patterson, A. *The Law Lords* [London 1982]

[5] Other evaluations of Lord Denning's contribution to the law made after his retirement in 1982 include: Jowell, J. and McAuslan, P. *Lord Denning: The Judge and the Law* [London 1984]; Heward, E. *Lord Denning* [London 1990] 2nd ed [London 1997]. The journal of the Law School of the University of Buckingham, the Denning Law Journal, published an edition entirely dedicated to Lord Denning in 1999. Many of these papers were delivered at a conference, organised by the Law School of the University of Buckingham to mark the 100th birthday of Lord Denning on 23rd January 1999.

[6] Daily Telegraph 6.3.99

[7] In 1990, in a letter to the Daily Telegraph, quoted by the leader writer, Lord Denning wrote: 'No longer is European law an incoming tide flowing up the estuaries of England. It is now like a tidal wave, bringing down our sea-walls and flowing inland over our fields and houses - to the dismay of all'.

[8] The Sunday Times 7.3.99

[9] The Daily Telegraph 6.3.99 Lord Goff of Chievely, Eton and New College, Oxford, Lord of Appeal in Ordinary 1986-2001

[10] Ibid

[11] Ibid

[12] Ibid

[13] Ibid

[14] Ibid

[15] Ibid

[16] The Guardian 6.3.99

[17] QC, author of *Freedom, the Individual and the Law* [London 1989] and *Crimes against Humanity* [London 1999]
[18] [1977] 1 WLR 766
[19] High Court [1992-2002] Court of Appeal [2002-]
[20] Sedley went on to qualify this judgment with a nice piece of irony: 'When, not long after his retirement, he appeared in full wig and gown on 'Jim'll Fix It' and tried Little Noddy for knocking down PC Plod, what stuck in the mind was not the incongruity but the homogeneity of it - the same benign moralism as the legal profession had known for 40 years, in prose begotten by Samuel Smiles upon Enid Blyton'. Sedley also pointed out that: 'Such was his authority that lawyers now believe that Lord Mansfield, giving judgment in favour of the slave James Somersett, said: 'The air of England is to pure for any slave to breathe: let the black go free'. But the line appears in no contemporary report of Mansfield's judgment: the phrase has a long lineage, but the attribution originates, so far as is known, in Lord Denning's celebrated 1949 Hamlyn Lectures, *Freedom under the Law*.
[21] *The Politics of the Judiciary* 5th edition [London 1997]
[22] Griffith places a quotation by Lord Denning from Anthony Sampson's *The Changing Anatomy of Britain* [London 1981] p. 159 on the first page of his book: 'The most politically influential of the judges however, has been the Master of the Rolls, Lord Denning.....with his own modest roots he dismisses the attacks on a class-based judiciary: 'The youngsters believe that we come from a narrow background - it's all nonsense - they get it from that man Griffith'.
[23] Griffith, J.A.G. *The Politics of the Judiciary* 5th Edition [London 1997] p. 289
[24] 1973-1984 Political Editor of the Times; 1981-1984 Joint Deputy Editor of the Times; 1984-2003 Political Editor of the Guardian; Chairman of the Scott Trust [1989- 2003]; author of *This Blessed Plot: Britain and Europe from Churchill to Blair* [London 1998]
[25] *One of Us: a Political Biography of Margaret Thatcher* [London 1989]
[26] Obituary The Guardian 23.9.03
[27] The Sunday Times 30.5.82, also quoted in Lord Denning *The Closing Chapter* [London 1983 p. 13
[28] Dicey, A.V. Op. cit. lv
[29] Between April 1962 and September 1982 1072 judgments of Lord Denning were reported in the All England Law Reports. The argument of this study is based on a close analysis of all of these judgments.
[30] Commonwealth Immigration Act 1962, Peerages Act 1963, Race Relations Act 1965, Parliamentary Commissioner Act 1967, Representation of the People Act 1969, Equal Pay Act 1970, Industrial Relations Act 1971, European Communities Act 1972, Local Government Act 1972, Northern Ireland [Temporary Provisions] Act 1973, Border Poll Act 1973, Northern Ireland Constitution Act 1973, Trade Union and Labour Relations Act 1974, Referendum Act 1975, Sex Discrimination Act 1975, Race Relations Act 1976, British Nationality Act 1981, Northern Ireland Act 1982.

[31] Lord Denning made a series of public statements about the law during a period of judicial reticence. Although Lord Radcliffe, *The Law and its Compass* [London 1960]; *Not in Feather Beds* [London 1968]; Lord Devlin, *The Enforcement of Morals* [London 1965]; Lord Reid, 'The Judge as Law-maker' Journal of the Society of Public Teachers of Law [1972] 12 pp. 22-29 and Lord Scarman, *English Law: the New Dimension* [London 1974] made important interventions during this period, Lord Denning's interventions were arguably more significant. The Hamlyn Lectures, published as *Freedom under the Law* [London 1949], the Romanes Lecture of 1959, the *Report into the Circumstances Leading to the Resignation of John Profumo the Secretary of State for War* Cmnd 2152, *The Discipline of Law* [London 1979], *The Due Process of Law* [London 1980], the Richard Dimbleby Lecture, *The Misuse of Power* [London 1980], *The Family Story* [London 1981] and *What Next in the Law* [London 1982] amount to a unique set of public interventions by a judge sitting in the Court of Appeal and the House of Lords during the period of the so-called 'Kilmuir rules'.

CHAPTER ONE

LORD DENNING AS AUTHOR

The Family Story [1981]

The Family Story[1] was Lord Denning's attempt at autobiography. In some respects, this work is a conventional work of family piety combined with a brief outline of his legal career. However, it also reveals Lord Denning's understanding of the nature of English history and the English legal order not least by placing his own life and work within the larger English story, of which his own family story is an epitome.

For Lord Denning, 'family' is the foundation of society. The family maintained a 'united front',[2] thereby creating a stable foundation for the social order. Divorce therefore posed a threat to the maintenance of that order: 'A broken home leaves an indelible mark - a dark, dark mark - on the character and temperament of the child'.[3] The English constitution, the body of the nation, was founded on the family: 'Family trees only take root in a marriage bed'.[4] The line of descent from the past maintained the continuity of that order: 'Descent by blood counts a good deal. Heredity it is called'[5]. Family and the descent through the generations by way of the 'marriage bed' combined to produce 'our native English race'.[6] The origins of that line of descent were lost in 'time immemorial' but preserved in the continuity of the name: 'The first beginnings are myth - derived only from names'.[7]

The English race[8] was located in a specific geographical place whose influence was also of fundamental importance: 'Surrounding play their part - fields, hills, rivers and mills'.[9] In the English towns, everyone knew everyone else, as a result there was no wrong doing.[10] Education, based on language, literature and history, also played its part: 'The teachers who taught us. All go to the making of us'.[11] Religion 'perhaps the chiefest influence of all...faith in God handed down from generation to generation',[12] completed the English constitution which, growing out of its 'root' in the 'marriage bed', embraced the whole land of England.

Family, land, language,[13] history, literature[14] and religion,[15] for Lord Denning these were the elements which made the England which he knew and loved

In 1957, when appointed to the House of Lords, he took the title Denning of Whitchurch, the place of his birth. In 1960, Lord Denning returned to Whitchurch, the town of his birth, buying a house, the Lawns, where he was able to live in the style of a seventeeth or eighteenth century judge such as Coke or Mansfield, 'in the sort of establishment which judges of olden days used to live'.[16] As he put it: 'I am back in the place where I was born. It is good for a man to have his roots deep down. It is good for him to return to the place of his childhood. It is good for him to meet and talk with those whom he knew when he was a boy. And to feel that he has done something to keep its character as a period piece'.[17] As Master of the Rolls, from 1962 to 1982, Lord Denning lived in the place of his birth and felt that his life, and therefore his judgments, were at one with England herself.

Within this framework, Lord Denning told his own 'family story' in such a way that that 'family story' was made congruent with the history of England thereby placing him, its most recent descendant, in the line of a tradition which conferred the authority to 'speak for England'. The establishment of such a genealogy gave its inheritor the authority to claim that as a judge, as Coke put it, he could speak the law which was a living thing within his breast.[18]

Lord Denning defined the descent of the English as issuing from the Saxon, the Viking and the Norman.[19] From the Saxon comes 'fair dealing', from the Viking 'hardihood to withstand the storm' and from the Norman the 'capacity to lead'.[20] He aligned his own 'family story' with these elements by linking his name 'Denning' with 'Dane-ing', 'son of the Dane'[21] suggesting that his maternal forebear, living in Somerset, as a West Saxon, must have married a Dane during the Danish invasions of the ninth century.[22] He pointed out that 'law' has a Danish etymology thereby associating his legal career with a Danish, paternal forebear. However, his Christian name Alfred associated him with the Anglo-Saxon king and lawgiver, Alfred the Great. Lord Denning noted that he was born, and christened, in 1899, a thousand years after the death of Alfred the Great:

> I was born in 1899, just one thousand years after King Alfred's death. He was being remembered here in Wessex. A fine statue was set up to his memory in Winchester. My father and mother decided that I should be christened Alfred. Our connection with him is not proved. But he took shelter in Somerset where the Dennings were. I like to think that there the

son of the Dane may have married into the family of Alfred the Great.[23]

Having associated his genealogy with both the origins of the word 'law', by means of his Danish forebears, and the first great English lawgiver Alfred, Lord Denning proceeded to associate his family with the Normans, who imported the conceptions of feudal tenure, trial by jury, Norman French and Magna Carta into the English legal order, by tracing his descent from two Norman families named 'Newdigate' and 'Poyntz'.

Lord Denning wrote about the English Civil War, the great disruption of the continuity of the English history, as if it were a 'family story'. His forebears fought on both sides of the Civil War. Newdigate Poyntz fought for the King and was killed, early in the war, at Gainsborough. His brother, Sir Sydenham Poytz became 'one of Cromwell's most famous generals'.[24] Lord Denning made it quite clear that, with regard to the Civil War, his sympathies were with the Parliament and Cromwell rather than the King. When writing about his brother Norman, an officer of the Royal Navy, he noted that, on the conclusion of peace in 1945, he quoted from Milton's letter to Lord General Cromwell in May 1652: 'Peace hath her victories no less renown'd than war'.[25] Writing about his brother Reg's career in the Army after the war Lord Denning quoted Cromwell's famous words 'Put your trust in God and keep your powder dry'.[26] In 1934, Lord Denning gave a copy of John Buchan's recently published biography of Cromwell to his wife. He commented: 'Oliver Cromwell has always been a hero in our family.....some people regard Charles I as a saint and a martyr. I would not so describe him myself'.[27] On another occasion, writing about the trial of Charles I, Lord Denning noted that the King rejected the authority of the Court 'like the Nazi war criminals at Nuremburg'.[28] Commenting on the trial itself, Lord Denning observed: 'He disputed with John Bradshaw. All very unseemly. He was sentenced to death. John Bradshaw was the first to sign the death warrant'.[29] For Lord Denning, John Bradshaw was no regicide, but a judge, like himself, applying the law without fear or favour. Lord Denning was no Royalist, for him the legacy of the disruption of the Civil Wars was the limitation of the powers of the Monarchy and the establishment of the independence of the judiciary.[30]

The crucial moment in the resolution of the constitutional conflicts of the seventeenth century for Lord Denning was the reign of James II: 'James II was a bad king. It was he who dismissed the judges'.[31] It was the jurors in the case of the Seven Bishops, in particular the King's brewer who changed his mind, who by delivering a verdict against the King 'saved the English constitution' and so defended the principles of trial by jury[32] and the independence of the judiciary.[33]

Having associated his 'family story' with the triumph of Parliament, judicial independence and trial by jury, Lord Denning had secured his genealogy in relation to English history. He could claim in his own person the authority of the Anglo-Saxon lawgiver Alfred who gave him his Christian name, that of the Danes, from whom 'law' itself came, who gave him his surname, that of the Normans, who brought in trial by jury and were his forebears in line of direct family descent and finally that of Oliver Cromwell and the Parliament, for whom his ancestor Sir Sydenham Poyntz fought as a General, and whose victory ensured the preservation of trial by jury and established the principle of judicial independence.

From that time, until the lifetime of Lord Denning and his brothers, the family lapsed into obscurity, ceasing to play a role in the great dramas of English history. In 1720 there was an elopement and in a series of legal disputes over inheritance which began in 1807, all the estates, like those of the Manor of Marr, in Charles Dickens' *Bleak House*, were lost in Chancery.[34] Having been notable and important, the Denning family lapsed into poverty and obscurity, victims of an unjust legal order, a wrong which Lord Denning was to devote himself to putting right by embracing the cause of legal reform and dedicating his life to the pursuit of justice.

The rest of *The Family Story* was concerned with placing Lord Denning and his brothers at the heart of the history of England in the twentieth century. The decisive event of that century, for Lord Denning, was the First World War. One brother, Jack, was killed at the Battle of the Somme, another, Reg, was wounded on the Somme. Gordon fought at Jutland and died of tuberculosis in 1918. Lord Denning himself fought in the decisive fighting in April 1918 which resulted in the collapse of the Ludendorff offensive and laid the basis for the Allied victory in September to November 1918. Linking his experience with that of an earlier period of English martial prowess, he said that he felt 'proud to have been there, as were those at Agincourt' and then quoted the speech[35] of Henry Von St. Crispin's Day from Shakespeare's play *Henry V*.[36]

The blood sacrifice of England's youth, in particular that of his two brothers, in the First World War remained a decisive experience for Lord Denning for the rest of his life.[37] At the Lincoln's Inn dinner held to mark his eightieth birthday in 1979, poppies from Picardy were displayed. Lord Denning, profoundly moved, said in his speech: 'Out of us, five brothers, three fought in Picardy. I was the youngest of the three - only there for the last nine months. Too young to go before, I came through unhurt. The other two were soldiers there from the beginning. Both were in the Battle of the Somme'. He then described how his mother fainted when she received the telegram informing the family of Jack's death and how another brother died at the end of the war: 'Jack and Gordon - they were the best of us'. He then quoted from Lawrence Binyon's *For the Fallen*:

> They shall not grow old as we that are left grow old.
> Age shall not weary them, nor the years condemn,
> at the going down of the sun and in the morning
> we shall remember them.

At that point: 'The poppies slipped from my hand to the floor. Eyes filled with tears. It was the eve of Remembrance Day'.[38]

The Second World War, by comparison, was a mundane matter. As Lord Denning put it: 'We all carried on'.[39] 'We kept bees for honey. We kept chickens for eggs. We had no car. We went without. We won through'.[40] His two surviving brothers, Reg and Norman, prospered in their careers in the armed services as a result of World War Two. Norman worked in Naval Intelligence becoming Director of Naval Intelligence in 1961 and Deputy Chief of Defence Staff [Intelligence] in 1967. In retirement, he ran the D-Notice system.[41] Reg, an army officer, became Chief of Staff Eastern Command in 1947, General Officer Commanding Northern Ireland in 1948; on retirement in 1952 he became the first Colonel of the Royal Anglian Regiment. The Denning 'family story', for all of its rootedness in the English tradition, may have languished in obscurity after the decisive disruption of the Civil War, but by the mid twentieth century, with one brother an Admiral and the other a General, it had found its way back, by way of the blood sacrifice of the Somme, to the very heart of English history.

Having taken a triple first, in Mathematics and Law, at Magdalen College Oxford, won an Eldon Scholarship, passed out first in the Bar examination in 1923,[42] assisted Sir Joseph Chitty in the preparation of a new edition of Smith's *Leading Cases*,[43] and embarked on a promising career at the Bar in the mid 1920s,[44] Lord Denning became a KC in 1938 and was elevated to the bench in the Probate, Divorce and Admiralty Division on the 6th March 1944. He became a trial judge on the Court of King's Bench in 1945. In October 1948, at the age of 49, he was appointed to the Court of Appeal. As he put it: 'It is in the Court of Appeal that a Judge has the chief opportunity of influencing the law......very few cases go to the House of Lords'.[45] From 1948 until 1982, Lord Denning was in a position to shape the law of England. His principles were to 'let justice be done', 'freedom under the law' and 'put your trust in God'.[46] He was determined to challenge the conservatism of his fellow judges: 'They give priority to the letter of the law; whereas I give priority to the doing of justice'.[47]

At this time, Lord Denning was particularly concerned about 'the vast new powers which had been entrusted to the executive'[48] as a result of the Second World War and the changes introduced by the Labour government of 1945. In 1952, he delivered a lecture at University College London entitled: 'The need for a new equity'. He saw the possibility of renewal and reform of the law being based in the resources of equity rather than those of precedent,[49] considering that the judges could use the resource of equity to reform the law, as he himself had done in his judgment in the High Court in 1947[50] which had used the equitable doctrine of promissory estoppel to avoid the unjust consequences of the application of the Common Law rules of contract[51] and to uphold the principle that men should be held to their promises. In his lecture, Lord Denning argued that the university law departments[52] could help the judges achieve the reform which would inaugurate a new Elizabethan age: 'They must raise up another Bentham to expose the fallacies and failings of the past and to point the way to a new age and a new equity. We stand at the threshold of a new Elizabethan era. Let us play a worthy part in it'.[53] Lord Denning considered that reform of the law, based on a new equity, which could remove rigidities which led to injustice and control abuse of power by the executive, was essential or 'else the oppressed will get to the point when they will stand it no longer. They will find their own remedy. There will be anarchy'.[54] It was for the judges to hold the balance between competing interests and to 'put freedom first', to give 'priority to the freedom of the individual'.[55]

In April 1957, Lord Denning was appointed to the House of Lords. 'It was only when I was in the Lords that I got to know the working of our Constitution....the Palace of Westminster is itself the physical embodiment of our Constitution...we have had many changes but nevertheless the spirit of the Constitution remains the same'; it is 'to be felt rather than seen, to be experienced rather than learnt'.[56] Clearly there was something mysterious about the English Constitution which defied rational analysis as far as Lord Denning was concerned. It was a thing of history, literature and imagination, but it was also founded on the principles of the judges which were 'more powerful than anything else in creating the spirit of the British Constitution'.[57] This spirit was a very precious thing: 'The English people are heirs of a spiritual worth which is a greater power in the world than armies or navies or atomic bombs'.[58] This spirit was an 'instinct for justice', a belief in 'right, not might, as the true basis of society' and that 'free will, not force is the true basis of government'. It was a 'practical instinct leading us to balance rights with duties, and powers with safeguards, so that neither rights nor powers should be exceeded or abused'.[59] Its two pillars were the 'sovereignty of Parliament' and the independence of the judiciary'.[60] 'The people of this country.... trust Parliament- and the members of it - always to be guided by those instincts of for justice and liberty of which I have written'.[61]

However, for Lord Denning, the 'keystone' of the rule of law in England was the independence of the judges....it is the only respect in which we have any real separation of powers'.[62] The judges could be trusted because trust 'is born in them.....they know it in their bones'.[63] Metaphors of birth, family, race and descent were deployed to justify the role of the judges in the English constitution. Religion was also a vital part of that order, the judges were bound by an oath, sworn to God, to 'do justice to all manner of people, according to the laws and customs of England, without fear or favour, affection or ill will'.[64] On the basis of this oath, and their independence, the judges could determine the scope of the powers of Parliament and of the government.[65] According to Lord Denning, this ability of the judges to supervise and control those who wielded power was one 'of the most formidable principles of our constitution'.[66] He discussed these powers in his first published work about the nature of the English legal system *Freedom under the Law*.[67]

Freedom under the Law [1949]

In October and November 1949, Lord Denning, recently appointed to the Court of Appeal, delivered the first series of Hamlyn lectures[68] at Senate House in the University of London. The lectures were published as *Freedom under the Law*[69] and constitute Lord Denning's first public statement of his conception of the English legal order. He began, consistently with the purpose of the Hamlyn lectures, by emphasising the importance of knowledge of the law by the 'common people of England'.[70] He stressed the privilege which was attached to birth as one of the 'common people' of England: 'Not that it is any discredit to any of us to be one of the common people of England. It is indeed the greatest privilege that any man can have; for the common people of England have succeeded to the greatest heritage of all - the heritage of freedom: and it is that that I have come to talk about - freedom under the law'.[71] Lord Denning associated race, law and freedom, identifying the English race with its law and defining that law as being founded on the principle of freedom.

Lord Denning proceeded to explain what he meant by freedom and, in particular, how that freedom was protected by the law. He began with the principle of *habeas corpus*, emphasising that freedom was protected by the procedures of the courts rather than an abstract guarantee of right and that in applying those procedures the courts would always balance freedom with the duty owed by the individual to society.[72] Lord Denning defined freedom as follows: 'What matters in England is that each man should be free to develop his own personality to the full: and the only duties which should restrict that freedom are those which are necessary to enable everyone else to do the same'.[73]

Lord Denning then set this freedom, and its protection by the procedures of the courts, within the context of contemporary society referring to 'the social revolution of today',[74] by which he meant the reforms initiated by the Labour government of 1945, and 'the hated gestapo and the police state',[75] by which he meant the enemy which had threatened the existence of the English legal order in 1940, but which had been overcome by the victory of 1945. In order to emphasise the distinctiveness of the English legal order and its capacity to protect freedom in contrast with that of Nazi Germany and the challenges which it might face from the 'social revolution of today', he identified two contrasting legal decisions of the English courts: *Darnel's Case*[76] and *Somersett's Case*.[77] The first was made before the principle of *habeas corpus* had been established, in the 'evil days when the judges took their orders from the executive';[78] the second, in which a slave was freed, in the period after that principle had been established. For Lord Denning, it was the fact that the courts could protect the subject's liberty by means of the procedure of *habeas corpus* rather than an abstract right to freedom set out in a written constitution that distinguished the English legal order from those of continental Europe which had recently succumbed to the Nazi tyranny. To emphasise this point he discussed Regulation 18B, the emergency measure that allowed imprisonment without trial during the war. For Lord Denning, it was the fact that regulation 18B, for all that it suspended *habeas corpus*, was still subject to supervision by the courts that was the crucial point.[79] To emphasise this he quoted Lord Atkin's famous dissenting judgment concerning the scope of regulation 18B in *Liversidge v Anderson*[80] and contrasted that speech with the procedures current in the Soviet Union in 1949. He conceded that Article 7 of the Soviet Constitution was similar in spirit to regulation 18B, but in decisive contrast it was not subject to the procedures of the courts.

Although Lord Denning referred to the Nazi tyranny, his main focus in *Freedom under the Law* was the threat posed by the Soviet Union and the challenge of the 'social revolution of today'. Written in 1949, *Freedom under the Law* was as much a combative response to the challenge of the Cold War, and to the threat, as perceived by Lord Denning, posed to freedom by the increase in executive power which had accrued to the Labour government after the war, as a vindication of Britain's victory over Nazism. Lord Denning emphasised that 'freedom must be true to itself or it will perish'[81] and that the current conflict with the Soviet Union was 'a war of ideologies which is not to be won by throwing people behind bars, but by having your 'loins girt about with truth'.[82] If victory abroad in the Cold War was to be gained by preserving 'freedom under the law' then, on the home front, the 'social revolution of today', based on the increased powers of the executive, must be controlled by judicial supervision of the powers of the executive: 'The executive government must never be allowed more power than is absolutely necessary. They must always be made subject to the law....we taught the Kings that from Runnymede to the scaffold at Whitehall: and we have not had any serious trouble since. But we cannot afford, in these days, to be off our guard'.[83] It was plain that in Lord Denning's judgment it was the courts, and therefore the judges, that would guarantee the continuation of 'freedom under the law' in the face of the challenges posed by the Cold War and the 'social revolution of today'.

Having discussed *habeas corpus* and set it in a contemporary context, Lord Denning then proceeded to examine the police power of arrest, concluding that 'we have reason to be proud' because the potential conflict with the liberty of the subject posed by the police power of arrest has been 'solved by the judges'[84] thereby re-emphasising the role played by the judges in the protection of 'freedom under the law'. Lord Denning contrasted the French approach whereby the citizen must submit to the police with the English position whereby the police could only arrest a person if they had a valid reason and that the individual was entitled to resist any arrest which was not premised on such a reason, a principle established by the courts in *Christie v Leachinsky*[85] in 1947.[86] Lord Denning then proceeded to give a eulogy of the British Police: 'The Police are not regarded as the strong arm of the executive, but as the friends of the people……..such a fine body of men that they do not abuse the powers which they have'. They are of 'excellent character' and are recruited from 'sturdy country stock', able to ensure 'fair play' and showing 'calmness in emergency'.[87] As far as Lord Denning was concerned the potential threat to the liberty of the individual posed by the Police's power of arrest was neutralised by the supervision of the courts and the 'character' of the English policeman.

Lord Denning then examined the threat posed to freedom by the oppression which might occur when an individual was detained by the police. Referring incidentally to the torture of Cardinal Mindzenty and the Hungarian politician Rajk which had recently taken place, Lord Denning examined this issue by way of a brief history of torture in England, in the course of which he noted that Sir John Fortescue had proclaimed in the fifteenth century that torture was against the Common Law and that Charles I's government was the last to have used torture. The fact that that government had been overthrown by the 'common people', established that such practices were alien to the English constitution.[88] Another threat to 'freedom' identified by Lord Denning was the way in which an individual could be oppressed by the extortion of confessions by means of the promise of a pardon; such improperly obtained confessions were effectively prohibited by the courts which insisted on the need for 'free and voluntary' confessions and were able to exclude any confessions obtained in any other manner.[89]

Lord Denning argued that the freedom of the individual from arbitrary imprisonment, arrest, torture and subjection to all forms of improper pressure, freedoms which he stressed were not respected in those countries under the control of the Soviet Union, were guaranteed by the courts in England: 'So long as the judges hold the balance there will be no police state in England'.[90] The judges who protected the principle of 'freedom under the law' in the English constitution were 'men who have come of the common people themselves, they have evolved principles of law which express the spirit of the people - the spirit of freedom'.[91] 'Freedom under the Law', for Lord Denning the foundation of the English constitution, was guaranteed by the procedures of the courts rather than by abstract rights; the guardians of those procedures were the judges, the ultimate protectors of that order against the threat posed from without by the Soviet Union and from within by the powers of the executive.

'Freedom of mind and conscience' were also protected by the procedures of the courts. 'To our way of thinking it is elementary that each man should be able to inquire and search after the truth until he has found it'.[92] This principle had to be limited by rules which prevented an individual from speaking ill of his neighbour and from inciting others to violence or propagating ideas 'subversive of the existing constitution or a danger to the fabric of society'.[93] This balance was policed by the judges who were imbued with 'the practical genius of the Common Law' and by the jury system; acting together, judge and jury protected the individual from being prosecuted, as in the Soviet Union, for his 'state of mind'.[94] Lord Denning concluded that the combination of judicial supervision and jury trial have preserved 'freedom of mind and conscience' and that, since the eighteenth century, 'we have found little difficulty in criticising the government'.[95]

Having established that 'freedom of mind and conscience' were protected by the English constitution, Lord Denning proceeded to discuss the offence of 'public mischief', an offence with the potential to restrict 'freedom of mind and conscience' in that the offence was undefined.[96] Lord Denning contrasted, to its detriment, the French Code which upheld the principle of *nullum crimen, nulla poena, sine lege* with the Common Law. Unlike the French code, the Common Law did not accept a principle which allowed the courts to punish an individual for an act which was not an offence when committed but which was subsequently determined to be an offence.[97] However, 'public mischief' had the potential to create such a result in that it was an offence indeterminate in scope and capable of extension. The saving grace was that the offence of 'public mischief' was not defined by the government or by Parliament but by the judges; the English legal order was 'not contained in a code but in the breasts of the judges'.[98] The potential for abuse of such a power to define the law was, according to Lord Denning, negligible, given the fact that the judges were independent of the executive.

Lord Denning then noted that 'anti-semitism' could have been defined as a 'public mischief' and therefore excluded from jury trial. In 1949, this was a controversial example to choose in that many people would have felt that the law should prohibit 'anti-semitism' and that the offence of 'public mischief' would offer a means of achieving this end. In 1936 'anti-semitism' was defined as a 'public mischief',[99] but that decision was overturned in 1947 when 'anti-semitic' remarks were defined by the court as seditious libel, rather than 'public mischief', and therefore subject to trial by jury.[100] Lord Denning argued that although 'public mischief' could have been used to restrict freedom of expression by being applied to 'anti-semitism', the judges had not extended its scope in that way and had thereby protected 'freedom of mind and conscience' by allowing jurors rather than the judges alone to determine the scope of freedom of speech. For Lord Denning, the choice of the example of 'anti-semitism' was important in that, although many people would not have objected to it being made into an offence of 'public mischief', if that had occurred then many other, much more contentious, limitations on 'freedom of conscience and mind' could have been imposed by extending the scope of the offence of 'public mischief'. Lord Denning suggested that the judges would only use the offence of 'public mischief' to deal with attempts to 'overturn the state by force' and would not use that offence, as in theory they could, to limit 'freedom of mind and expression'. Again, the burden of his argument was that the protection of freedom lay in the hands of the judges and that it was safe in those hands. The judges had restricted the scope of 'public mischief' and prevented it from being applied to issues relating to freedom of speech. In relation to such issues, the jury, representative of the opinion of the 'reasonable man', retained its power to determine the scope of freedom of speech.

Lord Denning then proceeded to argue that freedom of religion was also securely protected in the English constitution; that Christianity was not enforced by law but by teaching and example.[101] The 'offence of blasphemy is a dead letter', he noted, because it would not, in practice, be enforced by the courts. Freedom of religion was not secured by means of an established right of toleration but by the fact that the English constitution was based on religion: 'When the state itself is religious as this country is - we have not only an established church, but religious instruction is part of the curriculum in all our schools - there is not the same danger' as in a society, such as the Soviet Union, in which the 'state demands undivided loyalty'.[102] 'If we are to maintain freedom of religion, we must keep the state religious'.[103] Lord Denning maintained that religious toleration was possible in England because of the establishment of religion and the self-imposed caution of the courts, symbolised by their reluctance to enforce the offence of blasphemy; an offence which could be, and had been, used to enforce religious conformity. For Lord Denning, religious intolerance was more likely to occur in a country such as that of the Soviet Union, where the state demanded undivided loyalty, loyalty which was incompatible with religious freedom, than in one such as England where the state was religious but the courts did not use their powers to enforce religious conformity. The courts, and therefore the judges, were the foundation on which the whole edifice of the English legal system was founded. The good sense of the judges would prevent the Blasphemy Act from being used but their inherent Christian commitment would ensure that the English constitution retained is link with a higher authority than that of the state.

In the course of discussing religious freedom, Lord Denning touched on racial freedom by adverting to the treatment of the Jews within the English legal order. He argued that the removal of legal disabilities from religious minorities in the nineteenth century meant that the law now treated all of its subjects equally. Jews, a religious minority, were therefore treated just like any other subjects of the legal order. On the basis of this argument, Lord Denning remarked that, in contrast with the United States and South Africa, the 'Common Law is colour blind'.[104] There is no other mention of 'race' in *Freedom under the Law*.

The central feature of Lord Denning's analysis of the way in which the English constitution protected 'freedom under the law' was that, in contrast with the Soviet Union where the courts were an instrument of the state, in England the courts stood between the individual and the state.[105] The principle of jury trial, in which unanimity was a requirement, safeguarded the individual from the effects of 'harsh laws, political prejudice and legal formalism'.[106] The law was 'controlled by the common people'.[107] Jury trial was of fundamental importance to the English constitution: 'To this charge he has pleaded not guilty and puts himself upon his country, which country you are. All our past struggles are bound up in that one sentence'.[108] The jury was an embodiment of the 'common people', an expression of the English nation itself.[109] 'It works in the English-speaking countries because of the temperament of the people, their sound good sense, which is not to be swayed unduly by emotion and prejudice. It does not work in the Latin countries with their mobile temperament, easily moved to pity or hate. The verdicts there given by juries were often fantastic'.[110] The English 'character', an essential aspect of English identity, was embodied, in Lord Denning's understanding, in the principle of trial by jury.

Having established that the English constitution, in sharp contrast with that of the Soviet Union, guaranteed 'freedom under the law' by means of the independence and good sense of the judiciary and the jury system, Lord Denning then proceeded to examine the question of 'justice between man and the state' in relation to 'the social revolution of today'.[111] He began by emphasising that, in the last 100 years, statutes had limited the scope of individual freedom in relation to property rights and freedom of contract. The courts had been strict in their protection of these rights in the nineteenth century but 'in this they were wrong. They weighed the scale too heavily in favour of the rights of man' and failed to balance those rights with the duties owed by the individual to society.[112] Freedom of contract was abused, inequality of bargaining power was not considered.[113] The balance was redressed by a series of Acts of Parliament which limited the scope of freedom of contract and the rights of the individual in relation to property.

One of the most important of these acts was the Crown Proceedings Act 1947 which allowed the individual to sue public authorities for breach of contract and in tort. Lord Denning stressed the importance of the Act: 'This Act is of profound significance in our constitutional law. It does a great deal to keep the balance between the individual and the state....no longer is the Crown a privileged person before the courts'.[114] However, the Act placed a negative duty on public authorities not to harm rather than a positive duty to take care. It did nothing to regulate and define the scope of the positive actions of the state which had expanded dramatically since the nineteenth century when those duties were limited to 'the bare necessities of the community as a whole, such as defence against aggression, the maintenance of order, and the provision of workhouses for the destitute...the state did not recognise any right to freedom from want. All was left to the charitable instincts of the few...the social revolution of today has changed all that'.[115]

Lord Denning was concerned about the extent to which the expanded scope of governmental power consequent on 'the social revolution of today' could be regulated by law. He made some positive comments, in notable contrast with the view taken by Dicey, and the tone of his own comments with regard to the shortcomings of the French Code, about the French system of administrative law which he deemed worthy of respect as 'a coherent system of courts which keeps a balance between the claims of the community on the one hand and the freedom of the individual on the other'.[116] Lord Denning was concerned that the expanded powers of the state should be subjected to the rule of law 'without which there is no freedom for any of us. We must see to it that the stream of British freedom - which has been kept clear by the decisions of the judges - does not perish in the bogs and sands of departmental decisions'.[117] 'I come at last to the most significant feature of our time - the increasing powers of the executive'.[118] 'All that the courts can do is to see that the powers are not exceeded or abused.....the Jack-in-office never realises that he is being a little tyrant'.[119]

Lord Denning emphasised the importance of the challenge posed by the increased powers of the executive by comparing the present situation with that faced by the English constitution in the seventeenth century: 'This problem bears considerable likeness to those which faced the courts in the great constitutional struggles of the past'.[120] He then discussed the Ship Money case[121] which was concerned with the power of the government to tax the individual and commented that, in the first instance, the courts found in favour of the King's right to levy tax: 'This contention [that there was no power to tax without Parliamentary consent] did not prevail with the court, as it ought to have done, and it needed a civil war to establish it'.[122] He continued that the problem today 'is in principle the same, and it must be solved by the courts and not by a civil war'.[123] Lord Denning was confident that the judges would be able to resolve the problems posed by the increase in the powers of government. 'This is not a task for Parliament'[124] but for the courts which could develop a new machinery to deal with abuse of power by the executive by means of the existing Common Law instruments of declarations, injunctions and actions for negligence.[125] His peroration was confident: 'We have in our own time to deal with changes which are of equal signficance to those which took place three hundred years ago. Let us prove ourselves equal to the challenge'.[126] However, despite this confidence, the reference to the Civil War suggested that Lord Denning was seriously concerned about the potential of the growth of discretionary governmental power to undermine the constitution. By comparing the government of Clement Attlee, by implication, with that of Charles I, Lord Denning was making it plain that he believed that this time, in contrast with the seventeenth century, the judges would use their power to restrain that of the government.

Lord Denning continued this theme concerning the dangers inherent in the growth of executive power, and the role of the courts in controlling that power, in *The Changing Law* which he published in 1953, the year of the Coronation of Queen Elizabeth II. In the first chapter entitled 'The Spirit of the British Constitution',[127] Lord Denning commented on the anxiety caused by the growth of executive power as a consequence of war, the need to control the exchange rate, rationing and the nationalisation of large sectors of industry.[128] He noted that 'in practice sovereignty no longer rests with Parliament'[129] but that 'once elected the leaders of the party are the sovereign power in the land'. The government might be morally bound by the duty to govern in the interests of all but that duty was not enforceable by the courts.[130] There was therefore a need for robust criticism of the government. 'Parliament is not infallible' and the judges had a duty to criticise Acts passed by Parliament if not the actual conduct of Parliament.[131] 'Only extreme danger would justify any restriction on freedom of discussion'.[132] The English constitution made 'no distinction between constitutional laws and other laws. We can change a fundamental law just as easily as a transient law. We may modify our law to meet changing needs but we keep the fundamental principles intact'.[133] Those principles depended on a strong Parliament, an independent judiciary and freedom of the press: 'So long as Parliament is vigilant, the Press is free, and the judges are confident, there can be no totalitarian state in England'.[134]

Lord Denning also reiterated his insistence on the importance of the relationship between law and religion. He was convinced that the separation of religion, law and morals had gone too far: 'Without religion there can be no morality, and without morality there can be no law'.[135] For Lord Denning, Christianity was a protest against a 'terrible despotism, the overwhelming domination of human life by the state'.[136] However, individualism could also be taken too far: 'No one doubts now that it is wrong to treat the rights of property as sacred'.[137] Although Lord Denning accepted the principle of the Welfare State, he stressed that it could also lead to too much power adhering to the government.[138] He stressed the importance of the family, in particular the indissolubility of marriage, condemning divorce as a threat to social stability: 'The only remedy is the growth of a strong public opinion condemning divorce, and I would add condemning infidelity'.[139] Sexual morality was not just a private matter of individual conscience, it should be enforced by society.[140] Lord Denning was unequivocal about the importance of religion and called for its role in society to be enhanced: 'If religion perishes in the land, truth and justice will also. We have already strayed too far from the faith of our fathers. Let us return to it, for it is the only thing that can save us'.[141] Lord Denning expressed these views in 1953, long before the advent of the 'permissive society'.

In his Romanes Lecture of 1959,[142] entitled 'From Precedent to Precedent',[143] Lord Denning, now a member of the Appellate Committee of the House of Lords, reviewed the role of the House of Lords in relation to the law since the seventeenth century in order to demonstrate that there was no constitutional reason why it should be bound by its previous decisions: 'In past times the House of Lords used to correct errors into which the lower courts had fallen - and indeed errors into which the House itself or its predecessors had fallen - it used to create new precedents so as to meet new situations'.[144] By means of considerable legal scholarship, he demonstrated how, when lay members of the House of Lords sat in judgment in the seventeenth and eighteenth centuries, the House of Lords had often overturned previous decisions in the interests of justice. The current doctrine that the House of Lords was bound by its previous decisions was, Lord Denning contended, an innovation of the nineteenth century; the result of the fact that lay members of the House of Lords had ceased to be involved in the judicial work of the House of Lords. Since the changes brought about by the Judicature Act 1876, the professional judicial members, the new fangled Life Peers, known as Lords of Appeal in Ordinary, had sole responsibility for the exercise of the judicial powers of the House of Lords and were consequently exceedingly cautious in using their inherent power to change the law. However, there was nothing to stop the House of Lords, argued Lord Denning, from reasserting its inherent power to change the law in the interests of justice. He concluded that the House of Lords must 'recapture this vital principle'.[145]

When he was appointed Master of the Rolls by Harold Macmillan in 1962, Lord Denning had spent thirteen years, in an era of judicial reticence, symbolised by the self-denying ordinance of the so-called

'Kilmuir Rules'[146], publicising his attitude to the law, in particular his conviction of the need for the law to adapt to the changing needs of society. No other judge had discussed the law so openly or been so clear about the role of the judges in changing the law so that it could adapt to changes in society, in particular in relation to the powers of the executive. In his published writings, Lord Denning had made it quite plain that he saw the judiciary as having a decisive role to play in reforming the law and in controlling the abuse of discretionary power by the government; a power which, in his opinion, had been developed to a potentially dangerous extent. As Master of the Rolls, Lord Denning was placed in a position from which he could reform and shape the law; at that time, most cases ended in the Court of Appeal. The House of Lords, in its judicial capacity, was practically inert. The Master of the Rolls could choose which cases he heard and only had to win over one of a bench of three to change the law. It is tempting to see Denning's appointment, along with the introduction of Life Peerages in 1958, the 'winds of change' speech in Capetown in 1960, the expansion of higher education following the Robbins Report and the application to join the European Community, as part of an attempt by Macmillan to radically modernise the United Kingdom.

In June 1963, Harold Macmillan gave Lord Denning the most public, and controversial, role that a judge had undertaken in recent memory. By asking him to make an inquiry into 'the circumstances leading to the resignation of the Minister for War and to report particularly on any danger to national security', Harold Macmillan not only gave Lord Denning what he was to call 'my most important case',[147] he also placed in the hands of a judge the fate of the government, even that of the Establishment itself. In the event, Lord Denning saved both the government and the Establishment. His report, published in September 1963, became the fastest selling official publication in history and the most remarkable intervention by a judge into political and constitutional controversy in the twentieth century. Whereas judges often dealt with political and constitutional issues in the courts, expressing their decisions in legal language which was opaque to anyone but a lawyer, the Denning Report was written, in the style of an editorial in the Daily Mirror, for the consumption of the public. The fate of a government depended upon its reception. No decision in the Court of Appeal, or the House of Lords, would ever be subject to such public scrutiny.

The Report on the Circumstances leading to the Resignation of the Former Secretary of State for War, Mr. J.D. Profumo [1963]

The Profumo affair was one of the most controversial episodes in late twentieth century British political history. Most of the files, including those relating to Lord Denning's inquiry, will remain closed to researchers until 2013. However, important details about the 'Profumo' affair continue to emerge; interpretations of the events surrounding the resignation of John Profumo,[148] and their significance, vary widely. For some the most important questions raised by the events of the summer of 1963 concerned national security,[149] for others it was a matter of a clash of moral values[150] between those who supported traditional Christian morality and those inclined to a more 'permissive' approach,[151] for others the main issue was that of scandal and the fact that Profumo's affair with Christine Keeler was just one of many instances of reprehensible behaviour which had been kept quiet on the basis of a hypocritical double standard whereby the private 'immorality' of the rich and powerful was concealed behind a facade of repectability.[152] Another issue raised by the Profumo affair concerned the freedom of the press. As a result of the Vassal inquiry, two journalists had been imprisoned[153] for failing to reveal their sources.[154] This led to a great deal of antagonism between the press and the government which made it very difficult for the hysteria that accompanied the media frenzy which accompanied the Profumo affair to be controlled. It was suggested by some government sources and reinforced in Lord Denning's report[155] that the press was acting irresponsibly, indeed was out of control.[156] There were those who argued that in effect Stephen Ward was the real victim; a scapegoat[157] hounded by a criminal prosecution based on deployment of the law against his lifestyle rather than on substantive offences.[158] In the end, Ward committed suicide[159] thereby taking the attention away from the problems of the government.

Such was the complexity, and potentially explosive nature, of the issues which were raised by the Profumo affair that it is impossible to predict what might have happened in the summer of 1963 had events unfolded in a slightly different manner, in particular if the immediate crisis had not been resolved by the appointment of Lord Denning to conduct an inquiry into the circumstances of Profumo's resignation. The publication of Lord Denning's report on 26th September 1963 effectively defused the whole scandal, enabling the government to continue its business and to restore some sense of normality to political affairs.[160] While it is not possible to say, unequivocally, that Lord Denning saved the government, and therefore the establishment, his report clearly contributed very substantially to resolving a major political crisis whose consequences were unpredictable and potentially extremely serious.[161] In 1966, Lord Salmon wrote, in the Report of the Royal Commission on Tribunals, of which he was the Chairman: 'Lord Denning's report was generally accepted by the public. But this was only because of Lord Denning's rare qualities and high reputation. Even so, public acceptance of the Report may be regarded as the brilliant exception to what would normally occur when an inquiry is carried out in such circumstances'.[162] The Denning Report was a unique event. Not until the very different circumstances which gave rise to Scott report of 1996, and the Hutton report of 2004, was a judge to be allowed to probe into the very heart of the workings of government.

Lord Denning called his inquiry into the Profumo affair my 'most important case'.[163] In *Landmarks in the Law*,[164] he described his Report as 'an inquiry to find out the truth'.[165] He claimed that the government was in 'jeopardy'.[166] 'The morale of the government was by this time at a low ebb. Something had to be done. It was done. The Prime Minister invited me to conduct an enquiry into the resignation of the Secretary for War'.[167] Lord Denning dismissed any criticism that he should not have accepted the Prime Minister's request because of the political sensitivity of the matter: 'Some have said that, as a judge, I should not have accepted the task - because of its political overtones. But I felt, and I still feel, that with the security of the state involved, it was my duty to do what I was asked'.[168] Not only did Lord Denning see his task in terms of a duty to protect the state, he was also quite clear that a judge was particularly well suited for such work: 'The government usually asks a judge to do such a task when it is in a quandry. There is public unease, and the only person who can be trusted to be impartial is a judge. He is independent of the executive and thus can speak his mind. Thus was I called upon in 1963. The government was indeed in a quandry'.[169] It is plain that Lord Denning saw himself, as a judge, as the ultimate guardian of the constitution.

With a strong sense of historical context, Lord Denning compared the mood in the country in the summer of 1963 with that which accompanied the Popish Plot in 1678: 'The end of it all was that Parliament was dissolved and a new Parliament elected. Something of the kind happened after the Profumo report'.[170] Referring to Shakespeare's depiction of 'Rumour, painted full of tongues' which stirred up 'the blunt monster with uncounted heads, the still discordant multitude', thus setting the whole episode firmly within the traditions of English history, he continued: 'In the story which I tell you, the people of England were 'the blunt monster with uncounted heads'.[171]

Lord Denning began his Report into 'the circumstances leading to the resignation of the former Secretary of State for War - Mr J.D. Profumo'[172] with Stephen Ward: 'The story must start with Stephen Ward'.[173] He described Ward as 'the son of a clergyman' who 'was prone to exaggerate the nature of acquaintanceships with people in high places'. He did not keep a 'banking account' and made 'many cash transactions which left no trace'. 'He admired the Soviet Regime and sympathised with communists'. Ward was 'at the same time utterly immoral', conducted sexual relationships with 16 and 17 year old girls[174] and participated in 'sexual orgies of a revolting nature'.[175] Right at the start of his report, Lord Denning established that Ward was, emphatically, not the kind of reasonable and decent citizen with whom, in his capacity as Master of the Rolls, he might have considered to be an attractive litigant. Ward was defined as someone quite beyond the pale of 'reasonable' behaviour by this description. He was a man with whom the 'reasonable' men and women of a jury would have had no sympathy. Lord Denning concluded his account of the events leading to Profumo's resignation with Ward: 'The story ends, as it began, with him'.[176] Ward was therefore presented as the villain of the piece, even though it was Profumo's behaviour, in particular his lie to Parliament, which brought about the crisis which led to his resignation. Profumo's behaviour should have been at the centre of Lord Denning's attention but it was Ward who 'stole the show' and who was condemned, without a fair hearing, by a judge who clearly assumed that he would be found guilty, without much discussion, by the jury. By the time the report was published Ward was dead. This was a fortunate happenstance.[177] Had he been alive then much of what Lord Denning had to say about him might, despite the criminal trial, have been considered libellous.[178]

Although it was Ward who was convicted and sentenced in Denning's Report, there was a modicum of formal criticism of the Prime Minister and the ministers who dealt with the affair: 'The conduct of Mr Profumo was such as to create, amongst an influential section of the people a reasonable belief that he had committed adultery with such a woman in such circumstances as the case discloses. It was the responsibility of the Prime Minister and his colleagues, and of them only, to deal with the situation: and they did not succeed in doing so'.[179] However, that criticism was framed within a narrative which always kept Ward, and his 'immorality', at the centre of the stage. The Prime Minister handled the situation badly, but he was deceived by Profumo who had been entangled with a 'thoroughly immoral man'. The blame was firmly attached to Ward. The failures of the Prime Minister and his colleagues, by contrast with the damnation of Ward, were effectively exonerated.[180] Lord Denning pointed out that: 'They could not conceive that any of their colleagues would have the effrontery to make a false statement to the House....the business of the country could not be carried on if a member of the government could not accept the word of another implicitly'.[181]

While Ward's character was blackened, those of the other participants, in particular Profumo and Lord Astor, were painted in glowing colours.[182] Ivanov was cleared of having sexual relations with Christine Keeler.[183] The Police were exonerated of any serious failings. Their role in enforcing the criminal law, as opposed to investigating the private lives of individuals, a role which, according to Lord Denning, they carried out effectively in this instance, was stressed as was their complete independence of the government.[184] Lord Denning found no evidence that the government had influenced the actions of the police; specifically he found no evidence that the government had applied pressure on the police to prosecute Ward. Lord Denning stressed that 'we do not live in a police state'.[185] Whereas the activities of Lord Astor and Profumo were confined to the realm of private life, Ward was defined as a criminal who was a legitimate object of police attention, not because he was persecuted by the government, but because he had broken various sections of the Sexual Offences Act 1956.

However, although the narrative of the Report succeeded in shifting the focus of attention from the government to Ward there remained a serious problem which Lord Denning had to address if the Report was to succeed in completely shifting responsibility away from the government for the events leading to the resignation of the Secretary of State for War. The leader of the Opposition, Harold Wilson, had ignored the moral issues raised by Profumo's conduct, and the failure of the Prime Minister to realise that Profumo had behaved in a disgraceful manner, and focused exclusively on the security aspects of the case. Wilson suggested that Profumo's relationship with Keeler, coincident with her having a sexual relationship with Ivanov, a charge denied by Lord Denning, meant that there was a danger that classified information relating to the deployment of atomic weapons in Germany might have been leaked to the Russians. While ignoring Wilson's allegations, Lord Denning acknowledged the importance of the security issue admitting that, as a result of the events which unfolded in 1963: 'The Security Service can be made to appear incompetent'. Even more damaging, the events could "weaken the confidence of the United States in our integrity and reliability', that the whole affair would 'work towards destroying confidence'.[186]

The context was important. The combination of the Vassall case, Philby's defection in January 1963 and the revelation to the CIA of Blunt's role in the Cambridge spy ring by Michael Straight[187] in the early summer of 1963 had created a crisis in relations between the United States and Britain entailing the possibility that confidence in the Security Services could be undermined. It was therefore essential that Wilson's line of attack was defused and that a clear line was drawn between the Profumo affair and the other spy scandals. At the same time, Lord Denning's report provided an opportunity to place in the public domain an authoritative statement about the integrity of the British Security Services.

Lord Denning devoted a considerable part of his report[188] to establishing the integrity of the Security Services and to making it clear that there were no security implications in the Profumo affair. Much of Lord Denning's case was based on mere assertion, but his assertions were given credence by the fact that, for the first time, in a published document, his Report described, in some detail, the workings of the Security Services. This unprecedented candour, whilst not revealing much of significance, lent a weight of credibility to Lord Denning's refutation of allegations about the integrity of the Security Services. It also meant that, for the first time, the Security Services, and the Secret Intelligence Service in particular, emerged from the shadows into the public domain, albeit be with a robust judicial endorsement of their competence and integrity. It was as if James Bond himself had received an encomium from the Bench.[189]

Lord Denning stressed that the Security Services had 'one purpose and one purpose only, the Defence of the Realm'.[190] He made it quite clear that, like the Police, they had no role in investigating the private lives of individuals: 'It would be intolerable for us to have anything in the nature of a Gestapo or Secret Police to snoop into all that we do, let alone into our morals'.[191] Lord Denning revealed, with striking supporting detail, that the Security Service had previously reported directly to the Prime Minister, but since the 25th September 1952 they had reported to the Home Secretary.[192] A Cabinet Directive of a day later, the 26th September, had explicitly confined their activities to the Defence of the Realm. He also revealed, with much relish, that he had been able to witness at first handpresent one of the Security Services' operations against enemy agents in London.[193]

Lord Denning concluded that the circumstances of the Profumo affair, involving as they did 'the moral misbehaviour of a minister' for which 'we do not have the machinery to deal', meant that: 'They [the Security

Services] took all reasonable steps to see that the interests of the country were protected....there is no reason to believe that there was any security breach whatever'.[194] By emphasising that neither the police nor the Security Services investigated the private lives of politicians, and were therefore not a 'Gestapo', Lord Denning was able to assert that 'none of the governmental services was to blame'.[195] Faced with 'an unprecedented situation for which the machinery of government did not cater....there is no machinery for reporting the moral misbehaviour of ministers....it is perhaps better thus, than that we should have a 'police state''.[196] In other words, if something did go wrong it was because England was not like the Soviet Union; it was a country founded on the rule of law in which privacy was respected. The integrity of the traditional order was reasserted. The 'thoroughly immoral' figure of Stephen Ward, who was depicted as being manifestly un-English, a man who had broken all the rules of English propriety and could therefore be the scapegoat for the whole business remained, alone, in the spotlight, after all the other actors had left the stage. The traditional order, and its respectable subjects, were validated and reaffirmed by Lord Denning's Report which used Ward's 'alien' and 'un-English' character as a foil against which to assert the intrinsic integrity of the English character and the established way of doing things.

Although Lord Denning made some stern comments about the press, even the press was eventually brought within this reassuring framework. Lord Denning noted that the circulation of rumour by the press had damaged the existing order: 'Rumours are circulating which affect the honour and integrity of public life in this country',[197] remarking that the situation was made worse by 'the trafficing of scandal for reward',[198] that large sums of money were paid by newspapers to those who purveyed scandalous rumours. Worse still, these rumours 'so shook the confidence of the people of this country that they were ready to believe rumours which previously they would have rejected out of hand. No longer was the denial of a Minister to be accepted'.[199] Lord Denning devoted a substantial part of the Report to dealing with the problem of rumours which had spread through the press.[200] Some of those affected were threatening to take legal action. Lord Denning said enough in his report to prevent such actions while at the same time stilling the rage of rumour that was sweeping the country. He achieved this by referring explicitly to two rumours, those concerning 'The Man in the Mask'[201] and 'The Man without a Head'.[202] Both were made to appear ludicrous and absurd. 'The Man in the Mask' was said to be 'now grievously ashamed of what he did'.[203] The rumour concerning 'The Man without a Head', which involved a polaroid photograph of an act of *fellatio*, was disposed of by a rigmarole about a photograph of the relevant genitalia being compared with those of a Cabinet Minister and the consequent exoneration of that Minister.[204]

Apart from these two, which were dealt with explicitly, and somewhat pruriently, all the other rumours were attributed to Ward whose reliability had been totally undermined by the Report and were therefore dismissed comparatively easily as being 'utterly without foundation'.[205] Rumours about the 'great and the good', some of which were well founded, were therefore successfully scotched. Lord Denning concluded that there was 'no decline in the integrity of public life'[206] thus reasserting the stability and decency of the established order of things.

Although the press was clearly involved in the gratuitous spreading of rumour and innuendo, and were castigated accordingly, in the end Lord Denning brought even the press back within the embrace of the reaffirmed traditional order. They were not defined as part of the problem; that distinction was reserved for Ward, and Ward alone. Lord Denning concluded the Report by saying that he had received 'the greatest co-operation and assistance from the newspapers and all those concerned with them...not least from those whose practice I hold open to criticism'.[207] By concluding the Report in this way, Lord Denning was attempting to draw a line under the conflict between the press on the one hand, and the government and the courts on the other, which had developed during the Vassal case and had led directly to the hysteria which had engulfed the nation on account of the Profumo affair. To some extent, Lord Denning was responsible for the ensuing imbroglio because of the way in which he had framed his judgment about the issue of the confidentiality of journalist's sources which had arisen from the inquiry into the Vassall case.[208] His refusal of the appeal by two journalists against their commital for contempt by the Chairman of the Vassal tribunal, Lord Radcliffe, had led to their imprisonment and the consequential outrage and intransigence exhibited by the press during the Profumo affair. By stating his belief that the press understood the rules of the game and that they would respect them, that a free press, provided it behaved responsibly and did not 'traffic in scandal', was part of the traditional order of things, Lord Denning drew a line under the conflict between the press, the courts and the government which had created the atmosphere in which the poisonous blooms of the Profumo affair had bloomed so luxuriantly.

Lord Denning's report validated all the traditional institutions of the English constitution and broke new ground by including within that order the Security Services, which he insisted were devoted exclusively to the

Defence of the Realm. Lord Denning was the first person, holding a senior position within the establishment, to make any official comment about the nature and structure of the Security Services. The tone of his comments in his Report made them appear to be entirely beyond suspicion.

The Report began, and ended, with the thoroughly un-English Stephen Ward, the scapegoat who could not answer back. The traditional order was validated by the disgrace of Ward. The rumours subsided, the government survived and the reputation of the Security Services, glamourized by Ian Fleming's James Bond, now endorsed by the august authority of the Master of the Rolls, appeared secure.[209] Lord Denning's intervention was decisive and entirely successful. The fact that it did not tell the whole truth about the events which led to the resignation of the Secretary of State for War was beside the point. The system was saved. It was not until the late 1970s and early 1980s, a period in which quite different issues were at the centre of political debate, that any information reached the public domain which could be used to challenge the interpretation offered by Lord Denning concerning the events which had taken place in 1963. By that time the whole issue was academic. Thanks to Lord Denning the damage caused to the established order of things by the resignation of John Profumo was limited, the potential crisis which might have arisen was defused.

Between September 1963 and January 1979, Lord Denning confined his public interventions to those that arose from his judgments in the Court of Appeal. However, on the occasion of his eightieth birthday, he published the first of a series of books about the Law[210] and the following year gave a lecture which was broadcast on television.[211] These interventions, which addressed issues of current political controversy directly, and in an uncompromising manner, were quite unprecedented for a senior judge. No judge in living memory had entered the political arena so openly. The third of these books, *What Next in the Law*, went a step too far and led directly to the enforced retirement of Lord Denning on the 29th September 1982.

The Discipline of the Law, The Due Process of Law and *What Next in the Law* [1979-1982]

When Lord Denning published *The Discipline of Law* in January 1979, the political system was facing a significant series of challenges deriving from the conflict between the trade unions and the government over economic policy, the impact of the disorders in Northern Ireland, the debate about devolution for Scotland and Wales, the accountability of ministers to Parliament and the courts, the role of the Security Services, the issues raised by immigration, violence associated with picketing and demonstrations and, not least, the implications of membership of the European Community.

The role of the judges in relation to these issues was coming under scrutiny, as a result of the publication in 1977 of the first edition of J.A.G. Griffith's *The Politics of the Judiciary*. In January 1979 conflict between the government and the trade unions was to lead to a major political crisis, known popularly as 'the winter of discontent', followed, two months later, in March, by referendums, both of which failed, on Scottish and Welsh devolution. The subsequent defeat of the Labour government on a motion of confidence, the first to be successful since 1924, led to a General Election. At the start of the campaign, Airey Neave, the shadow Secretary of State for Northern Ireland was assassinated by Irish terrorists in the precincts of the House of Commons. The Conservatives won the election leading to the formation of Margaret Thatcher's first administration. Lord Denning's intervention into these turbulent events, which took the form of the publication of the first of a series of books about the English legal order, was therefore timely and, inevitably, controversial.

The epigraph to *The Discipline of Law* consists of a quotation from a judgment given by Lord Denning in the Court of Appeal in 1954[212]: 'If we never do anything which has not been done before, we shall never get anywhere. The law will stand still whilst the rest of the world goes on; and that will be bad for both'. This set the tone for a book in which Lord Denning developed the argument that the law could be reformed most effectively by the judges, that Parliament would take too long.

Lord Denning began *The Discipline of Law* with a discussion about 'the construction of documents' in which he made the case for the adoption of an approach to the interpretation of the wording of documents, including statutes, 'which accords with reason and justice'.[213] rather than on the basis of strict construction. 'A judge should not be a mere mechanic in the power-house of semantics. He should be the man in charge of it'.[214] The judge should therefore interpret words in the interests of justice so as to fulfill the words of his oath 'to do therein what to justice shall appertain'.[215]

He moved on to consider ways in which the judiciary could control 'the misuse of ministerial powers'; first quoting from his 1949 Hamlyn lectures that: 'Our procedure for securing our personal freedom is efficient, but our procedure for preventing the abuse of power is not. Just as the pick and shovel is no longer suitable for the winning of coal, so also the procedure of mandamus, certiorari and actions on the case are not suitable for the winning of freedom in the new age.....we have in our time to deal with changes which are of equal constitutional significance to those which took place 300 years ago'.[216] Reviewing the development of the powers of the courts to control abuse of power since 1949, he concluded that the courts have acted 'in support of the rule of law. All done so as to curb the abuse of power by the executive authorities'.[217] As was the case with the construction of documents, the judges had used their power to reform the law and promote the cause of justice. Lord Denning particularly noted the role of the courts in relation to official discretion in immigration cases as a crucial aspect of the court's vigilance in relation to control of the abuse of power: 'The best guidance is, I think, to be found in the case of immigrants. They have no right to come in, but they have a right to be heard'.[218] He also stressed that the 'constitutional importance'[219] of the Laker Airways case of 1977[220] which demonstrated that the courts were 'alert to see that any coercive action is justified in law'.[221]

Lord Denning then proceeded to discuss the importance of *locus standi* in relation to the control of the abuse of power, stressing the 'high constitutional principle' at stake in the Blackburn,[222] McWhirter[223] and Gouriet[224] cases in which he set out the basis for *locus standi* in bringing an action to review the use of discretionary power.[225] 'In administrative law the question of *locus standi* is the most vexed question of all' and the courts must exercise 'eternal vigilance' to ensure that *locus standi* is not used to restrict the ability of the citizen to seek redress in relation to abuse of power.

Having argued that the courts had managed to effectively control the abuse of power by ministers and those able to exercise discretion in making decisions related to public policy, Lord Denning then turned his attention to 'abuse of 'group' powers'; by 'group' he meant the trade unions. 'It is the most important question affecting society today',[226] he concluded. Reviewing the decisions of the courts in relation to trade unions since the 1950s, Lord Denning asserted that 'a man's right to work....is just as important to him as....his rights of property'[227] and that the courts would use their power to protect this right. He contended that 'domestic bodies which control the destinies of thousands...can mar or make a man by their decisions'.[228] 'It was the task of the courts to prevent them from abusing such power: 'They are not above the law, but subject to it'.'[229] Discussing the use by the courts of 'public policy' in relation to controlling such abuse of power, Lord Denning insisted that 'with a good man in the saddle, the unruly horse can be kept in control. It can jump over obstacles. It can leap the fences put up by fictions and come down on the side of justice'.[230] However, having asserted that the courts ought to have the power to deal with abuse of power by the trade unions, he concluded that 'if these groups abuse or misuse their powers, the courts are often unable to do anything about it'[231] because 'these efforts of the Common Law have been set at naught in large measure by the intervention of Parliament',[232] thereby implying that the actions of Parliament had enabled the trade unions to undermine the rule of law. This was a very contentious position for a senior member of the judiciary to adopt in January 1979. The Labour government elected in 1974 had repealed the Industrial Relations Act 1971, introduced by the preceding Conservative government as a means of restricting and regulating trade union power, in particular by curtailing the scope of some of the immunities granted by the 1906 Trade Disputes Act, replacing it with the Trade Union and Labour Relations Act 1974 which had significantly extended the immunities granted by the 1906 Trade Disputes Act. Lord Denning concluded his discussion of the relationship between the trade unions and the courts by suggesting, as the Conservative opposition was proposing, that the statutory immunity of the trade unions should be removed if their demands were 'wholly extortionate or utterly unreasonable, or quite impossible to fulfil'.[233]

Moving on to discuss the 'doctrine of precedent', Lord Denning noted that: 'In the House of Lords it is no good to dissent. In the Court of Appeal it is some good'.[234] He then listed a whole series of his dissenting judgments which had later been adopted by the House of Lords to support the idea that the courts could take a lead in reforming the law. According to Lord Denning, Parliament was not interested in reforming the law because 'there were no votes in it'.[235] Law reform therefore depended on the judges taking the initiative in changing the law in the interests of justice. This was a vital task because if the law was not 'consonant with justice....it will forfeit the confidence of the people. The law will fall into disrepute; and if that happens the stability of the country will be shaken'.[236]

However, despite his belief in the role that the judges could play in reforming the law and ensuring the proper administration of justice, Lord Denning concluded *The Discipline of Law* on a pessimistic note: 'The strict constructionists still hold the fortress. The officious bystander still dominates the field. The Court of Appeal is still bound hand and foot. The powerful still abuse their power without constraint'. The solution to the disorders of the time, according to Lord Denning, was that the judges should have the power to restrain the abuse of power by the powerful, be they government ministers or trade unionists, and to ensure that the law was reformed in the interests of justice. This insistence that the judges, rather than democratically elected Members of Parliament, should have the task of safeguarding the constitution was striking and controversial.

In his Dimbleby lecture of 1980, *The Misuse of Power*.[237] Lord Denning dealt unequivocally with the role of the judges in controlling the abuse of power, asserting that 'the only admissable remedy for any abuse of power - in a civilised country - is by recourse to law'.[238] He stressed that, for the law to be effective in controlling the abuse of power, the judges must be independent[239] and that 'the judges are the guardians of our Constitution'.[240] 'Someone must be trusted. Let it be the judges'.[241] As far as Lord Denning was concerned, the judges were the only people who could administer 'a body of law to see that powers are not misused or abused'[242] and by exercising those powers ensure that the constitution was preserved. He concluded by quoting from John Milton's *Samson Agonistes*: 'Oh how comely it is and how reviving to the spirits of just men long oppressed when God into the hands of their deliverer puts an invisible might, the might of the law'.[243]

The Due Process of Law,[244] published a year after *The Discipline of Law*, following the election of a Conservative government, was concerned with the balance between the freedom of the individual, a traditional characteristic of the Common Law, and the need to constrain that freedom in the interests of social order. In discussing contempt of court, where the judge acted as both judge and jury, and could deprive the individual of his freedom, Lord Denning emphasised that 'the course of justice must not be deflected or interfered with. Those who strike at it strike at the very foundations of society'.[245] Interference with 'the course of justice' was prevented by the power of the judge to commit an individual to prison for contempt of court. Despite its potentially draconian nature, this power was necessary because 'if they strike at the course of justice in this land....they strike at the roots of society itself; and they bring down that which protects them'.[246] It was clear that Lord Denning conceived the courts as being an indispensible part of the constitution.

However, in two instances, which some judges considered to be contempt of court - the case of the three dockers who were imprisoned by Sir John Donaldson, President of the Industrial Relations Court, in June 1972 and that of the Sunday Times in relation to the Thalidomide case - Lord Denning reached a very different conclusion. In the case of the three dockers, his intervention in the Court of Appeal, which led to their release, was justified on the basis that, whether or not there was a contempt, had they not been released 'they would have been martyrs. The trade union movement would have called a general strike which would paralyse the country'. As a result of the intervention of the Court of Appeal 'a general strike was averted. Another emergency was over'.[247] In the case of the Sunday Times, the Court of Appeal, agreeing with the European Court of Human Rights, found that the newspaper was not guilty of contempt, whereas the House of Lords came to the opposite conclusion.[248] It is clear that, while Lord Denning believed that contempt of court was an important means of protecting the judicial process from abuse, he also considered that the power to imprison for contempt should not be used in circumstances which might precipitate a political crisis, or compromise basic freedoms. It was for the judges to determine how the power vested in them should be used to protect the constitution, of which he judges were the guardians.

However, there was one circumstance in which the judges should always defer to the executive: national security. Discussing the decision of the Court of Appeal in the Hosenball case in 1977,[249] Lord Denning stated: 'There is one type of inquiry in which natural justice is excluded. It is when it is necessary in the interests of national security. There is some information which is so secret that it cannot be disclosed, except to a very few....in one case [of which the public know nothing][250] many of our agents disappeared. They were lost without a trace. They had been 'eliminated' by a foreign power. The information is known to the security service but to no-one outside...we cannot allow men's lives to be endangered by foreigners. Our history shows that, when the state itself is endangered, our cherished freedoms may have second place'.[251]

Lord Denning was also prepared to abridge the rights of the individual in the interests of the control of crime. Police powers of arrest and search could override individual rights in the interests of preserving law and order.[252] Lord Denning admitted that 'on looking back over the cases of the intervening 30 years, I find that I have been concerned - not so much with freedom - as with keeping the balance between freedom and security'.[253] He continued: 'In safeguarding our freedoms, the police play a vital role.......One of the most disturbing features of life in our time is the way in which wrongdoers seek to discredit the guardians of the peace....the time has come when it is the duty of every responsible citizen to support the police and to recognise that they are the front line of defence against violence and intimidation'.[254] He carried on: 'In these present times, with the ever increasing wickedness there is about, honest citizens must help the police and not hinder them in their efforts to track down criminals'.[255] These remarks were published a few weeks after Lord Denning delivered his notorious judgment about the Birmingham Six.

In order to sustain his position as a defender of the rights of the individual, despite these comments which revealed that he was prepared to compromise those rights, Lord Denning spent some time describing his judgment in the Rossminster case of 1979;[256] in which the Court of Appeal severely criticised the actions of the Inland Revenue and declared that they had abused their powers in searching business premises.[257] In his judgment he invoked the case of *Entinck v Carrington*[258] and reasserted the values of the traditional constitution: 'As far as my knowledge of history goes, there has been no search like it - and no seizure like it - in England since that Saturday, 30 April, 1763, when the Secretary of State issued a general warrant by which he authorised the King's messenger to arrest John Wilkes and seize all his books and papers.....once a great power is granted there is a danger of its being abused....it is the duty of the courts to construe the statute so as to see that it encroaches as little as possible on the liberties of the people of England'.[259]

Later in the book, Lord Denning turned his attention to the relationship between the traditional liberties accorded to the individual in the English constitution and the challenges posed to that constitution by mass immigration from the former Commonwealth. The tone of his remarks was clearly hostile to immigration, as it had developed since the 1950s: 'In recent times England has been invaded - not by enemies - nor by friends - but by those who seek England as a haven. In our country there is no poverty....in England there is social security - a national health service and guaranteed housing - all to be had for the asking without payment and without working for it. Once here each seeks to bring his relations to join him. So they multiply exceedingly'.[260] 'In the last 25 years there has been much concern about the entry of immigrants into England. Previously there was little concern. No restriction was placed on immigrants either by the Common Law or by statute....the most liberal of all the countries in the world'.[261] As in the other cases where he had advocated restrictions on freedom, Lord Denning qualified his position by adverting to a resonant example of the traditional approach of the Common Law to the protection of individual liberty, in this instance he referred to Somersett's case of 1772 in which 'the 'black' was set free'.[262] However, having used Somersett's case to establish his 'liberal' credentials, Lord Denning then proceeded to refer to a series of immigration cases decided by the Court of Appeal making comments that were distinctly hostile to the whole idea of immigration. Commenting on his judgment in *R v Home Secretary ex parte Phansopkar*[263] in which he had given judgment in 1976, in a tone which implied strong misgivings about the consequences of mass immigration, he observed, in relation to the Commonwealth Immigration

Act 1971: 'It made a new man. It called him 'patrial'. Not a patriot, but a patrial. Parliament made him one of us: and made us one of them. We are all now patrials. We are no longer, in the eyes of the law, Englishmen, Scotsmen or Welshmen. We are just patrials. Parliament gave this new man a fine set of clothes. It invested him with a new right. It called it 'the right of abode in the United Kingdom'. It is the most precious right that anyone can have. At least I so regard it'.[264] Mr Phansopkar 'became a citizen of no mean country. He could say proudly, if he spoke Latin - *civis Angliae sum*'.[265]

Commenting on his judgment in *Thakrah v Secretary of State for the Home Department*,[266] a case of 1974, Lord Denning observed: 'This country would not have room for them. It is not as if it was only one or two coming. They come not in single files, but in battalions'.[267] Lord Denning suggested that it might have been better for Mr Thakrah to become a citizen of 'that great country' India, 'there may be more scope for him than here'.[268] 'This country is not large enough to take all those whom we would gladly accept'.[269] In conclusion he asserted that the Home Secretary had used his discretionary power in relation to immigration 'generously in the interests of humanity' and, referring to immigration officers, he pronounced that 'I have never known a case where they have been unfair'.[270]

Lord Denning concluded his discussion of immigration by quoting from a judgment concerning taxation of a trust based in Jersey in 1969, *Re Weston's Settlements*.[271] 'There are many things in life more worthwhile than money. One of these things is to be brought up in this our England, which is still 'the envy of less happier lands'. I do not believe it is for the benefit of children to be uprooted from England and transported to another country simply to avoid tax....children are like trees: they grow stronger with firm roots'.[272]

As far as Lord Denning was concerned it was clear that immigration was a threat to 'this our England' which was 'still the envy of less happier lands'. The last book which he published before his enforced resignation, *What Next in the Law*,[273] revealed, in even more explicit terms, his hostility to immigration and was to be the proximate cause of his enforced resignation on September 29th 1982.

What Next in the Law was completed in February 1982 and published on the 20th of May 1982. Since the publication of his two previous books about the law, serious disturbances had taken place in St Paul's Bristol in April 1980 and in Brixton in April 1981, followed by rioting in Toxteth and other inner city areas in July 1981. In the course of a discussion about jury trials in the book, Lord Denning made comments about the jury which tried those charged with riotous assembly during the disturbances in St Paul's in Bristol which suggested that the use of the right of preremptory challenge had produced more black jurors and therefore created a 'packed' jury which would not convict black defendants.[274] The black jurors in the case, which found the defendants not guilty, threatened to sue. These comments, combined with general comments in the book about the suitability of black people to be jurors on the grounds that: 'The English are no longer a homogeneous race. They are white and black, coloured and brown. They no longer share the same standards of conduct. Some of them come from countries where bribe and graft are accepted as an integral part of life: and where stealing is a virtue so long as you are not caught'[275] led to a furore in which legal action was threatened against Lord Denning by the Society of Black Lawyers. The book was withdrawn, the offending passages removed. On the 28th May Lord Denning announced that he would retire on the 29th September 1982, making a public apology for the comments on the 6th June.[276]

Despite this controversy which was instrumental in bringing Lord Denning's career as Master of the Rolls to an involuntary end, *What Next in the Law* was intended to be a tract about law reform; 'My book shall be the spur...perhaps then something may be done'.[277] 'Most of it is controversial - I have deliberately made it so. It is to set you thinking, talking and writing about what I have said'.[278] He concluded by saying: 'In this book I have stood the law on its head - in the hope that you may help get it the right way up'.[279]

Lord Denning stated his motive in seeking reform of the law quite plainly: 'The most important function of the law is to restrain the abuse of power by any of the holders of it - no matter whether they be the government, the newspapers, the television, the trade unions, the multi-national corporations or anyone else'.[280] He began by quoting Bracton's doctrine that 'the King is under no man, but under God and the Law' and then comparing Charles I's treatment of the Court which tried him for treason with that adopted by the Nazi leaders at Nuremburg.[281] He continued: 'He disputed with John Bradshaw. All very unseemly. He was sentenced to death. John Bradshaw was the first to sign the death warrant'.[282] The subordination of power to the law was thus made very clear. Sir Edward Coke, who challenged James I on this point, and was the author of the Petition of Right, was praised as the great exemplar of the tradition of the rule of law and the control of power by the law. Lord Denning quoted Sir William Holdsworth's encomium of Coke: 'What Shakespeare had been to literature, what Bacon has been to philosophy, what the translators of the Authorised version of the Bible have been to religion, Coke has been to the public and private law of England'. The rule of law and its control of power was thus placed right at the foundation of English identity. Invoking another patriarch of the Common Law to endorse the importance of Coke, Lord Denning quoted Sir James Fitzjames Stephen's judgment that Coke had more influence than anyone on the development of the law from the time of Bracton to that of Blackstone.

Lord Denning then proceeded to praise Blackstone, but to denigrate Bentham who he noted was born, like himself, in Whitchurch: 'One of the very few bad things to come out of it....the most pretentious person who ever lived'.[283] The tradition of the Common Law, as understood by Lord Denning, excluded anyone who attempted to reform the law on a rational, critical basis. Lord Denning explicitly condemned Bentham's critique of Blackstone's doctrine of 'natural rights',[284] before proceeding to praise Lord Mansfield's reforms of the civil law, noting that he was both a Scot and a Jacobite, but that these characteristics did not prevent him from contributing to the development of the law: 'Scotsmen now dominate us in most things. We no longer resent it'.[285] Lord Denning's treatment of Lord Mansfield's distinctly 'un-English' provenance – he was both a Scot and a Roman Catholic - allowed him to demonstrate the flexibility and tolerance of the Common Law.[286] He concluded this section of the book by a discussion of the career of the Whig reformer, and drafter of the Great Reform Act, Lord Brougham. In this way, Lord Denning's reading of the genealogy of the Common Law, despite its anathematisation of Bentham, ws firmly associated with progressive, liberal values, those of Victorian Whiggery.

Having set out the genealogy of the Common Law, associating that genealogy with both reform and, in particular, with restraint of the abuse of power, Lord Denning then proceeded to discuss the jury system, 'the strongest of all the forces making for the nation's peaceful continuity and progress'.[287] Referring to the jury's acquittal of the 7 Bishops in 1688, 'the most important State trial recorded in our annals', he noted that 'they had saved the English constitution'[288] by resisting the tyranny of James II.

However, having stressed the constitutional significance of the jury in relation to the control of power by law, Lord Denning expressed concern about the role of the jury in the contemporary legal system. He noted that until 1918, juries were not chosen at random but were 'a select band of the middle classes....each was educated and of good understanding.... reasonable men'.[289] Random selection of jurors led to a danger of bribery when jurors were 'drawn from all elements of the population'.[290] Juries may have been essential to the rule of law and the control of power, but they were not democratic institutions, rather they were expressions of a stable social order. Juries 'grew up in the ages when the English were an homogeneous race....by the time trial by jury became enshrined in our constitution - an unwritten constitution - the English were one race'.[291] Lord Denning considered that the right to trial by jury was a fundamental principle of the English constitution, directly associating the stability of the constitution with racial homogeneity. The clear implication was that any dilution of that homogeneity would threaten the integrity of the jury system and therefore that of the nation itself. He concluded by proposing that the constitutional role of the jury could be protected by the abolition of preremptory challenge, the trial of fraud by special assessors, the trial of more minor offences by magistrates, the ending of random selection of jurors and the introduction of a new selection procedure for jurors. The remarks about black jurors which led to his resignation were removed, but it was notable that those remarks were made in a section of the book which was concerned with the fundamental principles of the English constitution; in Lord Denning's understanding the stability of the constitution depended on the maintenance of racial homogeneity.

In his discussion of libel, an aspect of the law which had significant implications for the freedom of the press, Lord Denning maintained that 'the right of fair comment is one of the essential elements which go to make up our freedom of speech. We must ever maintain this right intact'.[292] He continued: 'If the newspaper or television receive or obtain information fairly from a valuable and responsible source, which it is in the public interest that the public should know, then there is a qualified privilege to publish it. They should not be liable in the absence of malice'.[293] However, the determination of whether the information was obtained 'fairly', whether the source was 'valuable and responsible' and whether 'it is in the public interest that the public should know' was to be made by the courts, not by the newspapers. Regulation of freedom of speech, definition of its limits, was to be subject to standards created by the courts.

Lord Denning was clear that the courts should retain the power to award exemplary damages against newspapers and broadcasters if they violated the standards established by the judiciary.[294] He concluded with a ringing endorsement of the principle of press freedom: 'It is of the first importance that the newspapers and the media should be free. So long as this freedom is exercised in the public interest - it should not be subject to undue restraint'.[295] It was made very plain that, for all its importance, this freedom should be policed by the courts, that it was not a freedom which stood on its own. The judges, not the press, were the ultimate guardians of the constitution.

In discussing the equitable doctrine of confidentiality, Lord Denning made this point very plain indeed. There was a conflict between confidentiality and disclosure in the public interest: 'These two public interests reached their climax in investigative journalism'.[296] Lord Denning made it quite clear that it was for the judges to determine how that balance was to be struck.[297] He concluded by asserting, emphatically, that it was for the courts, not Parliament, to strike the balance in cases involving confidentiality and investigative journalism.[298] Lord Denning's defence of the freedom of the press was balanced by an insistence that the press should act responsibly, in accordance with standards set by the courts: 'In order to be deserving of freedom, the press must show itself worthy of it. A free press must be a responsible press. The power of the press is great. It must not abuse that power. If a newspaper should act irresponsibly, then it forfeits its claim to protect the sources of its information.....if they should repeat their irresponsible conduct, they will find that curbs are put on their freedom'.[299]

Having discussed the role of the judges, juries and the press in preventing the abuse of power, Lord Denning then proceeded to discuss the merits of the introduction of a Bill of Rights.[300] He noted that 'there is a feeling among ordinary people that rights and freedoms of the individual have been eroded beyond measure',[301] commenting that the law seemed unable to protect individuals against abuse of power by 'the government, trade unions and powerful bodies'.[302] Lord Denning dealt with this question by returning to the genealogy of the Common Law, to the forefathers of the law: 'As usual I go back in time'.[303] He discussed *Magna Carta* and the 1689 Bill of Rights, described by Macaulay as 'the germ of every good law which has been passed during a century and a half'.[304] However, Lord Denning suggested that it was the judges rather than the paper law of a Bill of Rights, which had protected the freedoms of the English. He quoted the words of Sir Edward Coke: 'I will seek nothing out of my own head, but from my heart and out of Acts of Parliament' to remedy the 'consumption' of the State, an opinion which suggested that it was the law graven in the hearts of the judges which was crucial to the protection of rights. James II was defined as 'a bad king....it was he who dismissed the judges',[305] again suggesting that abuse of power could only be controlled by the judges.

Lord Denning then examined the UN Universal Declaration of Human Rights which he declared to be 'absolutely useless for one decisive reason. There was no means of enforcing it'.[306] Such a law required judges to administer and apply it, otherwise it was nugatory. The European

Convention of Human Rights might be used as a guide, but use of it in the English courts as an aid to interpretation must be subject to the discretion of the judges.[307] The statements of principle contained in the European Convention of Human Rights were 'not the sort of thing which we can easily digest',[308] 'to swallow it altogether, hook, line and sinker - would be too much of a mouthful',[309] the principles were often 'so wide as to be incapable of practical application'.[310] He continued: 'It is drawn in such vague terms that it can be used for all sorts of unreasonable claims and provoke all sorts of litigation. As so often happens with high-sounding principles, they have to be brought down to earth'.[311] It was the discretion of the judges in applying such general principles that would perform that task.

Lord Denning illustrated this point by discussing a series of cases which raised issues concerning rights protected by the European Convention of Human Rights, in particular the right to marry, the right to respect for family life and the right to freedom of religion.[312] The cases involving the right to marry and the right to respect for family life also involved immigration law, that involving freedom of religion concerned a Muslim teacher who wished to be able to say his Friday prayers, a desire which conflicted with the terms of his contract of employment. It was notable that all these cases involved issues of race and ethnicity, providing examples of the way in which England was ceasing to be an homogeneous society. Intensely aware of the tension between the enumerated rights of the European Convention and the preservation of an ethnically homogeneous identity, Lord Denning maintained that the strict application of the European Convention of Human Rights to those cases would have the result that 'the cause of racial integration would suffer'.[313]

Another way of putting this would be that the necessary ethnic and cultural homogeneity which underpinned the legal order would be disrupted by the legal protection of certain human rights. Lord Denning was emphatic that the scope of such rights must be decided 'in the light of circumstances prevailing in England' and not 'by judges who have no knowledge of the circumstances in England'.[314] It was clear that he considered that human rights law would prove to incompatible with the traditional values of the English legal system and that it was for the judges to protect it from the threat posed by such rights. The key to the protection of individual rights, according to Lord Denning, was the independence of the judges rather than the incorporation of the European Convention of Human Rights into English law.[315]

However, Lord Denning adopted a very different approach to the law of the European Community which had been incorporated into English law in 1972. Discussing the decisions of the European Court of Justice he noted: 'If I were to look at it with the eyes of an English lawyer I would be critical. But when I look at their work with the eyes of a good European, I think they have done - and are doing - great things for Europe.....we should cease to look at its work with English eyes.....We should look at it with European eyes. We should strive to wipe out the discord of the past and do all we can to build the new Federation of Europe based on a comprehensive Community law. As I have said before: 'The Treaty is like an incoming tide. It flows into the estuaries and up the rivers. It cannot be held back'.[316]

It seemed that Lord Denning accepted that the authority of the sovereignty of Parliament, to which the courts must defer, had been used to import European law into the English constitution. He also appeared to conceive this act of the sovereign Parliament as being concerned with ending the European conflicts which had dominated his adult life and, in 1940, threatened the very existence of the England as a nation. Earlier in the book, commenting on the Second World War, he had stated: 'In 1945 we won. Civilisation was saved'.[317] It is clear from Lord Denning's comments about the European Court of Justice that he considered the European Community to be part of the fulfilment of the victory of civilisation which had occurred in 1945. That victory had preserved the English constitution; membership of the European Community would therefore ensure that it would survive in the future. As Lord Denning put it in *Macarthys v Smith*[318] in 1979, the sovereign Parliament might repeal the European Communities Act but 'I do not however envisage any such situation'.[319] Membership of the European Community, and all the legal consequences that flowed from that membership, were conceived as being part of the constitution, part of the re-ordering of the world which followed from the victory in 1945. In Lord Denning's eyes, adhesion to the European Community underpinned the constitution which had almost been overwhelmed in the struggle which preceded that victory.

Lord Denning concluded *What Next in the Law* with an emphatic assertion of the centrality of the judges in the English constitution: 'To my mind the judges are the guardians of the constitution'.[320] If the unwritten conventions of that constitution were abused then the judges 'should be able to pronounce on the validity of these conventions. They should be able to interfere if they are misused or abused'.[321] He continued: 'They stand, as ever, between the executive and the subject.....alert to see that any coercive action is justified in law'.[322] 'They are the representatives of all that is best in our people'.[323] 'Someone must be trusted. Let it be the judges'.[324]

What Next in the Law was an uncompromising assertion of the importance of the judiciary in the English constitution. It was ironical that the controversy caused by some of its comments about race, comments which flowed inexorably from Lord Denning's understanding that ethnic homogeneity provided the necessary stability which underpinned the legal order, led to the end of his legal career and the departure from the bench of the most formidable advocates of the Common Law.

Lord Denning's enforced retirement coincided with the British victory over Argentina in the Falklands conflict. This was the first time, since the Suez invasion of 1956, that British armed forces had engaged in a war with another sovereign state, as distinct from colonial police actions. For Michael Foot and the Labour opposition, the Falklands war was a war fought to uphold the principles of the United Nations; a war of self-defence fought against a power which had used violence to occupy territory to which it had a disputed claim in international law. For Enoch Powell, and others who thought like him, it was a straightforward defence of national sovereignty. Lord Denning clearly inclined to Enoch Powell's point of view. When the Task Force returned to Portsmouth after the victory, he recorded that 'we had a large Union Jack flying from the window. We cheered and cheered'.[325] Commenting on the victory of British arms Lord Denning quoted lines from Shakespeare's *King John*: 'Come the three corners of the world in arms and we shall shock them. Nought shall make us rue if England to itself do rest but true'.[326] *King John* was a celebration of the defiance by a King of England of the authority of the Pope; the play was intended to be a justification of Henry VIII's defiance of the Pope in 1534 when Parliament enacted the Act of Supremacy which declared England to be an 'empire', a moment of crucial importance in the evolution of the English constitution. For Lord Denning, the victory in the Falklands war was a vindication of the traditional order, a victory which enabled him to accept his enforced retirement in the knowledge that the order which he sought to defend was still intact despite all the challenges which had emerged during the period of his tenure of the office of Master of the Rolls.[327]

Notes

[1] [London 1981]
[2] Ibid vi
[3] Ibid p. 31
[4] Ibid p. 5 Lord Denning, providentially for someone with such firm beliefs, was very fortunate in his married life. One contemporary, who shared Lord Denning's

values, but who was less blessed was Lord Hailsham who became Lord Chancellor in 1970. Hailsham's marriage broke down during the Second World War resulting in divorce. A similar fate befell Anthony Eden who became Prime Minister in 1956. Harold Macmillan, who appointed Lord Denning to both the House of Lords in 1957 and the Mastership of the Rolls in 1962, had a notoriously miserable marriage which did not result in divorce but amounted to a menage a trois with Lord Boothby. In 1930, Lord Denning married Mary, his childhood sweetheart, a vicar's daughter. 'I met the fairest in the land. But I never lost my heart to any. I had already given it away - beyond recall'. Ibid p. 84. Mary died of tuberculosis in 1941. Lord Denning was married again, again very happily, to Joan Stuart in 1945.
[5] Ibid v
[6] Ibid vi
[7] Ibid p.5
[8] Lord Denning was using the word 'race' in relation to its Latin etymology. *Radix*, *radice* meaning 'root' was the source of the word 'race' as used in this passage. The association of 'race' with the marriage bed in which 'seeds' are sown which then germinate to form the 'root' or 'radix' from which the English nation is sustained is plain.
[9] Ibid vi
[10] Ibid vi
[11] Ibid vi
[12] Ibid vi
[13] Language was central to Lord Denning's understanding of the law. Later in *The Family Story*, he referred to John Buchan's planned anthology of judgments of which he said: 'It would put most professional stylists to shame' and that it would 'be worthy to rank with the greatest literature which England holds'. Ibid p.216. Lord Denning argued that language had helped to save the English nation in the Second World War: 'That is how Winston Churchill helped us so much to win the war...by his speeches and writings rather than by his strategy or mental capacity'. Ibid p. 216 Referring to the literary style of his own judgments, Lord Denning said that he tried 'to make his judgments live', setting them out in the manner of a play by Shakespeare with a Prologue, followed by a sequence of Acts divided up into scenes peopled with characters with real names. Ibid p. 207
[14] Later in *The Family Story* Lord Denning quoted the words of Colonel Mannering to Counsellor Pleydell from Sir Walter Scott's *Guy Mannering*: 'These are the tools of my trade. A lawyer without history and literature is a mechanic, a mere working mason; if he possesses some knowledge of these he may venture to call himself an architect'. Ibid p. 217
[15] Religion was of particular importance to the English constitution according to Lord Denning: 'Without religion there can be no morality; and without morality there can be no law'. Ibid p.182 'Justice is not something you can see. It is not temporal but eternal, a product of spirit not intellect...if religion perishes in the land, truth and justice will also' ibid p.183. In a lecture in 1954, he said: 'We have already strayed too far from the faith of our fathers. Let us return to it, for it is the

only thing that can save us', ibid p. 183
[16]Ibid p. 154
[17]Ibid p. 157-8
[18]'The King judges by his judges, and they are the speaking law, *lex loquens*'. Coke, Institutes, First Part s130A [1823 Edition]
[19]Ibid v
[20]Ibid v
[21]Ibid p.5
[22]Ibid p.6
[23]Ibid p.7
[24]Ibid p.8
[25]Ibid p120
[26]Ibid p.128 Later he applied the same words of Cromwell to the law: 'It is not enough to keep your law books dry. It is as well to have a Bible ready to hand too'. Ibid p. 181
[27]*Leaves from my Library - An English Anthology* [London 1986] pp. 34-35
[28]*What Next in the Law* [London 1982] p.6
[29]Ibid p. 6
[30]*The Changing Law* [London 1953] p.4-5
[31]Ibid p.273
[32]'Trial by jury remains the bulwark of our liberties....the first object of any tyrant in Whitehall would be to make Parliament utterly subservient to his will; and next to overthrow or diminish trial by jury, for no tyrant could afford to leave a subject's freedom in the hands of 12 of his countrymen. So that trial by jury is more than an instrument of justice and more than one wheel of the constitution; it is the lamp that shows that freedom lives'. Lord Denning quoted these words from Sir Patrick Devlin's *Trial by Jury* [London 1956] at p. 164. ibid p.162
[33]Ibid p. 43
[34]*The Family Story* [London 1981] pp.9-10
[35]*Henry V* William Shakespeare Scene 3
[36]Ibid p.75
[37]'I wonder how long this Service of Remembrance will continue. I hope forever. It is to those men that we owe our freedom. Yet, if it comes to another war, they will, I am sure, do just as we did. Fight for freedom'. ibid p 254.
[38]Ibid pp. 249-251
[39]Ibid p.130
[40]Ibid p.134
[41]Ibid p.120
[42]Ibid pp. 36-39 Lord Denning just failed to become a Fellow of All Souls in 1922 and thereafter referred to All Souls as the 'college that refused me'. He claimed that it was his lack of proficiency in Latin which was the cause of his failure. In the 1920s and 1930s, All Souls was close to the heart of government, the City and the Law. It was a college which entertained Prime Ministers, Governors of the Bank of England and judges of the Court of Appeal and the House of Lords, quite

a few of which were fellows of the college. Lord Denning was also awarded a gamma jurisprudence in his final Law examinations. As he put it: 'The jargon of the philosophers of law has always been beyond me'. Ibid p.240 Lord Denning claimed that his law tutor at Magdalen was 'the most ignorant man I have ever met', but he was also taught by Geoffrey Cheshire, one of the editors of *The Law of Real Property*, who made sure that he studied the 1922 Law of Property Act. This enabled him to be right up to date in his legal knowledge and helped him secure high marks in his examinations. Ibid p. 32. Lord Hailsham, the other dominant figure in the law during the 1960s and 1970s won a prize Fellowship to All Souls in 1931 in preference to the future Lord Wilberforce and H.L.A. Hart who later became Professor of Jurisprudence at the University of Oxford.

[43] Ibid p.94. Lord Denning claimed that this experience 'taught me most of the law I ever knew'. It certainly laid the basis for his extensive, and scholarly, knowledge of case law which enabled him to be so creative in his use, or manipulation, of precedent to change the law later in his career. Lord Denning called case law 'the greatest of all collections of law. Far outdoing the Digests of Roman Law or the Codes of Napoleon'. Ibid p. 221

[44] During the General Strike in May 1926 Lord Denning served as a Special Constable [ibid p. 79]

[45] Ibid p.172

[46] Ibid p.172

[47] Ibid p.175 As he put it 'Judges do not go by the strict law at all. They go by the good sense of the case'. Ibid p. 164

[48] Ibid p.139

[49] Ibid p.176-177

[50] *Central Property Trust Ltd. v High Trees House Ltd* [1947] 1 K.B. 130

[51] Ibid p. 165

[52] Between 1952 and 1983, Lord Denning was President of Birkbeck College but at that time there was no School of Law at Birkbeck. The School of Law was established in 1992.

[53] Ibid p.177

[54] Ibid p.179

[55] Ibid p.179

[56] Ibid pp.189-190. This section of *The Family Story* in which Lord Denning discussed the nature of the English constitution, is taken, almost word for word, from *The Changing Law* [London 1953] pp. 1-7

[57] Ibid p. 190

[58] Ibid p. 190

[59] Ibid p. 191

[60] Ibid p. 191

[61] Ibid p. 191

[62] Ibid p. 191

[63] Ibid p. 192

[64] Ibid p. 192

[65] Ibid pp.192-195
[66] Ibid p. 195
[67] This was the published version of the first Hamlyn lectures which Lord Denning delivered at Senate House, University of London in October and November 1949.
[68] This series of public lectures, endowed by a wealthy philanthropist, continues to this day and is dedicated to increasing the awareness of the public about the law and legal issues.
[69] [London 1949]
[70] Ibid p. 3
[71] Ibid p. 3
[72] Ibid p. 4
[73] Ibid p. 4-5
[74] Ibid p. 5
[75] Ibid p. 6
[76] *The Five Knights Case* [1627] 3 How. St. Tr. 1 KB
[77] *Somersett v Stewart* [1772] Loft 1 19. The famous quotation from this case which Lord Denning excerpted in *Freedom under the Law*: 'The air of England is too pure for the slave to breathe' was actually a submission of counsel, Francis Hargreave, not a dictum of Lord Mansfield. Lord Mansfield merely stated: 'Therefore the Black must be discharged'. Lord Denning was quoting from Lord Campbell's *The Lives of the Chief Justices* [John Murray 1858] See Samuels, A. 'What did Lord Mansfield actually say?' LQR 2002, 118 [July] 379-381
[78] Ibid p. 7
[79] Lord Denning stressed that regulation 18B was a 'high water mark'. Lord Atkin's judgment was a dissenting judgment but regulation 18B, for all its potential to undermine 'freedom under the law' was supervised by KCs who advised the Regional Commissioners responsible for applying 18B and 'a conscientious and careful Home Secretary'. Ibid p. 16. Lord Denning was just such a KC. In 1939 he was appointed legal advisor to the Regional Commissioner for the North East. *The Family Story* p. 129
[80] [1942] AC 206
[81] Ibid p. 14
[82] Ibid p. 14
[83] Ibid p. 15
[84] Ibid p. 18
[85] [1947] AC 573
[86] Ibid pp. 18-22
[87] Ibid p. 24
[88] Ibid pp. 27-29
[89] Ibid p. 29
[90] Ibid p. 31
[91] Ibid p. 31
[92] Ibid p. 35 Lord Denning referred to Cromwell's insistence on this principle. This was another example of his tendency to consider that the rule of Cromwell rather

than that of the Stuart monarchy had embodied the basic principles of the English constitution.

[93] Ibid pp. 35-36

[94] Ibid pp. 35-39 Commenting on the case of the *Junius Letters* [*R v Almon* [1770] 5 Burr 2686 20, State Tr 803] in which a jury acquitted a publisher who had accused ministers of misleading the King and was charged with seditious libel, Lord Denning remarked: 'It would be interesting to speculate what would happen in Russia if someone said that Mr Stalin was not acquainted with the language of truth'. Ibid p. 39

[95] Ibid pp. 39-40

[96] In *R v Higgins* [1801] 2 East 5 the court defined public mischief very broadly: 'All offences of a public nature, that is, such acts or attempts as tend to the prejudice of the community are indictable'. Ibid p. 41 Lord Denning compared this broad definition with Article 16 of the Soviet Legal Code which prohibits all 'socially dangerous acts'.

[97] Ibid p. 41

[98] Ibid p. 41

[99] *R v Leese* unreported

[100] *R v Caunt* unreported

[101] Ibid p. 47

[102] Ibid p. 48

[103] Ibid p. 48

[104] Ibid p.50

[105] Ibid p. 52

[106] Ibid p. 55

[107] Ibid p. 58

[108] Ibid p. 59

[109] 'The system which has been built up by our forefathers over the last 1000 years'. Ibid p. 63. 'We must be free, or die, who spoke the tongue that Shakespeare spoke; the faith and morals hold which Milton held; in everything we are sprung of Earth's first blood, have titles manifold'. William Wordsworth, quoted ibid p. 64 In 1982, Lord Denning's comments in *What Next in the Law* that immigration had undermined the homogeneity of the English nation, in particular that the diversity of values consequent on the influx of people from the former Commonwealth had compromised the integrity of the jury system, led to a bitter controversy which resulted in the Society of Black Lawyers bringing a libel action against him. Despite his issuing a public apology, the affair led to Lord Denning's enforced resignation in September 1982.

[110] Ibid p. 59

[111] Ibid p. 67

[112] Ibid p. 67

[113] Ibid p. 70

[114] Ibid p. 73

[115] Ibid p. 74-75

[116] Ibid p. 80
[117] Ibid p. 96
[118] Ibid p. 99
[119] Ibid p. 100
[120] Ibid p. 101
[121] *R v Hampden* [1637] How. St. Tr. 825
[122] Ibid p. 101
[123] Ibid p. 102
[124] Ibid p. 126
[125] Ibid p. 126
[126] Ibid p. 126
[127] *The Changing Law* [London 1953] pp. 1-18
[128] Ibid p. 1
[129] Ibid p. 8
[130] Ibid p. 10
[131] Ibid p. 14
[132] Ibid p. 15
[133] Ibid p. 17
[134] Ibid p. 18
[135] Ibid p. 99
[136] Ibid p. 118
[137] Ibid p. 119
[138] Ibid p. 120
[139] Ibid p. 121
[140] Ibid p. 121-122
[141] Ibid p. 122
[142] Delivered on the 21st May 1959. The Romanes Lecture is an annual public lecture delivered in the Sheldonian Theatre in Oxford. Its contents would have been reported in the newspapers and widely disseminated amongst opinion formers. Members of Oxford University, such as Harold Macmillan, the Prime Minister, who had the power to appoint judges, attended. In April 1962, Macmillan, who appointed Lord Denning to the office of Master of the Rolls, and was to become Chancellor of Oxford University in 1960, succeeding the Earl of Halifax who had held the position since 1933, would have attended in person. Lord Denning's call in the lecture for law reform, in particular that the House of Lords should be able to change its previous decisions so as to enable the law to develop in response to the needs of changing times, would have been noted by the government. It is possible that Macmillan's appointment of Lord Denning to the office of Master of the Rolls in 1962 was part of his desire to encourage law reform at a time when, under the leadership of Lord Simonds, the House of Lords were not prepared to undertake that task. As Lord Denning pointed out in *The Family Story*: 'It is in the Court of Appeal that a judge has the chief opportunity of influencing the law.....very few cases go to the Lords'. p. 172
[143] 'A land of settled government,

A land of just and old reknown
Where Freedom slowly broadens down
From Precedent to Precedent'.
From *You can ask me why, though ill at ease* by Alfred Lord Tennyson.
[144]*From Precedent to Precedent* [London 1959] p. 33-34
[145]Ibid p. 34
[146]The 'Kilmuir Rules' were not rules at all but a self-imposed convention of judicial self-restraint. These so-called 'rules' were associated with David Maxwell-Fife, Viscount Kilmuir, Lord Chancellor from 1954 to 1962. Kilmuir was sacked as Lord Chancellor by Harold Macmillan in the 'night of the long knives' in July 1962 and replaced by a figure of abject mediocrity, Reginald Manningham-Buller, Viscount Dilhorne, reputedly the model for Anthony Powell's comic monster Kenneth Widmerpool who married the *uber-bitch* Pamela Flitton, mistress of the writer X Trapnel. Manningham-Buller's daughter, Eliza, a former student of English Literature at Lady Margaret Hall and quondam schoolmistress, served as Director of M15 from 2002 to 2007; the second female to hold that post. However, the Lord Chancellor had no power to constrain the actions of a High Court judge, a judge in the Court of Appeal or a Lord of Appeal in Ordinary. The tenure of these judges, *puisne* judges, was protected by the Act of Settlement 1701; they could only be dismissed by a free vote of both Houses of Parliament. If a judge, such as Lord Denning, decided to speak in public about the Law that was a matter for him. Lords of Appeal in Ordinary, and judges such as Lord Denning who were given Peerages, could speak as they wished in the House of Lords. It was only a convention, which was never rigorously observed, and has been increasingly disregarded in recent times, which inhibited *puisne* judges from speaking their minds in public. Of course, there were obvious reasons why public garrulity was a bad idea. People thus inclined would never be appointed to judicial office; careers in journalism were more suitable for persons of that bent.
[147]*Landmarks in the Law* [London 1984] p. 351
[148]Useful studies of the period which shed some light on the complex pattern of events are: Andrew, C.M. *Secret Service* [London 1990], Blake, R. *The Decline of Power* [London 1974] and *The Conservative Party from Peel to Thatcher* [London 1992], Bogdanor, V. [ed] *The Age of Affluence* [London 1970], Booker, C. *The Neophiliacs* [London 1969], Horne, A. *Macmillan Vol 2* [London 1990], Knightley, P. *An Affair of State* [London 1968], Levin, B. *The Pendulum Years* [London 1970], Pimlott, B. *Harold Wilson* [London 1990], Annan, N. *Our Age* [London 1990], Boyle, A. *The Climate of Treason* [London 1978], Dorril, S. *Smear: Wilson and the Secret State* [London 1990], Faulks, S. *The Fatal Englishman* [London 1996], Kennedy, L. *The Trial of Citizen Ward* [London 1964], Summers, A. and Dorrill, S. *Honeytrap* [London 1987] and Wright, P. *Spycatcher* [London 1986]. In 1989 a film about the Profumo Affair, entitled *Scandal*, was released by Palace Pictures. The film was directed by Michael Caton-Jones and featured John Hurt as Stephen Ward with Joanne Whalley as Christine Keeler. Leslie Phillips, in an inspired piece of casting, played Lord

Astor. The film provided a pleasingly intelligent interpretation of the events and was clearly well researched. The second impression of the paperback edition of *Honeytrap* by Anthony Summers and Stephen Dorril featured images from the film on its back cover and made a specific if rather perplexing acknowledgment to the producers of the film: 'Of those crucial to the project, we thank Palace Pictures, producers of the television series [sic] *Scandal*. For Palace, Joe Boyd opened up difficult research roads'. [ibid p.14] The nature of these 'difficult research roads' was not specified. Mr Boyd, who was involved with the Incredible String Band and the brilliant Fellow of All Souls Alasdair Clayre, who some years later committed suicide, in the mid 1960s, does not appear to have been resident in London in 1963 but may have had knowledge of the American dimensions of the imbroglio. It is not known if Lord Denning saw the film.

[149] One of the major allegations concerning Profumo, which was vigorously pursued by Harold Wilson, the new leader of the opposition, was that his affair with Keeler had led to secrets of state being communicated to the Russian Naval Attache Ivanov who was sleeping with Keeler at the same time. The Government was already involved in security scandals involving John Vassall, the subject of a tribunal of inquiry which reported in March 1963, and Kim Philby who had defected the Soviet Union in January 1963. The details of the Blunt affair, unknown to the general public until November 1979 when he was 'outed' as a Soviet spy, had also reached a critical point in that the CIA became aware of Blunt's role in relation to Philby, Burgess and Maclean in the early summer of 1963, just at the moment that Profumo resigned. These security problems had major implications for the relationship between the USA and Great Britain at a time of acute international tension over Cuba and Berlin. It was also the case that the US President, John F. Kennedy, had slept with Mariella Novotny, one of the girls who testified at the trial of Stephen Ward.

[150] One of the many aspects of the 'Profumo' affair was race. The whole scandal was triggered by a shooting incident in Wimpole Mews on December 14th 1962 when one of Christine Keeler's Jamaican boyfriends Johnny Edgecombe fired a gun at Stephen Ward's mews residence. This led to a court case as a result of which Edgecombe, and another of Keeler's black lovers, 'Lucky' Gordon, were imprisoned. It was Keeler's failure to give evidence at the trial, and her contemporaneous her 'disappearance' to Spain, that led to the media frenzy which resulted in the breaking of the story about her affair with Profumo. The affair also involved drugs in that, as the scandal developed during the spring of 1963, Keeler was revealed to be a user of marijuana which she had obtained from her black boyfriends in Notting Hill.

[151] The intense debate about morality, stimulated by the Wolfenden Report of 1957 and the Chatterley trial of 1960, had led to expressions of judicial unease about the overt public display of sexuality, in particular homosexuality, in the case of *Shaw v Director of Public Prosecutions* [1962] AC 220 HL. In this judgment, the House of Lords invented the offence of 'conspiracy to corrupt public morals' in a clear attempt to provide the law with a weapon which could be used to intervene in the

debate about public morality, in particular in relation to homosexuality. The judicial obiter dicta in *Shaw v Director of Public Prosecutions* were very striking: 'The law must be related to the changing standards of life, not yielding to every shifting impulse of the popular will but having regard to fundamental assessments of human values and the purposes of society'. [Lord Simonds at 261]. 'Gaps remain and will always remain since no one can forsee every way in which the wickedness of man may disrupt the order of society' [Lord Simonds at 268]. Concern about homosexuality was notable in the majority opinions in *Shaw v Director of Public Prosecutions*. Lord Simonds averred that if homosexuality were to be legalised then the courts could ensure that it remained an offence if 'it were publicly advertised and encouraged by pamphlet and advertisement' [268]. Lord Tucker was particularly exercised and produced a rare judicial reference to lesbianism: 'Is it to be said that a conspiracy to further and encourage such practices among adult males could not be the subject of a criminal charge fit to be left to a jury? Surely, with regard to a conspiracy to encourage and promote lesbianism today?' [285]. The moral panic expressed in the judicial rhetoric of *Shaw v Director of Public Prosecutions* reached a peak in the opinion of Lord Hodson who stated that 'the Common Law has its roots in Christianity' and that it must support the institution of marriage and make no encouragement of adultery or fornication [294]. This statement strongly echoed the views of Lord Devlin, appointed to the House of Lords in 1961, the antagonist of the liberal utilitarian H.L.A. Hart in the contemporary debate about morality and law, and manifested a determination to defend traditional moral values. In the debate on the Wolfenden Report in the House of Lords in December 1957 Lord Denning opined that the law should punish moral vice, by which he meant incest, abortion, bestiality, suicide and homosexuality, but that the judges should use their discretion with regard to the punishment of the offender. In other words, the punishment of 'moral vice' should be a matter for judicial determination, a position exactly congruent with the majority decision in *Shaw v Director of Public Prosecutions*.

[152]Cases of scandal involving government ministers which remained secret during this period included the adulterous relationship between the Duchess of Argyll and Winston Churchill's son-in-law Duncan Sandys, the affair between Lord Boothby and Macmillan's wife Dorothy and Boothby's homosexual relationship with Ronnie Kray together with his other forays, in the public conveniences at Victoria Station, into the world of 'cottaging'. Other politically sensitive cases of the time involving homosexuality included those concerning Anthony Blunt, Jeremy Thorpe and Norman Scott and Lord Wolfenden's son Jeremy. All of these examples were current between 1959 and 1964 and would have been devastating had they been revealed. *Argyll v Argyll* [1967] Ch 302 concerned an action taken by the Duchess of Argyll to prevent the Duke publishing secrets about their marriage in a Sunday newspaper. The timing was significant. In November 1964, the Conservatives lost the General Election. The articles were therefore due to be published under a Labour government and, given the links between the Duchess and Sandys, and many others, they could have proved to be politically explosive.

It was, to say the least, convenient that Mr Justice Ungoed-Thomas came up with a new approach to the equitable law of confidentiality which enabled him to prevent publication of the Duchess' diary on the basis that its contents were subject to marital confidentiality. The fact that *Argyll v Argyll* was so politically sensitive, in relation to the role of Duncan Sandys, that the Duchess had already shared some of her marital secrets with the press and that the behaviour of the Duke and Duchess when they were married was substantially more outrageous, and consequentially more scandalising of judicial attitudes to orthodox sexuality, than the pecadillos of Stephen Ward, made the decision to offer the Duchess the protection of marital confidentiality profoundly hypocritcal. The Duke and Duchess of Argyll were married in the technical letter of the law, but in every other way their behaviour was a disgrace to judicial conceptions of marital propriety. The fact that the highly significant doctrine of confidentiality should have been developed in a case of this kind suggests that the courts were more concerned with establishing the doctrine than in delivering anything resembling justice to the parties concerned.

[153] *Attorney General v Mulholland and Foster* [1963] 2 QB 477

[154] Lord Denning gave the leading judgment and the House of Lords refused leave to appeal. Lord Denning's reasoning was based on a nineteenth century case which arose as a result of the affair between Charles Stuart Parnell and Kitty O'Shea. On February 19th 1889 the managing editor of The Times, under threat of imprisonment, revealed the name of a source to the Parliamentary Commission of Enquiry into the Parnell affair. On that occasion the Conservative government successfully concealed its 'dirty tricks' with regard to Parnell. There was an obvious irony in Lord Denning's use of this precedent. It was also a doubtful one given that, in that instance, it was a Parliamentary Commission whose authority had been impugned whereas the Vassall Tribunal was set up under an Act of Parliament but not by Parliament itself. This turned out to be academic because Lord Reid refused an appeal to the House of Lords on the grounds of national security. For the first time in the twentieth century a journalist was required by the courts to reveal his sources or else go to prison; this was a major, very creative, innovation in the law which did nothing at all for 'freedom of expression'.

[155] Concluding his report [pp 214-216] Lord Denning asserted that 'there has been no lowering of standards' and then seemed to blame the whole business on the commercial exploitation of rumour and gossip by the press: 'Scandalous information about well-known people has become a marketable commodity. True or false, actual or invented, it can be sold...the unpublished part goes around by word of mouth....it crosses the Channel, even the Atlantic and back again, swelling all the time...when such deplorable consequences are seen to ensue, the only thing that is clear is that something should be done to stop the trafficing in scandal for reward. The machinery is ready to hand. There is a new Press Council already in being'. Having imprisoned a journalist for not revealing his sources, on the basis of a novel interpretation of the law, Lord Denning concluded his Report on the Profumo Affair by making a scarcely veiled threat to 'freedom of expression'. The tone of Lord Denning's remarks recalls the ancient statute of 1275 *De Scandalis*

Magnatum [repealed 1887] which was intended to punish the spreading of 'false news or tales creating discord between King, People and Great Men'. The Denning Report of 1963, though lacking statutory authority, was, in spirit, in complete accord with that ancient statute. Both dealt with the same mischief.

[156]In a speech at Lincoln, reported in The Times on June 1st 1963, just before his appointment to conduct the inquiry into Profumo's resignation, Lord Denning made the following remarks about the press: 'The only restrictions put on the freedom of the press were those designed to prevent the abuse of freedom....Press criticism of court decisions was usually ill formed....freedom must be preserved but it must be bound up with responsibility. It is only at the abuse of freedom that the law will strike'.

[157]Ward was placed right at the centre of Lord Denning's report. The Report began: 'The story must start with Stephen Ward, aged 50, the son of a clergyman' [p 1]. The Report concluded: 'the story ends, as it began, with him' [p 138]. Lord Denning was relentless in his determination to blacken Ward's name calling him 'utterly immoral' [p 2], accusing him of participating in 'sexual orgies of a revolting nature' [p 2], 'vicious sexual activities' [p 25] and 'sexual activities of a vile and revolting nature' [p 199]. In his condemnation of Ward, Lord Denning was expressing the moral orthodoxy of the 1950s in a particularly forthright manner. Ward's sexuality was mainly passive, voyeuristic and totally heterosexual, but this would not be obvious if Lord Denning's Report was the only evidence at hand. On less orthodox sexuality, Lord Denning was uncompromising: 'I would normally regard homosexual behaviour, or perverted practices with a prostitute, as creating a security risk' [p 190].

[158]Ward was charged under s 30[1] of the Sexual Offences Act 1956 which dealt with 'living off the earnings of prostitutes'. Ward was involved with those who were known as 'call girls'; prostitutes who did business by phone, to get around the restrictions of the Street Offences Act [1959]. 'Call girls', much discussed in relation to *R v Ward*, were a phenomenon that developed as a result of the Street Offences Act 1959. Indeed, by making prostitutes invisible, the 1959 Act created a new area of 'expression' for the law to regulate. Not only were new 'forms' of prostitution, such as 'call girls', hitherto unknown to the law, created but as *R v Ward* revealed, now that the obvious 'streetwalker' had been made 'silent' and 'invisible' all forms of heterosexual behaviour of any kind other than monogamy and fornication between friends of the opposite sex, could be expressed in terms of the categories of the Sexual Offences Act 1956. The definition of 'prostitution' was therefore, potentially, immeasurably broadened by the Street Offences Act 1959 which had silenced one discourse around unorthodox heterosexuality only to create a new set of legal regulations of sexuality, all of which were potentially subject to the regime of the criminal law. Ward, whose sexuality was eccentric but essentially harmless, was also charged with offences under s.22 [causing the prostitution of women] s.23 [procuration of a girl under twenty one] and s.30 [living on the earnings of a prostitute] of the Sexual Offences Act 1956, as well as with offences concerning the procuration of abortion. Note the significance in

relation to the 1956 Sexual Offences Act of the age of 21. The heterosexual age of consent of 16 was qualified by other laws concerning legal personality and rights with the effect that a person, male or female, under 21 was not considered to be sexually autonomous. For example s. 23 of the Sexual Offences Act 1956 concerns 'procuration of a girl under twenty one'. Stephen Ward was charged with offences under this section. The Age of Majority Act 1969 lowered the relevant age for offences under the Sexual Offences Act to 18; in 1963 that was of no assistance to Stephen Ward. Christine Keeler, Mandy Rice-Davies, and a number of the other girls with whom Ward was associated, were under 21 at the relevant time. Ward's association with these girls was therefore criminalised. In *R v Ward* the Sexual Offences Act 1956 was used with devastating effect to criminalise sexual behaviour that was merely unconventional. In this sense Stephen Ward could be seen as the intended exemplary victim by whose conviction the code of public morality embodied in the Act could be vindicated. Griffith-Jones QC's peroration made this very clear: 'What is this doctor, so-called, of 48 doing when he happens to mention these girls to Lord Astor one day?....Is this mere friendliness? Is this really brotherly concern about these two girls who are broke? Or do you think, with any knowledge of human life, and the ways of a thoroughly immoral man, the inference was that there was something more sinister than that? And that is the picture upon which all else builds up in this case'. The only reason that a quite different result occurred was the way in which the case became a focus for satire and prurience. In a literal sense Ward paid the ultimate price by taking his own life. The Judge sentenced him in his absence and excused the jury from service for twenty years. Ward was absent because he was dying! Lord Denning entirely concurred with Griffith-Jones' evaluation of Ward's conduct. Griffith-Jones also acted for the prosecution in the Chatterley trial, *R v Penguin Books*, in 1960.

[159] Ironically, suicide had just been legalised by the Suicide Act 1961.

[160] Lord Denning always rejected the more lurid conspiracy theories which developed in the aftermath of his report. Commenting on an article published in the Sunday Times on 28th November 1982 which alleged that Ward had been collaborating with the Security Service and MI6, Lord Denning was dismissive: 'I do not accept this for one moment....he was the villain of the piece. It is quite ridiculous to say that he was working for MI5' [Lord Denning *Landmarks in the Law* [London 1984 p. 361].

[161] On 7th March 2003, The Scotsman published the letter written by the Prime Minister Harold Macmillan to the Queen on 23rd June 1963 in which he made a personal apology for the events which had led up to Profumo's resignation: 'I feel that I ought to apologise to you for the undoubted injury done by the terrible behaviour of one of your Majesty's Secretaries of State upon not only the Government but, perhaps more serious, one of the great Armed Forces.......I begin to suspect in all these wild accusations against many people, Ministers and others, something in the nature of a plot to destroy the established system'. This letter, not known before its publication in The Scotsman reveals quite clearly the degree of panic generated by the Profumo affair at the time. Harold Macmillan asked Lord

Denning to conduct his enquiry two days before the writing of this letter, on 21st June 1963.

[162] Lord Denning *The Due Process of Law* [London 1980] p.73
[163] Lord Denning *Landmarks in the Law* [London 1984] p.351
[164] [London 1984]
[165] Ibid p. 351
[166] Ibid p. 351
[167] Ibid p. 358
[168] Lord Denning *The Due Process of Law* [London 1980] pp. 67-8
[169] Ibid p. 67
[170] Ibid p. 354
[171] Ibid p. 355
[172] Cmnd 2152 [Stationary Office 1999]
[173] Ibid p. 1
[174] Although the age of consent for heterosexual intercourse was 16 in 1963, a whole range of sexual offences, defined in the Sexual Offences Act 1956, were possible with girls under the age of 21. Ward was charged with most of these offences in June 1963.
[175] Ibid pp. 1-2
[176] Ibid p. 138
[177] Auric Goldfinger makes an amusing aside in Ian Fleming's *Goldfinger*: 'Mr Bond, they have a saying in Chicago: 'Once is happenstance, twice is coincidence, the third time it's enemy action'. Conspiracy theorists have argued vehemently that Stephen Ward, like Dr David Kelly, in rather different circumstances in 2003, was murdered by the authorities.
[178] It is important to note that Ward died, apparently of an overdose, before his trial was completed, on the 3rd of August 1963. Lord Denning could therefore blacken Ward's character as much as he needed to in order to shift the focus of attention. Had Ward lived, even though he would have been found guilty of criminal offences, he might have had ground for a libel suit against Lord Denning who would not have been able to rely on the protection of judicial privilege for statements made in the Report. During the 1960s, Lord Denning was particularly insistent that those who had been found guilty in a criminal trial should not be able to reopen the issue by means of a civil suit. This issue had arisen in relation to those who had been convicted as a result of the Great Train Robbery of 1963 which had taken place in August, while Lord Denning was preparing his report on the Profumo affair. 'A suburban housewife reveals how she was caught up in the great mailbag plot' was the headline in *The People* on July 29th 1964. Douglas Gordon Goody brought a libel action against Mrs Karin Field who said that she had been 'forced to help gang get away with haul'. *Goody v Odhams Press Ltd.* 1966 3 AllER 369 at 371. The problem was that a decision in the Court of Appeal in 1943 - *Hollington v F. Hewthorn and Co. Ltd.* 1943 2 AllER 35 - which was binding, had determined that, for the purposes of a libel action, a criminal conviction was not evidence of guilt. 'I argued that case myself', observed Lord

Denning. He had tried to persuade the court that conviction was evidence of guilt. He failed. 'I thought that the decision was wrong at the time', he remarked. To get round the problem, Lord Denning allowed The People to amend their defence which had hitherto been based on justification. If the defence was amended previous convictions would be relevant to mitigation of damage, 'they are the raw material on which bad reputation is built up'. In a related case *Barclays Bank v Cole* 1966 3 AllER 948 a claim for trial by jury with regard to a suit of action for 'money had and received' following a robbery, Lord Denning ruled that the trial should be heard before a judge without a jury because 'his honour and integrity is no longer at stake. It is gone altogether'. Had the case been heard before a jury then, following *Hollington* his criminal conviction would not be admissible and he would be more likely to get off than if he was heard before a judge alone.

[179] Ibid p. 184

[180] Despite his modest criticism of his conduct as Prime Minster during the affair, Lord Denning retained a substantial amount of respect for Harold Macmillan. He concluded his account of the whole business in 'Landmarks in the Law' by quoting from the letter which Harold Macmillan wrote to him on his retirement on 28th July 1982 in which he praised him for his 'commonsense, fair play and justice' and concluded 'as Lord Mansfield and Lord Camden, so Lord Denning'. Lord Denning then commented that 'Macmillan was a very great man' Lord Denning, *Landmarks in the Law* [London 1984] p. 365]. The closeness and warmth of the relationship between Macmillan and Lord Denning is plain.

[181] Ibid p. 115

[182] Ibid p. 5-6

[183] Ibid p. 10-11

[184] Ibid p. 39

[185] Ibid p. 40

[186] Ibid pp. 3-4

[187] Straight, an associate of Blunt's in Cambridge in the 1930s, had been nominated by President John Kennedy to be Chairman of the National Endowment for the Arts. Facing a background check prior to Congressional hearings, Straight decided to volunteer information about his activities during the 1930s and his friendship with Blunt. 'Because of the arts.....because our government finally decided to support the arts. Kennedy was going to make me head of his new Arts agency....that forced the question'. Carter, M. *Anthony Blunt: His Lives* [London 2001] p. 453

[188] Ibid pp. 141-176

[189] The first James Bond film, *Dr No*, had been released in 1962; the second film, *From Russia With Love*, opened on 10th October 1963, just two weeks after the publication of Denning's Report. President Kennedy, whose womanising entangled him with the fringes of the Profumo imbroglio, was a self-declared fan, having recently named *From Russia With Love* as one of his favourite books. *From Russia With Love*, published in 1957, just after the Suez crisis, was an intriguing example of fiction becoming fact. Fleming wrote the book earlier in

1956, before Suez, but in the aftermath of that fiasco, the Prime Minister, Anthony Eden, stayed at Goldeneye, his retreat in Jamaica. Bond never bothered with the Middle East, a scene of abject British humiliation; Fleming preferred to let him operate in more congenial locations – France, the Caribbean, the United States, Switzerland and Japan, places where little, if anything, was at stake as far as Britain's national interest was concerned. Istanbul, where much of the action in *From Russia With Love* takes place is a close as Bond gets to the Middle East; a dismal theatre of operations, the scene of British failure and disgrace. At the heart of *From Russia With Love* was a *konspiratsia* hatched by SMERSH to undermine the Secret Intelligence Service by means of a sex scandal which would destroy the reputation of a national hero. Bond had been filmed through a two-way mirror, *in flagrante delicto*, with the slyly named Tatiana Romanova, in a hotel in Istanbul. Tatiana had come to Istanbul with the offer of a Russian code machine which would enable SIS to crack the Russian ciphers; an interesting notion given that, at that time, all knowledge of SIS's code-breaking capacity was totally confidential, a state secret. It was not until 1976 that SIS's codebreaking capacity was revealed by an article in *Time Out*. Lord Denning was involved in tidying up the detritus of that imbroglio - *R v Secretary of State for the Home Department ex parte Hosenball* 1977 3 AllER 452. Denning's decision ensured that state secrets about codebreaking after 1945 were kept under wraps for a little longer. SMERSH was anxious to take the British down a peg or two. In the course of the discussions which preceded the initiation of the *konspiratsia*, General Vozdvishensky, representing the Foreign Ministry, observed of the British: 'Most of their strength lies in the myth - in the myth of Scotland Yard, of Sherlock Holmes, of the Secret Service. We certainly have nothing to fear from these gentlemen….but this myth is a hindrance which it would be good to set aside'. Fleming, I. *From Russia With Love* [London 1957] p. 38. Colonel Nikitin of the MGB, a predecessor of the KGB, dismissed the possibility of entrapping M in a sex scandal: 'He does not drink very much. He is too old for women. The public does not know of his existence. It would be difficult to create a scandal round his death. And he would not be easy to kill. He rarely goes abroad. To shoot him in a London street would not be very refined'. His colleague, General Grubozaboyschikov, the Head of SMERSH, concurs with this analysis, and says: 'Have they no one who is a hero…..someone who is admired and whose ignomimious destruction would cause dismay? Myths are built on heroic deeds and heroic people. Have they no such men?'…….It was Colonel Nikitin who broke the embarrassed silence. He said hesitantly, 'There is a man called Bond'. Ibid p.40. There was, of course, no hero in reality but John Profumo, Secretary of State for War, the Member for Stratford-upon-Avon in the heart of England, married to a beautiful actress, a man who had had a 'good war' and was a rising star in the Conservative government was as close as it got to the target identified by Colonel Nikitin. Fleming himself might have become the victim of a sex scandal at the time the book was written; his wife Anne was sleeping with the Leader of the Labour Opposition, Hugh Gaitskell.

[190]Ibid p. 141

[191] Ibid p. 142
[192] Ibid p. 147
[193] Ibid pp. 172-3
[194] Ibid pp. 168-9
[195] Ibid p. 180
[196] Ibid pp. 180-181
[197] Ibid p. 188
[198] Ibid p. 216
[199] Ibid p. 189
[200] Ibid pp. 187-216
[201] Ibid pp. 202-207
[202] Ibid pp. 208-211
[203] Ibid p. 206
[204] The Cabinet Member concerned was Duncan Sandys, Winston Churchill's son-in-law, at that time Secretary of State for the Colonies. In August 2000, a Channel 4 programme about the Duchess of Argyll, whose divorce was going through the courts contemporaneously, revealed that in June 1963, at the moment of Profumo's resignation, Duncan Sandys told Macmillan that he would be obliged to resign because, as a result of the proceedings in the Argyll divorce case, he would be likely to be revealed as the 'headless man' photographed in a mirror enjoying an act of *fellatio* with the Duchess, the taker of the photograph. The fact that the divorce had been granted in March of 1963 and that various newspapers were seeking to make a killing by publishing assorted 'confessions' consequent on the bitterly contested court case made Sandys extremely vulnerable. Had Sandys resigned at the same time as Profumo, the government might well have fallen and, in a mood of national crisis, Labour might have won a General Election by a landslide. Sandys was saved from resignation by the fact that Lord Denning was persuaded to expand the terms of reference of his enquiry so as to exonerate Sandys from the rumour that he was the 'headless' man. Lord Denning examined the photographs depicting the Duchess in an act of fellatio with an unidentified man and interviewed the potential candidates for the title of 'headless' man in the Treasury. There were in fact two distinct sets of photographs. One, depicting Douglas Fairbanks Jr, was accompanied by writing, the other was unmarked. The fact that the writing was not that of Sandys enabled Lord Denning to be conveniently 'economical with the truth'.
[205] Ibid p. 207
[206] Ibid p. 215
[207] Ibid p. 216
[208] *Attorney General v Mulholland and Foster* [1963] 2 QB 477
[209] In the real world, the fortunes of SIS were at their lowest ebb. Distrusted by the Americans, humiliated in the Middle East, even the Russians, their principal opponents, had little to fear from them until the expulsion of their agents in 1971, a *coup de theatre* which crippled KGB operations in the UK during the 1970s, a time when militant trade unionism and student radicalism, on a scale which

dwarfed the 1930s, when the Cambridge spies had been recruited, offered plenty of opportunities for subversion.

[210] *The Discipline of Law* [London 1979]; *The Due Process of Law* [London 1980] and *What Next in the Law* [London 1982]
[211] *The Misuse of Power*, the annual Dimbleby lecture given on BBC1 on 20th November 1980
[212] *Packer v Packer* [1954] 15 at 22
[213] Lord Denning *The Discipline of Law* [London 1979] p. 22
[214] Ibid p. 56
[215] Ibid p. 57
[216] Ibid p. 61-62
[217] Ibid p. 62
[218] Ibid p. 93
[219] Ibid p. 104
[220] *Laker Airways Ltd v Department of Trade* 1977 2 AllER 182
[221] Ibid p. 104
[222] *R v Greater London Council ex parte Blackburn* 1976 3 AllER 184
[223] *Attorney-General [on relation of McWhirter] v Independent Broadcasting Authority* 1973 1 AllER 689
[224] *Gouriet v Union of Post Office Workers* 1977 1 AllER 696
[225] Ibid pp.105-146
[226] Ibid p. 148
[227] Ibid p. 154
[228] Ibid p. 168
[229] Ibid p. 168
[230] Ibid p. 173
[231] Ibid p. 175
[232] Ibid p. 176
[233] Ibid p. 193
[234] Ibid p. 287
[235] Ibid p. 289
[236] Ibid p. 293
[237] [London 1980]
[238] Ibid p. 5
[239] Ibid p. 6
[240] Ibid p. 10
[241] Ibid p. 19
[242] Ibid p. 19
[243] Ibid p. 19 Lord Denning slightly adapted the words of John Milton in *Samson Agonistes*. The original words are:
    Oh how comely it is and how reviving
    To the spirits of just men long oppress'd,
    When God into the hands of their deliverer
    Puts invincible might

> To quell the mighty of the Earth, th' oppressor,
> The brute and boist'rous force of violent men,
> Hardy and industrious to support
> Tyrannic power, but raging to pursue
> The righteous and all such as honour truth;
> He all their ammunition
> And feats of war defeats
> With plain heroic magnitude of mind
> And celestial vigour arm'd;
> Their armouries and magazines contemns,
> Renders them useless, while
> With winged expedition
> Swift as the lightning glance he executes
> His errand on the wicked, who surpris'd
> Lose their defence distracted and amaz'd.
> (John Milton *Samson Agonistes* 1268-1286)

In Milton's poem, God has put an 'invincible might' into the hands of the righteous but does not specify that the law is that 'might', describing it in terms of 'plain heroic magnitude of mind and celestial vigour', qualities which Lord Denning elided into 'the might of the law'

[244] [London 1980]
[245] Ibid p. 8
[246] Ibid p. 10
[247] Ibid pp. 37-39
[248] Ibid pp. 45-56
[249] *R v Secretary of State for the Home Department ex parte Hosenball* 1977 3 AllER 452
[250] Lord Denning was referring to events which had taken place in Albania in 1950. Kim Philby, whose flight to the Soviet Union from Beirut, via Mount Ararat, in January 1963, had taken place just before the Profumo affair, in which Lord Denning had played a notable part, was still in post at that time, indeed considered by those 'in the know' to be a likely future candidate for the role of C. Philby had been able to 'tip off' Moscow centre about an attempt to destabilise the government of Enver Hoxha by parachuting in a group of Albanian exiles. All of the men were rounded up and executed. See Dorril, S. *MI6: 50 Years of Secret Operations* [London 2000] pp. 354-403 Lord Denning's decision in the Hosenball case was an attempt to preserve the secrecy of SIS's code-breaking capacity by preventing disclosure of the existence of GCHQ. Although it had recently become known that the German codes had been cracked at Bletchley Park during the War, one of the most closely guarded secrets in British intelligence from 1945 to 1973, nothing at that time was known about SIS's capacity to break Soviet Codes. In 1946, an agreement between the US and the UK over sharing code-breaking secrets was secretly negotiated. From 1946 onwards, codebreaking, or signals intelligence, was the most important aspect of intelligence work. Co-operation

between the UK and the US in this vital area was threatened by the series of spying scandals which began with the flight of Burgess and Maclean to Moscow in 1951, reaching a climax in 1963 when Philby left Beirut and Blunt was exposed to the CIA. These events coincided with the Profumo affair and explain Lord Denning's anxiety to give the Security Services a clean bill of health in his Report. Lord Denning's brother Norman became Director of Naval Intelligence in 1961. During the War Ian Fleming had been the personal assistant of the Director of Naval Intelligence, Admiral Godfrey. After he retired in 1967, Vice-Admiral Sir Norman Denning was in charge of the D notice system. This became highly controversial because it was used by the Wilson government to prevent any information concerning British signals intelligence capacity from being published in the press. The Hosenball case was a desperate attempt by the government to maintain this secrecy. Lord Denning, as in the Vassall and Profumo affairs, was concerned that the information should be excluded from the public domain. Given his family associations with Naval Intelligence, it was not surprising that he should adopt this approach. The exposure of Anthony Blunt as a Soviet spy in November 1979 created a hysterical atmosphere in which, among many other detrimental developments, knowledge of the existence of GCHQ and of SIS's signals intelligence capacity entered the public domain just as tensions with the Soviet Union, following the invasion of Afghanistan in December 1979, began to increase. These considerations explain why Margaret Thatcher's governments were so anxious to prevent the publication of Peter Wright's memoirs. By that time, of course, Lord Denning had retired.

[251] Ibid pp. 84-85
[252] Ibid pp. 101-116
[253] Ibid pp. 101-102
[254] Ibid p. 102
[255] Ibid p. 114
[256] *R v Inland Revenue Commissioners ex parte Rossminster* 1979 3 AllER 385
[257] Ibid p. 116-121
[258] [1756] 19 How. St. Tr. 1030
[259] Ibid pp. 119-120
[260] Ibid p. 155
[261] Ibid p. 157
[262] Ibid pp. 157-159. Sir Stephen Sedley, in his obituary of Lord Denning, claimed that Lord Denning's interpretation of this case, to be found in his 1949 Hamlyn Lectures, *Freedom under the Law*, was tendentious. Sedley claimed to have found no evidence, in the original law report, of Lord Denning's claim that the case was a landmark in the history of the abolition of slavery. For further discussion of this matter see Samuels, A. LQR 118[July] 379-81
[263] *R v Secretary of State for the Home Department ex parte Phansopkar* 1975 3 AllER 497
[264] Ibid p. 168
[265] Ibid p. 170

[266] *Thakrah v Secretary of State for the Home Department* 1974 2 AllER 261
[267] Ibid p. 176
[268] Ibid p. 177
[269] Ibid p. 177
[270] Ibid p. 177-178
[271] *Re Weston's Settlement Trusts* 1968 3 AllER 338
[272] Ibid p. 180-181
[273] [London 1982]
[274] The Guardian 23.5.82, quoted in 'The New Racism', Barker, M [London 1981]
[275] The Times 22.5.82 quoted in 'The New Racism', Barker, M [London 1981] The principle of jury trial, in which unanimity was a requirement, safeguarded the individual from the effects of 'harsh laws, political prejudice and legal formalism'. The law was 'controlled by the common people'. Jury trial was of fundamental importance to the English constitution: 'To this charge he has pleaded not guilty and puts himself upon his country, which country you are. All our past struggles are bound up in that one sentence'. The jury was an embodiment of the 'common people', an expression of the English nation itself: 'The system which has been built up by our forefathers over the last 1000 years'. 'It works in the English-speaking countries because of the temperament of the people, their sound good sense, which is not to be swayed unduly by emotion and prejudice. It does not work in the Latin countries with their mobile temperament, easily moved to pity or hate. The verdicts there given by juries were often fantastic'. Denning, A. *Freedom under the Law* [London 1949] pp. 55-63 The English 'character', an essential aspect of English identity, was embodied, in Lord Denning's understanding, in the principle of trial by jury.
[276] Some would argue that this controversy allowed Lord Hailsham, the Lord Chancellor, to put pressure on Denning to retire. Lord Denning was the last judge sitting on the bench to whom the new rules about compulsory retirement at 75 introduced in the Judicial Pensions Act 1981 did not apply on account of the fact that his appointment as a judge long predated the legislation. Until 1959, judges were appointed for life, after that date appointment for life was no longer the norm, but those judges who were appointed before 1959 who wished to remain on tenure for life were permitted to do so. Wade, E.C.S and Bradley E.W. *Constitutional and Administrative Law* 11th Edition 1993. pp. 377-8. Lord Denning had been appointed to the High Court in 1944 and to the Court of Appeal in 1948.
[277] *What Next in the Law* [London 1982] pp. v-vi
[278] Ibid p.p. vi-vii
[279] Ibid p. 336
[280] Ibid p. vi
[281] Ibid pp. 5-6
[282] Ibid p. 6
[283] Ibid p. 17
[284] Ibid p. 17
[285] Ibid p. 19

[286] Lord Denning's coat of arms, chosen when he was appointed to the House of Lords in 1957, was emblazoned with the words *Fiat Justitia* and was flanked by the figures of Coke and Mansfield.
[287] Ibid p. 33
[288] Ibid p. 43
[289] Ibid p. 57
[290] Ibid p. 62
[291] Ibid p. 75
[292] Ibid p. 187
[293] Ibid p. 192
[294] Ibid p. 202-209
[295] Ibid p. 213
[296] Ibid pp. 216-217
[297] Ibid pp. 221-258
[298] Ibid p. 268
[299] Ibid pp. 328-329
[300] In 1981, a Bill of Rights which would have incorporated the European Convention of Human Rights into English law without qualification passed all of its stages in the House of Lords, but was rejected by the House of Commons ibid p. 271
[301] Ibid p. 271
[302] Ibid p. 271
[303] Ibid p. 271
[304] Ibid p. 274
[305] Ibid p. 273
[306] Ibid p. 278
[307] Ibid p. 278-279
[308] Ibid p. 282
[309] Ibid p. 302
[310] Ibid p. 282
[311] Ibid p. 284
[312] Ibid pp. 280-285 *R v Home Secretary ex parte Bhajan Singh* [1976] QB 198]; *R v Chief Immigration Officer ex parte Bibi* [1976] 1 WLR 979 and *Ahmad v ILEA* [1978] 1 QB 36
[313] Ibid p. 284
[314] Ibid pp. 291-292
[315] Ibid p. 303
[316] Ibid p. 301
[317] Ibid p. 277
[318] *Macarthys v Smith* 1979 3 AllER 325
[319] Ibid p. 300
[320] Ibid p. 318
[321] Ibid p. 318
[322] Ibid p. 324

[323] Ibid p. 334
[324] Ibid p. 300
[325] *The Closing Chapter* [London 1983] p. 22
[326] *King John* Act 5 Scene 7
[327] Shortly after his retirement, Lord Denning spoke at the 30th anniversary of the opening of Agatha Christie's *The Mousetrap*, a symbol of the stability of English identity. Lord Denning was enthusiastic about the play: 'This Mousetrap thriller is a better thriller than any other. It has gone on for thirty years because each generation in England takes its children to see it and every tourist from overseas is sure of entertainment'. *The Closing Chapter* p. 40

CHAPTER TWO

ENGLISH THEMES AND VARIATIONS

Lord Denning was a patriot. 'Intensely loyal to this country...keeping all things bright, beautiful and British',[1] the words which he used to describe Jack Hayward, a Liberal party supporter who sued the Sunday Telegraph for libel over allegations about his relationship with Jeremy Thorpe, at the time of the latter's trial for murder in 1978-9, could have been used to describe himself. For Lord Denning, England was 'home', a word he used in a case concerning a Bangladeshi who had brought over his family from Sylhet and then been evicted by his landlord.[2] Suggesting that the plaintiff's home was in Bangladesh, rather than England, Lord Denning said that his situation was like that of many English families: 'The menfolk go off to work in countries overseas and leave their wives and children at home in England'.[3]

The 'home' of England was of course an island. The image of England as an island and the role of the sea in her national life recurs in Lord Denning's judgments. 'English is the language of the sea and seafarers'.[4] 'A sea captain may be away from his home for months at a time but it is none the less his home'.[5] The name of Lord Nelson, whose victory at Trafalgar over France and Spain in 1805, ensured the security of the island 'home' was invoked in a judgment concerning the issue of whether fire engines, machines which could save English homes from destruction, could pass through a red light: 'The public interest may demand that, when all is clear, they should follow the precedent set by Lord Nelson'.[6] In a dissenting judgment about the rights of property owners in relation to the building of a sea wall, Lord Denning argued that property rights should give way to the need to defend the island against the sea and was dismissive of the plaintiff's claim that their property rights should prevail over the defence of the coastline asserting: 'I cannot see that they have any complaint at all'.[7]

The image of England as an island was deployed most famously by Lord Denning when he used the image of an 'incoming tide' which 'flows into the estuaries and up the rivers' and which 'cannot be held back' in one of the first judgments of an English court concerning the impact of the Treaty of Rome.[8] A few years later he developed that image to show how the tide of European law had inundated the shoreline of England: 'It has not stopped at the highwater mark. It has broken the dykes and the banks. It has submerged the surrounding land. So much so that we have to learn to become amphibious if we are to keep our heads above water'.[9] Such inundations have occurred throughout English history, most notably in the great floods of 1953, but the English people have always survived.

The reassuring continuities of English life were also invoked in Lord Denning's judgments. In a judgment concerning the extent to which pharmacists could engage in trade other than the traditional kind involving medicines, Lord Denning described a pharmacist as 'a qualified man dressed in a white coat' assisted by 'shop girls dressed in their neat overalls'[10] and compared their professional body to a medieval guild,[11] asserting that 'most people, when they go for their medicines, would prefer to go to an old-time chemists shop with its green and red carboys in the window'.[12] In a judgment concerning the status, for income tax purposes, of a premium paid to the owner of a tied service station, Lord Denning used a metaphor from traditional drapery, the business of his father: 'The yardstick is different from the cloth which it measures'.[13]

Lord Denning's understanding of the continuities of English life is revealed by the way in which a number of themes recur in his judgments.

Literature and the Stage

The authority of William Shakespeare was invoked by Lord Denning, praying in aid the persuasion of rhetoric, to support and underpin the legal argument at crucial moments in several of his judgments. In a judgment concerning the freedom of the press to report proceedings in a magistrates court, in which Lord Denning decided emphatically in favour of the freedom of the press,[14] he used a quotation from Shakespeare to make a disobliging comment about the self-importance of some magistrates:

> Drest in a little brief authority,
> most ignorant of what he's most assured
> plays such fantastic tricks before high heaven
> as make the angels weep.[15]

In another judgment concerning the freedom of the press,[16] Lord Denning, dissenting, compared the way in which the journalist used information, a use of which he approved, with the manner in which

Shakespeare made use of Holinshed's Chronicles in his History plays.[17] In resolving a dispute about land involving a restrictive covenant, Lord Denning referred to one of Shakespeare's most famous comedies: 'Counsel for the vendor refers to this case as a comedy of errors. It is no comedy but a history of errors'.[18]

Lord Denning adverted to the language of Shakespeare on a number of occasions when he needed the aid of potent rhetoric to support a controversial line of argument with an authority whose weight would be hard to challenge. In a judgment concerning a trade union which had used its power to close down all the schools in Haringey for several weeks in the winter of 1979, Lord Denning indicated that he would issue an injunction against any union which undertook such action in the future but would not have to take such action on this occasion because the union had ended their action before the case was brought to court and therefore 'all's well that ends well'.[19] In a judgment concerning a variation in a trust which had been made to avoid paying tax in Britain by moving the trust to Jersey[20], Lord Denning, deciding that such a variation was unlawful, quoted from John of Gaunt's speech in *Richard II* when he referred to England as 'the envy of happier lands'.[21]

Dissenting from his brethren in a judgment[22] concerning a planning application in relation to new building in Kent, Lord Denning made a series of references to *A Midsummer Night's Dream* referring to the propositions submitted in favour of allowing the planning application as 'pure moonshine'[23] and 'fine-spun arguments'.[24] In another dissenting judgment in which he found that the devaluation of sterling ought to be taken into account in a salvage case,[25] Lord Denning quoted from *Julius Caesar* to support his argument that although sterling was once a stable currency 'of whose true-fixed and resting quality there is no fellow in the firmament',[26] it was no longer so and therefore a salvage award should take its changing value into account. Once again invoking the authority of *Julius Caesar*, in a judgment finding that Robert Maxwell had not been denied natural justice by a Board of Trade Inspector,[27] Lord Denning observed that such inquiries were not to be shackled by legal niceties: 'To borrow from Shakespeare,[28] [the Inspector] is not to have all his faults observed, set in a note-book, learned and conned by rote, to make a lawyer's holiday'.[29]

Weighing the arguments for and against the waiver of a right to withdraw from a charterparty which would thereby save the charterer from paying a very high penalty,[30] Lord Denning, finding for the charterer, remarked 'need I mention the forfeit which the moneylender sought to enforce against the Merchant of Venice'.[31] In a case involving dismissal of an action for want of prosecution,[32] alluding to *Hamlet*, Lord Denning referred to the 'whips and scorns of time'.[33] In a judgment which broke new ground in that it found that an unmarried woman could be protected under the rent acts as a member of her deceased partner's 'family',[34] Lord Denning said that she was a member of the deceased's family in a 'popular' sense, using that word as Shakespeare used it in *Henry V* when he described a man as 'base, common and popular'.[35] Considering that actions of a local council which had led to the deprivation of a market trader in Barnsley of his pitch for urinating in the market square,[36] Lord Denning, finding for the market trader, used the words of Touchstone, the jester in *As You Like It*, to describe the altercation between Mr Harry Hook and the security officer. The security officer gave the 'reproof valiant' and Mr Hook gave the 'countercheck quarrelsome'.[37] In a judgment finding that sovereign immunity was no longer available for acts of state which were essentially commercial dealings, Lord Denning, arguing that English law should follow international law,[38] quoted from *Julius Caesar*, clearly one of his favourite plays, in support of the position that he was taking: 'We must take the current when it serves, or lose our ventures'.[39]

Finally, Lord Denning turned for Shakespeare for support in a judgment arising out of the extremely controversial Grunwick dispute in which he refused to issue an injunction against the Post Office because, if the injunction were enforced, the Post Office would be obliged to take back employees whom it had suspended for failing to deliver mail to the Grunwick processing laboratory.[40] If this happened then the injunction would have endorsed an unlawful action, namely the failure of Post Office employees to deliver the mail. Refusing to issue the injunction, Lord Denning quoted from *The Merchant of Venice*, another of his favourite plays: 'Twill be recorded for a precedent: and many an error by the same example, will rush into the state, it cannot be'.[41] For many in 1977, the Grunwick dispute and the violence which accompanied it, was seen as posing a threat to the state and to the stability of the constitution. At this fraught moment, Lord Denning turned to the authority of William Shakespeare, invoking the shade of Portia, a figure of justice, to enhance the authority of a controversial judgment.[42]

The authority of William Shakespeare, a contemporary of Sir Edward Coke, was invoked by Lord Denning to provide the extra weight of authority needed to buttress his reasoning in controversial cases. Shakespeare, the embodiment of English identity as expressed in language, was a crucial ally for an English judge bent on delivering justice. However, in the judgments which Lord Denning handed down as

Master of the Rolls these were the only occasions in which he overtly invoked the language of Shakespeare. On some occasions his language was used to support an innovative argument; on others the authority of Shakespeare was used by Lord Denning in a loose, throwaway manner, providing colour and spice but little else. Lord Denning's use of Shakespeare was erratic, veering from the portentous to the merely whimsical.

Only seven other English writers, and a single American, were used by Lord Denning to support the legal reasoning of his judgments: Charles Dickens, William Cowper, William Wordsworth, Alfred, Lord Tennyson, W.S. Gilbert,[43] Lord Acton, Anthony Hope, Lewis Carroll and William Longfellow.[44] Dickens was deployed in one of a series of judgments in the late 1960s concerning the dismissal of actions for want of prosecution.[45] In this instance, Lord Denning's rhetoric was vigorous: 'In these three cases the law's delays have been intolerable. They have lasted so long as to turn justice sour'.[46] The cases were struck out and the fault was laid at the door of the legal advisors; the clients were advised to sue them for negligence. Lord Denning then quoted from Charles Dickens' *Bleak House*, the obvious source, to support the decision saying, using the words of the writer, that such delays: 'exhaust finances, patience, courage, hope'.[47] This reference was perhaps an indication of the degree to which, in the late 1960s, Lord Denning felt that such delays were threatening the authority of the law. Lord Denning referred to *Bleak House* in his judgments on only one other occasion. This was in the course of a judgment concerned with a complex family dispute about property involving a conspiracy between a husband and wife to disinherit one of their sons.[48] Lord Denning remarked that the dispute 'bids fair to rival in time and money the story of *Jarndyce and Jarndyce*'.[49] There are no other references to Dickens in his judgments.

The words of the eighteenth century poet William Cowper were used by Lord Denning in one of a series of judgments in the mid to late 1970s in which the scope of the *Mareva* injunction[50] was developed. In this particular case, the court ordered the service of a *Mareva* injunction on a party whose principal assets were outside the jurisdiction of the court.[51] However, the ship concerned had sunk and the insurance monies, to which the *Mareva* injunction would attach, could only be paid in England. Lord Denning argued that the court could extend the scope of the injunction from physical assets to include legal or equitable rights, such as a prospective insurance claim, on the basis of its inherent authority, without waiting for the approval of the Rules Committee. Aware that the House of Lords might disagree, which in the event they did, he turned to the authority of the poet: 'To the timorous souls I would say in the words of William Cowper: 'Ye fearful saints fresh courage take. The clouds you so much dread are big with mercy, and shall break in blessings on your head'. Instead of saints read judges. Instead of mercy read justice. And you will find a good way to law reform'.[52] It is striking that Lord Denning should support a claim to inherent jurisdiction, which he knew would be overturned by the House of Lords, with the words of a poet rather than the authority of the law. The principled legal argument that he used to support this judgment was that it would harmonise English law with that of the European Community. The authority of a poet was used to bridge the gap between EC law and English law!

The authority of the English Catholic historian Lord Acton was deployed in another case concerning the *Mareva* injunction.[53] This was the first case before the Court of Appeal in which a *Mareva* injunction was approved after full legal argument. Lord Denning's judgment also deployed the argument that approval of the *Mareva* injunction would harmonise English law with EC law.[54] However having made the argument for the principle of the *Mareva* injunction, Lord Denning refused to grant it in the instant case which involved General Ibhnu Sutowo, a former Indonesian Head of State and an American adventurer called Bruce Rappaport, two thoroughly unattractive plaintiffs. To justify this refusal to grant a powerful new legal weapon, a potent aid to justice, to such plaintiffs, Lord Denning turned to the authority of Lord Acton. The authority of the historian was used to underpin the denial of justice to unworthy plaintiffs: 'It was said by Lord Acton that 'all power tends to corrupt. Total power corrupts absolutely.....I am tempted to say 'a plague on both your houses'.'[55] It is interesting that in a judgment involving a former head of state whch relied in part on the harmonisation of English law with that of the European community, Lord Denning should have prayed in aid the authority of an English Catholic historian who lived for most of his life in Rome!

In another case concerning the scope of the *Mareva* injunction which set out the guidelines for third parties such as banks which might be affected by the injunction,[56] Lord Denning deployed the words of Anthony Hope, a late nineteenth century author of whimsical romances, the most famous of which are *The Prisoner of Zenda* and *Rupert of Hentzau*. These are stories which Lord Denning would have read as a boy, in the years before the First World War. The judgment set out the guidelines for the five clearing banks which would have to 'freeze' the assets of two companies to which a *Mareva* injunction had been attached. The companies had been identified by counsel by the letters A and Z.

Unattracted to this concealement of identity, Lord Denning announced that he would 'adopt a different device', borrowed from the author of *The Prisoner of Zenda*, Anthony Hope: 'Ruritania is an imaginary country....I will use it to conceal the identity of a real country and its people'.[57] He proceeded to identify the head office of the companies as being in Ruritania; their main banking accounts being held in Hentzau. The companies had been indicted as conspirators to defraud; the judgment ordered the English banks which held their accounts to refuse to honour any of their cheques on pain of committing a contempt of court. The power of the *Mareva* injunction over companies outside English jurisdiction was made plain by reducing the country in which the companies were based to the status of the ridiculous Ruritania of Anthony Hope's romance. In common English usage Ruritania[58] is an absurd alpine or Balkan land of no account, a land fit for subjection by the imperial authority of the *Mareva* injunction.

In another case involving a *Mareva* injunction, Lord Denning used the words of Lewis Carroll whose *Alice in Wonderland* and *Alice through the Looking Glass* he would also have read as a child. This case involved the attachment of a *Mareva* injunction to an overdrawn bank account in which there were no current assets.[59] Despite the fact that the company argued that the attachment of a *Mareva* injunction to their overdrawn bank account would affect their business and oblige them to no longer use the United Kingdom as a base for their operations, Lord Denning ordered that a *Mareva* injunction be attached to their bank account. In a similarly denigrating tone to that which he had used in the 'Ruritanian' case, Lord Denning asserted that some companies were registered in countries whose law was so 'loose' that their registrations were 'nothing more than a name grasped from the air, as elusive as the Cheshire Cat'.[60]

The *Mareva* injunction, which allowed the seizure of assets and the freezing of rights held in England of companies and individuals outside the jurisdiction of the English courts, was a major innovation in English law. It was also very similar to the *saisie conservatoire* of French and European law; its development by the English courts harmonised English law with EC law. It is very striking that in four of the eight occasions in which Lord Denning used the words of writers, other than William Shakespeare, to support the authority of his judgments their words should be deployed in judgments concerning the authority and scope of the *Mareva* injunction and in a manner which suggested a dismissive attitude towards the countries in which those companies were registered. The imperial power of English law was imposed, by means of the *Mareva* injunction, on persons otherwise beyond the reach of its jurisdiction.

England may have lost its empire, but the City of London was open to business from all over the world. The *Mareva* injunction was designed to be a means of controlling those businesses. It is notable that the legal authority for that injunction should have been buttressed by the authority of a Catholic Englishman living in Rome, the author of romances and a writer who wrote books for children.

On three other occasions, Lord Denning turned to the authority of writers to support his legal reasoning. In one case, concerned with an attempt to prevent Marylebone Grammar School from being turned into a comprehensive, Lord Denning quoted from William Wordsworth's *On the Extinction of the Venetian Republic* to underline his conviction that the abolition of Grammar schools was a highly detrimental action.[61] The Venetian Republic had been abolished by Napoleon, the enemy of England, after the Treaty of Campo Formio in 1797. One of the other cases was concerned with the refusal of a town council to allow the National Front to rent one of their premises for their national conference.[62] Lord Denning invoked the authority of the Victorian Poet Laureate, Alfred Lord Tennyson to support his decision to allow the National Front to use the hall. The lines of Tennyson which he quoted were a eulogy of the English constitution: 'A man may speak the thing he would in a land of settled government, a land of just and old reknown, where freedom slowly broadens down from precedent to precedent'.[63] Lord Denning used the words of Tennyson to support his contention that, in England, the right of free speech, even that of the National Front, must be protected.

The only other occasion in which Lord Denning used the words of a writer was in his final judgment in the Court of Appeal.[64] The writer, once again, was Lewis Carroll, clearly a favourite. The case concerned cabbage seeds. The subject matter provided Lord Denning with a golden opportunity to make a valedictory invocation of Lewis Carroll by quoting from *Alice through the Looking Glass*:

'The time has come, the Walrus said
to talk of many things:
of shoes - and ships - and sealing wax -
of cabbages - and Kings'.[65]

Many of Lord Denning's judgments had been concerned with shoes, in the sense of goods whose ownership, and quality, were regulated by the law of contract. Others were concerned with ships, in the form of charterparties. Sealing wax could be taken to be a symbol of legal documents. Kings could be taken to represent the English constitution itself. In this way, Lord Denning used the words of Lewis Carroll as a valedictory summation of his life in the law.

There were no other occasions in which Lord Denning used the words of writers to support the arguments of his judgments. Each judgment in which he used the words of other writers was of considerable legal importance. The words of writers were used to support fragile moves in the argument. In these crucial moments, the authority of English literature was used to supplement the authority of law. The English language, as used by its writers, an embodiment of English identity, became, on occasional, highly charged moments, a source of legal authority in the judgments of Lord Denning.

On two occasions, the importance of the stage in English culture was alluded to by Lord Denning. As has been noted, the authority of Shakespeare was more frequently invoked by Lord Denning than that of any other writer. Both cases involved disputes arising from the commercial life of the theatre. One was a libel case in which Lew Grade sued a man for writing a letter in which he accused four actors, who had resigned from a West End production at the same time, of conspiring to bring the run of a successful play to an end.[66] In his judgment, Lord Denning maintained that there was a legitimate public interest in the affairs of actors and of the theatre: 'Many people are interested in what happens in the theatre. The stars welcome publicity...the comings and goings of the performers are noted everywhere'. Lord Denning was acknowledging the central role that had been played by theatre in English life since the time of Shakespeare; the stage was part of English identity. The other case concerned whether the fixtures of a theatre, the seating, lighting and so forth, were part of the demised premises for the purpose of fixing rent.[67] In the course of a judgment which decided that the fixtures were not a part of the demised property, Lord Denning commented that Her Majesty's Theatre, 'one of the most famous in London'[68] had been built in 1896 by Sir Herbert Beerbohm Tree thereby making plain both his knowledge of the history of theatre in England and emphasising its cultural importance.

Although there are no other explicit remarks about the stage in Lord Denning's judgments, a number of the cases in which he was involved concerned the affairs of quintessentially English actors such as Charles Chaplin,[69] Sir John and Hayley Mills[70] and Trevor Howard.[71] Other cases concerned the copyright in J.M. Barrie's *Peter Pan*,[72] a play which embodied certain aspects of English identity, and the impressario Howard Fielding who produced *Half a Sixpence*, a musical based on H.G. Wells' novel *Kipps*, a very English story, set in Kent, the 'garden of England'.[73]

Kipps' fortunes are saved by an investment which he makes in a play. Another case involved the Boulting Brothers who produced and directed a series of popular and quintessentially English films during the 1940s and 1950s.[74] Lord Denning almost certainly saw these films in the cinema. Given the fact that the Master of the Rolls would have had some influence over the cases which he heard, the subject matter and personnel of this range of cases supports the proposition that Lord Denning considered the theatre to be a vital part of English life.

The style and presentation of many of Lord Denning's judgments made explicit reference to the conventions of the theatre. Many of Lord Denning's judgments were constructed as narratives in which the various participants play their allotted roles, as on the stage. Lord Denning made this aspect of his style of judgment explicit in a libel case which turned on the question of whether the use of a document by clerical staff constituted 'publication'.[75] Lord Denning introduced his judgment thus: 'This case reads like a play that has many acts and scenes. On the stage now the principal characters are Mr Alfred Teddy Smith, a financier in London, and Mr Jude de Vries, a diamond tool manufacturer. In previous scenes there appeared Lord Carbery, the 11th Baron'.[76] We could be in the West End in the 1920s rather than in Court No 3 in the Royal Courts of Justice! Lord Denning considered the case to be one which raised fundamental issues about the right to free speech of shareholders and their ability to voice their concerns about business malpractice. As he put it: 'This raises a question of freedom of speech....we have in this court seen cases lately where those in control of a company plunder its funds and then seek to gag the minority. This should not be allowed. Shareholders should be allowed to speak their minds at meetings'.[77]

At that time confidence in the institutions of the City of London was at a low ebb following the financial collapse of 1974. The case was heard just a few months after an even more dramatic case in which the law of libel had been used in an attempt to 'gag' a shareholder who was attempting to expose a major series of frauds.[78] In that case Lord Denning had made some very robust remarks about the right of shareholders to expose fraudulent activities in their companies. The heightened rhetoric used in both judgments, in particular that which invoked the theatre, was intended to indicate the importance of the issues raised by the cases. The image of the stage, a central part of English identity, deployed as a metaphor in Lord Denning's judgment, reinforced the importance of the principles which Lord Denning believed would sustain the integrity of the City of London and prevent the whole economic system from being undermined. In the mid 1970s there were real fears of a major financial and economic collapse. These judgments were intended to help prevent that eventuality, reinforcing the reputation of the City of London by protecting shareholders who wanted to speak out against fraud. The image of the Theatre, part of England's identity since the time of Shakespeare, was prayed in aid to support Lord Denning's defence of the reputation of the City of London. Shakespeare's Globe theatre, now rebuilt, was situated just opposite the City, over the river in Southwark.

Theatrical narratives, of a melodramatic variety, were explicitly invoked in a judgment which turned on the question of whether a husband and wife could be guilty of conspiracy, a possibility hitherto prevented by the doctrine of unity.[79] Lord Denning began his judgment thus: 'This story might be called the Green saga'.[80] Many of his judgments depict the plaintiffs, defendants and other participants in vivid terms, as if they were characters in a play, appearing on the stage rather than in Court No 3 at the Royal Courts of Justice. Here is a selection of some of the more vivid of these 'characters'. 'The appellant, Miss Miriam Nothman, is a woman of intellect....she is a teacher of mathematics'.[81] 'Sir Philip Lee Brocklehurst, the second baronet of Swythamley Hall near Macclesfield....was born with a silver spoon in his mouth....the most unconventional of men...an autocrat if ever there was one [who said] when the time comes, I shall be like a fox. I shall have gone to ground'.[82] 'Joseph Langston is playing a lone hand. He is at odds with the other workers in the factory. He claims two rights of fundamental importance: First the right not to be a member of a trade union, or of an organisation of workers; second the right to work at his job'.[83] 'He found James Pannett all afire, his shoes and his hair all burning, and screaming'.[84] 'In 1964, Mr Thornton, the plaintiff, who was a freelance trumpeter of the highest quality, had an engagement with the BBC at Farringdon Hall'.[85]

One of the most poignant 'characters' to appear in Lord Denning's judgments was a woman called Margaret. He began her story thus: 'This case is of legal significance, but more of human interest. I will start with the human side; because that always has its bearing on the legal side...it is about Margaret...born in November 1955. 24....she never learned to read or write. At 16 she went out into the world, mentally handicapped, becoming by turns waitress, cleaner and chambermaid'.[86] Margaret's story continued as follows. At the age of 19 she met Fred who was aged 30 and married. They had two children which Margaret brought up as a good mother. However, Fred absconded from the family home. Margaret went off to find Fred who had run away to London only to discover that he had stolen a car, got caught and been sent to prison. Fred's father then came to look after Margaret. He was an old age pensioner of 66. He taught her to read and write. They fell in love and she had a child by him. In September 1977 they married. The case turned on the question of whether the decision of the local authority to deny Margaret access to her two children by Fred, taken into care when she went off to find him in London, could be construed as 'maladministration' and hence be reviewed by the Local Government Ombudsman. Lord Denning decided in favour of Margaret.

Two judgments even involve that stock character of English comedy the mother in law. In one of these cases Lord Denning observed: 'I am afraid that mothers and daughters do not always get on when they are living in the same house'.[87] In the other, the husband is described as a man who had attained 'the distinguished and responsible rank of Corporal of Horse' and who spent his time 'designing badges and heraldry'.[88] However, 'in 1963, the wife's mother inflicted herself on them. She was a disturbing influence. The wife gave up helping in the shop'.[89] The man had shut up the shop for the day to defend his right to the property which his former wife was claiming. He was unable to attend the reading of the judgment because he could not afford to have the shop closed for another day. In finding for the man, Lord Denning remarked that 'it is quite unacceptable to me that this wife, who has deserted her husband, should be entitled to a share of the property and bring him to ruin....it would indeed be quite intolerable that she should, for instance, be able to sell her interest to her mother and get her to turn him out'.[90] This particular drama ended with Lord Denning seeing off the wicked mother in law just as might have happened in a West End farce of the 1920s.

The Church of England

Lord Denning remarked, in the course of a judgment which turned on a point about the certainty of the objects of a trust,[91] that although 'it is not possible to define with certainty the qualifications necessary to be a member of the Church of England', a trust which was for the benefit of members of the Church of England would not be void for uncertainty because there were people who clearly were members of the established church.[92] In other words, although the Church of England was not defined by any specific doctrinal requirements, there was no doubt that many people belonged to that church and that their membership could be determined.

Deciding that a Mormon temple should be excluded from the benefit of a rating exemption under the provisions of the Places of Worship Registration Act 1855,[93] Lord Denning remarked that in practice the Church of England was open to everyone 'who chooses to come and is ready to be well behaved'.[94] The Church of England was the national church and did not seek to exclude any section of the community from access to its buildings and to its worship; it was comprehensive and all-embracing, in contrast with a religious sect like the Mormons. In the course of ordering that a Building Preservation Order could not apply to a Church of England rectory because it was an 'ecclesiastical building',[95] Lord Denning observed that 'a rectory of the Church of England has for centuries been recognised to have special attributes connected with the Church. It is vested in the incumbent for the time being as a corporation sole. It is a house set apart....the centre of all the spiritual and pastoral activities of the rector in regard to the parish'. The property of the established church was thus set apart from all other property and could not be the subject of a Building Preservation Order.

These judgments recognised the special legal status of the Church of England in English life. In another judgment, this time dissenting, Lord Denning, argued that a small plot of land which had been used as a garden by the Rector since 1938 had not become part of the 'glebe' as a result of adverse possession. Lord Denning's brothers accepted the argument that the rector had established ownership by adverse possession and that the land could be used as a place for the display of motor vehicles on the basis of the permission granted by the present incumbent. In his dissenting judgment Lord Denning argued that in 1938, the Rector had been allowed to use the plot as a garden by a 'staunch supporter of the church' who had allowed the use without demanding rent on the basis that he 'would not ask the Church for 10 shillings per year' but would rather have put the money 'in the offertory box'. Whereas the other judges applied the law in relation to adverse possession and found that there was evidence that the plot had been used by the Rector since 1938 in a manner which established possession, Lord Denning argued that the use of the land had always been based on an act of charity to the Church and that possession could not be claimed when the permission to use the land and not to ask for any rent was the result of, in effect, a charitable gift which waived the rent. Had rent been paid, the owner of the land would have given that rent back to the Church as an offertory donation. Unlike his brothers, Lord Denning maintained that an act of charity could not be the basis for a claim to land based on adverse possession. The law of charity, the rule of the Church, countermanded, in Lord Denning's dissenting argument, the strict application of the rules of land law.

Lord Denning's firm adhesion to the established Church was revealed in remarks about the vocation of a Catholic priest made in the course of a judgment concerned with innuendo in the law of libel.[96] A Catholic would consider that a priest who broke his vows was a man whose conduct had fallen well below the standard of acceptable behaviour. However, the Church of England did not recognise the validity of Catholic orders and therefore its members would not be likely to think less of the man who broke the vow which he took at ordination. Lord Denning, speaking in the voice of that church, asserted: 'No one thinks any the less of a man who becomes 'laicized' as it is called. Any one can change his career if he likes'.[97] The vocation of a priest in the Catholic Church was thus dismissed as being a career like any other. The importance of the rejection of the Church of Rome in 1534, on which the legal position of the Church of England was founded, was voiced very plainly by Lord Denning.

The disregard for the pieties of other faiths which was inherent in the nature of an established church was also expressed in a judgment concerning natural justice in relation to a compulsory purchase order.[98] The argument that because the hearings in relation to the compulsory purchase order took place on the 7th Day of Passover, and therefore could not be attended by devout Jews, was dismissed by Lord Denning out of hand. Noting that the hearing was held on the Wednesday following Easter, a normal working day for members of the established Church, and other Christians, and that reasonable notice of the date had been given, Lord Denning maintained that since all of the other relevant parties had received good notice and had arranged their affairs so that they could attend the hearing, and that administrative enquiries, by their nature, had to be organised a long time before the actual date of the hearing, the objection that the date, being the 7th Day of Passover, meant that devout Jews could not attend, was dismissed as irrelevant. Whereas a hearing held at a time when members of the Church of England could not attend as a consequence of their religious obligations would have amounted to a denial of natural justice, a hearing held when devout Jews could not attend did not amount to any such denial. The calendar in England was based on the requirements of the established church, and therefore determined the timing of Anglican religious holidays. This fact, which ensured that a clash between religious obligation and administrative convenience was impossible for Anglicans, but all too possible to those of other faiths, was ignored by Lord Denning's judgment. The position of the established church was so fundamental to the English constitution that its requirements could not be balanced against the religious obligations of other faiths in assessing whether natural justice had been breached as a result of the timing of a hearing which meant that devout Jews could not attend.

The intolerance of the established church towards any religious belief that could be defined as a sect, an attitude which dated back to the 1660s but which had been mitigated by statute in relation to Christian dissenting sects during the nineteenth century, was made very plain by Lord Denning in a series of judgments concerned with the cult of Scientology. Although Christian dissenting sects had statutory protection, that protection did not extend to non-Christian sects. Lord Denning approached Scientology in the same spirit of rigorous intolerance that an eighteenth century judge would have approached the claims of Methodism, Protestant Dissent and Unitarianism.

Confirming the Home Secretary's decision to deport an alien, in this case an American Scientologist, on the grounds that his presence was harmful to the country,[99] Lord Denning began by remarking that 'Scientology is a word which has recently been invented'. He then referred to a statement by the Minister of Health in the House of Commons which maintained that Scientology was 'a pseudo-religion' which was 'socially harmful' and 'a danger to health' which broke up families. Having thus defined Scientology as a cult which threatened the social order, a definition which an eighteenth century judge would have applied to any form of religious dissent, Lord Denning proceeded to argue that the Home Secretary's decision to expel the American alien was entirely fair and that it had been exercised in 'the interests of ordinary people in this country'. The action to overturn the Home Secretary's decision was dismissed as 'quite unsustainable'.

Deciding that a chapel of the Church of Scientology should not be exempted from the payment of rates under the provisions of the Places of Worship Registration Act 1855,[100] Lord Denning made the congruence between his approach to Scientology and that of an eighteenth century judge towards religious dissent explicit. He remarked that the law concerning places of worship other than those of the established church went back to 1688 when 'the Church of England was the established church of the land. All other denominations were persecuted'.[101] He then proceeded to set out the history of the development of the law with regard to the toleration of Protestant dissent, a process which culminated in the Places of Worship Registration Act of 1855 whereby 'all denominations were made free'. He then proceeded to argue that the protection of the 1855 Act would extend to 'a place where people come together as a congregation or assembly to do reverence to God. It need not be the God which Christians worship. It may be another God, or an unknown God, but it must be reverence to a deity'. Scientology did not qualify for protection because it was 'more a philosophy of the existence of man or of life than a religion' and 'there is nothing in it of reverence for God'. 'It emphasises man not God....it seems to me that God does not come into their scheme of things at all' and therefore their chapels are 'not a place for meeting for religious worship' and therefore not protected under the 1855 Act.[102]

Considering the use of writings protected by copyright in a work of criticism on the basis of fair dealing and the use of information gained in confidence if there was a public interest in its publication,[103] Lord Denning permitted himself to make some pungently dismissive comments about the nature of Scientology. He described its techniques as 'dangerous in untrained hands'[104] and the whole cult as being based on 'medical quackeries of a sort which may be dangerous if practiced behind closed doors', so dangerous that it was a matter of public interest that information about them should be published.[105] Scientology was based on 'dangerous material' and the dangers of the cult 'should be exposed'.[106] Just as an eighteenth century judge would have used the law to proscribe dissenting protestant sects on the basis that they posed a threat to the social order upheld by the established church, so Lord Denning used the law to proscribe Scientology by denying it the right to any protection.

Lord Denning's robust intolerance of sects and cults was extended to the Exclusive Brethren. In a dissenting judgment which concerned the issue of whether the proceedings in a local valuation court could be defined as legal proceedings for the purposes of the law of contempt,[107] Lord Denning gave an account of the Exclusive Brethren in which he stressed that 'everyone who is not one of them is evil'.[108] He explained that the activities of the sect had been the cause of 'much distress and unhappiness among deeply religious people' and have lead to families being 'split asunder', separating husbands from wives and children from parents.[109] As was the case with the Scientologists, Lord Denning considered that the sect posed a threat to the social order and thereby forfeited any claim to legal protection.

The Family

During the 1960s and 1970s, sex, and the nature of family life, became a subject of sharp contention and controversy. Starting with the Chatterley trial in 1960,[110] the traditional consensus about sex and the nature of family life was challenged. The stigma which had attached to divorce, the opprobrium directed towards illegitimacy, disapproval of sex before marriage and the treatment of homosexuality as a crime; all of which, as Lord Devlin pointed out in his Maccabean lecture delivered at the British Academy in 1958 might once have been assumed to be a reflection of the prejudices of the 'man in the Clapham omnibus', were, increasingly disregarded as attitudes towards sex and family life became more liberal and 'permissive'.[111]

Following the victory of the Labour Party in the 1964 Election, the law relating to divorce and homosexuality was reformed.[112] During the 1970s, further changes in the law with regard to the status of women were enacted.[113] The development of reliable methods of birth control created an atmosphere well described in Philip Larkin's poem *Annus Mirabilis*.[114] Lord Denning, as befitted a man born in the reign of Queen Victoria, defended traditional values with regard to sex and family life in a manner broadly consistent with the approach adopted by Lord Devlin. However, it would be a mistake to see his views as merely reactionary and out of date. Sex and the problems of family life were often present in cases which he heard in the Court of Appeal during this period; an interesting and nuanced picture of his attitude to such matters emerges from a close study of his judgments. A better way of considering Lord Denning's understanding of sex and family life would be to envisage his judgments as enacting the disquieting tension, experienced in varying ways by his contemporaries, between traditional values and the liberalism embodied in the statutory changes which was a feature of that era.

Male sexuality was the subject of a series of judgments which revealed a strikingly traditional attitude on the part of Lord Denning In a case concerning the right to a jury trial in relation to personal injury,[115] Lord Denning ruled that the trial judge's decision to allow a jury trial, rather than a hearing before a judge alone, was a valid instance of the 'exception' which had been allowed for in the recent guidelines set out by the Court of Appeal.[116] Despite the fact that a man's penis and scrotal skin had been 'avulsed'[117] he retained the sexual urge without the capacity to fulfil it. The judge had said: 'This is a unique case'. Lord Denning wholeheartedly agreed, saying: 'So it is'.[118] However, in a case heard the year before,[119] in which a woman had asked for jury trial in circumstances where her left hip had been dislocated, her left pelvis fractured and as a result she was unable to have sexual intercourse and therefore could not conceive a child, Lord Denning described the facts as constituting 'a very ordinary running down case' in which there was 'a rather unusual claim for inability to have sexual relations'[120] and refused to allow a trial by jury. In that case, the man had wanted a trial before a judge alone for 'loss of consortium', a loss which, presumably, a male judge would have understood and for which he would have felt sympathy. The contrast between Lord Denning's attitude to a man who had lost the ability to enjoy sexual intercourse and a woman faced with a comparable loss was very plain.

The dominating importance, and irresistible nature, of the male sexual urge, as Lord Denning understood it, was made clear in two cases in which judgment was given early in 1966. The first case concerned the issue of whether an act of sexual intercourse between a couple amounted to a condonation of adultery.[121] In 1958, when the act of sexual intercourse took place, an act of sex was conclusive evidence that the prior adultery of the wife had been condoned by the husband. Section 1 of the Matrimonial Causes Act 1963 had changed the law so that the condonation could be rebutted. In a complex judgment which involved distinctions between retrospectivity in relation to 'vested rights' and procedural or evidential issues and discussion as to the exact standard of proof required for the proving of a negative, Lord Denning quoted from the evidence given by the man of his perception of the nature of the act of sexual intercourse in question thus: 'Within a short time she had undressed herself and placed herself on a rug in front of the fire. She invited me to have intercourse with her. As a man, torment get the better of me, and we did have intercourse. We had a cup of tea, and I left the house'.[122] The irresistible quality of the male sexual urge was made plain by these words. Lord Denning continued, in the words of the man, that as to forgiveness 'we did not even trouble about it'.[123] An act of sexual intercourse had taken place but it had been driven by nothing more than male lust. As Lord Denning put it: 'No forgiveness. No reinstatement. No condonation'.[124] In the other case,[125] which concerned the issue of whether the refusal by a husband of sexual intercourse for six years amounted to cruelty, Lord Denning remarked in similar vein: 'What young man of normal instincts, in bed with his wife, will go on refusing for years to have sexual intercourse with her unless he gets satisfaction elsewhere?'[126]

The intrinsically irresponsible and automatic nature of male sexuality, as it was understood by Lord Denning, was made clear in another case which concerned affiliation proceedings by a woman of 32 in relation to a boy of 16.[127] The boy and the woman had had sexual intercourse at Butlins in Minehead in the summer of 1964 and the woman had become pregnant. In the eyes of the law the boy was an infant, but his parents had paid some money to the woman. This could be taken as evidence that he was acknowledging paternity on the basis of the equitable principle that if an infant does an act which he ought to do then it will be binding on him. In this case, Lord Denning refused to follow that principle and did not grant an affiliation order. Commenting on the weaknesses in the presentation of the woman's case he remarked: 'The mother was so much older than the defendant that, if she seeks to make him pay money for the child, she should prove her case properly'.[128] It is clear that Lord Denning was sympathetic with the boy who lost control of his sexual urges and was not willing to make him pay the woman for the child through an affiliation order. The boy could not control himself, the woman should have known better. On the other hand, if a girl of 15 was sexually errant, Lord Denning had less sympathy. In a case concerned with contempt of court by a newspaper which published an article about a runaway daughter, who was sexually involved with an older man, and who was the subject of wardship proceedings,[129] Lord Denning found that there was no contempt because it had not been proved that the newspaper was aware of the proceedings. He made the following comments about the girl: 'This is about a distressed father and mother. They have an errant daughter who has worried them greatly'.[130] Lord Denning emphasised the bad character of the man who was having sexual relations with the girl: 'He took drugs and wore long hair. He was one of a 'hippy' gang who did no work but squatted in empty premises. He gave the young girl drugs. He had sexual intercourse with her, knowing that she was only 15. She thought she was in love with him'.[131] Lord Denning plainly disapproved of 'free love' but, in contrast with his attitude to the sexual activity of the boy in the previous case, it was also clear that Lord Denning considered that the girl's behaviour was reprehensible. Hippies, male or female, were not people towards whom he felt any sympathy.

Lord Denning clearly endorsed a traditional view of male sexuality as impulsive, not responsive to conscious control and considered that women were in need of protection from the consequences of that sexuality. However, although he considered male sexuality to be irresponsible and uncontrollable, Lord Denning was firmly opposed to the overt visual display of the fantasies of male desire as his judgments in two cases concerning pornography made very plain. In a case concerning whether an order of *mandamus* could be made to oblige the Metropolitan Police to enforce the law with respect to the display and sale of pornography,[132] Lord Denning made some strong condemnatory remarks about pornography. He described pornography as 'powerful propaganda for promiscuity'[133] and described the images of male desire displayed and sold in Soho as 'disgusting in the extreme', 'as examples of the sordid side of life, they are deplorable'.[134] While praising the technical skill of the photographers, he condemned the subject matter of the images: 'The photographers have crowded close - inches close - to them and to their most private parts....apparently in the very act...in bright colours'.[135] The visibility of sexual intercourse produced by pornography was unacceptable to Lord Denning. Commenting on the letters published in the magazines, he remarked that the letters 'tell of it all, gloatingly, without shame, as if to commend the readers to do likewise, or worse'. Although Lord Denning accepted ordinary male sexuality, despite its raw importunity, provided it was indulged in private, and within the confines of marriage, he clearly regarded its visibility, and open discussion about its nature, as being highly detrimental to the good ordering of society. He declared that 'the law of England has always condemned pornography and sought to suppress it'.[136]

In a lengthy discussion of recent cases concerned with the control of pornography, Lord Denning made it quite clear that the Obscene Publications Act 1959 had completely failed to control pornography and that the 'expert witness' defence in particular had created a loophole through which pornographic works had been able to be widely disseminated. He was scathing about a series of recent judgments in which works which 'I should have pronounced....extremely obscene', had not been prosecuted on the grounds that they were of therapeutic value. In his opinion an 'immense amount of time, manpower and money' had been wasted' which 'had done nothing to stop pornography'.[137] Confident that the magistrates would 'know pornography when they see it' he advised that the police should make more use of the Customs and Excise and Post Office Acts which would enable them to deal with pornography effectively by avoiding the problems created by the Obscene Publications Act 1959 which, despite its apparent intention, 'had done nothing to stop pornography'. However, while admitting that the plaintiff, in asking for a *mandamus* to oblige the Police to enforce the law, had 'a point worthy of serious consideration', Lord Denning concluded that the Police were doing as much as could be expected and that it was for Parliament to change the law so as to make it possible for pornography to be eliminated from society: 'The police may well say to Parliament: 'Give us the tools and we will finish the job[138]......without efficient tools,[139] they cannot be expected to stamp it out'.[140]

Lord Denning's anxiety about the threat posed by pornography to the social order was reiterated in a case concerning the application for a *prohibition* to prevent a local authority from acting *ultra vires* by allowing cinemas to show indecent films.[141] Lord Denning asserted that 'it has been established for centuries that it is an offence at Common Law to show in public an indecent exhibition',[142] declaring that the Common Law offence of 'outraging public decency', revived in *DPP v Shaw*[143] and reiterated in *Knuller v DPP*,[144] would provide the most effective means of dealing with pornography. Lord Denning quoted, approvingly, Lord Reid's dictum in *Knuller v DPP* that indecency was 'anything which an ordinary decent man or woman would find to be shocking, disgusting or revolting'[145] and suggested that the rigorous application of this standard would ensure the elimination of pornography from the public domain and so provide a 'far better way of stopping pornography than the 1959 Act'.[146] He even proposed that he should look at Hansard[147] in order to establish that the real intention behind the 1959 Act had been to allow the Common Law prohibition on pornography to be applied to films, even though they were excluded from the provisions of the Act. Lord Denning concluded that the case for a *prohibition* had been made out, but that he would not impose one immediately, allowing time for the GLC to take action to ban the indecent films. However, should the GLC fail to act: 'It will be imperative for Parliament itself to take action so as to place the censorship of films on a proper footing'.[148]

These two cases make it very clear that Lord Denning did not consider that the law was being effectively used to control pornography and that, while he believed that the Common Law and the Customs and Excise and Post Office Acts, could be used to eliminate pornography, it would probably be necessary for Parliament to take further action. The comments which he made in these two cases from the mid 1970s when, in fact, control over the dissemination of pornography was being relaxed, suggest that Lord Denning was completely unreconciled to the more liberal approach to pornography and considered that the authorities should use the law more vigorously and that Parliament should strengthen the law still further.

Although homosexual acts between consenting adults had been decriminalised in July 1967, with the sole exception of his clear sympathy for the World War One veteran who faced forfeiture of his lease for running a male brothel,[149] Lord Denning's comments about homosexuality, acceptance of which was another aspect of the 'permissive' society, were as consistently hostile as those which he made about pornography. In a case concerning a defendant, charged with buggery, who wanted to bring evidence into court about the character of the young man with whom he was charged with committing buggery,[150] Lord Denning ruled that evidence of the appellant's previous convictions for sexual offences should also be presented to the jury. The appellant was trying to argue that the young man, who was 23, was a male prostitute and that their sexual relations had been consensual. The case was heard in September 1967, two months after the passing into law of the Sexual Offences Act 1967 which had decriminalised consensual homosexual acts committed by consenting adults in private. Lord Denning's lack of sympathy with the appellant was made clear immediately. He began his judgment with the statement: 'The facts are distasteful'[151] and went on to describe appellant's claims about the character of the young man as 'grave imputations',[152] despite the fact that sexual relations between adult males over the age of 21 had been decriminalised. The admission of evidence of the appellant's previous convictions would ensure his conviction for buggery whereas the exclusion of that evidence, and the admission of evidence that the young man was a male prostitute, would support the appellant's contention that the two of them had had consensual sex in private, an action which was no longer criminal. In a case concerned with the right of a wife to remain in the matrimonial home,[153] having stated the fact that the husband was living in the matrimonial home with a male friend, Lord Denning deployed strong emotive language both to suggest that the relationship between the two men was homosexual and to emphatically disapprove of such relations; even though the case was heard in 1969 when such relationships were no longer criminal. Lord Denning described the situation of the wife as a 'dire plight' and repeatedly described the husband's behaviour as 'deplorable' and 'outrageous'. He used the phrase, 'some features of family life are elemental in our society'[154] to describe the right of the wife to remain in the matrimonial home; the use of the word 'elemental' suggested that, in this case, the husband had done something worse than merely exclude the wife from the home.

In the course of considering an allegation of libel which turned on the interpretation of a particular word,[155] Lord Denning discussed the meaning of the word 'bent'.[156] Having stated that 'bent' was used as a piece of slang and that it had no precise meaning, he added that it could mean 'perverted in a sexual sense' or in 'an even worse sense'.[157] Lord Denning's disapprobation of a state of being which was no longer criminal could not have been made more plain. However, his attitude to the sexuality of the former leader of the Liberal Party, Jeremy Thorpe, which was revealed during his trial for conspiring to bring about the attempted murder of Norman Scott, was rather different. Thorpe's sexuality was dismissed as a youthful indiscretion which had taken place 'many years ago' and 'should have been erased and forgotten long since'.[158] Whereas homosexuality as a way of life was considered to be completely unacceptable, a youthful homosexual indiscretion by a public figure was considered, by Lord Denning, to be something which could be overlooked. Indeed, he must have been well aware that a very large number of public figures, including some sitting on the bench, had indulged in such indiscretions.[159] Lord Denning clearly considered that homosexuality was an aberration, indulged in by some young men but then superseded by normal heterosexual relationships. As far as he was concerned, it was not a normal condition, still less a viable way of life.

Two judgments shed light on Lord Denning's approach to conception and birth, the inevitable consequence of heterosexual intercourse in the absence of contraception. Given his view that male sexuality was effectively uncontrollable,[160] and that the production of children was the natural result of such relations,[161] heterosexual acts were bound to result in conception and birth. In a case concerned with an allegation of negligence by a doctor in the delivery of a baby,[162] Lord Denning started his judgment with the statement that 'being born is dangerous for the baby'.[163] This proposition was supported by the words of an unamed 'eminent professor' who stated that: 'Throughout history birth has been the most dangerous moment in the life of an individual and medical science has not yet succeeded in eliminating that danger'.[164] Lord Denning's judgment concentrated on the legal consequence of these propositions which was that the birth of a damaged or deformed baby did not imply negligence because, in the words of the Bible, women were condemned to bring forth children in 'pain' with all the inevitable risks associated with that 'pain'. In the instant case, he was completely satisfied that the doctors had done everything within their power to ensure a safe delivery. Whereas the doctors were presented by Lord Denning in the most favourable light, the woman who brought an action for negligence was described as 'very, nervous, tense'[165]; he noted that she had an 'instinctive revulsion against her vagina being examined'.[166] Lord Denning commented that 'she was not in a state to know what was going on'.[167] He concluded that the woman 'should be grateful for all that has been done for her without her trying to lay the blame on the doctors';[168] commenting adversely on the fact that her case had been paid for by legal aid at 'colossal'[169] expense which was borne by the taxpayers'. It was quite clear that Lord Denning took the traditional Biblical view that women gave birth in pain and that birth was an inherently dangerous event. For all that medical science might attempt to mitigate the danger, the danger remained and, in this case, it might have been better if medical science, though not to blame for the deformities of the child, had not intervened. Lord Denning remarked: 'What a pity they did not let him die'.[170]

It was clear that Lord Denning thought that a charge of negligence was completely inappropriate with regard to birth; indeed he compared the charge that doctors could be negligent in such circumstances with the accusation that he might have been negligent because one of his judgments was overturned by the House of Lords.[171] For Lord Denning, birth was an inherently dangerous aspect of the natural order; its dangers could only be marginally mitigated by medical science. Birth, the inevitable consequence of sexual intercourse without contraception, was an event to which women must submit, accepting the consequences, whatever they might be. If the doctors in the instant case had been to be found negligent then, according to Lord Denning, every doctor in England would say, in the words of John Bradford[172] as he witnessed a criminal being taken away for execution: 'But for the grace of God, there goes John Bradford'.[173] In a judgment which concluded that birth was inherently dangerous and that little could be done to mitigate that danger, Lord Denning deployed some very powerful rhetoric. He invoked the natural order, the execution of criminals and the nature of judgment. Life, death and the nature of law itself haunted this judgment in a manner which suggested that Lord Denning treated birth, the consequence of sexual intercourse, as something which was beyond regulation by either medical science or the law.

Lord Denning's understanding of sexual intercourse, conception and birth was made even more plain in a judgment concerning the legality of an abortion procedure which was supervised by a nurse rather than a doctor.[174] In this judgment, Lord Denning's use of language made it very plain that he considered abortion to be an unacceptable practice. He noted that he had passed 'severe sentences of imprisonment for this offence'[175] before the passing of the Abortion Act 1967. His use of language in describing abortion reflected that of anti-abortion campaigners. He described it as a 'soul-destroying task', a 'heart-rending task' which 'destroyed life'. The procedure had the result that the 'child is expelled from the body, usually dead, but sometimes at the point of death'. He stated at the outset that he was going to refer to the 'unborn child' rather than the foetus and invoked the old Common Law description in Law French, *en ventre de sa mere*',[176] thereby explicitly linking his view of the unacceptable nature of abortion with the authority of the Common Law as established from 'time immemorial'. It was quite clear, from the evidence of these two judgments, both directly concerned with conception and birth, the inevitable consequences of sexual intercourse without contraception, that Lord Denning, in accord with the doctrine of the Catholic Church, considered that the sole purpose of sexual intercourse was procreation and that neither the law nor medical science should intervene in that process other than to mitigate its effects at the margins. Sex, conception and birth were mysteries of the natural order beyond the authority of law or science.

Although Lord Denning plainly disapproved of abortion, he made no direct comments about contraception, in particular with regard to the contraceptive pill, in his judgments. However, some indication of his attitude towards contraception might be gained from a dissenting judgment,[177] made in the 1950s, which involved consideration of the implications of the sterilisation of a husband after the birth of his first child. The issue before the court was whether the sterilisation of the husband amounted to cruelty for the purpose of securing a divorce. The husband and wife were married in 1934 when the wife was 21 years of age; the only child of the marriage was born in 1936. In 1938 the husband submitted to a sterilisation operation with the wife's knowledge. The husband and wife continued to live together, although there was increasing discord and regular quarrels in the home, for 13 years until 1951, when the wife left. Sexual intercourse continued throughout this period. The wife petitioned for a divorce on the ground of cruelty. Lord Denning began his judgment thus:

> The parties married on October 25, 1934, when the husband was 25 and the wife 21. They lived very happily together for two years until a son was born to them on December 19, 1936. About 18 months later, in 1938, a shocking thing took place. The husband underwent an operation to have himself sterilised.[178]

The judgment continued as follows:

> This operation provokes several questions. The first is: Why did the husband have this done? Let me give his answer in his own words. Counsel asked him: "What was the immediate cause of the operation? (A.) It was because of my wife's attitude towards the boy. He was not a baby to be caressed and loved. He was a show-piece." Again: "Why did you agree to have an operation for sterilisation? (A.) Because my wife was so installed. She was so installed with the home, and with this baby she had. (Q.) You said the baby was a show-piece? (A.) Yes. (Q.) In what way? (A.) She wanted to have him perfectly dressed, and when he was tiny, if there was the least thing missing, she would be absolutely beside herself." Those answers throw a flood of light on the husband's mentality. Why did he object to the wife treating the baby as a show-piece? Although he did not realize it, he must in some strange way have been jealous of the place which the child had in the wife's affections; and his jealousy found expression in a determination not to give her any more children, seeing that was the way she treated this baby…….. It is, as the commissioner said, "an amazing story"; and it was done simply because he was jealous of the baby. He did it so as to "pay her out" for making so much of it. That seems to me to be cruelty in itself………What was the effect of the operation on the wife……..She could not bear him near her. Let me give

their answers in their own words: When the wife was asked "How did this operation affect you in your relationship to your husband and your married life? (A.) Well, I was disgusted with him, and for some time after the operation I could not bear him near me, and especially since the operation he has become really effeminate......" And as for the husband, he was asked: "How do you say things went on from 1942? (A.) Things became very difficult. (Q.) In what way? (A.) My wife could not bear me near her. If I tried to embrace her, she became frivolent (sic) to begin with, and then she refused, and I had to give up." I must say that that is just what I should expect. I cannot think of anything more disruptive of a marriage than for a party to sterilise himself in his way......The husband had some unpleasant and distasteful domestic habits, and he was dirty and untidy. He also kept Indian idols and burnt incense in the sitting-room; but the wife seems to have acquiesced in this. These incidents by themselves could not be said to have been cruelty. The important question is the effect of the sterilisation......There was no just cause or excuse for this operation at all. If the husband had undergone it without telling his wife about it beforehand, no one could doubt that it would have been cruelty. It was an act most disruptive of the married state, and she was the victim of it........when this husband was sterilised, the effect of it was not over and done with at once, like a blow with the fist or like an act of adultery. This operation had an effect which continued, day in and day out, year in year out, throughout the marriage. No act of sexual intercourse could result in a child.......An ordinary surgical operation, which is done for the sake of a man's health, with his consent, is, of course, perfectly lawful because there is just cause for it. But when there is no just cause or excuse for an operation, it is unlawful, even though the man consents to it. The classic instance is a case reported by Lord Coke, tried at Leicester in 1604, when a "young strong and lustie rogue, to make him impotent," got his companion to cut off his left hand so that he might avoid work and be able the better to beg. Both were found guilty on indictment of a criminal offence. A later instance can be given from early Victorian days when soldiers, as part of their drill, had to bite cartridges. A soldier got a dentist to pull out his front teeth so as to avoid the drill. In the opinion of Stephen J. both were guilty of a criminal offence. (See Stephen's Digest of Criminal Law, 3rd ed., p. 142.).........Take a case where a sterilisation operation is done so as to enable a man to have the pleasure of sexual intercourse, without shouldering the responsibilities attaching to it. The operation then is plainly injurious to the public interest. It is degrading to the man himself. It is injurious to his wife and to any woman whom he may marry, to say nothing of the way it opens to licentiousness............If a husband undergoes an operation for sterilisation without just cause or excuse, he strikes at the very root of the marriage relationship.........It is severe cruelty.[179]

Lord Denning's approach to sexual intercourse, conception and birth had implications for his application of the law to disputes concerning paternity and legitimacy. The issue of paternity in relation to the ownership of offspring in the case of sheep arose in a case concerned with a dispute between a farmer who had purchased some sheep by means of hire-purchase and the finance company to whom he was paying instalments to repay the debt incurred by the hire-purchase agreement.[180] Deploying the authority of Blackstone who, on this issue invoked the authority of Pufendorf, Lord Denning stated that the principle of *partus sequitur ventrem* determined the ownership of offspring in relation to the brute creation, though for the most part in the human species the Common Law disallowed the maxim'.[181] This was because, in the animal world, the father was usually not known beyond reasonable doubt or even on the balance of probabilities. However, there was one exception to this. In the case of swans, who mated for life, the father was known and therefore the presumption that the offspring belonged to the owner of the mother did not apply. The authority for this proposition was a case reported by Coke,[182] the patriarch of the English legal order. As Lord Denning put it: 'Swans, as we all know, are faithful unto death and beyond'.[183] For Lord Denning, the human father, like the male swan, had a relationship with his offspring whether or not that offspring was conceived within lawful marriage.

The importance of paternity to Lord Denning, and of the responsibilities which it entailed, whether or not the man was lawfully married to the woman, was made plain in a dissenting judgment in a case concerned with the interpretation of the word 'descendant' in a Group Life Assurance Scheme.[184] Unlike his brethren, who interpreted 'descendant' as legitimate descendant, Lord Denning interpreted the word as meaning 'blood' descendant and invoked Biblical authority to support this proposition: 'When we say that we are descended from Adam and Eve we mean that we are descended by blood not marriage'.[185] To the authority of the Bible, he added that of *Magna Carta*. Descent from one of the Barons who signed *Magna Carta* was not 'to be rejected because his escutcheon has been de-bruised with a baton sinister'.[186] In contrast with 'Victorian fathers who thought they were doing right when they turned their erring daughters out of the house' and who 'visited the sins of the father on his children - with a vengeance',[187] Lord Denning sought to use the law to protect the interests of an illegitimate child by arguing that paternity, by blood, was as important as legitimacy in establishing a claim to the benefits of a Life Assurance policy, that 'descent' was a matter of blood, of intercourse, conception and birth, rather than a consequence of legitimacy. Lord Denning argued that a rule which barred such a child from receiving the benefit of the policy was not a rule of law but a mere guide to the construction of documents which could be set to one side in the interests of justice. The invocation of the authority of both the Bible and *Magna Carta* in Lord Denning's rhetoric was an index of the strength of his feeling about this issue.

The legal importance of paternity, considered in terms of sexual intercourse, conception and birth, as opposed to those of marriage and legitimacy, was considered by Lord Denning in a series of cases between 1967 and 1970 which concerned the power of the court to order a blood test to establish the paternity of a child. In the first of these cases,[188] Lord Denning noted that there was no longer a requirement that the presumption of legitimacy could only be rebutted on the basis of an evidential standard of 'beyond reasonable doubt', but that that presumption could now be overturned on the basis of a 'balance of probabilities'. Observing that this meant that the 'sins of the fathers were no longer visited on their children' and that illegitimacy had become less of a stigma, Lord Denning stated that the question of whether a particular child was the son or daughter of the husband in a divorce case could be reconsidered. A blood test could not establish with certainty that the child was the son or daughter of the husband, but it could establish that they were not. Lord Denning ruled that the decision whether to order a blood test would be a matter for the High Court's discretion based on the court's inherent jurisdiction as *parens patriae*. In the second case,[189] Lord Denning used that discretion to refuse to order the husband to take a blood test when he would not allow his wife to have custody of his son; the wife had gone off with another man claiming that the man with whom she had committed adultery was the father. Lord Denning argued that if all three adults had taken the blood test then it would have been in the interests of the child to know who his father was, but the refusal of the husband to take the test was not unreasonable in the circumstances because the established position, based on the presumption of legitimacy, could be jeopardised if a forced blood test revealed that the other man was in fact the father. In this case, it was clear that Lord Denning was unwilling to contemplate the risk that a blood test might disrupt the *status quo* and enable the errant wife to take away the boy from the man who was content to be his father whether or not he was the blood father. Adultery on the part of the woman displaced the putative claim of a possible blood father.

In the third case,[190] the woman had gone off with a 'coloured' man and given birth to a child. Her husband had refused to accept the child and the mother had applied for an order of affiliation against the other man who had refused a blood test. Lord Denning stressed that the three sons which she had had with her husband were 'ordinary white children' but that the daughter who was the subject of the affiliation proceedings was 'said to be coloured'. The other man had refused a blood test. The problem was that whereas a blood test could establish with certainty that a man was not the father of a child, there was only a 70% possibility of it establishing that a given man was the father. Lord Denning ruled that it was in the financial and social interests of the child that she should know who her real father was and the man's refusal of a blood test was unreasonable. A blood test was ordered. What was interesting was that the husband's claim that the child was coloured was accepted on his say-so, without a blood test, but the other man's refusal of a blood test was considered unreasonable. The facts suggested the woman might well have slept with more than one other man and that, on that basis, the man would have had a good reason for refusing a test given that it could not establish, for certain, that he was the father. Lord Denning seemed willing to accept the assertion that the child was coloured without considering it necessary to confirm that claim by ordering a blood test that could resolve the question of whether the husband was the father with certainty in that it could establish beyond doubt that he was not the father. Blood may have been important to Lord Denning as a factor in establishing paternity but when it came to using a test which could resolve the question of whether a coloured man was the father of a child by establishing that the husband was not the father, a man's word took precedence over a blood test. Colour was a stronger factor than blood.

Lord Denning may have placed considerable emphasis on the importance of paternity by blood, and therefore on the significance of the relationship between sexual intercourse, conception and birth in human life, but he did not subscribe to the legal doctrine of unity whereby the man and the woman, joined in marriage, become a single person. Indeed, in two judgments of 1981, he effectively terminated the legal life of that doctrine. In a case which turned on the possibility of the existence of a joint conspiracy by a husband and wife,[191] Lord Denning stated that the doctrine of unity, which would have made any such conspiracy a legal impossibility, 'was a fiction then. It is a fiction now' and that 'it should be discarded'.[192] Instead he defined a man and woman who were married as 'equal partners in a joint enterprise' which involved maintaining a home and bringing up children 'maintaining and desiring the trust of each other', but otherwise, in the eyes of the law, they went their own separate ways. In the other case, which concerned the liability of an absent husband for the rates due on a property,[193] he ruled that the wife's actual occupation of the house meant that she was liable for the rates even though, under the doctrine of unity, the husband would have been considered to be in occupation rather than the wife. These two judgments effectively brought to an end the Common Law doctrine which had been the counterpart of the Catholic doctrine that a married couple were one flesh, a single person.

Lord Denning also brought to an end the doctrine that a wife's domicile was determined by that of her husband, another aspect of the old doctrine of unity. In a case which turned on the domicile of the woman,[194] a man was claiming that under Maltese law, where he was domiciled, the marriage, which took place in a registry office in England, was a nullity and, consequently, the woman, who was on national assistance, could not obtain a divorce, and therefore financial support for her three children, on the grounds of desertion, because the Maltese courts did not recognise the marriage. If her domicile was that of her husband, as the law traditionally would have ruled, then she could not obtain a divorce and could not obtain a financial settlement. If she were domiciled in England then under English law she could obtain a divorce and settlement. Lord Denning referred to the woman as an 'Englishwoman' and firmly rejected the law of domicile as it had been conceived up to that time, describing it as 'the last barbaric relic of a wife's servitude', concluding that he 'did not think that these courts are bound to declare this English marriage no marriage.'[195] Another case concerning the validity of a Czechoslovakian divorce decree,[196] also turned on the doctrine of domicile because, under that doctrine, a woman seeking a divorce would have had to apply for a divorce in the country in which her husband was living and in this instance he was living in England at the time of the issue of the Czechoslovakian decree. The point was crucial because if the Czechoslovakian marriage was valid then the man's marriage to an English woman would be bigamous and therefore she would be unable to obtain a financial settlement from him because, in the eyes of the law, they would never have been married. In order to protect 'the English Rose' as Lord Denning called the second wife, and to prevent her from being 'reduced to the status of a woman living with a man who is not her husband', he declared that the rule that a woman could only apply for a divorce in the country where her husband was domiciled was redundant. In these two judgments, Lord Denning set aside the old rule on domicile which had treated the man and woman as legally one person in order to protect the woman and ensure that she received justice.

Lord Denning was clear about the importance of marriage: 'The family relation is at the foundation of all society'.[197] In another judgment he remarked: 'It is the husband's duty to provide the wife with a roof over her head; and, by providing the matrimonial home he gives her the authority to be there. It is an authority he cannot revoke, so long as it remains the matrimonial home. He certainly cannot revoke it on his desertion'.[198] Again: 'Some features of family life are elemental in our society' – duty of a husband to provide a home for a wife. So long as the wife behaves herself she is entitled to remain in the matrimonial home'.[199] Children should be brought up by two parents in a secure home: 'In the ordinary way, the longer they can be brought up together in one house, with the parents, the better for them'.[200]

Lord Denning's traditional view of marriage was revealed in comments made in the course of judgments: 'The wife was an excellent wife is some ways.....husband's meal always ready'.[201] 'They spent Christmas together in the house. They had a happy day. The wife prepared the meals. The children enjoyed themselves. We have seen their letters telling what they did. It was a normal happy family Christmas'.[202] In his last volume of autobiography, *The Closing Chapter*,[203] he painted a picture of the 'happy family Christmas'. 'Christmas Day is a family day. It is the day on which sons and daughters – of all ages – gather together with their parents. They come from near. They come from far. To be at home with the family. Yes – at home – with the family and with the children. The future of the country depends on the upbringing of the children. Their home-life depends on their family ties. These ties are bonded by Christmas. The family is the microcosm of society. As bricks go to make a house, so do families go to make a people'.[204]

However, despite his enthusiasm for traditional marriage, Lord Denning exhibited a surprisingly broad range of sympathy for decidedly unconventional family arrangements: 'In 1966 there was a scripture rally in Trafalgar Square'. A man met a woman. 'He was not much to look at'. 'He looked like a tramp' she said, 'He had been picking up fag ends'. They got on well enough to exchange addresses. He gave her 'a rose wrapped up in a newspaper'. The woman smartened him up. They shared a house. The man wanted the woman to marry him, she rejected the offer. Despite this, Lord Denning, in a dissenting judgment, argued that a resulting trust in the man's favour had been created because both had contributed to a joint tenancy even if they had different purposes.[205] An unorthodox domestic arrangement received Lord Denning's approbation on another occasion:

> So far as we know, Jack Wright was a bachelor and Olive Agnes Fox was a spinster who met 40 years ago and lived happily ever after'. Jack died in

1961 after they had spent 21 years together. In Lord Denning's view Jack and Olive were a family in the popular sense; the lady was a member of the tenant's family though they were not married, she was therefore a statutory tenant.[206]

Lord Denning was disposed to protect women whose men, married or not, had not treated them properly. 'I will call her Janet because she has had four surnames already'. She married at 18 but changed her name to Eves by deed poll; she was not married to Stuart Eves. He promised to marry her but said she was too young because she was under 21. She did much more than many wives would do'. She broke up concrete, demolished a shed. However, 'he met Gloria when he got a job as a minicab driver'. She threatened violence. 'It was a poor return for all she had done'. However, he remarked, using what was, in the circumstances, a thoroughly appropriate metaphor, 'equity is not past the age of childbearing'. 'She trusted Stuart and he promised to marry her,' Lord Denning found no difficulty in finding that a constructive trust had been created for Janet whereby she was entitled to a quarter of the property.[207] 'In 1968 Mr Eric Tanner was a milkman during the day and a croupier at night......to use his own words, he got disgusted with his marriage and went out and had a good time'. Eric went out with three women at once. Then he met an 'attractive Irish girl, Miss Josephine McDermott'. Josephine became pregnant, took his name, gave birth to twins and gave up her flat. Lord Denning ruled that Josephine had an equitable license to continue in occupation of his flat.[208]

However, despite this evident sympathy with women who had been badly used, Lord Denning was inclined to evince marked hostility towards what he deemed to be an erring woman: 'Then in July 1961 this little family, the father, mother and the two girls went by themselves for their holiday to Westward Ho'. On holiday the husband intercepted a letter from wife to another man. There was a plan to take a flat and the children. The husband used his mother to take the children. In Lord Denning's view he was 'a man against whom no word can be spoken'. In so far as the wife, by her conduct, broke up with him she was not a good mother; she had little consciousness of her duty towards her husband or her children. 'It was a matter of simple justice between them that he should have care and control'.[209]

Lord Denning's doctrine of marriage was that of the joint enterprise rather than that of the unity of the flesh into one person. One of the consequences of this approach was that the woman, instead of being subsumed in the person of the man, acquired legal rights to property which could, according to Lord Denning, be protected by the courts. This was the so-called 'married woman's equity'. In a series of cases,[210] Lord Denning tried to argue that a combination of the woman's partnership in a joint enterprise, the man's duty to provide a home for the woman and their children and the court's discretion, under the terms of the Married Woman's Property Act 1882, to adjust the property rights of the two parties, enabled the courts to create an equitable jurisdiction which would provide a married woman with effective property rights in the event of divorce. Instead of the doctrine of unity, whereby the woman had no independent property rights, Lord Denning evolved a doctrine which assigned property rights where none had existed before. At the discretion of the court, and under its protection, a woman was given a right to property which she had not hitherto enjoyed.

Considered as a joint enterprise involving the creation of a home and the bringing up of children, the family was conceived by Lord Denning as an institution whose purpose was to provide the material protection necessary for children. Children were the inevitable consequence of sexual intercourse in the absence of contraception and, given Lord Denning's view of male sexuality, sexual intercourse was inevitable if a man and a woman lived together. Given the nature of male sexuality, as understood by Lord Denning, marriage was not a religious mystery involving the creation of one flesh out of two persons but an institution which protected women from the consequences of sexual intercourse which would, inevitably, lead to their giving birth to children who also needed to be protected by the law. The law ensured that the male, driven by his uncontrollable sexual urge, was obliged to fulfil his responsibilities towards the woman and the children that she would produce as a consequence of his lust. As he put it in a judgment refusing an injunction which would have excluded the husband from the marital home:[211] 'In the ordinary way, the longer the children can be brought up together in one house with their parents, the better for them'. This approach also provided a rational basis for deciding how to split up property in the event of a divorce because it enabled the court to follow the logic of marriage as a joint enterprise for the creation of a home in which to bring up children by ensuring that the woman, having been assigned an equitable property right in the matrimonial home by the court, would be able to continue to bring up the children who were the result of that joint enterprise. Seen in this light, the 'family relation is at the foundation of all society'[212] and, by means of the doctrine of joint enterprise and its necessary consequence of a married woman's equitable property rights, the courts could do something to mitigate the effects of divorce on the joint enterprise of creating a matrimonial home in which to bring up children.

Lord Denning understood marriage to be a social institution which protected vulnerable women from the consequences of sexual intercourse and ensured that the children produced as a result of that intercourse were provided with economic security. Marriage, in this sense, was fundamental since it was the institution which secured the reproduction of the nation. The collapse of marriage as an institution would therefore pose a threat to the social order. Lord Denning's development of the 'married woman's equity' was a legal device which ensured that children could be raised securely and therefore the reproduction of the nation would be safeguarded.[213]

Lord Denning acknowledged that 'in our time the concept of marriage, I am sorry to say, is being eroded. Nowadays many couples live together as if they were husband and wife, but they are not married'[214] and conceded, in a case which concerned the admissibility of interrogatories which asked whether a couple had had sexual intercourse,[215] a question which had previously been forbidden on the basis that it would result in self-incrimination, that 'the old ecclesiastical privilege arose at times when adultery was regarded as equivalent to a criminal offence', but that 'nowadays the thunders of the Church have lost their force. Even society does not condemn adultery as it once did. It is still a grave moral offence but not one which enables a person to object to answering questions about it'.[216] However, despite this recognition of changing values, in a series of cases[217] Lord Denning applied the law which he had developed in relation to protecting the proprietorial interests of married women so as to provide similar protection to unmarried women who had embarked on the joint enterprise of creating a home in which children could be raised. In this way, Lord Denning created a legal mechanism which could mitigate the effects of the breakdown of the institution of marriage on the social order and so create a modicum of stability during a time of rapid social change. Lord Denning did not approve of adultery or fornication in the least, he merely sought to limit the scope of their capacity to be 'detrimental to the good ordering of society'.

The most dramatic use by Lord Denning of the law to protect the interests of a woman concerned an unmarried woman who had been subjected to severe physical abuse by her partner.[218] In order to protect the woman, it was necessary to overturn decisions which had recently been made by the Court of Appeal, in effect to set aside the doctrine of precedent, and, by so doing, to deny the man an interest in property which, before that decision, had been protected by the Common Law. Both the doctrine of precedent and the sanctity of property rights were overruled in order to protect a woman from physical abuse. Lord Denning began his judgment by discussing the meaning of the term 'Common Law wife'. He insisted that 'no such woman was known to the Common Law' but accepted that in ordinary usage 'it means a woman who was living with man in the same household as if she were his wife. She is to be distinguished from a 'mistress' where the relationship may be casual, impermanent and secret'.[219] The patriarachal authority of Blackstone, who had allowed for 'moderate correction' of a wife by her husband was set aside with the comment 'those days are long past'.[220]

The rule of statutory interpretation whereby there was a presumption that property rights were not affected in the absence of express words was also set aside on the basis of the argument that 'social justice requires that personal rights should, in a proper case, be given priority over rights of property'.[221] Lord Denning also set aside the rule that Hansard and the Reports of Select Committees should not be used as aids to statutory interpretation in order to set out a purposive interpretation of the Domestic Violence and Matrimonial Proceedings Act 1976.

In order to get round the problem that two recent decisions of the Court of Appeal[222] had established precedents that the 1976 Act did not affect property rights, Lord Denning set out an unprecedented argument that the Court of Appeal had an inherent jurisdiction to overrule previous decisions if justice demanded that that should be done; that the rule that the Court of Appeal was bound by its previous decisions was based on 'comity between judges' and had no foundation in Common Law or in statute, and that the rule in *Young v Bristol Aeroplane Co. Ltd.*[223] had 'overruled the practice of a century'[224] but 'it is not a rule of law at all. It is simply a practice or usage laid down by the court for its own guidance...so we in 1977 can discard the guidelines of 1944 and set up new guidelines of our own or revert to the practice laid down by Brett MR[225]....nothing said in the House of Lords before or since can stop us from doing so...anything said about it there must needs be obiter dicta'.[226] He concluded that 'the list of exceptions [from the rule in *Young v Bristol Aeroplane Co Ltd]* is now getting so large that they are in the process of eating up the rule itself; and we would do well to follow the same practice as the House of Lords'.[227] Lord Denning knew perfectly well that these arguments would be rejected by the House of Lords out of hand, but what was striking was that he should have deployed an almost revolutionary doctrinal rhetoric to justify a decision which would protect a woman from abuse by excluding a man from a property in which he had a proprietary interest. The sanctity of property and a number of fundamental legal doctrines were set aside in order to allow the court to come to the aid of a woman. Lord Denning used the inherent power of the courts to do justice so as to shape the law in a manner that would enable them to mitigate the social disorder which, in his view, would follow if the law were not able to protect women and their children from the consequences of abuse by violent men.

Lord Denning considered that male sexuality was inherently uncontrollable; consequently, in the absence of contraception it was inevitable that men would have sexual intercourse with women and that this would result in conception and the birth of children. Marriage was an institution protected by law which ensured that men and women who had sexual intercourse were treated as being engaged in a joint enterprise to establish a matrimonial home in which children could be raised. The legal consequence of this was that married women were entitled to a proprietary interest in the matrimonial home. As divorce became more common, and as men and women lived together without getting married, Lord Denning extended this principle so as to assign proprietary interests to divorced and unmarried women. It was the fact that sexual intercourse inevitably led to conception and the birth of children that led Lord Denning to extend the protection of the law in relation to property rights to women who would otherwise have no such rights and therefore be unable to raise children in safety and security. In this way, Lord Denning shaped the law in such a way that it recognised women as independent legal subjects with proprietary rights. The Common Law had not conceived of women in this manner, but Lord Denning used his power to develop the law so that it could protect women from the consequences of sexual intercourse.

However, this approach to women was not remotely congruent with that espoused by feminists during the 1970s. Lord Denning's attitude to women was premised on the female biological role of being a mother and, given the nature of male sexuality, the fact that the women would inevitably conceive and give birth to children. This protective attitude co-existed with an emphatic rejection of abortion and the woman's right to choose. Although the Abortion Act 1967 had given women a legal right to abortion, Lord Denning's decision in *Royal College of Nursing of the United Kingdom v Department of Health and Social Security*[228] would have radically restricted a woman's access to abortion had it not been overturned by the House of Lords.[229]

Lord Denning shaped the law so as to enable the courts to protect women and to give them property rights so that, if necessary, they could raise children on their own, obliging the biological fathers to give them money and property so that they could do so in safety and security. Lord Denning's attitude to paternity was that a man should not escape the consequences of sexual intercourse; it followed that the rules on legitimacy should be set aside so that illegitimate children could receive money and property from their natural fathers. Lord Denning was a radical anti-feminist. For him women were defined by their role as mothers and should be treated by men with traditional courtesy so that the inevitable consequences of uncontrollable male desire, which would, as a matter of course, lead to sexual intercourse between men and women and therefore conception and birth,[230] could be subjected to some degree of social regulation.

In two cases concerning the Sex Discrimination Act 1975, Lord Denning expressed views which feminists would have found unacceptable. In a case concerning discrimination against men who were obliged to work overtime in unpleasant conditions whereas women were not obliged to work overtime in such conditions, in which he found that men had suffered discrimination,[231] he remarked that 'a woman's hair is her crowning glory, so it is said. She does not like it disturbed, especially when she has just had a hair-do'.[232] In the first case which he heard on the Sex Discrimination Act 1975,[233] he remarked: 'It would be very wrong to my mind if this Act were thought to obliterate the differences between men and women or to do away with the chivalry and courtesy which we expect mankind to give womankind. The natural differences of sex must be regarded even in the interpretation of an Act of Parliament....it is not discrimination for mankind to treat womankind with the courtesy and chivalry which we have been taught to believe is right conduct in our society'.[234]

Although Lord Denning conceived of women as autonomous legal subjects and extended the scope of their proprietary interest in the matrimonial home, his attitudes could not be described as progressive by the standards of 1970s feminism. While his approach to sexuality was radical in its rejection of the traditional doctrines of unity and domicile and in his disregard of the legal rules about legitimacy, in all other respects his approach was traditional. He emphasised the uncontrollability of male desire, rejected abortion, and probably also contraception, considered women to be defined by their role as mothers and conceived of sexual intercourse exclusively in terms of procreation. His approach to education, the means whereby the children who were the products of sexual intercourse were shaped into members of the social order, was equally unprogressive. In a series of judgments, Lord Denning made plain his support for traditional grammar schools, institutions which the Labour governments of 1964-70 and 1974-79 sought to transform into comprehensive schools.

Education

On July 12th 1965 the Labour government initiated a major change in the English educational system. The Education Act 1944 had created a system of grammar schools, supported by state funding but based on the principle of selection by examination, and secondary modern schools. A third tier of technical schools had not been successfully established due to problems with funding. The Labour party had criticised this system when in opposition on the basis that it was socially divisive and had indicated that they would change the structure of education provision, if they won an election, so as to create a system which was no longer based on selection and which catered for all abilities in a single school. This system was called comprehensive education.

Unusually for a judge, Lord Denning had been educated at a grammar school, in Andover, and had proceeded from there to Magdalen College, Oxford. In three judgments concerning the implementation of the Labour government's policy of abolishing state grammar schools and replacing them with comprehensive schools, he made very plain his views about the superiority of the grammar schools, and their place in English tradition.

The first case concerned the requirement that a local authority should give adequate notice of the change in status of a school from being a state grammar school to being a comprehensive school.[235] Lord Denning began his judgment thus: 'The best and brightest pupils are allocated to the grammar schools. These are often old foundations going back to the reign of Edward VI'.[236] He then explained that the London Borough of Enfield, following the order of the Secretary of State for Education, had set a target date for the existing state grammar schools to become comprehensive of 1st September 1967 but had failed to issue notices of the change to eight schools. Lord Denning then said, perhaps over-protesting the political neutrality of the judiciary: 'I pause to say that this is solely a question of law. We are not in this court concerned with the policy of the Secretary of State....nor have we to consider whether it is an good thing to change from a selective system of education to a comprehensive one. We have to consider only whether the requirements of the law have been fulfilled'.[237] He then argued that because the change from grammar school to comprehensive was a 'fundamental change', the existing schools would no longer be 'maintained'. The local authority had a statutory duty to 'maintain' schools in its area and therefore could not change the status of a school on the orders of the Secretary of State unless a notice was formally issued. It followed that the eight schools in question could not be changed from grammar schools into comprehensive schools unless proper notices were issued. As a result the target date of September 1st 1967 for establishing a comprehensive system in the London Borough of Enfield could not be met. Lord Denning concluded his judgment thus: 'Even if chaos should result, still the law must be obeyed'.[238]

The law had been used to disrupt the policy of the government, but Lord Denning had insisted, perhaps over much, that the decision was entirely a matter of statutory interpretation. However, it is not difficult to see how a different judge might have decided that the change was not 'fundamental', or that the schools were still being 'maintained', that the requirement to issue notices was directory rather than mandatory or that a balance between strict adherence to the letter of the law and consequential administrative chaos should be struck so as to prevent 'chaos' thereby reaching a conclusion which would have allowed the London Borough of Enfield to meet their target date.

In 1974, Labour returned to government, determined to complete the process of transforming state grammar schools into comprehensives. In a case which concerned the question of whether a local authority had acted *ultra vires* by deciding not to implement a plan which had been drawn up by the previous council and approved by the Secretary of State for Education,[239] Lord Denning once again made his own preferences plain and reached a decision which prevented the implementation of the plan to abolish grammar schools and replace them with comprehensives. As in the previous case, Lord Denning set out his understanding of the nature of grammar schools: 'Most educationalists and parents know what the controversy is about but for others who do not know the background perhaps I may say a word'.[240] He then proceeded to describe the pupils who were selected for the grammar schools as being of 'marked ability or aptitude'. At the grammar schools they would be able to 'mingle with other bright youngsters'. He then quoted words of the historian G.M. Trevelyan[241] describing 'the typical unit of Elizabethan education', the grammar school, as a place in which there could be found the 'inherited virtues of sound learning and hard work leading to fine achievement'[242] thereby associating the grammar schools with a tradition of English culture dating back to the time of Sir Edward Coke, a significant association which linked the grammar schools with the Common Law.

As in the previous case, Lord Denning protested, with decided emphasis, that the courts were completely neutral in the debate about the future of education: 'We, of course, in this court support neither side in this controversy but we have to take notice that the political parties are concerned in it'. This was an important step in his argument because the council which had decided not to implement the change from grammar schools to comprehensive schools was a Conservative council, elected in May 1976. The Conservatives had campaigned on the issue during the election and had included an explicit commitment not to implement the plan to create comprehensive schools in its manifesto. The existence of an electoral mandate was a crucial factor which allowed Lord Denning to contend that the decision of the council not to implement the plan was 'reasonable' and therefore within their powers. He was then able to argue that the Minister's application for a *mandamus* to force the council to implement the change was unreasonable. Lord Denning pointed out that the Minister's power to overrule the council was based on statutory authority and that it was not a 'reasonable' use of such authority to use it to overrule a council with which the minister merely disagreed: 'He must be very careful....not to fall into the error - a very common error - of thinking that anyone with whom he disagrees is being unreasonable'.[243] Satisfied that the council's decision could be considered 'reasonable', Lord Denning refused to provide the Minister with a *mandamus* on the basis that it was 'unreasonable' of him to consider a council 'unreasonable' on the basis that, as he saw it, they merely disagreed with him.

The Court of Appeal was called upon to consider the issue of an injunction to prevent a grammar school being changed into a comprehensive on the basis that the change would be incompatible with the duty of the local authority to provide a 'variety of instruction and training'.[244] Lord Denning ruled that the injunction should not be granted but also made a series of remarks which revealed his strong sympathy for the grammar school system. He began his judgment thus: 'The St. Marylebone Grammar School has a proud record'. It was part of 'a system of education, the grammar school system, which has served this country so well'.[245] He then stated that this system was 'under sentence of death,'[246] using the metaphor of execution to underpin the rest of his argument. He noted that 'it has all been done with complete legality' but that 'they ask for a stay of execution,' no doubt hoping that there may be a change of government which may result in a 'reprieve'. Perhaps a new government might even 'quash the sentence...so that the school may live, and not die'.[247] However, the courts could not intervene to prevent the carrying out of this sentence of execution because it was founded on statute and this could not be overturned because 'such is the sovereignty of Parliament which is fundamental in our constitution'.[248] Having made his sympathies plain, Lord Denning explained that the courts were powerless because the change was based on sovereignty of Parliament. Although the 1944 Act, which provided for the system of state grammar schools, was 'passed in time of war when we were struggling for our survival as a nation',[249] the doctrine of sovereignty of Parliament meant that any Act could be altered or repealed by a subsequent Act. Despite the link between the grammar schools and national survival, the sovereignty of Parliament had now been used to pass a 'sentence of death' on those schools and the courts could do nothing to interfere with this legitimate use of power. Lord Denning concluded his judgment thus: 'Many will grieve 'when that which once was great is passed away'. But so it must be'.[250] The quotation, for which Lord Denning did not give a source, came from William Wordsworth's poem 'On the extinction of the Venetian Republic'.[251] The Venetian Republic was dissolved by Napoleon in 1797. If the analogy were followed it would link Napoleon with 'sovereignty of Parliament' which had extinguished the grammar schools. Like the Venetian Republic, the grammar schools, and the courts, were powerless before the Napoleonic potency of Parliament which had been deployed to extinguish Liberty, the quality with which Venice, and therefore the grammar schools, were associated in the poem.

It was clear from these three judgments that Lord Denning considered the grammar schools to be an intrinsic part of English tradition and identity. He used the power of the courts to disrupt the change into a comprehensive system on two occasions. When, on the third occasion, he had to concede defeat, his rhetoric was very robust, not least in associating the sovereignty of Parliament with Napoleon, a figure indelibly associated, in English tradition, with tyranny. England had overcome the threat to its existence posed by Napoleon in the wars against France between 1793 and 1815. Lord Denning's use of Wordsworth's poem about the extinction of the Venetian Republic, written during the struggle against Napoleon, together with his invocation of the Second World War as a 'struggle for national survival', associated the grammar schools with the English nation itself. Lord Denning made it quite clear that he would use the power of the courts to defend the grammar schools, but that that power had to give way before a greater power, that of Parliamentary sovereignty. The suggestion of his rhetoric was that that power had, in this instance, been wrongly used.

The association, in Lord Denning's mind, between the English education system and the traditional order of things was made clear in a case concerning the conditions under which a non-patrial could be educated in England.[252] In deciding that a 12-year-old Iranian boy could study in England until he had completed his degree, Lord Denning observed that 'to be educated in England is an advantage'.[253] He went on to note that many people had studied in England and then returned to their own countries 'often to exercise much influence there, for good'.[254] He gave as examples Nehru, Gandhi and Ayub Khan, a prime minister of Pakistan, emphasising the 'value of this beneficent service to the world'.[255]

The English education system was radically transformed during the 1960s and 1970s in a manner which, it is clear, did not meet with Lord Denning's approval but which he was obliged to accept because of its authorisation by Parliamentary sovereignty. Another integral part of the English nation, the currency, was undermined during this period by inflation and by the volatility of its value in relation to other currencies.

The Currency

Inflation began to affect the economy in the late 1950s but with the exception of Enoch Powell, who resigned as Chief Secretary of the Treasury in January 1958 because of what he perceived to be the government's failure to make the control of inflation a priority,[256] continuing to call for tough policies against inflation thereafter,[257] every government and every leading politician of the time argued that a balance should be struck between the need to control inflation and the importance of maintaining economic growth and reducing unemployment. It was not until 1981 that a government made control of inflation its priority and was prepared to pursue this priority regardless of the impact on short term rates of growth and unemployment. Lord Denning's comments on inflation, in a series of judgments from as early as 1965 suggest that, like Enoch Powell, he considered inflation to pose a major threat to the stability of the nation.

In a judgment concerning the level of damages awarded in a personal injury case in February 1965,[258] Lord Denning remarked: 'We all know how the value of money has changed since that time, wages have gone up, money has altered'.[259] A few months later, in a judgment concerned with Estate Duty,[260] he observed: 'In these days of inflation if the value went up during the twelve months, the owner would benefit considerably from the value being taken at the time of death'.[261] Apart from Enoch Powell, none of the leading politicians of the time would have placed such emphasis on the importance of inflation. Five years later, in a case concerned with a notice raising the rent payable for a council tenancy,[262] Lord Denning remarked: 'In these days money diminishes in value continually'.[263] In 1975, in a case concerned with the level of damages to be awarded as compensation for personal injury,[264] Lord Denning noted that 'in the intervening 15 months there has been a big drop in the value of money; and the rate of inflation has increased greatly'; but also pointed out that 'this compensation could become altogether excessive if it were based on expectation of future inflation. To keep it within bounds it must be based on the value of money at the date of the trial'.[265] Lord Denning's approach to compensation in personal injury cases was similar to that later adopted by the Conservative government which came to power in 1979 in relation to public sector wages.

Two years later, in 1977, in a case concerned with damages in relation to a fatal accident,[266] he reiterated the point having first noted the serious impact of inflation: 'Now that inflation has become rampant, and looks like continuing, the practice should be altered....in determining the multiplier, no regard should be had to the possible, nay probable, inflation ahead of us....the law is that future inflation should be disregarded'.[267] Lord Denning's approach to inflation was exactly congruent with that of the Conservative opposition which was to implement a tough anti-inflationary policy when it came to power in 1979. After 1979, public sector wages and state pensions and benefits were held down and not increased in line with projected rates of inflation despite the fact that such policies, like those adopted by Lord Denning in relation to damages, led to an effective reduction in payments to those who were economically vulnerable. In 1978, in a case concerned with the interpretation of a contract made in 1929 for the provision of water,[268] Lord Denning remarked that costs increase 'with inflation through the rooftops', that 'times have changed' and 'we have since had mountainous inflation and the pound has dropped to cavernous depths'.[269] The strong rhetoric is indicative of Lord Denning's strong distaste for inflation, a distaste which he shared with Margaret Thatcher, the leader of the Conservative opposition. In a judgment of March 1981 concerned with the level of damages in a personal injury case, handed down at the same time as the announcement of the first Budget to make the reduction of inflation the absolute priority of government economic policy, Lord Denning remarked, commenting on the experience of the 1960s and 1970s in relation to inflation: 'In the succeeding years we met with racing inflation'.[270]

It was clear from his rhetoric that Lord Denning's attitude to inflation was congruent with that of Margaret Thatcher His approach to the volatility of the value of the Pound Sterling in the period which followed Devaluation in November 1967 and continued until his retirement in 1982, was also congruent with the approach of the Prime Minister of the Conservative government which came to power in 1979.

Like Margaret Thatcher, and Enoch Powell, Lord Denning considered that inflation posed a threat to the stability of the country. However,

Enoch Powell had always argued that, while the government had a duty to control domestic inflation, it should not intervene in the money markets to support a particular value of the Pound Sterling. In June 1979, Margaret Thatcher's government followed this policy by abandoning Exchange Controls and allowing the Pound Sterling to find its own level in the international currency markets. Lord Denning's approach to Devaluation and currency volatility was compatible with the abandoning of Exchange Controls. He believed that the courts should be able to do justice to those, usually foreign, companies, which came to the English courts in search of justice by awarding them damages in currencies other than Sterling in instances where Sterling judgments would impose unfair losses or gains, consequent on the changes in values of Sterling relative to other major currencies, which were unrelated to the merits of the case. However, it was necessary to change the law to make this possible. Lord Denning played a major part in making this change possible.

In November 1967, when the Pound Sterling was devalued, the established rule was that English courts only awarded damages in Sterling. Devaluation, and the persistent instability of the value of the Pound Sterling which followed from the 'floating' of the Pound in 1972, meant that the rigid application of this rule would lead to injustice and, in all likelihood, have the consequence of making London unattractive as a place in which to do business and settle disputes. In a case concerned with a salvage award which had been affected by the devaluation of the Pound Sterling,[271] Lord Denning made a dissenting judgment in which he argued that the rule which restricted the power of the courts to make awards in currencies other than Sterling should be abandoned. After noting that the Pound Sterling once possessed, in the words of Shakespeare's *Julius Caesar*, a 'true-fixed and resting quality' of which 'there is no fellow in the firmament', he stated that 'that enviable state of affairs has gone'.[272] He then argued that because Sterling was 'no longer the most stable currency in the world', the rule that the courts could only award damages in Sterling should be abandoned on the basis that it was nothing more than a procedural rule. He warned that if the rule were not abandoned then the courts would not be able to do justice and 'once justice is denied, confidence is lost. And once confidence is lost, it is hard to restore'. The change in the rule was, according to Lord Denning, necessary if the legal order itself was not to be undermined. It was notable that Lord Denning, like Enoch Powell, but unlike the Labour government, and the Conservative opposition, did not regard a stable Pound as being of fundamental importance. For Lord Denning, it was more important that the courts should be able to do justice, and retain their business, than that the Pound should be stable.

In 1969, Lord Denning's view that the rule about making awards in Sterling should be abandoned was a dissenting view. In 1971, in a case concerned with a cocoa contract whose value had been affected by devaluation of the Pound Sterling,[273] Lord Denning successfully avoided the rule by using an argument based on *estoppel* but pointed out that 'this was an important case. It concerns the effect of devaluation on contracts in the cocoa trade....so long as the exchange rate remains steady, no one worries'.[274] However, once the Pound was floated in 1972, it was inevitable that the question of abandoning the rule should be dealt with directly. In 1975, in order to give a judgment in Swiss Francs,[275] Lord Denning argued that the rule that the court could not make awards in foreign currencies was merely procedural rather than a matter of substantive law. The cases which had created that precedent involved the execution by a sheriff of a court order; the sheriff had no power to make an execution in a foreign currency. On this basis Lord Denning argued that the Court of Appeal was not prevented from making an award in a foreign currency when there was no need for the order to be executed by a sheriff. He was confident that the decision would be welcomed by the City of London.[276]

In 1978, Lord Denning extended the scope of this approach to include arbitration awards,[277] observing in the course of his judgment that 'Sterling is no longer a stable currency. Nor are US dollars. Nor French francs. No currency is stable. They all swing around with every gust that blows...it is always wise for the courts, in commercial matters, to follow the practice of the City of London'.[278] In 1980, Lord Denning extended the scope of the new rule still further by applying it to a garnishee order in relation to a debt in a foreign currency,[279] noting that 'this is a very desirable state of the law, especially now that exchange controls have been removed'[280] thereby explicitly approving the policy introduced by the Conservative government in June 1979. In a dissenting judgment in 1981, Lord Denning tried to argue that, as a result of the currency volatility which followed the 'floating' of the Pound, arbitrators should be able to make additional awards based on currrent interest rates so as to compensate for changes in the currency markets.[281] He began his judgment thus: 'At the time when under the Common Law courts were developing their rules about interest, Sterling was a stable currency. Inflation was unknown. Interest was regarded by many with opprobrium. It was stigmatised as usury'.[282] He concluded that 'during the last twenty years the money systems of the world have changed radically. Sterling is no longer a stable currency, it floats in the wind. It changes like a weathercock with every gust that blows....the value of money in every country depreciates each year...inflation is the order of the day'.[283] In these circumstances, the courts should take account of the value of Sterling in order to deliver justice thereby maintaining their place as an attractive place for international businesses to resolve their disputes.

Whereas domestic inflation was perceived by Lord Denning to be a threat to the legal order, the volatility of Sterling was perceived very differently as a challenge to which the courts could respond and as a possible benefit to the economy. In these respects, Lord Denning's views were congruent with those of Margaret Thatcher and Enoch Powell and fundamentally at odds with those of the Labour and Conservative governments of the 1960s and 1970s.

The Empire

When Lord Denning became Master of the Rolls in 1962, the process of decolonisation was almost complete. In a case concerning the issue of a libel writ in Ghana,[284] which had become independent in 1960, Lord Denning had to consider the argument that the writ could not be served in Ghana because it was no longer a British Dominion. In his judgment, Lord Denning drew a distinction between serving a writ and serving notice of a writ arguing that in the nineteenth century it had been considered that a writ could not be served in another country because to do so would be to affront the dignity of that country and therefore only notice of the writ could be given. This led him to consider whether Ghana was still a British Dominion. In 1957, Ghana had become independent within the British Commonwealth, but the Queen remained sovereign of Ghana. In 1960 Ghana had been declared a republic.[285] Ghana's status thereafter depended on the interpretation of the Ghana [Consequential Provisions Act] 1960; according to this Act, Ghana remained a member of the Commonwealth and its citizens remained British subjects, despite the fact that it had declared itself to be a republic. A libel writ could therefore be served in Ghana. According to Lord Denning's analysis, the 1960 Act had not changed the status of Ghana, despite the fact that a republic had been declared. Lord Denning's judgment ignored the fact that Ghana had declared itself to be a republic and treated it as if it were still, in effect, a Dominion.

In 1964, just before Gambia was given independence, the courts were asked to consider the validity of a retrospective validation by an Order in Council authorised under the British Settlements Act 1887. This concerned elections to the Gambian House of Representatives which had been elected by voters registered in old registers rather than the new registers which had recently been prepared.[286] The case turned on the question of whether, on the one hand, the British Settlements Act 1887 had swallowed up the Prerogative power of the Crown or, on the other, the Prerogative remained intact because it could not be renounced until effective legislative institutions, elected by the Gambian people and independent of Westminster, were able to function in Gambia. Lord Denning reviewed the history of the settlement in Gambia, stressing the fact it had 'been settled by the English a couple of centuries ago'[287] and that 'when English folk settled a colony they took their English law with them, that is to say, the Common Law and statute law as it existed at that time'.[288] The Common Law included the Prerogative and Prerogative power, Lord Denning argued, could not be used to impose on the settlers a legislature in which they were not represented. It therefore followed that the 1887 Act, which had set up a legislature in which English settlers were represented, had completely swallowed up the Prerogative. Under that Act it was possible for Orders in Council to regulate elections and therefore the 1962 elections were valid. Gambia was treated as a settlement of English subjects which had been given a constitution in 1887. The granting of this constitution precluded the use of the Prerogative to intervene in a question of constitutional law which was governed by the terms of the 1887 Act. The argument of the defendant, that there were no effective legislative institutions in place, because Gambia was not yet self-governing, and that the Prerogative could therefore overrule the provisions of the 1887 Act, was dismissed on the basis that, since 1887, Gambia had been an English settlement with English institutions in which the English settlers were represented. Consequently, the Prerogative was limited and could not be used to overturn the Orders in Council which had been issued under the 1887 Act. It is worth noting that, unlike Rhodesia and Kenya, where large white settler populations had developed since the late nineteenth century, the settler population in Gambia, whose climate was decidedly unattractive to those born in the temperate climate of England, was minute.

Both of these cases reflected the old Imperial assumptions that territories controlled by the British were subject to English law and that only an explicit Act of Parliament could alter that situation. Neither Ghana's declaration that it was a republic, nor the claim that Gambia did not have effective institutions because it was not self-governing, were acknowledged as having any legal substance by the court.

A similarly dismissive attitude to the legal claims of peoples and territories which might conflict with the imperial authority of English law, could be seen in a case concerned with a claim that an allegation that a party had conspired to bring about an Act of State from which it benefited, was slanderous.[289] Lord Denning began his judgment thus: 'In the days of Empire, the UK used to have some influence in the Persian Gulf and over the rulers or sheikhs that were there'.[290] The claim that one of the parties had conspired with one of those sheikhs to prevent the other party from making a claim to oil in the Persian Gulf, by persuading him to extend his territorial waters so that they included parts of the seabed claimed as a drilling concession by the other party, was dismissed by Lord Denning thus: 'I do not suppose that Sharjah has any developed system of law such as to permit an enquiry into the extent of civil liability for conspiracy'.[291] In the view of the Master of the Rolls, Sharjah was completely beyond the pale, a place without law.

In a dissenting judgment in 1976,[292] Lord Denning once again insisted that the legal empire of England remained intact. Lord Denning argued that the Rhodesian Unilateral Declaration of Independence in November 1965 had not affected the jurisdiction of the courts in Rhodesia, that they remained British courts, despite the fact that in 1969 the Rhodesian judges had sworn an oath to uphold the new Constitution. Following this reasoning, he argued that a letter of request for assistance to the English High Court by the Chief Justice of Rhodesia in relation to an action under the Bankruptcy Act 1914 should be honoured and acted on so that assets of a Rhodesian bankrupt held in banks and in the form of property in England could be seized.

Lord Denning argued that 'the white settlers made no complaint against the lawful sovereign, the Queen of England. They pledged their loyalty and allegiance to her. They rebelled against her ministers in Whitehall....But they left the judges undisturbed. They left the judges still pledged under their oath of allegiance to the Queen and under their judicial oath well and truly to serve her in the office of a judge. They left the courts to carry on with their daily tasks...they left the existing law as it was. After all, they were as much concerned as anyone to see that law and order were maintained...in this too, they were supported by the lawful sovereign, the Queen of England'.[293]

According to this argument, the judicial oath sworn by the judges meant that the courts in Rhodesia remained legitimate despite the Unilateral Declaration of Independence and therefore a request by the Rhodesian Chief Justice for assistance from the High Court in a bankruptcy case should be honoured and acted upon. 'The implication was irresistible that the lawful sovereign authorised the judges to continue in office, and the courts to continue to function'.[294] 'The judicial branch remained subject to the lawful sovereign, the Queen of England'.[295] As far as the courts were concerned, at any rate in Lord Denning's opinion, it was as if UDI had never occured; the empire of law remained intact despite the rebellion of the politicians in Salisbury.[296]

Lord Denning made a number of comments in the course of the judgment which related to current negotiations for a settlement in Rhodesia. It was highly unusual for a judge to make comments on contemporary political developments. Lord Denning's remarks revealed that he strongly supported the negotiation of a settlement with the rebel government in Rhodesia. Lord Denning's judgment was delivered in October 1976 when negotiations involving Britain, the United States and the government of Ian Smith in Salisbury seemed to be on the point of achieving a major breakthrough. In fact, no such breakthrough occurred, but Lord Denning's comments, which strongly supported the argument of the judgment that UDI had not disturbed the authority of the courts and that, legally, Rhodesia remained subject to the empire of English law, suggested that he was convinced that such a breakthrough was imminent. He stated in his judgment that 'the outlook is now altered beyond measure'[297] and 'in the last few weeks hopes have risen that the rebellion in Rhodesia will come to an end. The economic blockade is to be lifted. So too should the legal blockade'.[298] Lord Denning's judgment assumed that Rhodesia remained a British colony and that, despite UDI, Rhodesia remained subject to the legal sovereignty of the Crown: 'The judicial branch remained subject to the lawful sovereign, the Queen of England....the country remained, in the eyes of the law, a British colony'.[299] For Lord Denning, the Empire, at any rate in Rhodesia, had never ended. The minor matter of a colonial rebellion, which had taken the form of a Unilateral Declaration of Independence, could be glossed over and the authority of the Empire re-established. Final decolonisation was matter for the sovereign Parliament of the United Kingdom rather than the people of Rhodesia.

However, despite his insistence on the continuation of the *imperium* of English law until it was formally disrupted by an Act of Parliament, a view decisively expressed in his dissenting judgment about the nature of legal authority in Rhodesia in 1976, Lord Denning did concede that, as regards Canada, the Crown had become divisible and therefore the Indian peoples of Canada could no longer petition the Queen in the right of England but would have to petition her in the right of Canada.[300] The question of the divisibility of the Crown arose in a case concerned with the relationship between the rights of the Canadian Indian peoples, as protected by the Royal Proclamation of 1763, and the status of those rights under the Charter of Rights which was enacted by Canada following the 'repatriation' of the Canadian constitution in 1981.[301] The Indian Association of Alberta attempted to petition the Crown in the right of England to enforce the 1763 Royal Proclamation. Lord Denning stated that the Royal Proclamation of 1763 'was ranked by the Indian peoples as their Bill of Rights, equivalent to our own Bill of Rights in England 80 years before'.[302] However, he then argued that 'by constitutional usage and practice', the Crown had become 'separate and divisible'.[303] The creation of 'autonomous communities' owing a 'common allegiance' by the Statute of Westminster 1931 had created a situation in which the Crown was represented in each Dominion by a Governor-General and took advice from the government of the Dominion rather than from the government of the United Kingdom. This meant that, in effect, the Crown was divisible, taking different advice from different governments, a position acknowledged in the Royal Titles Act 1953 consequent on the 'usage and practice' which followed from the passing of the Statute of Westminster. For this reason, the only remedy available to the Indian Association of Alberta was to petition the Crown in the Right of Canada. Given that the Canadian constitution had been 'repatriated' in 1981, the Charter of Rights could only be challenged in Canada. The English courts could not accept a petition in the right of England to review the Charter in relation to the 1763 Royal Proclamation.

The disruption of the unity of the Crown, a consequence of 'constitutional usage and practice' following the enactment of the Statute of Westminster 1931, was plainly decisive in relation to the *imperium* of English law. Although Rhodesia remained subject to that unity in 1976, not having become a Dominion and only claiming to be independent on the basis of the illegal Unilateral Declaration of Independence, Canada, Australia, South Africa, and any other former colony which had progressed via Dominion status to independence, under the sanction of an Act of Parliament, had clearly passed beyond the legal authority of the *imperium* of English law. The introduction of Devolution Bills in relation to Scotland and Wales in 1976, combined with the attempts to resolve the conflict in Northern Ireland by the constitutional innovations of the Sunningdale Agreement of 1973, began to raise the question of whether the Union of England, Wales, Scotland and Northern Ireland under the undivided authority of the Crown would be maintained indefinitely. Lord Denning's approach to the Union was revealed in a series of judgments during the 1960s and 1970s.

The Union

In a case concerned with a conflict of laws in relation to an arbitration agreement,[304] in which Scottish law did not provide for an arbitrator to state a 'special case' for the decision of the court whereas English law did provide for a 'special case' to be stated, Lord Denning ruled that although the land in question was in Scotland, and therefore Scotland was the 'country' with the closest association with the contract, the 'system of law' with which the contract had the closest association was English law, and that the link with the 'system of law' rather than that with the 'country' should be decisive in determining where the case should be heard. In making this ruling he claimed to have made a 'slip' in his *obiter* remarks in a previous judgment that he had given in the House of Lords [305] in which he had said that the 'country' with which the contract had the closest association rather than the 'system of law' should be decisive.

Despite this example of English chauvinism, Lord Denning showed a good deal of respect for Scots law in his judgments. In a case concerning 'conceptual uncertainty' in relation to a provision in a trust,[306] Lord Denning made some critical remarks about the distinctions made by some English lawyers between 'evidential' and 'conceptual' certainty and between 'subsequent' and 'precedent' conditions which had been used to defeat the intentions of testators. Referring to the power of the House of Lords to create uniformity in the law and to overcome such technical distinctions, Lord Denning noted that Scottish judges sat in the House of Lords and that, as a result, Scottish legal principles could influence English law as had happened most notably in *Donoghue v Stevenson*.[307] Lord Denning remarked that 'the very constitution of the House shows that each system of law has much to learn from the other; and that a decision on a point of principle should reflect the best of both'.[308] The judgment in this case was given in November 1977, coincident with the introduction of the Devolution Bill which became law in August 1978. In a judgment given earlier in the same year, Lord Denning made explicit reference to the issue of Devolution in relation to the law.

The case turned on the question of whether a plaintiff could seek a stay of proceedings in the Scottish courts to pursue a claim in the English courts.[309] In a dissenting judgment, Lord Denning ruled that the plaintiff should not be able to get a stay of proceedings and must pursue his claim in the Scottish courts. The judgment expressed, in emphatic terms, the view that the plaintiff had every right to be proud of the Scottish legal system. Lord Denning began thus: 'As you might guess, Peter McKinley MacShannon is a Scotsman....proud, no doubt, of his native land and its laws'.³¹⁰ He continued in the same vein, describing the defendant thus: 'Likewise with another good Scotsman, Kenneth Duncan Fyfe. His name betrays him too. No doubt he was born and bred in Scotland too, and proud of its laws'. Lord Denning then proceeded to acknowledge that English lawyers had once looked down on other systems of law, such as that of Scotland, but had now changed their attitude: 'Previously we were disposed to think too much of our own legal system. It was so superior to all others that, if a plaintiff managed to serve a defendant while he was in this country, we nearly always let him continue with it.....in so laying down the law we were going back to the days which Lord Reid described as the good old days when inhabitants of this island felt an innate superiority over those unfortunate enough to belong to other races. Those good old days are gone'.³¹¹ He concluded that the plaintiff 'has lived under Scots law all his life. He should take its legal system, like his wife, for better or for worse. All the Scots lawyers that I have met have a great sense of the superiority of their system over ours. Let it be so. A Scotsman should be in no better position than a Frenchman'. He ended the judgment with an explicit reference to the Devolution Bill which made it clear that, as far as the law was concerned, there was no need for devolution since the law had always been devolved: 'There is no need to wait for Parliament to give Scotland its own legal system, devolution of legal systems took place in the Act of Union 1706'.³¹²

Lord Denning took care to make clear his respect for the Scottish legal system at a crucial moment in Anglo-Scottish relations. He took similar care to show his respect for the Welsh in a case which concerned the imprisonment for contempt of court of a group of Welsh students who had disrupted the proceedings in the High Court in order to draw attention to their campaign to preserve the Welsh language.³¹³ Lord Denning paid tribute to the patriotism of the Welsh students from the University of Aberystwyth: 'There is no violence, dishonesty or vice in them. On the contrary, there is much that we should applaud. They wish to do all they can to preserve the Welsh language. Well may they be proud of it. It is the language of the bards - of the poets and the singers - more melodious by far than our rough English tongue'.³¹⁴

Lord Denning's approach to Ireland was altogether less deferential. In the notorious judgment which refused leave to the Birmingham Six to reopen the issue of their treatment by the police,³¹⁵ treatment which they claimed had been so brutal that it had forced them to confess to the bombing, Lord Denning concluded that the whole case 'shows what a civilised country we are',³¹⁶ not least because the state had expended large sums of money in paying for the defense and the appeal of the accused. It was notable that Lord Denning's judgment began by telling the story of the Birmingham Bomb in a manner which emphasised its barbarous nature and then proceeded to set out a long and complex argument, based on the principle of *estoppel*, which concluded that there were no grounds for the case to be reopened. In the course of that argument, which ranged over the whole history of the Common Law in relation to *estoppel* from the Norman Conquest to the present day, Lord Denning referred to some of the patriarchal authorities of the Common Law: Littleton, Coke and John William Smith of *Smith's Leading Cases*.[317] Even Bentham's name was invoked, although usually Lord Denning was dismissive of him as an authority. It was quite clear that the full weight of the authority of the Common Law was being used to crush the barbarity of the Irish who had dared to set off a bomb in the heartland of England.

Lord Denning only referred to Ireland in three other cases, in each of them the reference was detrimental. In a case concerned with the confidentiality of journalist's sources,[318] Lord Denning argued, on the basis of very little authority, that journalists could be imprisoned for contempt of court if they refused to reveal their sources to a judicial inquiry set up under the Tribunals of Enquiry [Evidence] Act 1921. It was notable that one of the authorities which gave some support to Lord Denning's argument concerned the ruling by the President of the Parliamentary Inquiry into the Parnell affair that the Editor of the Times should reveal the source of a letter which he had published about Parnell. Charles Stuart Parnell, the Leader of the Irish Home Rule Party, which had posed a significant threat to the Union between Britain and Ireland during the 1880s, was destroyed by the scandal about his relations with Mrs Kitty O'Shea. Lord Denning's use of this authority suggested a negative attitude to Ireland. Even more derogatory were his remarks about the plaintiff in a personal injuries case[319]: 'Michael Kelly is a plausible Irishman and a chronic alcoholic'.[320]

The only other case in which Lord Denning had to deal with Ireland was a case concerned with an application for *habeas corpus* which arose from the policy of internment introduced by the government of Northern Ireland in August 1971.[321] Lord Denning noted that internment had been introduced because 'very serious attacks were being made against the army, police and civilians of Northern Ireland'.[322] Lord Denning then proceeded to review the history of the jurisdiction of the English courts in Ireland concluding that, since 1782 when an Act of 1719 which had, in his words, created a 'confused' situation, the English courts had no jurisdiction in Ireland and therefore could not hear a case of *habeas corpus* brought by someone in Northern Ireland. Ireland was judicially independent of England and 'since 1782 the English courts have no jurisdiction to send a writ of the High Court into Ireland'.³²³ It was notable that, in coming to this conclusion, Lord Denning was explicitly overruling the opinion of Blackstone who had maintained that a writ of the High Court could run 'into all parts of the King's dominions' except for Scotland.³²⁴ Lord Denning concluded his judgment by stating that 'this course of proceeding is so obviously right that, even if we had jurisdiction ourselves, I would doubt very much the propriety of exercising it'.³²⁵ It was interesting that, although a few years later, Lord Denning ruled that Rhodesia was still part of the *imperium* of English law',³²⁶ this judgment took as its starting point the fact that Ireland was not a part of that order. Comity existed between the High Court of Rhodesia and the English courts, despite UDI, but not with those of Northern Ireland.

Lord Denning's approach to the Empire was to emphasise the fact that the *imperium* of the English legal order continued to run, unless explicitly disrupted by an Act of Parliament, as was the case with regard to Ireland. With regard to the Union, which was coming under pressure during the 1970s, he expressed respect for the Scots and the Welsh, while treating Irish, some of whom were in a state of rebellion against the authority of the Crown, with contempt.

Aliens and Foreigners

Lord Denning's inherent patriotism was made very clear by the uniformly disparaging references to France, England's traditional enemy, which occur in his judgments. Lord Denning was born in 1899, some five years before the 'Entente Cordiale' established the pattern of Anglo-French alliance which dominated the twentieth century. The traditional approach of the English to the French, which he would have absorbed from his education, was one of hostility. Dating back to the time of Louis XIV, Blenheim and Marlborough, the Seven Years War and the American rebellion and that of Napoleon, Trafalgar, Waterloo and Wellington, the French had been the prime antagonists of the English. Indeed, the French had been the enemy of the English from the time of Crecy and Agincourt in the fourteenth and fifteenth centuries, long before the time of Sir Edward Coke. The loss of Calais was, famously, said to have been engraved on Mary I's heart. Lord Denning grew up in a world in which it was France, not Germany, which typified the 'enemy' against whom the English defined themselves. Several of his judgments reveal traces of this antagonism which was so central to the creation of an English identity. However, there was one notable occasion on which Lord Denning resorted to the use of the French language to support the position which he had taken up in a judgment. In that instance, he was confronted by an enemy even more unattractive to his tastes than the French; a trade union which was abusing its power. In 1975, in a prelude to the dispute which closed *The Times* in 1978, the National Graphical Association was disputing an attempt by the Newspapers Publishers Assocation to enforce contracts of employment on some of its members who were keen to go on strike. Expressing his contempt for this manoeuvre, Lord Denning lapsed into French in order to describe the attitude of the Newspaper Publishers Association: *Cet animal est tres mechant; quand l'on attaque, il se defend.*[327]

Lord Denning's attitude to the French was normally less friendly. In a case concerning a dispute between two French companies turning on an arbitration clause which involved a conflict of laws,[328] Lord Denning remarked: 'It would not be at all convenient that English arbitrators sitting in London should listen to an exposition of French law by experts in French law'.[329] In another case concerning the interpretation of the 1961 Carriage by Air Act[330] which necessitated reference to the French text, from which the English text of the 1961 Act had been translated, in order to clarify the meaning of the word *avarie*, Lord Denning made some revealing remarks, in a dissenting judgment, about the level of knowledge of the French language which could be expected of an English judge. Commenting on the need to refer to the French text to resolve an ambiguity in the English text, he remarked: 'That is a funny sort of thing to tell us English lawyers. Some of us have no French. Others have schoolboy French. None of us has sufficient French to detect any inconsistency'.[331] He then added: 'I do not suppose that the members of Parliament were any more linguistically accomplished than we'.[332] On this basis he stated: 'So for the present, I propose to go by the English text'.[333] A little later, he reinforced this point by observing that: 'To my schoolboy French, the French text is also ambiguous'.[334] The authority of the original French text, on which that of the 1961 Act was based, was completely disregarded on the basis that the English courts had no knowledge of French and did not need to have any knowledge of that language to apply the law.

This hostility towards France, a determining feature of English identity at the time of Lord Denning's birth, was plainly expressed in a judgment in contract law concerning the determination of which of two innocent parties should bear the loss consequent on the fraud of a third party.[335] The case turned on the doctrine of mistake in contract law, in particular whether a mistake could make a contract void. Lord Denning's view was that because the rogue appeared to be the owner of the property, the contract was voidable rather than void. As he put it: 'We look to outward appearances'.[336] The argument that because the rogue, who called himself Richard Greene, the name of the actor who played Robin Hood in the popular television series, was passing himself off as someone he could not possibly have been and that, in consequence, the contract was based on a mistake which rendered it void was dismissed out of hand, not least because that argument was based on the views of the French jurist Pothier. Lord Denning was dismissive of Pothier: 'This argument has been supplied by a reference to the French jurist Pothier's *Traite des obligations*[337] s.19 but I have said before, and I repeat now, his statement is no part of English law'.[338] He continued: 'The statement by Pothier has given rise to such refinements that it is time that it was dead and buried altogether...these fine distinctions do no good to the law'.[339] The common sense of the English was asserted against the theoretical absurdities of the French; as Lord Denning put it: 'We look to outward appearances'. If the rogue seemed to be genuine then he must be assumed to be so, unless it could be proved otherwise. The contract was therefore voidable rather than void *ab initio*.

Lord Denning permitted himself to make dismissive remarks about the French system of law in a case which involved *champerty*.[340] A Frenchman was paid £4,000 by a Yugoslav businessman to instruct English solicitors to act in a liquidation case. On the basis of a contract drawn up in French, the Frenchman was to receive 25% of the funds which were recovered in the action if it was successful. The English solicitors then drew up a contract in English which would, if necessary, have allowed the Frenchman to enforce the French contract against the Yugoslav. When the Yugoslav withdrew, the English solicitors tried to claim costs for the work that they had done in drawing up the English contract; a supplementary defence for the Frenchman and which might never have been used. Lord Denning remarked at the beginning of his judgment; 'I understand *champerty* is lawful in France'.[341] On this basis, the French contract made by the English solicitors would be enforceable. However, Lord Denning ruled that the solicitors might not recover their costs, for drawing up a contract which was never used, because *champerty* was not lawful in England and in drawing up the contract they were parties to a *champertous* agreement. However, having stated at the outset that *champerty* was lawful in France, the country where the contract was made, and in whose language it was drafted, he proceeded to deliver a lengthy, and highly rhetorical, condemnation of *champerty*, setting out its history and nature in terms which made it plain that the English legal order was patently superior to that of France, a legal order which permitted an activity which, as his judgment made clear, was utterly subversive of the rule of law.[342] The solicitors who had drawn up a contract to protect an agreement which was lawful in France were denied their costs on the basis that what was lawful in France was not only not lawful in England, but repugnant to the English legal order itself.

In the course of considering the interpretation of the French text of a European directive on Company law,[343] Lord Denning was once again dismissive of the French legal order. The point at issue in the case concerned whether an advance paid to the agent of a company that was in fact never formed could be repayable. The relevant Directive was issued in 1968 and was written in French. England was not, at that time, part of the European Community and therefore the Directive could not have been written in English. The French text of the Directive could be interpreted to imply that a company *en formation* would be liable to repay the advance. In his judgment Lord Denning remarked, 'interpreting the French text as best I can', that *en formation* meant that a company which was in the same state as a baby between conception and birth would be liable, even though, following the analogy, it had not been born, not achieved existence as a legal person. Lord Denning rejected this analogy of a company to a foetus as being utterly unacceptable and irrelevant. Engish company law was organised on the basis of the concept of adult 'personhood' defined by words with precise legal meaning, rather than the organic metaphors of sexual intercourse and its consequences favoured by the French which enabled a company to be conceived of as a foetus. He then proceeded to use the 1972 European Communities Act, which incorporated Article 189 of the Treaty of Rome which allowed national authorities to have the choice of 'forms and methods' used to implement the Directive, as authority to use English company law, rather than the organic and sexual French law, to decide whether or not the agent was liable to repay the advance.[344] English law was presented as being conceptually radically different from French law which, in this case, was depicted, to its considerable detriment as being based on organic, sexual metaphors in contrast with the sober metaphors of adult personhood around which English company law was organised. The French legal order was portrayed by Lord Denning as allowing the 'evil' of champerty and as embracing a repugnant sexual conception of the nature of a company.

However, despite these vivid expressions of contempt for the French legal order, against which the integrity and coherence of the English legal order could be asserted, Lord Denning was disposed to extend the protection of the English courts to the worthy, and vulnerable, French legal subject. In a case which turned on the interpretation of the meaning of 'intentional homelessness', Lord Denning expressed great sympathy for a French widower, a bookseller from Grenoble, who was trying to educate his three daughters in England.[345] Lord Denning noted that 'Rene Lambert is a real Frenchman. He cannot speak English'.[346] In the course of a very sympathetic judgment for this worthy and upstanding widower trying to educate three daughters, Lord Denning noted again that, despite living in England for some time: 'he was still struggling with his bad English'.[347] Clearly M. Lambert was a weak and vulnerable 'real' Frenchman who was a worthy recipient of the court's sympathy in decided contrast with those of his compatriots who indulged in champerty and embraced sexual notions of company law.

Lord Denning believed that the courts of England should be open to the whole world: 'This right to come here is not confined to Englishmen. It extends to any friendly foreigner...you may call this 'forum shopping' if you please, but if the forum is England, it is a good place to shop in, both for the quality of the goods and the speed of the service'.[348] It was notable that the metaphor of the market was used to typify the nature of English justice; Lord Denning clearly associated the aspect of English culture and identity which had been famously denigrated by Napoleon with the intrinsic virtue of English law. The market of English justice was open to all provided that 'they come in good faith'. The foreigner who came to England for justice 'must not do it from an unworthy motive; such as to vex or to harass his opponent'.[349]

Any foreigner who came to England to settle lawfully 'had rights equal to those of anyone born in England of ancient stock'.[350] The lawfully settled foreigner was entitled to those rights because he owed allegiance to the Crown and that allegiance created a consequent duty on the Crown to protect him.[351] In a case concerned with the scope of the *parens patriae* jurisdiction of the courts in relation to the children of aliens,[352] Lord Denning argued that children of aliens 'ordinarily resident' in England were subject to that jurisdiction as a consequence of the fact that their parents owed allegiance to the Crown. He supported this argument by reference to the law of treason. Under the law of treason, aliens resident within the realm of England owed allegiance to the Crown; that allegiance was not broken if they left the realm.[353] It followed that if the father of the children in the instant case were to leave the realm, but leave his children behind, then he would still be bound by that allegiance and his children would be subject to the *parens patriae* jurisdiction. In this case, the father had taken the children out of the realm, but since the status of 'ordinary residence' with regard to children could only altered by consent of both parents, and that consent had been witheld by the wife, the courts retained *parens patriae* jurisdiction with regard to the children.[354] Allegiance to the Crown was obligatory to any alien lawfully resident in England, that allegiance conferred protection equal to that of 'anyone born in England of ancient stock'[355] but also subjected the alien to the authority of the law. The family in the instant case was Jewish. As Lord Denning put it: 'We received them and gave them shelter here'.[356]

Lord Denning considered that the Jews were distinguishable from the English entirely on the basis of race: 'There is nothing in their culture or language or literature to mark out Jews in England from others. The Jews in England share all of those characteristics equally with the rest of us. Apart from religion, the one characteristic which is different is a racial characteristic'.[357] Lord Denning emphatically condemned anti-semitism, describing the actions of the German government during the Second World War in relation to the Jews of Europe as 'fiendish',[358] insisting that 'anti-semitism must not be allowed'.[359] However, he also stated that 'the wandering Jew had no nation. He is a wanderer on the face of the earth'.[360] This comment suggested that Lord Denning did not consider the state of Israel to be legitimate and that Jews were stateless unless they were lawfully resident in England, or some other country; if ordinarily resident in England then they owed allegiance to the Crown and in return were protected by the Crown.

This emphasis on the importance of allegiance with regard to the status of aliens and foreigners was made explicit in case concerned with the nationality of German Jews.[361] Lord Denning began his judgment thus: 'These two cases arise out of the persecution of the Jews in Nazi Germany'. The issue at the heart of the case was whether the plaintiffs could be taxed in England on a pension which they had been awarded by the German government in 1953. If they had dual nationality then they would be exempted from the duty to pay English taxes on the German pension. Although in 1968, the German government declared that the 1941 decree which had deprived German Jews of their citizenship was void *ab initio*, that decree did not act retrospectively. On this basis the plaintiffs remained German citizens until 1968. However, Lord Denning argued that although the 1941 decree 'was an objectionable law....it was still the German law at the time....however objectionable or atrocious that decree might be, we have to some extent to recognise it'.

This meant that when the plaintiffs came to England in 1948, they were, arguably, not German nationals because nationality was determined by municipal law. However, he continued his argument by maintaining that if the plaintiffs were British nationals then the German law would not be decisive in relation to the question of whether they could have dual nationality; that issue would be determined by English law if they were British nationals, whatever their status in German law. In 1941, England and Germany were at war, the 1941 decree would therefore not have been recognised at that time on account of the state of belligerency between the two nations. In 1948, when the plaintiffs had been naturalised, they had taken the oath of allegiance to the Crown. The crucial point was that England was still at war with Germany at that point. There was no legal peace between the two nations until 1951. As Lord Denning put it: 'Nationality and allegiance are twin bedfellows...one cannot exist without the other...protection and allegiance are reciprocal'.[362] The result was that the plaintiffs were not exempt from English taxation on their German pensions because they were English subjects. Their allegiance to the Crown, sworn when England was still at war with Germany, displaced any possibility of their being German subjects after 1948. Had the plaintiffs not sworn allegiance in time of war, when no German decree made during the existence of a state of war between the two nations would have been recognised, then the impact of the 1941 decree would have been considered by the court. However, allegiance sworn by an alien in time of war displaced all other legal considerations and established that the aliens were now subjects of the Crown, thereby entitled to its protection but also bound to pay the taxes demanded under the authority of the Crown.

The importance which Lord Denning attached to the protection, and consequent rights which attached to the loyal subject, which flowed from an oath of allegiance sworn by a Jew to the Crown, was revealed in a case concerned with an attempt by such a Jewish subject of the Crown to move a trust fund to Jersey.[363] If the trust were valid then the intended beneficiaries would be able to benefit from the fact that, based in Jersey, the fund would avoid Capital Gains Tax if they were no longer British subjects. Lord Denning refused to sanction the variation in the trust that would be necessary if the trust were to be moved to Jersey on the grounds that such a move would be detrimental to the interests of the beneficiaries since the financial gains that would accrue to them could not outweigh the detriment that they would suffer by their loss of English nationality. In the course of his judgment, Lord Denning made a series of remarks which indicated the very high value which he placed on the privileges which adhered to the Jews who became English subjects: 'There are many things in life more worthwhile than money. One of those things is to be brought up in this our England which is still 'the envy of less happy lands'.[364] The children of the Jewish emigrants who had sworn allegiance to the Crown would inherit English nationality; as Lord Denning put it: Children are like trees, they grow stronger with firm roots',[365] adding that 'many a child has been spoiled by being given too much'.[366] Financial advantage could not outweigh detriment which would accrue to a Jew who gave up his or her English nationality.

It was quite clear from these remarks about Jews who became loyal subjects of the Crown, that Lord Denning considered allegiance to be the prime determinant of status. Once a foreigner swore an oath of loyalty to the Crown and came within the allegiance they were entitled to 'rights equal to anyone born in England of ancient stock'. Until 1962, anyone born within the British Empire was automatically a subject of the Crown within the allegiance. Any such person could therefore come to England and enjoy the full protection of the Crown. Starting with the Commonwealth Immigration Act 1962, a series of changes to the law, culminating in the British Nationality Act 1981, had the effect that those who were born in territories which were once part of the British Empire were no longer entitled to the protection and rights which adhered to anyone who was a subject of the Crown.

Aliens had no rights in English law. Anyone who was not a subject of the Crown, not born within the allegiance, was, in the eyes of the Common Law, an alien. It is notable that when giving judgment in a case in which the question of whether a judge could be sued for exceeding his jurisdiction was considered,[367] Lord Denning began by stating that 'Michael Sirros is an alien'.[368] The case had been brought by the North Kensington Law Centre which argued that a judge had unlawfully imprisoned Sirros when he fled from court after being issued with a repatriation order. Lord Denning rejected the argument; a judge could only be sued if he exceeded his jurisdiction in bad faitth. In the instant case there was no evidence of bad faith; the judge had made an honest mistake about the extent of his jurisdiction. Sirros' detention may have been technically unlawful but there was no question of countenancing an attempt by an alien to sue an English judge.

Lord Denning's approach to the status of aliens was clearly expressed in *Schmidt v Secretary of State for Home Affairs*[369] in which he remarked that the Home Secretary 'can exercise his power for any purpose which he considers to be for the public good or to be in the interests of the people of this country'.[370] Lord Denning was content to allow the Home Secretary to use his discretionary powers in relation to immigration without significant review by the courts. When Quintin Hogg,[371] acting for the defence in *Schmidt*, tried to argue that the Home Secretary's discretion to exclude an alien should only be used to secure the safety of the realm, the observance of the law of the land and the preservation of standards of morality, in other words that the discretion should be to some extent limited, Lord Denning ruled that this particular discretion could not be limited in that way and would be lawful provided that it was 'exercised in the interests of the ordinary people of this country'.[372] The discretion to exclude aliens should not be fettered by any general policy, no matter how broadly that policy might be framed. Lord Denning concluded that aliens were only present in England 'by license of the Crown' and therefore had no 'legitimate expectation'[373] of natural justice or any other protection. As he put it: 'Once his time is expired he has to go'.[374] Lord Denning dismissed the plaintiff's arguments categorically: 'I see no trace of unfairness at all...this action is quite unsustainable'.[375]

The combination of a restrictive interpretation of the immigration statutes and a 'liberal' approach to the Home Secretary's extensive residual discretion in this area would have been sufficient to restrict the numbers of immigrants who were able to establish a lawful right to reside in England. Any other form of immigration would be unlawful and therefore, in the eyes of the law, as interpreted by Lord Denning, any such immigrant would be an 'alien' subject to the effectively unregulated discretionary power of the Home Secretary.

On three occasions Lord Denning had to deal with the antecedents of the British National Party as plaintiff or defendant. The first case concerned a libel action brought by a Member of Parliament.[376] The defendants sought to use a series of defences ranging from arguing that their remarks were not defamatory, to pleading that they were fair comment on a matter of public interest and, finally, amending their defence to claim qualified privilege on the basis that the defendants had a common interest with the electors in the constituency.

In his judgment Lord Denning read out the allegedly defamatory words used by a candidate for office in local government in an electoral address which went as follows: 'Your pro-black MP. The help you can expect from our Labour opponents is shown by their boss, Sir Leslie Plummer - Deptford's Labour MP. Plummer has tried several times to get a bill through Parliament to send you to prison if you oppose coloured immigration in public. Commenting on one of Plummer's attempts to get this bill through, the South London Press of Feb 2 1960, stated: 'One of the reasons for the bill is the increasing friction between white and coloured people in Deptford. Clubs run by coloured people have been opening in the area causing many white people to complain'. That is a quotation from the South London Press and the election address goes on: There you have it! Your Labour MP comes down solidly on the side of the coloured spivs and their vice dens as opposed to the white people of Deptford'.[377]

Lord Denning then noted that the defendants had amended their defences of denial of defamatory meaning and fair comment on a matter of public interest, on the basis that 'the words were published to the electors of Deptford, that the electors of Deptford had an interest in good housing, and that an influx of coloured people into Deptford had aggravated the housing shortage in Deptford'.[378] In response to this point, Lord Denning stated: 'Let me say at once that, if the decision of this court in *Braddock v Bevins* had remained good law, it would have afforded a firm basis for this plea of qualified privilege' before continuing to observe that s.10 of the Defamation Act 1952 had effectively removed the defence of qualified privilege from material published in electoral addresses. Lord Denning added: 'I do not exclude the possibility that there might be a case where a person might conceivably say: 'I am an elector; I made the communication to the other electors on a matter of common interest to us in such circumstances that it is privileged', and is not caught be s. 10'.[379] However, Lord Denning declined to apply the principle to the facts in the instant case.

What was notable about this judgment was that it turned on a technical point about amendment to a defence and whether the amendment was founded in law. The decision was that the appearance of the material in an election address meant that, because of s.10, the particular defence of qualified privilege would not be available. It was plain, from the way in which Lord Denning quoted the words, indicating that most of the factual information came from the South London Press, that he did not necessarily consider the statements to be defamatory and, by pointing out that the same words, not included in an election address, but addressed, in some other form, to electors on the basis of common interest might escape s. 10, he reinforced the suggestion that he did not consider the words to be defamatory. The attack on Sir Leslie Plummer was, interestingly, based on the fact that he had supported a bill very similar to that which was eventually enacted as the Race Relations Act 1965; from his comments in later judgments, we know that Lord Denning was highly critical of that legislation.

The second case in which Lord Denning had to deal with the antecedents of the British National Party, by this time rebranded as the National Front, concerned a case in which a Parliamentary candidate sought to prevent the BBC from broadcasting a filmed report of his campaign in which he appeared with a National Front candidate.[380] Lord Denning ruled that the candidate could only prevent the broadcast of the film if he had 'actively participated' in some way with the National Front candidate. This was because the mischief addressed by the Representation of the People Act 1969 was the possibility that a candidate who had agreed to be interviewed by the BBC might be tricked by the interviewer into making statements which, as a result of editing after the conclusion of the interview could result in misrepresentation of his position. In the present circumstances, the National Front had been caught on camera while the candidate's campaign had been filmed, but he had not 'actively participated' with them. This circumstance was not the kind of mischief addressed by the statute. That mischief involved active participation in an interview. It followed that the exclusion of this footage would effectively oblige the BBC not to broadcast material about the National Front and that would undermine their duty to be impartial: 'They would be forced by the veto to be partial'.[381] In this case, Lord Denning's purposive interpretation of the Representation of the People Act 1969 allowed him to refuse the demand that footage of the National Front should not be broadcast on the basis that the BBC's duty to be impartial meant that it was up to them to decide what to broadcast, provided that they did not exclude a political party because another candidate objected to them for some reason. The suggestion was that the National Front had the right to free speech and access to broadcast media on the basis of the BBC's duty to be impartial.

The right of the National Front to free speech, a principle which was implicit in these two judgments, was made explicit in a case in which the National Front applied for an order of specific performance to correct the wrongful repudiation of a contract.[382] The Conservative council of Great Yarmouth had made a contractual arrangement with the National Front to hire a hall in Great Yarmouth for their 1979 national conference. In May 1979, a Labour council was elected which sought to repudiate the contract on the basis that the proposed conference would cause major law and order problems. The council offered to compensate the National Front by refunding their deposit. The National Front sought to enforce the contract by specific performance, a discretionary remedy. The trial judge had made an order for specific performance. The Court of Appeal ruled that, since the trial judge had taken all the relevant considerations into account in making his decision, there were no grounds on which they could interfere and overturn the decision. As a result, the council was obliged to honour the contract and could not escape it by paying damages to the National Front.

Lord Denning began his judgment by stating that 'the National Front is a political party' and then proceeded to outline their policies of opposition to all non-European immigration, repatriation of immigrants, 'preservation of the national and ethnic character of the English people' and opposition to Communism and all forms of Marxism. He then noted that 'these principles are abhorrent to many', but insisted that the National Front was entitled to 'make its views known, so long as it does so peaceably and without inflaming others to violence'.[383] Lord Denning then said that the trial judge, Tasker Watkins VC, had decided to order specific performance 'because of the importance of freedom of speech and assembly. They are amongst our most precious freedoms....freedom for the views of which you most heartily disapprove'.[384] He then quoted the words of the Poet Laureate of Queen Victoria, Alfred Lord Tennyson, words which specifically invoked, in particular by the use of the word 'precedent', the values of the Common Law: 'A man may speak the thing he will, a land of settled government, a land of just and old reknown where freedom slowly broadens down from precedent to precedent'.[385]

Lord Denning conceded that freedom of speech could be abused 'to propagate race hatred and class warfare', emphasising that both Hitler, and the Communists, the specific foes of the National Front as he had earlier noted, had abused that freedom, but found no evidence that the National Front were abusing freedom of speech in that way and insisted that 'freedom of assembly is another of our precious freedoms'.[386] He added that the threat of violence did not come from the National Front, which was organising 'a private meeting of a political party', but from their opponents the Anti-Nazi League. 'It would then be those interruptors who would be the destroyers of freedom of speech', not the National Front.[387]

Lord Denning concluded a judgment suffused with rhetoric which emphasised the importance of freedom of speech in the English constitution, a freedom whose benefits, in the opinion of the court, should extend to the National Front, with this peroration: 'In the interests of our fundamental freedoms, freedom of speech, freedom of assembly, and the importance of holding people to their contracts, we ought to grant specific performance'.[388] Provided they did not break the criminal law, the National Front were entitled to the full protection of the Common Law. It is quite clear from this judgment that Lord Denning, while he had no use for the ideas of the National Front, was not prepared to deny them access to the protection of the law. Provided they did not commit any criminal acts, the National Front, like any other English people, were entitled to exercise their right to freedom of speech. Lord Denning's judgment made no reference whatsoever to the Race Relations Legislation, legislation whose provisions the National Front persistently breached; the consequences of such breaches were civil, not criminal.

Notes

[1] *Hayward v Thompson* 1981 3 AllER 450 at 453
[2] *R v London Borough of Hillingdon ex parte Islam* 1981 2 AllER 1089
[3] Ibid at 1092
[4] *Monterosso Shipping Co Ltd v International Transport Workers Federation* 1982 2 AllER 841 at 846
[5] *Herbert v Byrne* 1964 1 AllER 882 at 885
[6] *Buckoke v Greater London Council* 1971 2 AllER 254 at 259
[7] *Webb v Ministry of Housing and Local Government* 1965 2 AllER 193 at 203
[8] *H.P. Bulmer Ltd v J. Bollinger SA* 1974 2 AllER 1226 at 1231
[9] *Shields v E. Coombes [Holdings] Ltd.* 1979 1 AllER 456 at 460-1
[10] *Dickson v The Pharmaceutical Society of Great Britain* 1967 2 AllER 558 at 563
[11] Ibid 565
[12] Ibid 568
[13] *Strick [Inspector of Taxes] v Regent Oil Co Ltd.* 1964 3 AllER 23 at 27
[14] *R v Horsham Justices ex parte Farquharson* 1982 2 AllER 269
[15] Ibid 284; *Measure for Measure* II ii 117
[16] *Schering Chemicals Ltd v Falkman Ltd* 1981 2 AllER 321
[17] Ibid 318
[18] *Re Stone and Saville's Contract* 1963 1 AllER 353 at 354
[19] *Meade v London Borough of Haringey* 1979 2 AllER 1016
[20] *Re Weston's Settlement Trusts* 1968 3 AllER 338
[21] Ibid 341 *Richard II* II i
[22] *Kingsway Investments [Kent] Ltd v Kent County Council* 1969 1 AllER 601
[23] Ibid 613
[24] Ibid 613
[25] *The Teh Hu* 1969 3 AllER 1200
[26] Ibid 1202 *Julius Caesar* III i
[27] *Maxwell v Department of Trade and Industry* 1972 2 AllER 122
[28] *Julius Caesar* IV iii
[29] Ibid 129
[30] *The Mihailos Xilas* 1979 1 AllER 657
[31] Ibid 664
[32] *Allen v Sir Alfred McAlpine and Sons Ltd* 1968 1 AllER 543
[33] Ibid 547 *Hamlet* III i
[34] *Dyson Holdings Ltd v Fox* 1975 3 AllER 1030
[35] Ibid 1031 *Henry V* IV i
[36] *R v Barnsley Metropolitan Borough Council* 1976 3 AllER 452
[37] Ibid 455
[38] *Trendtex Trading Corporation Ltd v Central Bank of Nigeria* 1977 1 AllER 881
[39] Ibid 891
[40] *Harold Stephen and Co Ltd v the Post Office* 1978 1 AllER 939
[41] *Merchant of Venice* IV i 220

[42] At the climax of the play, Portia, disguised as a Doctor of Law, invokes the morality of law, rather than legal technicality, to rescue Antonio, whose argosy has sunk to the bottom of the ocean, from the enforced redemption of the pledge of a pound of flesh which he has lodged with Shylock:
'The quality of mercy is not strained,
It droppeth as the gentle rain from heaven
Upon the place beneath. It is twice blest:
It blesseth him that gives and him that takes'.
The Merchant of Venice IV i

[43] In a dissenting judgment concerned with the issue of an Anton Piller order in relation to the 'pirating' of video tapes, Lord Denning quoted from *The Pirates of Penzance*: 'It is, it is a glorious thing, to be a pirate king'. *Rank Film Distributors Ltd v Video Information Centre* 1980 2 AllER 273 at 277

[44] In a judgment concerned with the right to work in relation to trade unions, Lord Denning quoted the words of the village blacksmith in Longfellow's poem *The Village Blacksmith* to illustrate his conception of the value of work: 'Something attempted, something done, has earned a night's repose'. *Langston v AUEW* 1974 1 AllER 980 at 987

[45] *Allen v Sir Alfred McAlpine and Sons Ltd* 1968 1 AllER 543

[46] Ibid 546

[47] Ibid 547

[48] *Midland Bank Trust Co Ltd v Green* 1979 3 AllER 29

[49] Ibid 32

[50] Lord Denning's judgment, which approved the developing practice of the Commerical Court to order the *saisie conservatoire* of the assets of a party of whom it was suspected that he might move his assets out of the jurisdiction of the English courts, to avoid execution in the event of a judgment against him, was made on 26th June 1975 but reported in 1980 [*Mareva Companionera Naviera SA v International Bulk Carriers SA* 1980 1 AllER 213]

[51] *The Siskina* 1977 3 AllER 803

[52] Ibid 815

[53] *Rasu Maritima SA v Perusahaan Pertambangan Minyak Dan Gas Bumi Negara [Partamina] and Government of Indonesia [as interveners]* 1977 3 AllER 324

[54] Ibid 332

[55] Ibid 335

[56] *Z Ltd v A* 1982 1 AllER 556

[57] Ibid 560

[58] *The Concise Oxford English Dictionary* [Tenth Edition Revised 1999] defines Ruritania as 'relating to or characteristic of romantic adventure or its setting' and gives its origin as being derived from an imaginary kingdom set in SE Europe used as the setting for the novels of courtly intrigue and romance written by the English novelist Anthony Hope.

[59] *Third Chandris Shipping Corporation v Unimarine SA* 1979 2 AllER 972

[60] Ibid 985

[61] *Smith v ILEA* 1978 1 AllER 411
[62] *Verrall v Great Yarmouth Borough Council* 1980 1 AllER 839
[63] Ibid 845
[64] *George Mitchell [Chesterhall] Ltd v Finney Lock Seeds Ltd* 1983 1 AllER 109
[65] Ibid 111
[66] *London Artists Ltd v Littler* 1969 2 AllER 193
[67] *New Zealand Government Property Corporation v HM and S Ltd* 1982 1 AllER 624
[68] Ibid 626
[69] *Chaplin v Leslie Frewin* 1965 3 AllER 764
[70] *Mills v Inland Revenue Commissioners* 1972 3 AllER 977
[71] *Howard v Borneman [No 2]* 1974 3 AllER 862
[72] *Board of Governors of the Hospital for Sick Children v Walt Disney Productions Inc* 1967 1 AllER 1005
[73] *Fielding v Variety Incorporated* 1967 2 AllER 497
[74] *Desert Victory* [1943], *Burma Victory* [1945], *Brighton Rock* [1947], *Private's Progress* [1956], *Lucky Jim* [1957], *Brothers in Law* [1958], *Carlton Browne of the FO* [1959] and *I'm All Right Jack* [1959]
[75] *Bryanston Finance Ltd v De Vries* 1975 2 AllER 609
[76] Ibid 612
[77] Ibid 620
[78] *Wallersteiner v Moir* 1974 3 AllER 217
[79] *Midland Bank Trust Co Ltd v Green* 1979 3 AllER 29
[80] Ibid 30
[81] *Nothman v London Borough of Barnet* 1978 1 AllER 1243 at 1244
[82] *Re Brocklehurst [deceased]* 1978 1 AllER 767
[83] *Langston v Amalgamated Union of Engineering Workers* 1974 1 AllER 980
[84] *Pannett v P. McGuiness and Co Ltd* 1972 3 AllER 137
[85] *Thornton v Shoe Lane Parking Ltd* 1971 1 AllER 686
[86] *R v Local Commissioner for Administration for the North and East Area of England ex parte Bradford Metropolitan City Council* 1979 2 AllER 881
[87] *Hussey v Palmer* 1972 3 AllER 746
[88] *Bedson v Bedson* 1965 3 AllER 307
[89] Ibid 310
[90] Ibid 314-5
[91] *Re Gulbenkian's Settlement Trusts* 1967 3 AllER 15
[92] Ibid 18
[93] *Henning [Valuation Officer] v Church of Jesus Christ* 1962 3 AllER 364
[94] Ibid 366
[95] *Phillips v Minister of Housing and Local Government* 1964 2 AllER 824
[96] *Fulham v Newcastle Chronicle and Journal Ltd* 1977 3 AllER 32
[97] Ibid 34
[98] *Ostreicher v Secretary of State for the Environment* 1978 2 AllER 82
[99] *Schmidt v Secretary of State for Home Affairs* 1969 1 AllER 904

[100] *R v Registrar General ex parte Segerdal* 1970 3 AllER 886
[101] Ibid 887
[102] Ibid 887-90
[103] *Hubbard v Vosper* 1972 1 AllER 1023
[104] Ibid 1025
[105] Ibid 1029
[106] Ibid 1030
[107] *Attorney-General v British Broadcasting Corporation* 1979 3 AllER 45
[108] Ibid 48
[109] Ibid 48
[110] *R v Penguin Books Ltd.* 1961 Crim. L.R. 176; see also *The Trial of Lady Chatterley* ed. Rolph, C.J. [London 1961]. This was a test case following the Obscene Publications Act 1959 which, while attempting to regulate pornography more strictly, allowed, for the first time, under s.4, a defence of public good: s.4 (1) A person shall not be convicted of an offence under section two of this Act, and an order for forfeiture shall not be made under the foregoing section, if it is proved that publication of the article in question is justified as being for the public good on the ground that it is in the interests of science, literature, art or learning, or of other objects of general concern. (2) It is hereby declared that the opinion of experts as to the literary, artistic, scientific or other merits of an article may be admitted in any proceedings under this Act either to establish or to negative the said ground.
[111] This lecture was a response to the publication of the Wolfenden Report in 1957 which recommended a reform of the law with regard to prostitution and homosexuality based on John Stuart Mill's contention that acts between consenting adults in private should not attract the attention of the criminal law. This position was strongly supported by H.L.A. Hart who engaged in a public debate with Lord Devlin about these issues which culminated in the publication of his *Law, Liberty and Morality* in 1963. In response Lord Devlin published *The Enforcement of Morality* in 1965.
[112] Sexual Offences Act 1967; Divorce Law Reform Act 1969
[113] Equal Pay Act 1970; Sex Discrimination Act 1975
[114] Sexual Intercourse began
   In nineteen sixty-three
   [Which was rather late for me] –
   Between the Chatterley ban
   And the Beatles first LP.

   Up till then there had only been
   A sort of bargaining.
   A wrangle for a ring,
   A shame that started at sixteen
   And spread to everything.

Then all at once the quarrel sank:
Everyone felt the same.
And every life became
A brilliant breaking of the bank,
A quite unlosable game.

[115] *Hodges v Harland and Wolff Ltd* 1965 1 AllER 1086

[116] *Ward v James* 1965 1 AllER 565

[117] 'It caught his trousers and tore them. It tore off his penis and severely injured him and that part of the body'. Ibid 1087

[118] Ibid 1087

[119] *Watts v Manning* 1964 2 AllER 267

[120] Ibid 268

[121] *Blyth v Blyth* 1966 1 AllER 524

[122] Ibid 537

[123] Ibid 537

[124] Ibid 537

[125] *Sheldon v Sheldon* 1966 2 AllER 257

[126] Ibid 260

[127] *G[A] v G[T]* 1970 3 AllER 546

[128] Ibid 550

[129] *Re [F] [a minor][publication of information]* 1977 1 AllER 114

[130] Ibid 117

[131] Ibid 117

[132] *R v Metropolitan Police Commissioner ex parte Blackburn [No 3]* 1973 1 AllER 324

[133] Ibid 327

[134] Ibid 327

[135] Ibid 327-8

[136] Ibid 327

[137] Ibid 328-9

[138] This reference to Churchill's speech to Congress in December 1941 gave added authority to Lord Denning's condemnation of pornography.

[139] This phrase was an illusion to a phrase used by Churchill during the Second World War in relation to Lend-Lease. The invocation of the Second World War was perhaps an index of the degree of anxiety engendered by the issue of pornography in the mind of Lord Denning.

[140] Ibid 332

[141] *R v Greater London Council ex parte Blackburn* 1976 3 AllER 184

[142] Ibid 189

[143] 1962 AC 220

[144] 1972 2 AllER 898

[145] Ibid 189

[146] Ibid 189

[147] In 1976 the convention was that judges did not use Hansard to interpret the

provisions of an Act of Parliament.
[148]Ibid 193
[149] *Central Estates [Belgravia] Ltd v Woolgar [No 2]* 1972 2 AllER 610
[150] *R v Selvey* 1968 1 AllER 94
[151]Ibid 9
[152]Ibid 98
[153] *Gurasz v Gurasz* 1969 3 AllER 822
[154]Ibid 823
[155] *Allsop v Church of England Newspaper Ltd* 1972 2 AllER 26
[156]An informal, derogatory word for homosexual. Concise Oxford English Dictionary 10th Ed 1999
[157]Ibid 30
[158] *Hayward v Thompson* 1981 3 AllER 450 at 452
[159]Harold Macmillan, who appointed Lord Denning to conduct the Profumo inquiry, had enjoyed such an indiscretion when he was at Balliol. H.L.A. Hart had also indulged in such indiscretions when he was at New College and afterwards when he was practising as a young barrister in London. See A. Horne, *Macmillan: Volume One* [London, 1987] and N. Lacey, *The Life of H.L.A. Hart* [Oxford, 2004]
[160]See above
[161] In *Sheldon v Sheldon* 1966 2 AllER 257, Lord Denning found that a man's refusal to have sexual intercourse with a wife who wanted to have a child amounted to cruelty.
[162] *Whitehouse v Jordan* 1980 1 AllER 650
[163]Ibid 652
[164]Ibid 652
[165]Ibid 652
[166]Ibid 652
[167]Ibid 656
[168]Ibid 658
[169]Ibid 652
[170]Ibid 654
[171]Ibid 658
[172]It is interesting that Lord Denning stated that John Bradford said these words 'over 450 years ago'. That would mean that they were said in the 1520s, at a time when England was still part of the Roman Catholic Church. The presence of words from the time in which England was a Catholic country in a judgment concerned with birth is suggestive, given Catholic doctrine in relation to contraception and abortion. For Catholics, in contrast with Protestants and non-believers, sexual intercourse and its consequences of conception and birth were mysterious and sacred aspects of the natural order.
[173]Ibid 658
[174] *Royal College of Nursing of the United Kingdom v Department of Health and Social Security* 1981 1 AllER 545
[175]Ibid 554

[176] Ibid 554. Contast this approving use of French with the disobliging reference to the use in French law of the metaphors of conception and birth in relation to company law in a case of the same year - *Phonogram Ltd v Lane* 1981 3 AllER 182. It would seem that Lord Denning considered that the use of French in a Common Law court was appropriate in matters related to sex, but not in matters concerned with company law.
[177] *Bravery v Bravery* 1954 1 WLR 1169
[178] Ibid 1176
[179] Ibid 1176-1181
[180] *Tucker v Farm and General Investment Trust Ltd* 1966 2 AllER 508
[181] Ibid 509
[182] *The Case of Swans* 1592 7 Co Rep 156
[183] Ibid 510
[184] *Sydall v Castings Ltd* 1966 3 AllER 770
[185] Ibid 772
[186] Ibid 772
[187] Ibid 773
[188] *Re L* 1968 1 AllER 20
[189] *B. v B. And E. [B intervening]* 1969 3 AllER 1106
[190] *S v McC [formerly S] and M [intervening]* 1970 AllER 1162
[191] *Midland Bank Trust Co Ltd v Green [no 3]* 1981 3 AllER 744
[192] Ibid 748
[193] *Routhan v Arun District Council* 1981 3 AllER 752
[194] *Formosa v Formosa* 1962 3 AllER 419
[195] Ibid 422
[196] *Indyka v Indyka* 1966 3 AllER 583
[197] *Re Valentine's Settlement* 1965 2 AllER 226 at 230
[198] *National Provincial Bank Ltd v Hastings Car Mart* 1964 1 AllER 688
 Ibid 693
[199] *Gurasz v Gurasz* 1969 3 AllER 822 at 823
[200] *Hall v Hall* 1971 1 AllER 762 at 764
[201] *Jackson v Jackson* 1971 3 AllER 774 at 776
[202] *Hall v Hall* 1971 1 AllER 762 at 763
[203] [London 1983]
[204] Ibid p. 50
[205] *Burgess v Rawnsley* 1975 3 AllER 142
[206] *Dyson Holdings Ltd v Fox* 1975 3 AllER 1030 at 1031-1034
[207] *Eves v Eves* 1975 3 AllER 768 at 769-771
[208] *Tanner v Tanner* 1975 3 AllER 776 at 777-780
[209] *Re L [an Infant]* 1962 3 AllER 1 at 2-4
[210] Most notably in *National Provincial Bank Ltd v Hastings Car Mart* 1964 1 AllER 688 and *Williams and Glyn's Bank Ltd v Boland* 1979 2 AllER 697
[211] *Hall v Hall* 1971 1 AllER 762
[212] *Re Valentine's Settlement* 1965 2 AllER 226

[213] In 1946 Lord Denning had sat on the Committee for the Reform of the Law of Divorce which had produced, with great rapidity, a series of changes to the law to deal with the consequences of the rise in the number divorces during the Second World War. The findings of the committee were of great importance in creating stability in this area in the aftermath of the war.
[214] *Bernard v Josephs* 1982 3 AllER 162
[215] *Nast and Nast v Walker* 1972 1 AllER 1171
[216] Ibid 1175
[217] *Cooke v Head* 1972 2 AllER 38; *Burgess v Rawnsley* 1975 3 AllER 142; *Eves v Eves* 1975 3 AllER 768; *Tanner v Tanner* 1975 3 AllER 776; *Dyson Holdings Ltd v Fox* 1975 3 AllER 1030
[218] *Davis v Johnson* 1978 1 AllER 841
[219] Ibid 846
[220] Ibid 846
[221] Ibid 849
[222] *B v B* 1978 1 AllER 821 and *Cantliff v Jenkins* 1978 1 AllER 836
[223] [1944] K.B. 718
[224] Ibid 855
[225] *The Vera Cruz [No 2]* 1884 9 PD 9 at 98
[226] Ibid 855
[227] Ibid 857
[228] 1981 1 AllER 545
[229] In deciding that a nurse was not a 'medical practitioner', Lord Denning ruled that abortion could only be carried out if a doctor was present throughout the procedure, a decision which would have had profound implications for the cost, and therefore the availability, of abortion.
[230] Lord Denning made no judicial comment on contraception, but a decision in the 1950s - *Bravery v Bravery* 1954 1 WLR 1169 - in which he stated that any may who sterilised himself was behaving unnaturally, and that such an action would constitute grounds for divorce, suggested that he did not approve of it. The decision in *Sheldon v Sheldon* 1966 2 AllER 257 that refusal of sexual intercourse to a woman who wanted to conceive supports the probability that Lord Denning did not approve of contraception.
[231] *Ministry of Defence v Jeremiah* 1979 3 AllER 833
[232] Ibid 835
[233] *Peake v Automotive Products Ltd* 1978 1 AllER 106
[234] Ibid 108
[235] *Bradbury v London Borough of Enfield* 1967 3 AllER 434
[236] Ibid 437
[237] Ibid 438
[238] Ibid 441
[239] *Secretary of State for Education and Science v Metropolitan Borough of Tameside* 1976 3 AllER 665
[240] Ibid 667

146   Chapter Two

---

[241] It was unusual, to say the least, for a judge to invoke the authority of a historian to support his legal reasoning. However, G.M. Trevelyan was well placed within the established order to act as an authority, particularly in relation to education. G.M. Trevelyan [1876-1962] was the great nephew of Lord Macaulay, the historian of the events of 1688, Master of Trinity College Cambridge between 1940 and 1951, a trustee of the British Museum and the National Portrait Gallery and a recipient of the Order of Merit.
[242] Ibid 667
[243] Ibid 671
[244] *Smith v Inner London Education Authority* 1978 1 AllER 411
[245] Ibid 415
[246] Ibid 415
[247] Ibid 415
[248] Ibid 415
[249] Ibid 417
[250] Ibid 418
[251] Once did she hold the gorgeous east in fee;
And was the safeguard of the west; the worth
Of Venice did not fall below her birth,
Venice, the eldest child of Liberty.
She was a maiden city, bright and free;
No guile seduced, no force could violate;
And, when she took unto herself a Mate,
She must espouse the everlasting Sea.
And what if she had seen those glories fade,
Those titles vanish, and that strength decay;
Yet shall some tribute of regret be paid
When her long life hath reached its final day;
Men are we, and must grieve when even the Shade
Of that which once was great is passed away.
[252] *Chief Immigration Officer, Gatwick ex p Kharrazi* 1980 3 AllER 373
[253] Ibid 375
[254] Ibid 375
[255] Ibid 375
[256] Heffer, S. *Like the Roman: the Life of Enoch Powell* [London 1998] pp. 225-241
[257] Powell, J.E. *Freedom and Reality* ed. Wood, J. [London 1969] pp. 136-192
[258] *Senior [an infant] v Baker and Allen Ltd* 1965 1 AllER 818
[259] Ibid 819
[260] *Duke of Buccleuch v Inland Revenue Commissioners* 1965 3 AllER 458
[261] Ibid 460
[262] *Greater London Council v Connolly* 1970 1 AllER 870
[263] Ibid 874
[264] *Taylor v British Omnibus Co Ltd* 1975 2 AllER 1107
[265] Ibid 1111

[266] *Cookson v Knowles* 1977 2 AllER 820
[267]Ibid 823
[268] *Staffordshire Area Health Authority v South Staffordshire Waterworks Co* 1978 3 AllER 769
[269]Ibid 775-7
[270] Ibid 712
[271] *The Teh Hu* 1969 3 AllER 1200
[272]Ibid 1202
[273] *Woodhouse AC Israel Cocoa Ltd SA v Nigeria Produce Marketing Co Ltd* 1971 1 AllER 665
[274]Ibid 667
[275] *Miliangos v George Frank [Textiles] Ltd* 1975 1 AllER 1076
[276]Ibid 1081
[277] *The Folias* 1978 2 AllER 764
[278]Ibid 768-772
[279] *Choice Investments Ltd v Jeromnimon* 1981 1 AllER 225
[280]Ibid 228
[281] *Techno-Impex v Gebr van Weelde Scheepvartkantoor BV* 1981 2 AllER 669
[282]Ibid 673
[283]Ibid 677
[284] *Gohoho v Guinea Press Ltd* 1962 3 AllER 785
[285]Kwame Nkrumah [1909-1972] was Ghana's first president. He made an alliance with the USSR and was outspoken in his condemnation of British imperialism. He developed a 'cult of personality' and was the first 'dictator' to emerge in the former African possessions of what had been the British Empire. In 1966 he was deposed in a military coup.
[286] *Sabally v Attorney-General* 1964 3 AllER 377
[287]Ibid 378
[288]Ibid 381
[289] *Buttes Gas and Oil Co v Hammer [No 2]* 1975 2 AllER 51
[290]Ibid 54 The Persian Gulf was the last part of the former Empire to be decolonised. It was not until 1971 that Britain finally left the Gulf, a region in which it had established a presence in the early nineteenth century, first to protect the Indian Raj and later to protect British oil interests.
[291]Ibid 59
[292] *Re James [an insolvent] [Attorney-General intervening]* 1977 1 AllER 364
[293]Ibid 369
[294]Ibid 370
[295]Ibid 375
[296]In 1980, British imperial rule was restored during the period between the ending of UDI and the election of a Parliament chosen by both black and white Rhodesians.
[297]Ibid 369
[298]Ibid 374

148   Chapter Two

[299] Ibid 375
[300] In the debate on the Royal Titles Bill 1953, Enoch Powell had described the 'divisibility' of the Crown as an 'evil' because the 'realm was a unity'. Lord Denning disagreed: 'By constitutional usage or practice' the Crown had become separate and divisible' [ibid 137-8]. Whereas Powell had argued that the Royal Titles Bill was an innovation, Lord Denning recognised that 'divisibility' of the Crown had emerged as a doctrine some years before as a result of usage and practice rather than statutory authority.
[301] *R v Secretary of State for Commonwealth Affairs ex p Indian Association of Alberta* 1982 2 AllER 118
[302] Ibid 124
[303] Ibid 137-8
[304] *Whitworth Street Estates [Manchester] Ltd v James Millar and Partners Ltd* 1969 2 AllER 210
[305] *Re United Railways of Havana v Regla Warehouses Ltd* 1960 2 AllER 333 at 335
[306] *Re Tuck's Settlement Trusts* 1978 1 AllER 1047
[307] 1932 AC 562
[308] Ibid 1053
[309] *MacShannon v Rockware Glass Ltd* 1977 2 AllER 449
[310] Ibid 451
[311] Ibid 451
[312] Ibid 453
[313] *Morris v The Crown Office* 1970 1 AllER 1079
[314] Ibid 1084
[315] *McIlkenny v Chief Constable of West Midlands Police* 1980 2 AllER 227
[316] Ibid 240
[317] Lord Denning had edited these in 1929
[318] *Attorney-General v Mulholland; Attorney-General v Foster* 1963 1 AllER 767
[319] *Kelly v London Transport Executive* 1981 2 AllER 842
[320] Ibid 845
[321] *Re Keenan* 1971 3 AllER 883
[322] Ibid 885
[323] Ibid 889
[324] Ibid 886
[325] Ibid 889
[326] *Re James [an insolvent] [Attorney-General intervening]* 1977 1 AllER 364
[327] *Chappell v The Times Newspapers Ltd* 1975 2 AllER 233 at 239. The quotation comes from an old French song *La Menagerie* which Lord Denning would have learnt at school.
[328] *Compagnie Tunisienne de Navigation SA v Compagnie d'Armament Maritime SA* 1969 3 AllER 589
[329] Ibid 591
[330] *Fothergill v Monarch Airlines Ltd* 1979 3 AllER 445

[331] Ibid 448
[332] Ibid 449
[333] Ibid 449
[334] Ibid 449
[335] *Lewis v Averay* 1971 3 AllER 907
[336] Ibid 911
[337] Published in 1806, a year after the battle of Trafalgar.
[338] Ibid 910
[339] Ibid 910-11
[340] *Re Trepka Mines Ltd* 1962 3 AllER 351
[341] Ibid 354
[342] Ibid 354-6 The words and phrases 'strife', 'evil', 'improperly stirring up', 'without just cause or excuse', 'inflame damages', 'suppress evidence', 'suborn witnesses' were deployed in the judgment with telling effect.
[343] *Phonogram Ltd v Lane* 1981 3 AllER 182
[344] Ibid 186-7
[345] *Lambert v Ealing Borough Council* 1982 2 AllER 394
[346] Ibid 396
[347] Ibid 396
[348] *The Atlantic Star* 1972 3 AllER 705 at 709
[349] Ibid 709
[350] *Nissan v Attorney-General* 1967 2 AllER 1238 at 1243
[351] Ibid 1243
[352] *Re P [G.E.] [an infant]* 1964 3 AllER 977
[353] Ibid 981 The authority for this point was *Joyce v DPP* [1946] AC 347 William Joyce, Lord 'Haw Haw', a stateless person, had been issued with a British passport which entitled him to return within three months thereby confirming his status of 'ordinary residence'. On this basis he was found guilty of treason for his adherence to the German Nazi government and hanged.
[354] Ibid 982-3
[355] *Nissan v Attorney-General* 1967 2 AllER 1238 at 1243
[356] Ibid 979
[357] *Mandla v Dowell Lee* 1982 3 AllER 1108 at 1112
[358] Ibid 1112
[359] Ibid 1113
[360] Ibid 1113
[361] *Oppenheimer v Cattermole* 1972 3 AllER 1106
[362] Ibid 1111
[363] *Re Weston's Settlement Trusts* 1968 3 AllER 338
[364] Ibid 341
[365] Ibid 341
[366] Ibid 341
[367] *Sirros v Moore* 1974 3 AllER 776
[368] Ibid 779

[369] 1969 1 AllER 904
[370] Ibid 908
[371] Quintin Hogg was Lord Chancellor as Lord Hailsham between 1970 and 1974 and 1979 and 1987. It is interesting that Lord Hailsham was one of the bitterest opponents of Enoch Powell's approach to immigration and a leading proponent of a more 'liberal' approach to immigration. In April 1968, he advised Heath to sack Powell from the Shadow Cabinet and hardly ever spoke to him again after 1968.
[372] Ibid 908
[373] This was the first occasion on which the phrase 'legitimate expectation' was used in a judgment in the English courts. It was later to develop into an important principle of administrative law. It was notable that on this occasion Lord Denning used the phrase in order to exclude the possibility of judicial review of administrative discretion in relation to immigration law.
[374] Ibid 909
[375] Ibid 909-10
[376] *Plummer v Chapman* 1962 3 AllER 823
[377] Ibid 825
[378] Ibid 825
[379] Ibid 826
[380] *James Marshall v BBC* 1979 3 AllER 80
[381] Ibid 81
[382] *Verrall v Great Yarmouth Borough Council* 1980 1 AllER 839
[383] Ibid 842
[384] Ibid 844-5
[385] Ibid 845
[386] Ibid 845
[387] Ibid 845
[388] Ibid 845

CHAPTER THREE

THE HISTORY OF ENGLAND 1962-1982

As Master of the Rolls, Lord Denning was able to influence the development of the law in significant areas; shaping the way in which the English legal system responded to the challenges of adhesion to that of the European Community and mass immigration from the former Commonwealth; defining the rights of the individual and the powers of the Police; extending the scope of the equitable doctrine of *estoppel*; increasing the capacity of the Court of Appeal to depart from its own precedents and advocating the purposive approach to statutory interpretation; controlling the abuse of power by trade unions, local government officials and ministers of the Crown, even to the extent of reviewing actions taken under the authority of the Royal Prerogative. In all of these ways, Lord Denning contributed significantly to the reform of the law.

As well as dealing, on a daily basis, with routine issues involving the law of personal injury[1], industrial injury[2], fatal accident[3], contract[4], charterparties[5], shipping[6], arbitration[7], land[8], leasehold[9], agricultural tenancy[10], landlord and tenant[11], planning[12], compulsory purchase[13], rating[14], tax[15], wills[16], divorce[17], trusts[18], legal aid[19], contempt[20] and libel[21], all the day to day routine matters of the civil law, Lord Denning also heard cases which reflected the social changes, political conflicts, even major historical events of the time. Consideration of his judgments as Master of the Rolls therefore not only provides insights into major reforms and developments in the law, as well as the way in which he was able to shape the more routine aspects of the civil law, it also sheds light on the way in which English society, and politics, were being transformed during the turbulent years spanned by his tenure of the office of Master of the Rolls.

During the period in which Lord Denning was Master of the Rolls, most cases were finally decided in the Court of Appeal. Only a small proportion of cases were appealed to the House of Lords. Even though the House of Lords asserted its inherent authority to depart from its own, hitherto, binding precedents in 1966, it was not until the 1980s that the

House of Lords began to develop its role as a final court of appeal, a supreme court in all but name; a position it finally attained in 2009 when its members ceased to be members of Parliament. It was therefore the Court of Appeal which had the decisive role in shaping the law during the period in which Lord Denning was Master of the Rolls, a point of which he was well aware.

As Master of the Rolls, Lord Denning had considerable discretion over which cases he heard, choosing those which attracted his interest, in particular those which he could use to shape the law. Cases which reached the Court of Appeal were either those which involved controversial or technical points of law, or else those which concerned the resolution of legal issues raised by dispute and conflict about matters of considerable economic, social and often political importance such as the position of trade unions, the control of immigration, the scope of the law of contempt, the freedom of the press, the rules governing *locus standi*, or the regulation of gambling and pornography, to take a selection of the subject matter of cases decided by Lord Denning.

Seen in this light, Lord Denning's judgments in the Court of Appeal provide a valuable source of evidence for the history of a period which began with the end of Empire and ended with the advent of the radical economic and social reforms associated with the governments of Margaret Thatcher; a time in which it could be argued that England manifestly failed to respond to the challenge posed by Dean Acheson's acerbic assessment of her role in the world.[22] Although the political, social and economic state of the country may have been disturbed, and decidedly unsatisfactory, during this period, the legal system retained the prestige and authority with which it had been associated since the days of Coke and Blackstone. As Master of the Rolls, Lord Denning worked to maintain that prestige and authority; his judgments in the Court of Appeal reveal both the manner in which he sought to achieve that objective, and the extent to which the Common Law, the greatest tradition and inheritance of England, was able to shape her destiny in an era characterised, according to some tastes, by cynicism, fatuity, decline and disillusion.

The premiership of Harold Macmillan entered a fraught period, from which it did not recover, with the shock victory of the Liberal, Eric Lubbock, in the Orpington by-election on the Ides of March in 1962; Orpington was next door to the Prime Minister's own Bromley constituency. Lord Denning was appointed Master of the Rolls just over a month later, on April 19th 1962, becoming, over the years, a renowned figure who represented the Common Law in our national life. This was in marked contrast with the man who appointed him; a sad, even tragic, figure who was transmogrified from 'Supermac' at the time of his remarkable victory in the General Election of 1959[23] to the broken down actor-manager, memorably depicted by Peter Cook.[24]

Just over a year after his appointment as Master of the Rolls, Lord Denning conducted the inquiry into the resignation of John Profumo, the Secretary of State for War. The publication of his report, on September 25th 1963, effectively defused a scandal which had the capacity to undermine a government, even to destabilise the political system itself. From the autumn of 1963, until his retirement in September 1982, Lord Denning was never far from the centre of the political life of the country; his decisions in the Court of Appeal frequently touched on, even shaped, some of the decisive political events of that era, as well as influencing more mundane, if no less important, aspects of social and economic life. The Common Law has been at the centre of political, economic and social life in England since the time of King Alfred whose Christian name Lord Denning shared. Between 1962, when Lord Denning became Master of the Rolls, and 1982, when he retired, the political leadership of the country was troubled, uncertain and, it is arguable, in many respects incompetent but the Common Law remained an icon, possessed of real substance, which represented stability and continuity.

After a deceptively bright start, Harold Wilson, prone to gimmickry and, in the eyes of some of his colleagues, and many of his opponents, 'too-clever-by-half', to use the phrase by which Lord Salisbury described Iain Macleod, found himself out of his depth. Presiding over a Cabinet filled with, what one commentator has called, 'the wisest fools in Christendom',[25] Wilson soon found himself adrift in a decidedly choppy sea which became ever more turbulent from the time of the Unilateral Declaration of Independence by Rhodesia on November 11th 1965. Edward Heath, his successor, a man, according to some caustic commentary at the time, more fitted to be a Permanent Secretary than a Prime Minister,[26] lost power ignominiously following an election called in February 1974 on the issue 'Who governs Britain?' Succeeding governments led by Wilson and James Callaghan floundered in a state of continuous economic crisis, industrial strife and social disorder. It was not until the victory over Argentina in the South Atlantic in June 1982, a few months before Lord Denning's retirement, that some semblance of authority was returned to the political leadership of the country by the government of Margaret Thatcher.

Throughout this period, the Common Law, embodied in the figure of the Master of the Rolls, retained a prestige and authority patently lacking in the country's elected leadership. From the time that his report into the resignation of John Profumo became a best-seller, an unique distinction for a publication of HMSO, the presence of Lord Denning in the national life of the United Kingdom offered reassurance that, to quote from *Julius Caesar*, one of his favourite plays, in the midst of all the 'hurly burly', to invoke the Scottish play, whose mood was apt for the times, there remained a figure of whom it could be said that to his 'true-fixed and resting quality' there was 'no fellow in the firmament'.[27]

Resonances emanating from events taking place in the world beyond the confines of the United Kingdom were felt in Lord Denning's court. In 1969, a property dispute required consideration of the impact the German invasion of Greece in 1941.[28] The Anglo-French invasion of Egypt in November 1956, described by Lord Denning as 'the seven days war in 1956',[29] was at the root of three cases heard in his court, one as late as 1975. The first case concerned a charterparty and the question of whether it had been frustrated by the war.[30] Lord Denning described the situation facing the litigants as follows: 'On July 26th 1956, the Government of Egypt nationalised the Suez Canal. Soon afterwards the UK and France began to build up military forces in Cyprus. It was obvious to all mercantile men that English and French forces might be sent to seize the Canal, and this might lead to its becoming impassable to traffic'.[31] He concluded, as suggested in his introduction, that there was no frustration because the events which had affected the charterparty were foreseeable. The second case[32] concerned the impact of the war on shipping freight rates; the final case was about compensation for the sequestration of property during the crisis by the Government of Egypt.[33]

Events in Cyprus, the base from which the Anglo-French invasion was launched in 1956, led to cases heard in Lord Denning's court. Lord Denning described Cyprus as 'an island torn with dissension'.[34] On Christmas Day 1963, the United Nations, supported by British, Turkish and Greek troops, came to the aid of the Government of Cyprus which had been established in 1960 and was facing an incipient civil war. The problem which came before Lord Denning's court concerned the issue of compensation for damage caused by the use of the Royal Prerogative[35]; the intervention had not been authorized by Parliament but had taken place in response to a request to the UN by the Government of Cyprus. The Court of Appeal authorized the payment of compensation for the damage caused to a hotel by British troops. The invasion of Northern Cyprus by Turkey in July 1974 led to an action in the English courts[36]; the plaintiff arguing that a Turkish Cypriot had committed an act of trespass in taking over a hotel in the northern part of the island. Describing the defendant, Mr. Muftiazde, as 'a man of distinction who holds the Queen's

Medal for Gallantry',[37] Lord Denning dismissed the case as non-justiciable.

The consequences of Harold Macmillan's 'winds of change' speech, delivered in Cape Town on February 3rd 1960, loomed large among the cases heard in Lord Denning's court. Within five years of the speech, almost all of Britain's African colonies had been granted independence. In 1962, Lord Denning heard a case concerning the validity of a libel writ issued in England concerning a libel committed in Ghana which had been independent since 1957. [38] In 1964, his court had to consider the validity of election registers in Gambia[39] which was to gain its independence the following year. Although Nigeria had gained its independence in 1960, the year of Macmillan's speech in Cape Town, between 6th July 1967 to 15th January 1970 the new country was convulsed by a violent and bitter civil war. The consequences of this reached Lord Denning's court in a dispute over the eviction of a Biafran diplomat from premises owned by the Government of Nigeria.[40] Lord Denning introduced his judgment as follows: 'There is a civil war flaring in Nigeria. Sparks from it have come down in London. Some have landed on number 35 Woodstock Road, London NW11'.[41]

Although independence was granted, perhaps with undue haste, to Britain's African colonies during the last years of Macmillan's Conservative government, one intractable problem remained, to be inherited by the succeeding Labour government of Harold Wilson. Rhodesia, with a large white settler minority, was governed by a political party, the Rhodesian Front, led by Ian Smith, which was determined to resist majority rule, a requirement insisted on by the British government as a condition for the granting of independence. On November 11th 1965, the Rhodesia government made a Unilateral Declaration of Independence, an action condemned as unlawful by the British government. UDI precipitated a major crisis for the Labour government. Despite attempts at negotiations in 1966 and 1968, and the introduction of sanctions in 1965, there was no resolution of the problem until the initiation of successful negotiations by Margaret Thatcher's government in 1979 resulting in independence, with majority rule, in 1980. The Rhodesian crisis led to three cases in Lord Denning's court. The first, in 1968, was a routine matter, involving a tobacco company, about the implications of sanctions.[42] Lord Denning introduced his judgment thus: 'In November 1965, the men in control of Southern Rhodesia made a unilateral declaration of independence, the plaintiffs have been very badly hit by the steps taken against the men in Rhodesia'.[43] The second case, involving a claim against the Bank of England for interest on colonial stock held in

Rhodesia, on which no interest had been paid since 1965, concerned the first Petition of Right[44] to have been made since the 1850s, a matter of considerable legal interest which was treated with relish by Lord Denning. Reviewing the history of such actions, dating back to the reigns of Edgar II and Canute II, long before the emergence of Parliament, Lord Denning noted that a Petition of Right was a demand that 'Right be done' and that it led not to a judgment but to an order on the Crown 'which it will honour'.[45]

A case concerned with insolvency, heard in October 1976,[46] led Lord Denning to consider the relationship between the courts in Rhodesia and those in the United Kingdom and, in the course of his dissenting judgment, reach some notable conclusions and make some striking obiter remarks. The Rhodesian High Court had asked for the assistance of the High Court in London in the prosecution of a solicitor. The Attorney-General had intervened, arguing that the English courts should not recognise those of Rhodesia and therefore offer no assistance. Lord Denning concluded that UDI had had no effect on the Rhodesian courts, that even judges appointed since UDI retained their legitimacy, despite the imposition of sanctions and the refusal of the British government to recognise that of Rhodesia. Lord Denning insisted that justice was more important than the temporary political disruption caused by UDI and that, despite the economic blockade, there was no legal one.

Lord Denning introduced his judgment thus: 'David Emlyn James is a lawyer who has gone astray'. His firm, 'Green, Moxon, Quirk and Hadden....sound as if they came originally from England'.[47] Commenting on the current situation in Rhodesia he remarked that 'the outlook is now altered beyond measure' and that there was a 'reasonable prospect that the illegal regime will come to an end' as a result of pressure applied by the United States and South Africa[48]. Reviewing the impact of UDI, Lord Denning maintained that 'the white settlers made no complaint against the lawful sovereign, the Queen of England. They pledged their loyalty and allegiance to her. But they rebelled against her ministers in Whitehall....they left the judges still pledged under their oath of allegiance to the Queen; and under their judicial oath well and truly to serve her in the office of a judge. They left the courts to carry on with their daily tasks...they left the existing law as it was. After all, they were as much concerned as anyone to see that law and order were maintained....in this too, they were supported by the lawful sovereign, the Queen of England...otherwise there would be utter chaos....the implication[49] was irresistible that the lawful sovereign authorized the judges to continue in office, and the courts to continue to function....to see that law and order is maintained'.[50]

Lord Denning then invoked the authority of Grotius to support the contention that, if a lawful sovereign was ousted by an alien, the new ruler had a duty to maintain law and order.[51] Provided that the authority of the new regime was not used to enforce new laws passed subsequent to UDI the Rhodesian courts had full authority to enforce existing law and to apply to the courts in the United Kingdom for aid in that duty. The relevant law with regard to insolvency was made before UDI, the High Court of Rhodesia could therefore ask English courts for aid; as far as the courts were concerned Rhodesia was still a colony, the Queen sovereign and her courts legitimate. Judges appointed after 1965 were legitimate. Lord Denning remarked that in 1944 a man lifted his hat to him saying: 'I raise my hat, if not to you, at any rate to the office'.[52] UDI had done nothing to undermine the authority of judicial office in Rhodesia. Lord Denning observed that 'in the last few weeks hopes have risen that the rebellion in Rhodesia will come to an end. The economic blockade is to be lifted. So too should the legal blockade'.[53] Referring to courts in the Southern States after the American Civil War, he noted that the Confederate courts had the power to do that which was 'necessary to peace and good order among citizens'.[54] He concluded that the 'judicial branch remained subject to the lawful sovereign, the Queen of England.....the country remained, in the eyes of the law, a British colony'.[55]

Lord Denning's court also heard a number of high profile cases arising out of the activities of the Anti-apartheid movement in the United Kingdom. Following the Soweto rising of 1976, and its suppression by the government of South Africa, the Post Office Workers attempted to disrupt the sending of mail to South Africa. When the Attorney-General refused to intervene to prevent the disruption of the postal service between Britain and South Africa in response to a relator action initiated by John Gouriet, Mr Gouriet applied to Lord Denning's court, arguing that, as a member of the public, he had the necessary *locus standi* to apply directly to the courts to enforce the criminal law.[56] Lord Denning noted that 'there is an association called the National Association for Freedom of which we know nothing except that it has a secretary, Mr John Gouriet[57]. It is said by its critics to be a right wing pressure group. But that is no concern of ours'.[58] He continued, allowing Mr Gouriet's appeal, observing that 'the Post Office operates a great public service. It is essential to the well being of the community. I feel sure that all from the humbler grades, the postmen and telegraph boys, up to the top, they are those who would wish to abide by the law of the land. It is as well that the law of the land should be known to everyone concerned in the Post Office. It is enacted, not by old Acts of Queen Anne [as someone seems to have supposed on the television][59] but by statutes passed by governments of various colours in the last 20 or 30 years'.[60]

A few months later, a similar situation arose when the Association of Broadcasting Staff tried to disrupt the broadcast of the FA Cup final on 21st May 1977 to South Africa by closing down the Indian Ocean satellite.[61] The BBC applied for an injunction to prevent the disruption and the court had to consider whether the proposed action by the trade union could be considered as a 'trade dispute' and therefore permitted by law. The trade union argued that their action was justified by UN resolutions against Apartheid and by race discrimination law in the United Kingdom. Lord Denning introduced his judgment authorising the injunction against the action as follows: 'Half the world will not see the game if a trade union has its way…..the story starts with Mr. Peter Hain, the chairman of a group which calls itself the Action Committee against Racism…..in three recent acts….Parliament has conferred more freedom from restraint on trade unions than has ever been known to the law before. All legal restraints have been lifted so that they can now do as they will'.[62] However, he considered the proposed action to be 'coercive action unconnected with a trade dispute' based on the principle that 'we don't like the article which you are going to publish abut the Arabs, or Jews, or on this or that political issue'. It was 'unlawful interference with the freedom of the press…a self-created power of censorship'.[63]

The other occasion on which Lord Denning's court had to consider the situation in South Africa arose from an advertisement for nurses in the Daily Mail which offered the information that applicants would be caring for 'All White patients'.[64] Lord Denning noted that 'although the act of discrimination is itself perfectly lawful, it is unlawful to advertise it'.[65] The question for the court was whether the way in which the advertisement was framed would mean that no coloured nurses would apply. He considered it to be 'a nicely balanced question',[66] but it was a matter of fact which should be considered by the court of first instance; the Court of Appeal would not interfere with its decision to dismiss the action on the basis that the ordinary reader would not consider that the advertisement bore the discriminatory meaning attributed to it by the Race Relations Board.

Although Britain had formally withdrawn its forces from 'East of Suez' at the end of the 1960s, relationships with the Gulf States remained of great importance because of the oil reserves buried beneath their territory. Despite the formal withdrawal announced by the Labour government in 1968, British forces were heavily involved in supporting the government of Oman against an insurgency between 1962 and 1976. Lord Denning's court was involved in a small sideshow of the major engagement of British, and American, interests in the Persian Gulf in a libel case which ran from 1971 to 1980,[67] the protracted nature of which caused Lord Denning to comment that 'it looks like outdoing *Jarndyce v Jarndyce* except that these litigants are not likely to run out of money'.[68] When the litigants first appeared in his court,[69] Lord Denning commented as follows: 'This case takes us to the Persian Gulf...Each of the two Sheikhs had their foreign affairs managed by Britain...these oil companies are international in character. They operate across the world. The City of London is as much interested in their actions as Los Angeles'.[70] When the litigants reappeared four years later,[71] he remarked: 'Two American oil companies are locked in battle....in the days of Empire, the UK used to have some influence in the Persian Gulf and over the Sheikhs that were there'.[72] In 1970, there was a show of force on the part of the United Kingdom. Men from HMS Yarnton had boarded a derrick to prevent Occidental Oil, owned by Armand Hammer, from persuading the Sheikh of Sharjah to change its territorial boundaries. The United Kingdom had withdrawn from the region in 1971. Hammer accused Buttes of conspiring to make Sheikh of Sharjah change his boundaries; Buttes launched a slander action; Hammer relied on the Act of State by United Kingdom in 1970 as part of his defence of justification. Lord Denning was perplexed, observing: 'I do not suppose that Sharjah has any developed system of law such as to permit of an inquiry into the extent of civil liability for conspiracy'.[73] The case returned to his court in 1980.[74] Appalled at the dilatoriness of the proceedings, Lord Denning exclaimed: 'Let it hang about no longer. For goodness sake get rid of it one way or the other'.[75]

Two of the major conflicts of the 1960s and 1970s were involved in shipping cases heard by Lord Denning. As a result of the 1973 Arab-Israeli War, Libya banned all oil exports; the charterers of the tankers claimed repudiation.[76] In March 1966, the South Vietnamese government confiscated a ship, claiming that it was carrying contraband, this led to another shipping dispute[77] which eventually reached Lord Denning's court. He introduced the case laconically: 'In 1966 Vietnam was in turmoil. The man in charge was Marshal Ky'.[78]

One of the major international developments of the 1970s was the rapprochement between the United States and China. On December 15th 1978 the United States formerly recognised the People's Republic as the legitimate government of China. One of the consequences of this rapprochement was a resolution to expel Taiwan from the International

Athletics Association. Lord Denning's court had to consider whether the Association had acted *ultra vires*.[79] It was a matter of construing the rules of an unincorporated association. Lord Denning began by declaring: 'I put on one side any thought of international politics'.[80] Taiwan had been elected a member of the IAA in 1956, China had withdrawn in 1958. Lord Denning pointed out that Wales was a member of the IAA and that, like Wales, Taiwan could be considered a country. He accepted that states such as Iowa could not be members but saw no reason why Taiwan should not be a member. It followed that the election of Taiwan in 1956 was lawful and its expulsion in 1978 was unlawful.

One of the major political events of the 1970s was the Watergate scandal which led to the resignation of President Nixon in August 1974. Lord Denning referred to the scandal, and its legal consequences in two judgments. The first judgment[81] concerned the issue of whether untransmitted film recorded by Independent Television News at the Windsor Park Free Festival, at which there had been serious disturbances, could be used as evidence by police. Lord Denning was anxious that the police should be able to use this evidence in court remarking that 'these new inventions are capable of producing most valuable evidence and the courts should have the means of making them available....we are masters of our own procedure and have authority to adapt it to meet the needs of the time'.[82] To support his argument he quoted, at length, from his own judgment in *Attorney-General v Mulholland and Foster*,[83] a judgment which had resulted in the imprisonment of two journalists for refusing to reveal their sources to the Committee of Inquiry into the Vassall case:

> The journalist puts forward as his justification the pursuit of truth. It is in the public interest, he says, that he should obtain information in confidence and publish it to the world at large, for, by so doing, he brings to the public notice that which they should know. He can expose wrongdoing and neglect of duty which would otherwise go unremedied. He cannot get this information, he says, unless he keeps the source of it secret. The mouths of his informants will be closed to him, if it is known that their identity will be disclosed. So he claims to be entitled to publish all his information without ever being under any obligation, even when directed by the court or a judge, to disclose whence he got it. It seems to me that the journalists put the matter much too high. The only profession that I know which is given a privilege from disclosing information to a court of law is the legal profession, and then it is not the privilege of the lawyer but of his client. Take the clergyman, the banker or the medical man. None of these is entitled to refuse to answer when directed to by a judge. Let me not be mistaken. The judge will respect the confidences which each member of

these honourable professions receives in the course of it, and will not direct him to answer unless not only it is relevant but also it is a proper and, indeed, necessary question in the course of justice to be put and answered. A judge is the person entrusted, on behalf of the community, to weigh these conflicting interests—to weigh on the one hand the respect due to confidence in the profession and on the other hand the ultimate interest of the community in justice being done or, in the case of a tribunal such as this, in a proper investigation being made into these serious allegations. If the judge determines that the journalist must answer, then no privilege will avail him to refuse.[84]

He then referred to a case arising from the Watergate affair, *Democratic National Committee v McCord*[85] which, he conceded, pointed in the other direction, towards allowing ITN to refuse to hand over their film to the police:

Democratic National Committee v McCord [D.D.C. 1973] 356 F. Supp. 1394 involved an attempt to compel reporters to reveal the identity of sources who supplied information concerning the Watergate burglary, information which eventually led to the resignation of President Nixon. In denying disclosure, the court stated that it "cannot blind itself to the possible 'chilling effect' the enforcement of these broad subpoenas would have on the flow of information to the press, and so to the public.[86]

Despite the American precedent, Lord Denning upheld the stance which he had taken in *Attorney-General v Mulholland and Foster*, ordering ITN to hand over the untransmitted film to the Police.

In a later case, concerned with the 1980 Steel Strike[87], Lord Denning referred again to *Attorney-General v Mulholland and Foster* and to *Democratic National Committee v McCord*. Granada Television had obtained confidential documents owned by the British Steel Corporation from a confidential source who thought that the government had blocked a deal between BSC and the leadership of the trade union; based on these documents, Granada had made a TV documentary in which serious allegations were made of government interference in the strike. Referring to the Poulson scandal of the early 1970s, Lord Denning conceded that there could be circumstances in which disclosure of such information could be justified, but he emphasized that broadcasters must behave responsibly in such circumstances. He was not satisfied that Granada had done so. As in the earlier case, Lord Denning referred to *Attorney-General v Mulholland and Foster* and *Democratic National Committee v McCord* and, in the same way, came down against the press.

Lord Denning was well aware of the role of the press in the Watergate scandal and declined to use the American decision, which supported press freedom, as a persuasive precedent. The Watergate affair, as far as Lord Denning was concerned, could not be used to justify what he regarded as irresponsible and politically motivated behaviour by the press. The 1960s and 1970s were a time in which the activities of spies were a subject of considerable public interest. Shortly before the Profumo affair, in January 1963, Kim Philby had absconded from Beirut to the Soviet Union. At the height of the scandal associated with Profumo, the CIA had learnt the truth about Anthony Blunt; this revelation, communicated to the British government at the time of Profumo's resignation, led to a series of 'molehunts' conducted by the MI5 officer Peter Wright who later wrote a book of memoirs called *Spycatcher*. In the course of his report into the Profumo affair, Lord Denning had, for the first time, openly acknowledged the existence of the Security Services, whose identity and activities had hitherto been a closely kept secret[88]. At the end of the 1970s, and beginning of the 1980s, the exposure of Anthony Blunt led to a deluge of stories in the press concerning the activities of spies culminating in the *Spycatcher* affair of the mid 1980s which revealed the full extent to which the Cambridge spies - Philby, Burgess, Maclean, Blunt and Cairncross - had penetrated the British establishment. On three occasions, Lord Denning's court was directly involved in issues emanating from these events.

In December 1960, Dr Robert Soblen, a psychiatrist who had immigrated to the United States from Lithuania in 1940, was arrested by the FBI and charged with having committed espionage in wartime, an offence which carried the death sentence. In August 1961, he was sentenced to life imprisonment but released on bail pending appeal. At that time he was diagnosed with leukaemia. In June 1962, after his final appeal was rejected, he fled to Israel, relying on the Right of return, the basis of the Israeli state. Expelled from Israel, he stabbed himself on the plane forcing it to land at Heathrow in London. The Court of Appeal refused his application to remain in Britain, rejecting the argument that he was entitled to *habeas corpus*.[89] Dr Soblen took a fatal overdose of barbiturates. Lord Denning approached the matter from the starting point that Dr Soblen was an alien: 'There is no doubt that if he is "An alien to whom leave to land is refused," he is properly detained. The whole question in the case, therefore, is whether he is such an alien to whom leave to land has been refused. That he is an alien there can be no question. He is a doctor of medicine. He was born in Lithuania and lived there practising as a doctor of medicine until 1941, but for the last 20 years or thereabouts he has been in the United States of America. So he is not a British subject; he is an alien'.[90] He continued: 'On the facts of this case I see no possible ground for any implication that the applicant was ever given leave to land in the proper sense of the word. To "land" does not mean physically to land a body on the land of this country. To "land" in these articles means to land as a free man, free to move about in this country, either subject to conditions or not. The applicant was certainly not given leave to land in that sense at all. This is really the end of the case'.[91]

A few months after these events, Lord Denning gave judgment in a case arising from the Vassall affair.[92] In 1954, John Vassall, an Admiralty clerk, had been posted to Moscow as Naval Attache to the British Ambassador. Vassall, a homosexual, was compromised by the KGB and blackmailed into handing over classified information. On September 12th 1962, Vassall was arrested, charged with spying and confessed. A tribunal of inquiry, headed by Lord Radcliffe, exonerated the government of any failures with regard to intelligence. In the course of the inquiry, two journalists refused to disclose their sources. The tribunal convicted them of contempt, a sentence which was confirmed by the Court of Appeal. The significance of the case was that it alienated the press to such a degree that, when the allegations about John Profumo began to circulate, the government was unable to control the reaction of the press. The resulting furore came close to bringing down the government. Lord Denning was appointed by Harold Macmillan to investigate the circumstances which had led to Profumo's resignation.

Starting with Soblen, continuing with the Vassall case, Lord Denning found himself at the centre of the controversies concerning espionage which dominated the early 1960s. In 1977, Lord Denning had, once again, to consider the role of the Security Services in a case which, like those of the early 1960s, went to the heart of the British government's concerns about national security.[93] It was not until the early 1970s that information about the code-breaking operation at Bletchley Park began to enter the public domain. Post-war signals intelligence and code-breaking remained a matter of this highest confidentiality. The existence of GCHQ was not a matter of public knowledge. In 1976, the magazine *Time Out* published an article called 'The Eavesdroppers' which revealed, for the first time, the existence of GCHQ. Lord Denning remarked that 'we have been told very little about that journal'[94] but he had no doubt that the workings of GCHQ must be kept secret. Referring back to his experience at the time of the Profumo affair, he said: 'Little has been written and little is known about the work of this service. I had to consider it in the report[95] which I made in

1963 in relation to the former Secretary of State for War, Mr. Profumo. As I there said: 'The function of the Security Service is to defend the Realm as a whole from dangers which threaten it as a whole, such as espionage on behalf of a foreign Power, or internal organisations subversive of the State'.[96] Lord Denning went on to make it plain that the Security Services were solely concerned with national security, they had no authority over individuals; that was a matter for politicians:

> For this purpose it must collect information about individuals and give it to those concerned. But it must not, even at the behest of a Minister or a Government Department, take part in investigating the private lives of individuals except in a matter bearing on the Defence of the Realm as a whole. [I went on to say that] if the Director General of the Security Service ... gets information about a Minister or senior public servant [or, I would now add, a journalist] indicating that he may be a security risk—he should consult the Home Secretary. The Home Secretary then will have to take the responsibility for further action, that is to say, whether to take steps to eliminate the security risk or to put up with it. If a mistake is made, it is the Home Secretary who will be responsible to Parliament.[97]

Lord Denning was quite clear that national security outweighed any other interest: 'It is a case in which national security is involved, and our history shows that, when the state itself is endangered, our cherished freedoms may have to take second place. Even natural justice itself may suffer a set-back'[98]. He added: 'Times of peace hold their dangers too. Spies, subverters and saboteurs may be mingling amongst us, putting on a most innocent exterior. They may be endangering the lives of the men in our secret service'.[99] Confidentiality, in matters of national security was paramount:

> The information supplied to the Home Secretary by the Security Service is, and must be, highly confidential. The public interest in the security of the realm is so great that the sources of the information must not be disclosed, nor should the nature of the information itself be disclosed, if there is any risk that it would lead to the sources being discovered. The reason is because, in this very secretive field, our enemies might try to eliminate the source of information. So the sources must not be disclosed. Not even to the House of Commons. Nor to any tribunal or court of inquiry or body of advisers, statutory or non-statutory, save to the extent that the Home Secretary thinks safe. Great as is the public interest in the freedom of the individual and the doing of justice to him, nevertheless in the last resort it must take second place to the security of the country itself. So much so that arrests have not been made, nor proceedings instituted, for fear that it

may give away information which must be kept secret. This is in keeping with all our recent cases about confidential information. When the public interest requires that information be kept confidential, it may outweigh even the public interest in the administration of justice.[100]

The case specifically concerned the deportation of an American citizen, Mark Hosenball, who, like Dr Soblen, was an alien. Lord Denning was clear about the way in which such people should be treated: 'If they are British subjects, we must deal with them here. If they are foreigners, they can be deported. The rules of natural justice have to be modified in regard to foreigners here who prove themselves unwelcome and ought to be deported'.[101]

It is clear from these three cases that, as far as Lord Denning was concerned, when it came to national security, the rights of the individual, and the freedom of the press, took second place to the defence of the realm. His report on the Profumo affair, while admitting the existence of the Security Services, said very little about them. By 1977, fourteen years later, in Lord Denning's judgment, nothing had changed. National security was not a matter for public discussion; aliens who threatened it were given short shrift.

Lord Denning called his Report into the resignation of John Profumo his 'most important case'.[102] By a strange irony, one of the first cases which he heard as Master of the Rolls concerned a Whitsun Fair at Wraysbury in Buckinghamshire, near Windsor and Runnymede, where Christine Keeler had lived as a girl.[103] Oddly, another of the first cases which he head as Master of the Rolls concerned Harley Street osteopaths.[104] Stephen Ward practiced as an osteopath in Devonshire Street, just off Harley Street. Keeler had lived with Ward, and enjoyed her affairs with John Profumo and Eugene Ivanov, close by in Wimpole Mews.

Christine Keeler lived in a converted railway carriage which had been set on wheels. It was not precisely a caravan but near enough. In the early 1960s, as a result of the post-war housing problems, many people lived in caravans. Caravans were also popular as a means of accommodating holiday makers by the seaside. In 1960, the Caravan Sites and Control of Development Act had been passed in order to regulate the large number of caravan sites which had sprung up over Britain since the War. Between 1964 and 1969, Lord Denning heard a large number of cases concerning enforcement notices authorized by the 1960 Act and other matters ranging from rating to rights of way which had arisen as a result of the growth in the numbers of caravan sites.[105] Lord Denning noted the complexity of the

Act and the scope which it gave to challenges by those who wished to continue living on caravan sites which local authorities sought to close: 'It is an unfortunate feature of the legislation about caravans that it is exceedingly complicated. It is very easy to get lost in the maze of procedure that it sets down. Even the most diligent of planning authorities must be discouraged from taking proceedings against infringers. There seems to be no end of obstacles which the ingenuity of lawyers can place in their way'.[106]

The damage caused by the War was still visible in the early 1960s. Not only did this contribute to the housing shortages which led to the proliferation of caravan sites, it also created the need for new development and rebuilding. Wartime bomb damage is specifically mentioned in a number of cases heard by Lord Denning.[107] Slum clearance is another prominent theme in cases of the 1960s and 1970s.[108] Lord Denning was not impressed by the quality of Parliament's attempts to regulate this area: 'I must say that rarely have I come across such a mass of obscurity, even in a statute. I cannot conceive how the ordinary person can be expected to understand it. So deep is the thicket, that before the Lands Tribunal, both of the very experienced counsel lost their way.....It might happen to anyone in this jungle'.[109]

In a notable case of the 1970s, Lord Denning made plain his distaste for some of the activities of the developers. The case concerned a demonstration in May 1975 by social workers outside an estate agent's offices in Islington.[110] In a strong dissenting judgment which supported the right of the social workers to demonstrate, adverting pointedly to the Peterloo Massacre of 1819 where the right to demonstrate had been disregarded by the magistrates who ordered the Yeomanry to charge an unarmed crowd with fatal results, Lord Denning referred, disparagingly, to an 'invasion of professional people', a 'middle class influx' which had changed the character of the area. He continued: 'some years ago Islington was run down in the world.....In recent years Islington has become a desirable area.....Property men have stepped in. They have bought up houses and persuaded tenants to leave. Now they are occupied by families who are well to do...a group of social workers deplored this development'.[111] The future Prime Minister Tony Blair was one of these 'professional' invaders who attracted Lord Denning's distaste.

Legal issues arose from the planning of new developments. Lord Denning had to consider the impact of the development of Basingstoke on the property of Lord Camrose.[112] Lord Denning's lack of sympathy with development was made particularly clear in a case concerned with the development of Milton Keynes.[113] He began his judgment thus: 'In 1962 life was peaceful in Buckinghamshire. We mean in the northern part of it. Bletchley was the little market town serving the villages and farms round about...He [Mr Bernard Myers] made of it a place to be envied'[114] ...but the peace was doomed'.[115] The Walton Manor Estate, the future home of the Open University, was subjected to a compulsory purchase order by the Milton Keynes Development Corporation. The problem confronting the court concerned the quantum of compensation. The compensation could not include an estimate of the value added to the site by the proposed development involving Hoechst Ltd and the Open University. As Lord Denning put it: 'The valuation has to be done in an imaginary state of affairs in which there is no scheme...he must let his imagination take flight to the clouds. He must conjure up a land of make-believe, where there has not been, nor will not be, a brave new town, but where there is to be supposed the old order of things continuing'.[116]

Lord Denning's sympathies were with 'the old order of things continuing' but the Court of Appeal had to respond to the needs of a rapidly changing, ever more modern world. During the 1960s, when Lord Denning was Master of the Rolls, Britain enjoyed a consumer boom, a phenomenon reflected in the number of cases concerning the hire-purchase of motor vehicles heard by Lord Denning between 1963 and 1971.[117] Lord Denning himself was not a driver. Confronted by a situation in which a husband used his wife's car to give a lift to a friend after an evening spent together in a pub and then crashed the car, an accident in which both died, Lord Denning found that the wife was vicariously liable for the accident and its consequences. In giving his judgment he expressed his own view about the nature of the motor car: 'Whenever the law imposes vicarious liability, it does so for reasons of social policy, reasons which commend themselves to the people at large....it is distributed amongst the community in a way that is fair to all....A motor vehicle is a powerful engine of death and destruction....when I was first called to the Bar the law was still the same as it was in the days of horses and carts...In the 1920s the motor vehicle made its tremendous impact'.[118]

The rapid growth in the number of cars on the road was reflected in vigorous, often cut-throat competition between the big oil companies for access to a rapidly developing market. This commercial battle was reflected in a series of cases, mainly in the 1960s, heard by Lord Denning concerning *solus* agreements whereby the big oil companies sought to control as many garages and petrol stations as they could by negotiating deals, often based on financial inducements, with garage and petrol station proprietors, on the basis that they agreed to be supplied exclusively by a particular oil company.[119] These deals, raising serious questions concerning restraint of trade, were regularly considered by the Court of Appeal. Lord Denning described the situation thus: 'Very few of the garages or filling stations in England and Wales are 'free' to buy and sell any brand of petrol that they like. Most of them are 'tied'...so as you go on your way you may pass a garage or filling station which is tied to Shell, the next one to Esso and so on'.[120] Rarely impressed by *solus* agreements, favouring the traditional independent trader rather than the big oil companies, he commented pointedly in one case: 'There is quite a small garage in Cheshire called Lostock Garage'. Geoffrey Clark runs it as his father did before.[121] Lord Denning was determined to prevent the big oil companies from exploiting the small, independent trader: 'The law does not permit a man to barter away his freedom for money, no matter whether it be by cash down, or by way of loan, or a mortgage'.[122] Striking down the *solus* agreement, he pointedly referred to such agreements amounting to a 'badge of slavery' by invoking an earlier case when a man mortgaged his earnings to a moneylender, agreeing that he would not change his job until repaid.[123]

The consumer boom of the 1960s was not just a matter of motor cars. Many other new scientific and technological developments affected people's lives; some of them were the subjects of litigation heard before Lord Denning. Before the 1960s, chicken was relatively expensive but the introduction of battery farming changed that, turning chicken into a cheap, easily available form of protein. Two cases concerning the rateable value of broiler houses were heard in Lord Denning's court.[124] In one of the cases, where the plaintiff was appealing against a decision to deny broiler houses an exemption, Lord Denning adopted a traditional approach to agricultural matters which suggested skepticism about the new, intensive, methods of farming: 'The only agricultural operations in this area [Local Government Act 1929] are the ordinary occupations of ploughing, sowing, grazing of animals and the like. They have nothing to do with the broiler house....one must always find some connexion between the use of the buildings and the agricultural operations on the land'.[125]

New artificial fabrics were the subject of consideration in his court; in 1967, a tax case concerned the status of 'a new fibrous material which they called Terylene'.[126] More ominously, the dangerous side effects of two drugs – Thalidomide and Primodos – were the subject of extended litigation,[127] the first in relation to damages and a contempt of court committed by a newspaper, the second with regard to a television programme drawing attention to the perils inherent in its use. In 1966 Lord Denning had to deal with a new invention, which is now all too familiar: the Ansaphone. He commented that 'it is something of a 'robot'.

It operates when there is no-one in the house to answer a telephone call'.[128] In 1971, his court was confronted with the legal implications of a mistake made by a computer: 'The computer is not infallible', noted Lord Denning, and then quoted the evidence of a witness who remarked that 'computers are fast, reliable and stupid. Human beings are slow, unreliable and intelligent'. Lord Denning continued: 'When controverted by human evidence, the computer cannot speak. It cannot give evidence. It may be disbelieved. The judge here thought that the computer had made a mistake. He found that in two cases at least the computer had failed to include the notes. He accepted the evidence of the farmers, who were respectable and responsible men'.[129] Lord Denning concurred with the judge.

The development of cheap air travel was also the subject of litigation in Lord Denning's court. A rating case in 1962 was an indication of the expansion of Heathrow.[130] In 1977, Lord Denning's decision in the Laker Airways case[131] was a landmark on the road to cheap air travel, opening the door to competition and the development of 'no frills' budget airlines. Lord Denning was clearly impressed by Freddie Laker: 'Mr. Laker is a man of enterprise. He has an exciting project for travel by air'.[132]

The development of the package holiday industry also figured in two judgments of the 1970s in which Lord Denning awarded damages in contract for what amounted to emotional distress consequent on the poor quality of the holiday provided by the travel company. These judgments acknowledged that, in an increasingly driven and commercial society, when people were coming to treat their holidays as one of the most important aspects of their lives, the idea, image and dream of the holiday mattered as much, if not more, than anything else. Disappointment in these matters could be emotionally disastrous to the victims who worked hard all year round looking forward to an escape from reality. In the first of these cases,[133] Mr Jarvis, a hard working solicitor aged 35, had booked a winter sports holiday. The holiday turned out to be a great disappointment:

> There was no welcome party. The ski-runs were some distance away and no full length skis were available except on two days in the second week. The hotel owner did not speak English and in the second week there was no one to whom the plaintiff could talk. The cake for tea was only potato crisps and dry nutcake. There was not much entertainment at night; the yodler evening consisted of a local man in his working clothes singing a few songs very quickly, and the hotel bar was an unoccupied annexe open only on one evening[134].

At the beginning of his judgment Lord Denning read out an extract from the brochure:

> HOUSE PARTY CENTRE with special resident host ... Mörlialp is a most wonderful little resort on a sunny plateau ... Up there you will find yourself in the midst of beautiful alpine scenery, which in winter becomes a wonderland of sun, snow and ice, with a wide variety of fine ski-runs, a skating-rink and an exhilarating toboggan run ... Why did we choose the Hotel Krone ... mainly and most of all, because of the "GEMUTLICHKEIT" and friendly welcome you will receive from Herr and Frau Weibel ... The Hotel Krone has its own Alphütte Bar which will be open several evenings a week ... No doubt you will be in for a great time, when you book this houseparty holiday ... Mr. Weibel, the charming owner, speaks English[135].

He described Mr Jarvis's ordeal in some detail, noting that:

> There were many other matters, too. They appear trivial when they are set down in writing, but I have no doubt they loomed large in Mr Jarvis's mind, when coupled with the other disappointments. He did not have the nice Swiss cakes which he was hoping for. The only cakes for tea were potato crisps and little dry nutcakes. The yodler evening consisted of one man from the locality who came in his working clothes for a little while, and sang four or five songs very quickly.[136]

Lord Denning had no hesitation in awarding Mr Jarvis damages for mental distress, a notable development in the scope of damages in contract. In setting out his argument Lord Denning made the following point:

> A good illustration was given by Edmund Davies LJ in the course of the argument. He put the case of a man who has taken a ticket for Glyndbourne. It is the only night on which he can get there. He hires a car to take him. The car does not turn up. His damages are not limited to the mere cost of the ticket. He is entitled to general damages for the disappointment he has suffered and the loss of the entertainment which he should have had. Here, Mr Jarvis's fortnight's winter holiday has been a grave disappointment. It is true that he was conveyed to Switzerland and back and had meals and bed in the hotel. But that is not what he went for. He went to enjoy himself with all the facilities which the defendants said he would have. He is entitled to damages for the lack of those facilities, and for his loss of enjoyment.[137]

The other case involved a holiday in Ceylon.[138] Lord Denning introduced his judgment thus:

> Mr Jackson is a young man, in his mid-twenties. He has been very successful in his business. He is married with three small children. In November 1970 there were twin boys of three years of age; and his wife had just had her third child. He had been working very hard. They determined to have a holiday in the sun. He decided on Ceylon[139].

He then described the reality of this dream holiday:

> They were greatly disappointed. Their room had not got a connecting door with the room for the children at all. The room for the children was mildewed—black with mildew, at the bottom. There was fungus growing on the walls. The toilet was stained. The shower was dirty. There was no bath. They could not let the children sleep in it. So for the first three days they had all the family in one room. The two children were put into one of the single beds and the two adults in the other single bed. After the first three days they were moved into what was said to be one of the best suites in the hotel. Even then, they had to put the children in to sleep in the sitting room and the parents in the bedroom. There was dirty linen on the bed. There was no private bath but only a shower; no mini-golf course; no swimming pool, no beauty salon, no hairdressers' salon. Worst of all was the cooking. There was no choice of dishes. On some occasions, however, curry was served as an alternative to the main dish. They found the food very distasteful. It appeared to be cooked in coconut oil. There was a pervasive taste because of its manner of cooking[140].

Lord Denning had no hesitation in awarding damages for the distress and disappointment caused by an experience that is not unfamiliar to contemporary tourists. Whereas Mr Jarvis had been a single man of 35, on this occasion, the quantum of damage included the distress of Mr Jackson's wife and children; the whole family was compensated for their disappointment. By 1975, Lord Denning had established the principles on which such holiday makers, of which there would be countless thousands, even millions, over the coming years, could receive redress for ruined excursions.

There were other indications of the development of a more vigorously commercial society in cases appearing before Lord Denning. A case about Sunday trading in 1977[141] led to him remark: 'This case is about an activity which has developed a great deal lately, Sunday market trading'.[142] The case was indicative of a growing tendency to flout the rules which prevented Sunday trading, a tendency which was eventually, after a series of flagrant breaches in the law condoned by the authorities, legitimized by statute in the late 1980s; a surrender to flagrant illegality which destroyed forever the English Sunday, creating the relentless, year round, indulgence in shopping which is a deleterious feature of contemporary English life. The development of containerization which drastically changed the nature of English dock work, enhancing the development of commerce, but leading to bitter industrial conflict through the 1960s and 1970s was also reflected in a series of cases heard in Lord Denning's court.[143]

Fierce competition in the newspaper industry leading to closures of established titles, bitter industrial conflict and, in the 1980s, the domination of the industry by the relentlessly commercial, trivialized and ferociously amoral world of tabloid journalism, was evident in cases heard by Lord Denning. During the 1960s and early 1970s Lord Denning heard a series of cases concerned with restrictive practices by the newspaper industry.[144] In the 1970s, the cases were concerned with strikes and bitter industrial conflict, culminating in the closure of The Times for a year in 1978.[145] The growth of celebrity culture, the daily *pabulum* of the tabloid press, was also evident in cases heard before Lord Denning. Contractual disputes led to the appearance of the pop musicians Fleetwood Mac and Rod Stewart before Lord Denning.[146] In 1977, some well-known popular entertainers - Tom Jones, Engelbert Humperdinck and Gilbert O'Sullivan - attempted, unsuccessfully, to use the law of confidence[147] to prevent disclosures about what Lord Denning described as 'a very unsavoury incident on a Jumbo jet'; the protagonists were 'inebriated' and 'behaved outrageously'; there were 'discreditable incidents'.[148] Lord Denning believed that the public had a right to know what had transpired in the course of the 'very unsavoury incident on a Jumbo jet': 'As there should be 'truth in advertising' so there should be truth in publicity....the public should not be misled'.[149]

Lord Denning also had to deal with the problem of 'bootlegging'.[150] He described the practice thus:

> If you would like a caption for this case, I can suggest it. It is 'Pop Artists want to stop bootleggers'. It needs explanation for the innocents. Take a popular group who play and sing live in a theatre or in a broadcasting studio. They give an exciting performance....there is a person in the audience or beside the wireless set who is listening to the performance. He has in his hand or his pocket one of the latest scientific devices. It is a tiny machine by which he records on tape this exciting performance. It is called a condenser microphone. Having recorded it on the one tape, he then uses the tape to make hundreds of copies and sell them in the form of cassettes

and cartridges or gramophone records. Sometimes these are poor in quality. Sometimes they are as good as the records made by the recording companies themselves.....No matter how brilliant the performance, which no one else could rival, nevertheless it is so intangible, so fleeting, so ethereal, that it is not protected by the law of copyright.....Those who engage in this trade are called 'bootleggers'. That is a term which was coined in the United States a hundred years ago. Those engaged in illicit trading in liquor used to hide it in the upper part of their tall boots, the leg of the boot.[151]

The consumers of popular music, indeed of the produce of the 'bootleggers', were the young, in particular students. The growing presence of the 'student' in English life can be traced through a series of judgments in Lord Denning's court. The expansion of the universities, and of student places, was apparent in a case of 1964.[152] Lord Denning's judgment, which concerned a lease in Tavistock Square which would enable UCCA, which processed applications for university places, to move into larger premises, revealed that the number of students had grown from 70,000 in October 1955 to 190,000 in October 1961, two years before the Robbins Report which recommended further, dramatic expansion in student numbers and the opening of a series of 'new' universities.

A case in 1970[153] revealed one particular aspect of the impact of this growth in student numbers. The Electoral Officer for Cambridge had ruled that only scholars and exhibitioners, as members of the foundations of their colleges, would be considered as residents for the purposes of Parliamentary elections. In 1970, for the first time, eighteen year olds would be able to vote. This meant that, potentially, large numbers of students might wish to vote in their university town rather than at their home address. Lord Denning decided that the quality of residence of university students in towns and cities where there were universities amounted to a 'considerable degree of permanence'. However, the issue that decided him in favour of allowing university students to vote in their university constituencies was that currently students whose parents were not domiciled in the UK could vote in their university constituency; if students currently resident in the UK were not allowed to vote in their university constituency then, in Lord Denning's mind., an unacceptable anomaly would occur.

In 1975, Lord Denning had to deal with direct political action by students rather than the civilised issue of the Parliamentary ballot. He opened his judgment thus: 'This is the first case we have had in this court of a sit-in of students at a university...the majority did not approve of what was done...the examination programme was going to begin'.[154] Lord Denning also had to deal with the problem of students who claimed Supplementary Benefit when their grants ran out.[155] He noted that 'these are the first cases we have had under the Supplementary Benefit Act 1966. In each case it is a student who makes a claim'. Deciding that the Supplementary Benefits Tribunal should decide whether on not the claim was valid rather than the Court of Appeal, he remarked that Supplementary Benefit was an 'important part of the edifice of social welfare...this great piece of social welfare....should not become a happy hunting ground for lawyers'.[156] Lord Denning also had to consider whether Student Railcards should be rated at 0% for the purposes of VAT.[157]

The cases heard in Lord Denning's court registered the growth of crime as well as the rapid pace of social change. Peter Rachman enjoyed a notorious career as a slum landlord in Notting Hill, featuring as a bit player in the Profumo scandal. One of his enforcers, Norbert Fred Rondel, was the plaintiff in a notable case of 1966[158] which determined that barristers could not be sued for their actions in court. Rondel was a colourful character. He was employed as a rent collector and caretaker by Peter Rachman. On April 5th 1959, at 2.30 am, after a dance at 13 St Stephen's Gardens in Notting Hill, he bit off the doorkeeper's ear. Charged with assault and grievous bodily harm he was given a dock brief. Six years later he sued his barrister for negligence, arguing that the witnesses had not been properly cross-examined and that the barrister had failed to establish that Rondel was legally on the premises as rentcollector. Lord Denning summed up the situation as follows: 'He was looking for prostitution and acted in self-defence....he claims to be an expert in Judo and Karate. He said: 'I tore his hand in half and bit part of his ear off'. Even before the court he exulted in his achievement. He said 'it was difficult in cold blood but I can demonstrate it'. We did not accept his offer'.[159]

The Great Train Robbery of 8th August 1963, considered to be the 'crime of the century' by the popular press at the time, featured in a series of cases heard before Lord Denning. 'A suburban housewife reveals how she was caught up in the great mailbag plot' was the headline in *The People* on July 29th 1964. Douglas Gordon Goody brought a libel action against Mrs Karin Field who said that she had been 'forced to help gang get away with haul'.[160] The problem was that a decision in the Court of Appeal in 1943, *Hollington v F. Hewthorn and Co. Ltd.*,[161] which was binding, had determined that, for the purposes of a libel action, a criminal conviction was not evidence of guilt. 'I argued that case myself',[162] observed Lord Denning. He had tried to persuade the court that conviction was evidence of guilt. He failed. 'I thought that the decision was wrong at the time', he remarked.[163] To get round the problem, Lord Denning allowed *The People* to amend their defence which had hitherto been based on justification. If the defence was amended previous convictions would be relevant to mitigation of damage, 'they are the raw material on which bad reputation is built up'.[164] In a related case,[165] a claim for trial by jury with regard to a suit of action for 'money had and received' following a robbery, Lord Denning ruled that the trial should be heard before a judge without a jury because 'his honour and integrity is no longer at stake. It is gone altogether'.[166] Had the case been heard before a jury then, following *Hollington* his criminal conviction would not be admissible and he would be more likely to get off than if he was heard before a judge alone.[167]

The Great Train Robbery came up in another case heard before Lord Denning. Money from a story about the robbery had been paid to the wife of Charles Frank Wilson, one of the robbers, to pay for an insurance policy. This created a problem when the couple divorced which had to be considered by Lord Denning.[168] The story had been sold to the *News of the World* in 1968 for £39,000. In 1974, Mrs Wilson, who was living in Canada, faced a tax demand from the British authorities. The question was whether the payment for the story was a *chose in action* and therefore a taxable source of income or a right to demand payment for sum agreed in return for information, in which case it would not be taxable. Lord Denning decided that the payment was taxable.

The Mafia, the ultimate criminal gang of that era, showed up in a libel case,[169] involving the *Daily Mail*, about a bid for Butlins holiday camps. In an article published on 5th December 1968, the *Daily Mail* had referred to a 'mafia like bid', claiming that 'American gangsters could end up owning London'. Lord Denning felt it necessary to explain the meaning of the word 'Mafia': 'They assumed that everyone knows what the 'Mafia' is. I suppose most people do. The 'Mafia', we are told, used to be the name of a Sicilian Secret Society, but it has now come to designate a gang of American criminals, some of whom are of Italian origin'.[170]

Gambling, and the failure of the law to effectively regulate an activity which Lord Denning considered to be highly detrimental to the good ordering of society, was a major theme of his judgments during the 1960s and 1970s.[171] In a case concerned with Pool Betting,[172] Lord Denning noted that the Common Law had always condemned gaming houses. Referring to the 1541 Unlawful Games Act and the 1744 Gaming Act, he remarked that Blackstone had called it 'this destructive vice'.[173] However, attempts to regulate this vice had signally failed, the gamblers too quick witted; in particular the 1960 Betting and Gaming Act had 'lamentably failed to achieve' its object.[174]

Lord Denning was equally concerned about the failure of the law to effectively regulate the display and distribution of pornography, a serious problem during the 1960s and 1970s, which led to a number of cases in the Court of Appeal.[175] He declared that 'the law of England has always condemned pornography and sought to suppress it'.[176] In a lengthy excursus on recent cases concerned with the control of pornography, Lord Denning made it quite clear that the Obscene Publications Act 1959 had completely failed to control pornography and that the 'expert witness' defence in particular had created a loophole through which pornographic works had been able to be widely disseminated. He was scathing about a series of recent judgments in which works which 'I should have pronounced....extremely obscene', had not been prosecuted on the grounds that they were of therapeutic value. In his opinion an 'immense amount of time, manpower and money' had been wasted' which 'had done nothing to stop pornography'.[177] Confident that the magistrates would 'know pornography when they see it', he advised that the police should make more use of the Customs and Excise and Post Office Acts which would enable them to deal with pornography by avoiding the problems created by the Obscene Publications Act 1959 which, despite its apparent intention, 'had done nothing to stop pornography'. However, while admitting that the plaintiff, in asking for a *mandamus* to oblige the Police to enforce the law, had 'a point worthy of serious consideration', Lord Denning concluded that the Police were doing as much as could be expected and that it was for Parliament to change the law so as to make it possible for pornography to be eliminated from society: 'The police may well say to Parliament: 'Give us the tools and we will finish the job'[178]......without efficient tools[179], they cannot be expected to stamp it out'.[180]

On 16th January 1973, Lord Denning had to consider an application to prevent the showing of a film by Andy Warhol on television. According to the *News of the World* and the *Sunday Mirror*, whose journalists had not seen the film, it was 'the most permissive shocker to be shown on British screens'. Transvestism, lesbianism and fat girls exposing their breasts and sitting on the toilet would be shown on British screens for the first time.[181] When he saw the film, Lord Denning commented that it was 'dreary and dull', concerned with 'perverts and homosexuals who surround Mr Warhol' but 'taken as a whole it is not offensive'. He concluded that the lurid bits livened up the dullness.[182] However, despite his views as a judicial film critic, he noted that there were 'thousands sitting at home watching. All were entitled to have their privacy respected'.[183] 'They should always remember that there is a silent majority of good people who say little but view a lot. Their feelings are to be respected as well as those of the vociferous minority who, in the name of freedom, shout for ugliness in all its forms. So let the programme be shown. We will not stop it'.[184] The reference to the 'silent majority' was an allusion to a term used by Richard Nixon in a speech to the American people on November 3rd 1969.[185]

From the time of the Seamen's strike in July 1966, Britain faced a series of increasingly severe economic problems. The initial attempts of the Labour government to deal with these problems led to litigation in Lord Denning's court. A series of disputes over the interpretation of the Prices and Incomes Act[186] and Selective Employment Tax[187] of 1966 ended up in the Court of Appeal. Commenting on the Prices and Incomes Act, Lord Denning remarked that although they were 'no doubt justified by the economic conditions of the country at that time', with regard to the particular agreement before the court, the controls desired by the government were 'not justified by law'.[188] He continued, observing that 'the draftsman of the Act of 1966 was, it was suggested, a learned pedant who used words with meticulous accuracy...I decline to accept this invitation...We are not the slaves of words but their masters....no man's contractual rights are to be taken away by an ambiguity in a statute'.[189] Lord Denning was determined to ensure that the sloppy drafting of the Act could not be used to deny employees their right to a properly negotiated pay rise.

The continuing economic instability engendered serious industrial conflict and, during the 1970s, major strikes which threatened the future of the country. Many of these disputes ended up in the Court of Appeal. In 1971, the Conservative government attempted to use the law to control the power of the trade unions. The Industrial Relations Act 1971 led to even more serious conflict; Lord Denning's court played a major role in attempting to resolve the disputes which followed the introduction of the Act. In a case[190] which was heard before the Act became law, Lord Denning remarked, showing his sympathy for the principle that the trade unions should be subjected to regulation, that 'in 1871 the legal position of a trade union was not settled' but in the 1950s, *Bonsor v Musicians' Union* 1955 3 AllER 518 had settled that it was a legal entity 'which can sue and be sued and make contracts in the same way as any other legal entity'.[191]

The Industrial Relations Act came into force on February 28th 1972. It was soon put to the test. On 16th April 1972, acting under powers conferred by the Act, the Secretary of State for Employment imposed a 'cooling off period' on the rail unions, ASLEF, NUR and TESSA, ordering them to suspend their strike and hold a ballot before taking further strike action. This order was challenged by the unions. The Industrial Relations Court endorsed the Minister's action. The appeal[192] was heard by Lord Denning who made his feelings plain: 'There was much dislocation of services...misery, discomfort and loss...no possible doubt that the country is faced with an emergency...wages are to be paid for services rendered not for producing deliberate chaos...we are concerned here with a grave threat to the national economy'.[193]

The climax came on 16th June 1972.[194] On 14th June, the Industrial Relations Court issued an order for the committal to prison of three dockers for contempt; they had refused, offensively, to obey an order by the court to desist from industrial action. The dockers were sent to Pentonville jail. Relishing their status as martyrs, they did not challenge their imprisonment. On Friday 16th June, their case was heard by the Court of Appeal after Lord Denning had been approached by Peter Pain QC. The Secretary of the Industrial Relations Court had asked the Official Solicitor, who was empowered to intervene in the legal process on behalf of children, the incapable and prisoners, to consider the case of the Pentonville 3 on Monday 19th June. Lord Denning decided to take immediate action in order to defuse a situation which had the potential to escalate into a General Strike.

Lord Denning went straight to the point: 'The three dockers have not applied themselves, nor have they instructed anyone to apply on their behalf'. However, the Official Solicitor had authority to apply to the court 'on behalf of any person in the land who is committed to prison and does not move the court on their own behalf'.[195] Lord Denning, and his fellow judges in the Court of Appeal, overturned the conviction of the men for contempt by the Industrial Relations Court. The men were released. The crisis was over.

The Labour government elected in 1974, repealed the Industrial Relations Act, replacing it with the Trade Union and Labour Relations Act 1974. In a judgment concerned with the interpretation of that Act,[196] Lord Denning remarked: 'This case arises out of paragraphs 6 and 8 of section one of the Trade Union and Labour Relations Act 1974. I am not going to read it out. It is far too complicated for anyone to understand except a lawyer specializing in the task'.[197] Commenting on the 1974 Act in another judgment he observed that 'Parliament has conferred more freedom from restraint on trade unions than has ever been known to the law before. All legal restraints have been lifted so that they can now do as they will'.[198]

Lord Denning played an important role in preventing the industrial conflict of the early 1970s from getting out of control. His intervention in June 1972 may well have prevented a General Strike which would have had unpredictable consequences. In 1973-4, the City of London came close to collapse after a series of so-called 'fringe banks' collapsed and the stock market crashed to its lowest level since 1945, losing 73% of its value between January 1973 and December 1974. The FTSE hit a low of 146.0 on 6 January 1975, a sustained fall from a peak of 543.6 points on 1st May 1972. Lord Denning was anxious to support the reputation of the City of London during this difficult period. His comments on the nature of banking in a case of 1966[199] provide some insight into his approach to the City.

The problem facing the court was that United Dominions Trust, an organisation offering hire-purchase agreements to those who wanted to buy motor cars, while taking deposits and making loans, would be considered to be a moneylender unless it could show evidence to the contrary.[200] Lord Denning began his judgment thus: 'Bankers are a privileged class. They are exempt from the vexations and restrictions which are imposed on other moneylenders. They are an exclusive circle to which entry is limited'.[201] Lord Denning continued, noting that Parliament had never defined a 'bank' or 'banker', never 'told us what is the business of banking'.[202] Invoking the authority of Dr Johnson, he noted that, in his 1755 Dictionary, banks were defined as institutions which collected and utilised money, but there was no mention of cheques. Referring to the Law Reports, he remarked that, between 1910 and the present day [1966] the case law in relation to banks had been dominated by legal analysis of the meaning of the promise to repay embodied in a cheque. The Shorter Oxford English Dictionary entry on banks referred to cheques and current accounts.[203] With regard to the usual characteristics, it seem that United Dominions Trust was not a bank but there were other relevant considerations such as stability, soundness and probity; Parliament would not grant the privileges of a bank to 'a ramshackle concern which had not reserves or whose methods were dubious'.[204]

Lord Denning continued his analysis thus: 'Like many other beings, a banker is easier to recognise than define....reputation may exclude a person from being a banker; so also it may make him one'.[205] He added that 'our commercial law has been founded on the opinion of merchants',[206] noting that Lord Mansfield had empanelled his own special jurymen of the City of London; it followed that if Parliament offered no guidance then the courts should 'look to the reputation of the concern amongst intelligent men of commerce....when merchants have established a course of business which is running smoothly and well with no inconvenience or injustice, it is not for the judges to put a spoke in the wheel and bring it to a halt....so you will find it said for the time of Lord Coke that the law so favours the public good that it will in some cases permit common error to pass for right [see the Fourth Institute p 240]. *Communis error facit jus*, that is to say, when business has been regulated in the faith of it and the position of the parties altered in consequence [Lord Blackburn on several occasions so said], it is a maxim of English law to give effect to everything which appears to have been established for a considerable course of time and to presume that what has been done was of right, and not in wrong'.[207] Lord Denning concluded that United Dominions Trust was a banker by reputation; 'It is not rapacious, extortionate or unmerciful...it is sensible, moderate and reasonable'.[208] In reaching this judgment, Lord Denning adopted a conspicuously deferential attitude towards the City of London, respecting the way it did business, content to use its standards as a guide for the courts.

Deferential as he may have been towards the customs and practices of the City of London, Lord Denning was determined that businessmen and company directors whose standards fell below the requisite standard should be disciplined by the courts. This was made clear in a series of judgments concerned with the practice of 'dividend stripping'.[209] Lord Denning's comments in these cases could be quite acerbic: 'This case shows a series of somewhat surprising transactions between some associated companies'.[210] Whoever would suppose that any trader in his right mind would enter into transactions of this kind'.[211] 'This is yet another case about dividend stripping but of a new kind. It is forward stripping as distinct from backward stripping. He says it is all part of his trade. If so, it is a most discreditable part....It is dividend stripping and nothing else'.[212]

Lord Denning may, like his exemplar Lord Mansfield, have respected the good sense of the men of the City of London but he made little reference to the thoughts of economists, men held in high esteem by the Labour and Conservative governments of the day. However, on two rare occasions, Lord Denning referred to economists by name in his judgments. In one of his judgments concerned with 'dividend stripping', Lord Denning invoked the authority of Adam Smith to support his contention that fixed capital was 'what an owner turns to profit by keeping it in his power'.[213] In a case concerned with dubious transactions by an Italian called Terruzzi on the London Metal Exchange,[214] Lord Denning referred to another economist, John Maynard Keynes. Counsel for the defendant argued that the contracts were not enforceable because they were in violation of Italian exchange control rules; Lord Denning held them to be enforceable because exchange controls were concerned with currency rather than metals. In support of his argument, he referred to the Bretton Woods Conference of 1944 which had established the rules for the international financial system currently in force: 'At this conference the UK was represented by the distinguished economist, John Maynard Keynes'.[215] Noting that, according to his biographer Sir Roy Harrod, Keynes did not like lawyers, Lord Denning pointed out that lawyers played a big part in the Bretton Woods negotiations which were intended to stop the mischief of currency speculation. Illustrating the dangers posed by this mischief, he referred to rulings by Scrutton J in the 1920s. However, the Bretton Woods agreement had placed no restrictions on legitimate trade such as that in metals; it followed that losses in speculation in metals by Terruzzi must be honoured.

At the time of the economic crisis which severely affected the City of London in the mid 1970s, Lord Denning showed considerable concern for its reputation, making notable judgments which supported the right of shareholders to call corrupt and errant company directors to account. A judgment delivered on 21st May 1974,[216] at perhaps the lowest ebb in the fortunes of the City of London since the 1930s, gave vivid expression to Lord Denning's concerns about the reputation of the City of London and his determination to use the authority of the courts to protect it. He began thus: 'Mr Moir works in a stockbroker's office. He has taken on a big fight. He has challenged Dr Wallersteiner, a man of influence in the City of London'.[217] Mr Moir had brought an action of fraud, misfeasance and breach of trust against Dr Wallersteiner who, in an attempt to outmanoeuvre him, had provided no defence for 12 months. Judge Geoffrey Lane, sitting in Chambers, had ordered Dr Wallersteiner to pay £500,000; the order was challenged, Lord Denning's court heard the appeal. His response was vigorous: 'Some say that we should be neutral in the face of public scandal. I say, not so. If we say nothing .....it may be years before the truth is shown'.[218] He continued, invoking the authority of Lord Bacon: 'The principle duty of a judge is to suppress force and fraud....to denounce wrong doing....he speaks for all law-abiding citizens...his words uphold the opinion of the good and shake the confidence of the wicked. By condemning wrongdoing, he reinforces the moral sanction on which law and order so much depend'.[219] He then proceeded to describe the actions of Dr Wallersteiner: 'He made contracts of enormous magnitude on their behalf on a sheet of notepaper without reference to anyone else....the case discloses grave breaches of company law....[he] gained control of the board by means which were quite unlawful...puppet trusts in Liechtenstein....it would so exhaust courage, finances, patience, hope that those who have lost their money would say of this court: 'Suffer any wrong that can be done to you rather than go there'. Something must be done now. We must brook no further delay'.[220] Lord Denning approved the action taken by Geoffrey Lane J., ordering Dr Wallersteiner to pay the £500,000 to Mr Moir forthwith.

A judgment of the following year reiterated his concern for the reputation of City and his determination that shareholders must be able to bring errant company directors to heel.[221] He remarked: 'We have in this court seen cases lately where those in control of a company plunder its funds and then seek to gag the minority. This should not be allowed. Shareholders should be allowed to speak their minds at meetings'.[222]

Lord Denning's court dealt with the consequences of major financial disasters and the flamboyant businessmen who caused them. The collapse of the John Bloom empire in the early 1960s was the subject of one of his judgments.[223] John Bloom had created a profitable business by selling washing machines on hire purchase. He had then had branched out into fridges, televisions and, somewhat improbably, Bulgarian holidays. Bloom slashed his prices by cutting out middleman, making direct sales to the customer. His company was listed on the stock exchange in 1962 but, hopelessly overextended, it collapsed in July 1964. The 'rise and fall of the Bloom empire', as Lord Denning described it,[224] was an augury of the consumer boom of the 1960s.

Captain Robert Maxwell MP, MC, of infamous memory, appeared before Lord Denning in 1970 because of a Board of Trade investigation into the affairs of his Pergamon Press company.[225] Lord Denning was not impressed: 'They demanded further assurances. They had no colour of right to demand them....The judge was merciful to them....If they should seek to take again such unwarranted points, they can expect no mercy'.[226]

Lord Denning was more cautious when it came to one of the most flamboyant businessmen of the day but nonetheless found against him, as he had found against Maxwell. In 1976, following a libel action against *Private Eye*, the recently knighted James Goldsmith, a bizarre beneficiary of Harold Wilson's notorious resignation honours list, attempted to extend the action to include all those who distributed and sold the magazine. In a strong dissenting judgment,[227] Lord Denning disagreed with his brethren who considered that Goldsmith's action had not been directed against *Private Eye* in particular but was merely intended to prevent the circulation of the libel. Lord Denning described *Private Eye* as having an 'original style' and being inclined to make 'colourful allusions', publishing 'caricatures well-known people for the amusement of its readers'. He noted that 'it exposes wrongdoing but sometimes misses the mark and gets sued for libel'. In this particular instance it had made some 'unpleasant insinuations against Mr James Goldsmith'.[228] He went on: 'He has recently been honoured with the distinction of a knighthood. So I will hereafter call him Sir James'.[229] Lord Denning then referred to the alleged libel as concerning allegations about Sir James' associations with Lord Lucan, his failure to co-operate with the police investigation into Lord Lucan's disappearance, his proneness to 'dressing up the balance sheets' and his links to the collapse of Slater-Walker, T. Dan Smith and John Poulson, notorious figures of the day. Lord Denning commented that he was sure that 'everyone will sympathise with Sir James. It was very wrong of *Private Eye* to make these grave imputations against him'. 'He hit back hard'.[230] Goldsmith had sued *Private Eye* for criminal libel, in particular with regard to the allegations concerning Lord Lucan. Lord Denning was taken aback: 'I do not remember such a charge in my time'.[231] However, pointedly referring to his recent judgment in *Wallersteiner v Moir*,[232] he refused to support Goldsmith's attempt to join the distributors and sellers of *Private Eye* to the libel action, calling such a move a blatant 'gagging of press'.[233]

Lord Denning's judgments in the Court of Appeal reflected the high politics and low crimes of the time and also the social and economic changes which were transforming the country. However it is also possible to find traces of a quieter, more sober world in the prose of his judgments; an ordinary English world that was, perhaps, vanishing beneath the turbulent waves of the times, still appears, from time to time, in the pages of the judgments of Lord Denning as recorded in the Law Reports. For example, there were cases concerned with the assignment of pitches in Petticoat Lane:[234]

> Mrs Perilly, who traded under the name of Mrs Celia Franks, had a pitch, no 30, Wentworth Street, E1. Ever since 1942 she had had a licence for that pitch for the sale of hosiery and haberdashery on Sundays only. Year by year she applied for the licence. Year by year she was granted it. Her son helped her there. On 17 November 1970 she died. She was buried the next day, 18 November. On the morrow, 19 November, Mr Monty Perilly, her son, made application for pitch 30, Wentworth Street. You would have thought he had a good claim to it. But on 7 December the committee of the respondent council met and 'with regret' refused Mr Perilly's application, although he and his mother and the family had had that pitch for 30 years. The reason why the committee refused it, and with such regret, was this: a

gentleman called Mr Benny King had got in first. He had gone to the council on 18 November—the day of the funeral—and had put in an application. In it he said that he wanted to sell gramophone records. In answer to the question in which street he wanted to trade, he put 'Any vacant position Petticoat Lane E1'. The justices thought that Mr King had not satisfied that requirement, because on the evidence there is no such street as 'Petticoat Lane'. There may have been a lane of that name in olden times up to about the year 1830. But then the name was changed, and it was called Middlesex Street. It has been Middlesex Street ever since. Nowadays ten streets in that neighbourhood together are often called 'Petticoat Lane'. The Petticoat Lane market is the whole market area comprising these ten streets: Middlesex Street, Wentworth Street, Toynbee Street, Goulston Street, Cobb Street, New Coulston Street, Leyden Street, Bell Lane, Old Castle Street and Strype Street.[235]

Old Mrs Annie Levenson had one of the best pitches in the street market called Petticoat Lane. It was pitch 1. She ran it with the help of her son Harold and his wife Shirley. She had an annual licence for the pitch which was granted by the borough council. But she was getting on in years and the question was: what was to happen to the pitch on her death? By statute she was entitled to nominate a relative to succeed her. In her application for each of the years 1969 and 1970 she nominated her son Harold. But in her application for the year 1971 she nominated no one. The reason was because the borough council stated on the form: 'The relative so specified should NOT be a person holding a current licence in the Tower Hamlets area.' Now old Mrs Levenson's son Harold did hold a licence for another pitch. He held a licence for pitch 107. So old Mrs Levenson did not nominate him. And she could not nominate his wife Shirley because a daughter-in-law does not come within the category of 'relative' entitled to succeed. Likewise in her application for the following year, 1972, old Mrs Levenson nominated no one to succeed, and for the same reasons. But on 27 September 1972 her son and his wife had a baby daughter, Samantha. This baby was a grand-daughter of the old lady and did come within the category of 'relatives' entitled to succeed. So on 10 October 1972, when old Mrs Levenson applied for a renewal of pitch 1, she nominated her grand-daughter Samantha. Four months later, on 13 February 1973, old Mrs Levenson died. On 23 February 1973 Samantha's mother applied in Samantha's name for pitch 1. Someone at the town hall told her that Samantha was too young to be a licence-holder.[236]

There was also the matter of bad behaviour by estate agents in respect of a leasehold.[237] Lord Denning introduced the case as follows: 'Two ladies, Miss Lester and Miss Warrior, who carried on a business known at the Park Hill Café'.[238] He concluded: 'This is plainly an attempt by the agents to get commission contrary to the ordinary understanding of mankind in these matters...the one reason why all this litigation was necessary was because the agents were determined to hold onto the money'.[239] Although refusing his appeal for damages following an accident in which he fell into a hole dug by the London Electricity Board, Lord Denning was gracious to the plaintiff who he described as follows: 'John Haley, is now aged sixty-four. Twenty years ago he suffered a great misfortune. He was hit in the eye by a hard ball and he was rendered completely blind. But he overcame his misfortune with great perseverance and courage'.[240] A rather less worthy plaintiff in a personal injuries case was characterised thus: 'She was always pretty quick off the mark for her cup of tea'. The plaintiff had slipped and fell, she was wearing the wrong kind of shoes; it was 'a piece of misfortune...there was no default by anyone'.[241] In a divorce case, the facts were summarised, poignantly, thus: 'She left a note on the table: Dog at kennels, Chelmsford'.[242] She had left 31 years after being married in the Baptist tabernacle.

Lord Denning's description of the facts in one case brings the whole scene to life. Air Vice-Marshal Bennett wanted to run a civil airport at Blackbushe airport. There had been a Parish meeting but the question was not put to the vote. The Air Vice-Marshall had applied to Lord Denning's court for a declaration that there should be a poll on the issue of the airport; the parish council wanted the land 'to be kept in perpetuity as a public open space'. Lord Denning described the situation as follows: 'It was a noisy meeting...As you might expect of a military man he had considered his plan of campaign beforehand and he demanded a poll...The plaintiff put his case with the utmost ability, courtesy and conscientiousness before us'. Despite his ability, courtesy and conscientiousness, Lord Denning refused the Air Vice-Marshall's appeal.[243] Another plaintiff was more successful. A group of residents challenged an enforcement notice which authorised the demolition of a newly built house. Lord Denning began thus: 'This is a case for expedition. It concerns a part of St. John's Wood in which there are many high class residences'.[244] The appeal succeeded; the street in which the house was situated, near Lord's cricket ground, was renamed Denning Close.

Two plaintiffs appealed particularly strongly to Lord Denning, their plight leading him to make some strong remarks about the legal aid system.[245] One Reeves had bought a photographic business from Mr and Mrs Thew. He did not pay but claimed that Mr and Mrs Thew had been guilty of fraud when they sold the business to him, asking for a grossly inflated price. Lord Denning described Mr Thew as a young man, back from the War, who had started the business in 1945. The husband and wife were 'good honest folk that had never been treated like that before'. A 'hardworking husband and wife ruined by the fact that the other side were granted legal aid'. Lord Denning noted that much contemporary litigation was dominated by legal aid and that people of 'very moderate means' were often unassisted.[246] He continued: 'Unless carefully controlled legal aid may be used unfairly to harm the other side who is not assisted'.[247] In his opinion, legal aid was 'the unacceptable face of British justice'.[248] This was a highly charged phrase. Writing in *The Times* on May 15th 1973, Edward Heath had called the Lonrho affair, involving the flamboyant businessman 'Tiny' or Roland Rowland,[249] 'the unpleasant and unacceptable face of capitalism'.

The abuse of legal aid, a topic which had exercised Lord Denning since the 1960s, was, along with the other matters which attracted his disdain, not least the activities of flamboyant businessmen, a sign all was not for the best in modern England. There were other signs that all was not well, even in the rural shires where Lord Denning had grown up: 'On July 21st 1966 the peace of the ancient borough of Dorchester was disturbed....The people in the court did not like the sound a jukebox in the café. They also objected because the customers relieved themselves on the carpet in the courtyard'.[250] The defendant had built lavatories but 'relations were strained'. There was a public altercation in which abuse was hurled about. The defendant was heard to exclaim: 'Shut up you monkey faced tart'. He received 'a savage blow out of all proportion to the occasion'.[251]

Even the police were not immune from the noisome spirit of discontent.[252] 'Alton[253] is a quiet Hampshire town. Most people sleep well. But at 2.20 am they were awakened'. Three young men were drunk. PC Maynard said that one of them had been struck by a Sergeant and wanted to report it; the Sergeant accused him of being asleep on duty: 'It was a very disturbed night at Alton police station'.[254] Disciplinary proceedings were instituted against PC Maynard. There was a question of natural justice. Should he be given legal representation? Lord Denning felt that he should not. Representation by a fellow police officer would be adequate; as he put it in his Hamlyn Lectures in 1949, the Police are 'such a fine body of men that they do not abuse the powers which they have'; they are of 'excellent character' and are recruited from 'sturdy country stock', able to ensure 'fair play', showing 'calmness in emergency'.[255] Given such views, it was perhaps not surprising, that just two years later, in 1980, in the most notorious judgment of his career, Lord Denning should remark: 'If the six men win, it will mean that the police were guilty of perjury, that they were guilty of violence and threats, that the confessions were involuntary and were improperly admitted in evidence, and that the convictions were erroneous. That would mean that the Home Secretary would have either to recommend they be pardoned or he would have to remit the case to the Court of Appeal under s 17 of the Criminal Appeal Act 1968. This is such an appalling vista that every sensible person in the land would say: 'It cannot be right that these actions should go any further'.[256]

Much had changed in England since Lord Denning became Master of the Rolls in 1962. Perhaps the most disturbing of all these changes was the fact that, by 1982, when he retired, it was clear to many that the police could no longer be trusted. By 1982, statements about the police, like those made by Lord Denning in 1949, were no longer credible.

Notes

[1] The All England Law Reports for 1969 recorded the following cases on this area of law in which Lord Denning passed judgment: *Hewer v Bryant* 1969 3 AllER 578; *Scott v Green* 1969 1 AllER 849; *Greenhalgh v British Railways Board* 1969 2 AllER 114; *Connel v Motor Insurers Bureau* 1969 3 AllER 572

[2] The All England Law Reports for 1968 recorded the following cases on this area of law in which Lord Denning passed judgment: *R v Industrial Injuries Commissioner ex parte Cable* 1968 1 AllER 9; *Cross v British Iron, Steel and Kindred Trades Association* 1968 1 AllER 250

[3] The All England Law Reports for 1966 recorded the following cases on this area of law in which Lord Denning passed judgment: *Dietz v Lennig Chemicals Ltd* 1966 2 AllER 962

[4] The All England Law Reports for 1978 recorded the following cases on this area of law in which Lord Denning passed judgment: *H. Parsons [Livestock] Ltd. v Uttley Ingham and Co. Ltd.* 1978 1 AllER 525; *Western Excavating Ltd. v Sharp* 1978 1 AllER 713; *Howard Marine and Dredging Co. Ltd. v A. Ogden and Sons [Excavators] Ltd.* 1978 2 AllER 1134; *Photo Production Ltd. v Securicor Transport Ltd.* 1978 3 AllER 146; *Staffordshire Area Health Authority v South Staffordshire Waterworks Co* 1978 3 AllER 769; *Gibson v Manchester City Council* 1978 2 AllER 583

[5] The All England Law Reports for 1964 recorded the following case on this area of law in which Lord Denning passed judgment: *Ocean Tramp Tankers Corp. v v/o Sovfracht* 1964 1 AllER 161

[6] The All England Law Reports for 1977 recorded the following cases on this area of law in which Lord Denning passed judgment: *The Siskina* 1977 3 AllER 803; *The Maratha Envoy* 1977 2 AllER 41

[7] The All England Law Reports for 1982 recorded the following cases on this area of law in which Lord Denning passed judgment: *Italmare Shipping Co. v Ocean*

Tanker Co. Inc. 1982 1 AllER 517; *The Weijiang* 1982 2 AllER 437; *Paul Wilson and Co. A/S v Partenreederie Hannah Blumenthal* 1982 3 AllER 394; *European Grain and Shipping Ltd. v Johnston* 1982 3 AllER 989

[8] The All England Law Reports for 1979 recorded the following cases on this area of law in which Lord Denning passed judgment: *Williams and Glyn's Bank v Boland* 1979 2 AllER 697; *Midland Bank Trust Co. Ltd. v Green* 1979 3 AllER 29

[9] The All England Law Reports for 1962 recorded the following case on this area of law in which Lord Denning passed judgment: *Dellafiora v Lester* 1962 3 AllER 393

[10] The All England Law Reports for 1963 recorded the following cases on this area of law in which Lord Denning passed judgment: *Ministry of Agriculture, Fisheries and Food v Jenkins* 1963 2 AllER 147; *Bernays v Prosser* 1963 2 AllER 321; *Shepherd v Lomas* 1963 2 AllER 902

[11] The All England Law Reports for 1971 recorded the following cases on this area of law in which Lord Denning passed judgment: *Peck v Anicar Properties Ltd.* 1971 1 AllER 517; *Wolf v Crutchley* 1971 1 AllER 520; *Shell-Mex and BP Ltd v Manchester Garages Ltd.* 1971 1 AllER 841; *Feather Supplies Ltd. v Ingham* 1971 3 AllER 556 *R v Tottenham District Rent Tribunal ex parte Frazer Bros [Properties] Ltd.* 1971 3 AllER 563; *Central Estates [Belgravia] Ltd. v Woolgar* 1971 3 AllER 347; *Liverpool Corporation v Husain* 1971 3 AllER 651; *Total Oil Great Britain Ltd. v Thompson Garages [Biggin Hill] Ltd.* 1971 3 AllER 1216

[12] The All England Law Reports for 1970 recorded the following cases on this area of law in which Lord Denning passed judgment: *Ministry of Housing and Local Government v Sharp* 1970 1 AllER 1009; *Lever [Finance] Ltd. v Westminster Corporation* 1970 3 AllER 496

[13] The All England Law Reports for 1976 recorded the following cases on this area of law in which Lord Denning passed judgment: *R v Secretary of State for the Environment ex parte Ostler* 1976 3 AllER 90; *Munton v GLC* 1976 2 AllER 815; *DHN Food Distributors Ltd. v London Borough of Tower Hamlets* 1976 3 AllER 462

[14] The All England Law Reports for 1972 recorded the following case on this area of law in which Lord Denning passed judgment: *Bexley Congregational Church Treasurer v London Borough of Bexley* 1972 2 AllER 662

[15] The All England Law Reports for 1967 recorded the following cases on this area of law in which Lord Denning passed judgment: *Re Harmsworth [deceased]* 1967 2 AllER 249; *Campbell v Inland Revenue Commissioners* 1967 2 AllER 625; *Inland Revenue Commissioners v Educational Grants Association* 1967 2 AllER 891; *Mason [Inspector of Taxes] v Innes* 1967 2 AllER 926; *Macsaga Investment Co. Ltd. v Lupton [Inspector of Taxes]* 1967 2 AllER 930; *Murray [Inspector of Taxes] v Imperial Chemical Industries Ltd.* 1967 2 AllER 980; *Scott [Inspector of Taxes] v Ricketts* 1967 2 AllER 1009; *Wiseman v Borneman* 1967 3 AllER 1045

[16] The All England Law Reports for 1965 recorded the following case on this area of law in which Lord Denning passed judgment: *Re Jebb [deceased]* 1965 3 AllER 358

[17] The All England Law Reports for 1973 recorded the following cases on this area of law in which Lord Denning passed judgment: *Hector v Hector* 1973 3 AllER 1070; *Wachtel v Wachtel* 1973 1 AllER 829; *Trippas v Trippas* 1973 2 AllER 1; *Fuller v Fuller* 1973 2 AllER 650; *Kowalczak v Kowalczak* 1973 2 AllER 1042

[18] The All England Law Reports for 1975 recorded the following cases on this area of law in which Lord Denning passed judgment: *Burgess v Rawnsley* 1975 3 AllER 142; *Eves v Eves* 1975 3 AllER 768; *Tanner v Tanner* 1975 3 AllER 776

[19] The All England Law Reports for 1980 recorded the following case on this area of law in which Lord Denning passed judgment: *Hanlon v Law Society* 1980 1 AllER 763

[20] The All England Law Reports for 1974 recorded the following cases on this area of law in which Lord Denning passed judgment: *Balogh v Crown Court at St. Albans* 1974 3 AllER 283; *Danchevsky v Danchevsky* 1974 3 AllER 934

[21] The All England Law Reports for 1981 recorded the following cases on this area of law in which Lord Denning passed judgment: *Grapelli v Derek Block [Holdings] Ltd.* 1981 2 AllER 272; *Hayward v Thompson* 1981 3 AllER 450

[22] Speaking at West Point in December 1962, Dean Acheson observed that 'Great Britain has lost an empire and has not yet found a role', adding that a role based on the Commonwealth 'is about played out'. *The Times* 6th December 1962. In 1965, Acheson went further describing Britain's approach to the Rhodesian crisis as being 'the stupid policy of a bewildered country under a third-rate prime minister'. Hyam, R. *Britain's Declining Empire: The Road to Decolonisation 1918-1968* [Cambridge 2006] p. 327

[23] Macmillan's Conservatives had an overall majority of 100; their largest victory since 1945 until that of Margaret Thatcher in 1983.

[24] Jonathan Miller recalled that Cook did not write the sketch 'out of any sense of indignation…I think he found him rather adorable really'. *Tragically I Was An Only Twin–The Complete Peter Cook* [ed. Cook, W.] [London 2003] p. 43. The sketch, which was performed in the presence of President Kennedy in New York in October 1962, during the Cuban Missile Crisis, can be found on pp. 51-52. Cook's impersonation of the Prime Minister was the first occasion, in recent history, that he had been represented on the stage. When Macmillan came to watch Cook's performance, he improvised thus: 'When I've a spare evening, there's nothing I like better than to wander over to a theatre and sit there listening to a group of sappy, urgent, vibrant satirists with a stupid great grin spread all over my silly old face'. Ibid p. 51 'My impersonation of Macmillan was in fact extremely affectionate,' explained Cook twenty years later, 'I was a great Macmillan fan. He did have this somewhat ludicrous manner, but merely because it was the first time for some years that a living Prime Minister had been impersonated on the stage, a great deal of weight was attached to it'. Ibid p. 51

[25] Reviewing Noel Annan's *Our Age* in *The Independent* on Saturday 6th October 1990, Eric Christiansen memorably and succinctly described the Labour government of 1964-1970: 'The Wisest Fools in Christendom had stormed Downing Street and they quickly relieved the Lord Chamberlain and the public

hangman of their duties. They liberated the homosexuals and then it was all over. Dark, unforeseen shades of inflation, Union power, political corruption, industrial decay, student unrest and racial tension began to gather. The economists were discredited, the planners were hooted, the professors were pelted and the philosophers ignored. In the wings a grim figure was waiting....Margaret Thatcher had weighed Our Age in the balance and found it wanting'.

[26] The obituary of Edward Heath in the *Daily Telegraph* [18.7.05] contained this judgment: 'Sir Edward Heath, who died yesterday aged 89, achieved his great ambition of taking Britain into the European Economic Community, but proved unable to solve the many economic and labour problems which afflicted his administration between 1970 and 1974. The first Conservative Prime Minister to be born the son of a manual worker, Heath pursued his European vision against every discouragement. But in the face of almost continuous crisis he was unable to maintain policy at home. Elected on laissez-faire economics, his government found itself pouring out public money in all directions. Determined to reform industrial relations, he made matters worse through ill-considered legislation. Heath, moreover, conspicuously lacked the ability to charm his way out of trouble: for a leading politician he was an astonishingly inept communicator. His awkward mannerisms - the brusque retort, the shoulders heaving in mirthless laughter - repelled; his speeches were wooden in delivery and banal in phrasing; for almost a year, from November 1972 to October 1973, he gave no television interview. In consequence, "the Grocer" was pilloried as a heartless automaton, contemptuous of the poor and unemployed. In reality, his administration twisted and turned because the kind of Conservatism which Heath espoused - and which appealed to his instincts far more than did the prescriptions of the market-place - was corporatist rather than political, dirigiste rather than democratic. In some respects Heath was a permanent secretary manqué, more at ease with civil servants than with his own Cabinet. His creation of the Central Policy Review Staff, or Think Tank, to help him take the long strategic view, suggested his impatience with orthodox politics. Heath also differed from most prime ministers in his interests. A keen sailor, he had won the Sydney-Hobart race in his yacht Morning Cloud in 1969; and in 1971, as Prime Minister, he captained the British team which won the Admiral's Cup. That same year he conducted Elgar's Cockaigne overture at the Royal Festival Hall.

[27] William Shakespeare, *Julius Caesar* Act III Scene 1. During the 1960s and 1970s, no effective leadership was provided by the Church of England; the only other national institution besides the Monarchy, Parliament and the Law invested with any significant authority. Michael Ramsey [1961-1974] was a figure of ridiculous absurdity; Donald Coggan [1974-1980] lacklustre to the point of non-entity. It was not until the Silver Jubilee of 1977 that Queen Elizabeth II emerged from relative obscurity and modest propriety to become the figure of national unity which she has been since that time.

[28] *Westminster Bank Executor and Trustee Co. [Channel Isles] Ltd. v National Bank of Greece SA* 1969 3 AllER 504

[29] *Bevin v Whimster* 1975 3 AllER 706
[30] *Ocean Tramp Tankers Corporation. v v/o Sovfracht* 1964 1 AllER 161
[31] Ibid 163
[32] *The World Beauty* 1969 3 AllER 158
[33] *Bevin v Whimster* 1975 3 AllER 706
[34] *Hesperides Hotels Ltd. v Aegean Turkish Holdings* 1978 1 AllER 277
[35] *Nissan v Attorney-General* 1967 2 AllER 1238
[36] *Hesperides Hotels Ltd. v Aegean Turkish Holdings* 1978 1 AllER 277 at 280
[37] Ibid 280
[38] *Gohoho v Guinea Press Ltd* 1962 3 AllER 785
[39] *Sabally v Attorney-General* 1964 3 AllER 377
[40] *Agbor v Metropolitan Police Commissioner* 1969 2 AllER 707
[41] Ibid 708
[42] *Gallagher Ltd. v Commissioners of Customs and Excise* 1968 2 AllER 820
[43] Ibid 822
[44] *Franklin v The Queen* 1973 3 AllER 861
[45] *Franklin v The Queen* 1973 3 AllER 861
[46] *Re James [an insolvent] [Attorney-General intervening]* 1977 1 AllER 364
[47] Ibid 367
[48] In September 1976, a month before the case was heard, the Foreign Secretary, David Owen had appeared to persuade Ian Smith to accept Anglo-American proposals for majority rule in 2 years, an undertaking from with Smith resiled in January 1977.
[49] No Rhodesian judges had been dismissed following the Order in Council of 16th November 1965 which had imposed sanctions on Rhodesia.
[50] Ibid 369-70
[51] Ibid 370 Grotius *De Jure Belle et Pacis* 1621 ch. 4 515
[52] Ibid 374
[53] Ibid 374
[54] *Texas v White* 1868 74 US 700 at 733 Ibid 374
[55] Ibid 375
[56] *Gouriet v Union of Post Office Workers* 1977 1 AllER 696
[57] Campaign Director and founding member of the National Association for Freedom 1975-1978. The NAFF led by Gouriet was involved in Tameside case and the Grunwick dispute, both of which led to cases heard in Lord Denning's court: *Secretary of State for Education and Science v Metropolitan Borough of Tameside* 1976 3 AllER 665; *Grunwick Processing Laboratories Ltd v Advisory, Conciliation and Arbitration Service* 1978 1 AllER 338; *Harold Stephen and Co. Ltd v the Post Office* 1978 1 AllER 939. Ross McWhirter, a founding member of the NAFF, also appeared in Lord Denning's court: *Attorney-General [on the relation of McWhirter] v Independent Broadcasting Authority* 1973 1 AllER 689. Lord Denning later referred to Ross McWhirter as 'the late Mr McWhirter of courageous memory' in *R v Greater London Council ex parte Blackburn* 1976 3 AllER 184 at 191. Ross McWhirter was assassinated by the IRA Balcombe Street

gang on 2nd December 1975.
[58] Ibid 711
[59] Tom Jackson, the Postal Workers Union President, had said on the BBC on 13.1.77 that 'the laws relating to it dated from Queen Anne and were more appropriate for dealing with highwaymen and footpads'. Ibid 701
[60] Ibid 700
[61] *BBC v Hearn* 1978 1 AllER 111
[62] Ibid 114-116
[63] Ibid 117
[64] *Race Relations Board v Associated Newspapers Group Ltd.* 1978 3 AllER 419
[65] Ibid 420
[66] Ibid 422
[67] *Buttes Gas and Oil Co. v Hammer*
[68] *Buttes Gas and Oil Co. v Hammer [No 3]* 1980 3 AllER 475 Ibid 480
[69] *Buttes Gas and Oil Co. v Hammer* 1971 3 AllER 1025
[70] Ibid 1026-7
[71] *Buttes Gas and Oil Co. v Hammer [No 2]* 1975 2 AllER 51
[72] Ibid 54
[73] Ibid 59
[74] *Buttes Gas and Oil Co. v Hammer [No 3]* 1980 3 AllER 475
[75] Ibid 480
[76] *Antco Shipping Ltd. v Seabridge Shipping Ltd.* 1979 3 AllER 186
[77] *Panamanian Oriental Steamship Corporation v Wright* 1971 2 AllER 1028
[78] Ibid 1030
[79] *Reel v Holder* 1980 3 AllER 321
[80] Ibid 323
[81] *Senior v Holdsworth* 1975 2 AllER 1009
[82] Ibid 1014
[83] 1963 1 AllER 767
[84] Ibid at 771
[85] 1973 Feb. Supp. 1394
[86] Quoted in *Mitchell v Superior Court* (1984) 37 Cal.3d 268 , 208 Cal.Rptr. 152; 690 P.2d 625 [S.F. No. 24685. Supreme Court of California. November 19, 1984
[87] *British Steel Corporation v Granada TV Ltd.* 1981 1 AllER 417
[88] One of Lord Denning's brothers, Norman, had worked in Naval Intelligence during the War and had ended up being responsible for the D notice system in the 1960s. Ian Fleming worked with Norman Denning during the War.
[89] *R v Secretary of State for Home Affairs ex parte Soblen* 1962 1 QB 829 The Secretary of State for the Home Department, Henry Brooke, made the following statement to the House of Commons concerning Dr Soblen: 'When Dr. Soblen, who had been convicted of espionage in the United States of America and sentenced to life imprisonment, was on bail pending the hearing of an appeal, he absconded and made his way to Israel. He was expelled from that country, and was being returned by air to the U.S.A. when he stabbed himself. When his plane

landed at London Airport he had to be removed to hospital for the treatment necessary to save his life, though he was formally refused leave to land, and the airline were directed to remove him on the aircraft on which he had arrived. This was in strict accordance with the normal practice. Had he been fit to travel, this would have meant the immediate resumption of his journey to the U.S.A. As soon as Dr. Soblen was fit to be moved from the hospital, he was taken to Brixton prison, where he still is. A *habeas corpus* application to the High Court failed, and this decision was upheld on appeal. I have given anxious thought to this case, and to requests made to me about it, and to the representations of some hon. Members who were good enough to come and put their views to me. There is no ground for granting Dr. Soblen political asylum here. He is not in danger of persecution in his own country for his political opinions or on racial grounds. Dr Soblen is a convicted spy, a fugitive from a sentence imposed on him by the courts of a country whose life is based on democratic institutions and constitutional guarantees. I have concluded that my proper course is to re-establish the situation in which Dr. Soblen would have found himself on his arrival in this country but for his self-inflicted wounds. In that situation he would undoubtedly and properly have been refused leave to land, and the airline would have been required to remove him at once on the plane on which he arrived, which was bound for the U.S.A. Directions are accordingly being given to the airline now for Dr. Soblen's removal to the United States. Before reaching this decision I called for and studied medical reports on Dr. Soblen's health and gave the fullest weight to representations made to me that he should be sent to Czechoslovakia or some other country willing to receive him'. HC Deb 02 August 1962 vol 664 cc804

[90] Ibid 842
[91] Ibid 842-3
[92] *Attorney-General v Mullholland; Attorney-General v Foster* 1963 1 AllER 767
[93] *R v Secretary of State for the Home Department ex parte Hosenball* 1977 3 AllER 452
[94] Ibid 455
[95] Lord Denning's Report (1963) Cmnd 2152
[96] (1963) Cmnd 6152, paras 239(3), 240
[97] Ibid 460
[98] Ibid 457
[99] Ibid 457
[100] Ibid 460
[101] Ibid 457
[102] Lord Denning, *Landmarks in the Law* [London 1984] p. 351
[103] *Wyld v Silver [No2]* 1962 2 AllER 809
[104] *Gregson v Cyril Lord Ltd.* 1962 3 AllER 907
[105] *R v Axbridge Rural District Council ex parte Wormald* 1964 1 AllER 571; *British Railways Board v Glass* 1964 3 AllER 418; *James v Minister of Housing and Local Government* 1963 3 AllER 602; *Edsell Caravan Parks v Hemel Hempstead RDC* 1965 3 AllER 737; *Munnich v Godstone Rural District Council*

1966 1 AllER 930; *Field Place Caravan Park Ltd. v Harding* 1966 3 AllER 247; *Blow v Norfolk Council* 1966 3 AllER 579; *Webber v Minister of Housing and Local Government* 1967 3 AllER 981; *Jelbert v Davies* 1968 1 AllER 1182; *Garton v Hunter [Valuation Officer]* 1969 1 AllER 451

[106] *James v Minister of Housing and Local Government* 1963 3 AllER 602 at 606

[107] *Re King [deceased]* 1963 1 AllER 781; *Public Trustee v Westbrook* 1965 3 AllER 398; *E.R. Ives Investments Ltd v High* 1967 1 AllER 504; *Scott [Inspector of Taxes] v Ricketts* 1967 2 AllER 1009

[108] *Davy v Leeds Corporation* 1964 3 AllER 390; *Ashbridge Investments Ltd. v Ministry of Housing and Local Government* 1965 3 AllER 371; *Munton v GLC* 1976 2 AllER 815

[109] *Davy v Leeds Corporation* 1964 3 AllER 390 at 393

[110] *Hubbard v Pitt* 1975 3 AllER 1

[111] Ibid 4

[112] *Viscount Camrose v Basingstoke Corporation* 1966 3 AllER 161 John Seymour Berry, 2nd Viscount Camrose was the Deputy Chairman of the *Daily Telegraph* from 1939 to 1987

[113] *Myers v Milton Keynes Development Corporation* 1974 2 AllER 1096

[114] Walton Manor, an Elizabethan barn

[115] Ibid 1098

[116] Ibid 1102

[117] *Financings Ltd v Stimson* 1962 3 AllER 386; *Financings Ltd v Baldock* 1963 1 AllER 443; *Unity Finance Ltd v Woodcock* 1963 2 AllER 270; *Brady v St Margaret's Trust Ltd.* 1963 2 AllER 275; *Liverpool and County Discount Co. Ltd. v A.B. Motors Co. [Kilburn] Ltd* 1963 2 AllER 396; *Car and Universal Finance Co. Ltd. v Caldwell* 1963 2 AllER 547; *Capital Finance Co. Ltd. v Bray* 1964 1 AllER 603; *Premor Ltd. v Shaw Brothers* 1964 2 AllER 583; *Snook v London and West Riding Investments Ltd.* 1967 1 AllER 518; *Goulston Discount Co. Ltd. v Clark* 1967 1 AllER 61; *Wickham Holdings Ltd. v Brooke House Motors Ltd.* 1967 1 AllER 117; *Bennett v Griffin Finance* 1967 1 AllER 515; *United Dominions Trust [Commercial] Ltd. v Ennis* 1967 2 AllER 345; *Belvoir Finance Co. Ltd. v Stapleton* 1970 3 AllER 664; *Bentinck Ltd. v Cromwell Engineering Co.* 1971 1 AllER 33; *Eshun v Moorgate Mercantile Co. Ltd.* 1971 2 AllER 402; *Barker v Bell* 1971 2 AllER 867; *Worcester Works Finance Ltd. v Cooden Engineering Co. Ltd.* 1971 3 AllER 708

[118] *Launchbury v Morgans* 1971 1 AllER 642 at 645-6

[119] *Strick [Inspector of Taxes] v Regent Oil Co. Ltd.* 1964 3 AllER 23; *Regent Oil Co. Ltd. v Aldon Motors Ltd.* 1965 2 AllER 644; *Esso Petroleum Ltd. v Harper's Garage [Stourport] Ltd.* 1966 1 AllER 725; *Petrofina [Gt Britain] Ltd v Martin* 1966 1 AllER 126; *Cleveland Petroleum Co. Ltd. v Dartstone Ltd.* 1969 1 AllER 201; *Shell UK Ltd. v Lostock Garage Ltd.* 1977 1 AllER 481

[120] *Petrofina [Gt Britain] Ltd v Martin* 1966 1 AllER 126 at 129

[121] *Shell UK Ltd. v Lostock Garage Ltd.* 1977 1 AllER 481 at 484

[122] *Esso Petroleum Ltd. v Harper's Garage [Stourport] Ltd.* 1966 1 AllER 725 at

730
[123] *Horwood v Miller's Timber and Trading Co. Ltd.* 1916-17 AllER 842
[124] *Gilmore [Valuation Officer] v Baker-Carr* 1962 3 AllER 12; *W. and J.B. Eastwood Ltd. v Herrod [Valuation Officer]* 1968 3 AllER 389
[125] *Gilmore [Valuation Officer] v Baker-Carr* 1962 3 AllER 230 at 233
[126] *Murray [Inspector of Taxes] v Imperial Chemical Industries Ltd.* 1967 2 AllER 980
[127] *Re Taylor's Application* 1972 2 AllER 873; *Attorney-General v Times Newspapers Ltd* 1973 1 AllER 815; *Schering Chemicals Ltd v Falkman Ltd* 1981 2 AllER 321
[128] *Robophone Facilities Ltd. v Blank* 1966 3 AllER 128
[129] *Agricultural, Horticultural and Forestry Industry Training Board v Kent* 1970 1 AllER 304 at 306
[130] *Shell-Mex and British Petroleum v Langley [Valuation Officer]* 1962 3 AllER 433
[131] *Laker Airways Ltd v Department of Trade* 1977 2 AllER 182
[132] Ibid 186
[133] *Jarvis v Swans Tours Ltd.* 1973 1 AllER 71
[134] Ibid 71
[135] Ibid 73
[136] Ibid 73
[137] Ibid 74
[138] *Jackson v Horizon Holidays Ltd.* 1975 3 AllER 92
[139] Ibid 92
[140] Ibid 92
[141] *Stafford Borough Council v Elkenford Ltd.* 1977 2 AllER 519
[142] Ibid 526
[143] *Munson v British Railways Board* 1965 3 AllER 441; *National Dock Labour Board v John Brand and Co.* 1970 2 AllER 577; *Boal Quay Wharfingers Ltd. v King's Lynn Conservancy Board* 1971 3 AllER 597
[144] *Attorney-General v Butterworth* 1962 3 AllER 326; *Re Newspaper Proprietor's Agreement* 1963 1 AllER 36; *Daily Mirror Newspapers Ltd. v Gardner* 1968 2 AllER 163; *Registrar of Restrictive Trading Agreements v W.H. Smith* 1969 3 AllER 1065; *Re National Federation of Retail Newsagents, Booksellers and Stationers Agreement [Nos 3 and 4]* 1971 2 AllER 514
[145] *Chappell v The Times Newspapers Ltd.* 1975 2 AllER 233; *Express Newspapers Ltd v McShane* 1979 2 AllER 360
[146] *Clifford Davis Management Ltd v WEA Records Ltd.* 1975 1 AllER 237; *Warner Brothers Records Inc. v Rollgreen Ltd.* 1975 2 AllER 105
[147] *Woodward v Hutchins* 1977 2 AllER 751
[148] Ibid 753
[149] Ibid 754
[150] *Ex parte Island Records Ltd.* 1978 3 AllER 824
[151] Ibid 826-7

[152] *Wills v Association of Universities of the British Commonwealth* 1964 2 AllER 39
[153] *Fox v Stirk* 1970 3 AllER 7
[154] *Warwick University v De Graaf* 1975 3 AllER 284 at 285-6
[155] *R v Preston Supplementary Benefits Appeal Tribunal ex parte Moore* 1975 2 AllER 807
[156] Ibid 809-813
[157] *British Airways Board v Customs and Excise Commissioners* 1977 2 AllER 873
[158] *Rondel v Worsley* 1966 3 AllER 657
[159] Ibid 660
[160] *Goody v Odhams Press Ltd.* 1966 3 AllER 369 at 371
[161] *Hollington v F. Hewthorn and Co. Ltd.* 1943 2 AllER 35
[162] Ibid 372
[163] Ibid 372
[164] Ibid 372
[165] *Barclays Bank v Cole* 1966 3 AllER 948
[166] Ibid 950
[167] Ibid 950
[168] *Hargrave v Newton [formerly Hargrave]* 1971 3 AllER 866
[169] *Associated Leisure Ltd. v Associated Newspapers Ltd.* 1970 2 AllER 754
[170] Ibid 756
[171] *J.M. Allan [Merchandising] Ltd v Cloke* 1963 2 AllER 258; *J. and C. Moores Ltd v Commissioners of Customs and Excise* 1963 2 AllER 714; *Fisher v C.H.T. Ltd* 1966 1 AllER 88; *Avais v Hartford Shankhouse and District Workingmen's Social Club and Institute Ltd.* 1967 3 AllER 987;
[172] *Commissioners of Customs and Excise v Top Ten Promotions Ltd.* 1969 3 AllER 39 *R v Metropolitan Police Commissioner ex parte Blackburn* 1968 1 AllER 763; *Commissioners of Customs and Excise v Top Ten Promotions Ltd.* 1969 3 AllER 39; *R v Gaming Board of Great Britain ex parte Benaim* 1970 2 AllER 528; *Sagnata Investments Ltd. v Norwich Corporation* 1971 2 AllER 1441; *Tehrani v Rostron* 1971 3 AllER 790; *R v Leicester Gaming Licensing Committee ex parte Shine* 1971 3 AllER 1082; *R v Herrod ex parte Leeds City District Council* 1976 1 AllER 273; *Imperial Tobacco Ltd. v Attorney-General* 1979 2 AllER 592
[173] Ibid 766
[174] Ibid 767
[175] *R v Metropolitan Police Commissioner ex parte Blackburn [No 3]* 1973 1 AllER 324; *R v Greater London Council ex parte Blackburn* 1976 3 AllER 184 Between 1978 and 1984 Operation Countryman uncovered wide-ranging corruption in the Vice Squad of the Metropolitan Police; a state of affairs which meant that effective control of pornography was impossible. There was much substance to Mr Blackburn's complaints but it was noticeable that, despite his rhetoric, Lord Denning did not use the power of the courts to force the Metropolitan Police to deal with the problem.

[176] Ibid 327
[177] Ibid 328-9
[178] This reference to Churchill's speech to Congress in December 1941 gave added authority to Lord Denning's condemnation of pornography.
[179] This phrase was an allusion to a phrase used by Churchill during the Second World War in relation to Lend-Lease. The invocation of the Second World War was perhaps an index of the degree of anxiety engendered by the issue of pornography in the mind of Lord Denning.
[180] *R v Metropolitan Police Commissioner ex parte Blackburn [No 3]* 1973 1 AllER 324 at 332
[181] *Attorney-General [on relation of McWhirter] v Independent Broadcasting Authority* 1973 1 AllER 689 at 692
[182] Ibid 701
[183] Ibid 696
[184] Ibid 701-2
[185] 'I know it may not be fashionable to speak of patriotism or national destiny these days. But I feel it is appropriate to do so on this occasion. Two hundred years ago this Nation was weak and poor. But even then, America was the hope of millions in the world. Today we have become the strongest and richest nation in the world. And the wheel of destiny has turned so that any hope the world has for the survival of peace and freedom will be determined by whether the American people have the moral stamina and the courage to meet the challenge of free world leadership. Let historians not record that when America was the most powerful nation in the world we passed on the other side of the road and allowed the last hopes for peace and freedom of millions of people to be suffocated by the forces of totalitarianism. And so tonight, to you, the great silent majority of my fellow Americans, I ask for your support'.
[186] *Allen v Thorn Electrical Industries Ltd.* 1967 2 AllER 1137
[187] *C. Maurice and Co. Ltd. v Minster of Labour* 1968 2 AllER 1030; *Esso Petroleum Co. Ltd v Minister of Labour* 1968 3 AllER 425; *Prestcold [Central] Ltd. v Minister of Labour* 1969 1 AllER 69; *Fisher-Bendix Ltd. v Secretary of State for Employment* 1970 2 AllER 286
[188] *Allen v Thorn Electrical Industries Ltd.* 1967 2 AllER 1137 at 1140
[189] Ibid 1141
[190] *Keys v Boulter* 1971 1 AllER 289
[191] Ibid 292
[192] *Secretary of State for Employment v Associated Society of Locomotive Engineers and Firemen [No 2]* 1972 2 AllER 949
[193] Ibid 964-968
[194] *Churchman v Joint Shop Stewards Committee of the Workers of the Port of London* 1972 3 AllER 603
[195] Ibid 605
[196] *Stock v Frank Jones [Tipton] Ltd.* 1978 1 AllER 58
[197] Ibid 59

[198] *BBC v Hearn* 1978 1 AllER 111 at 114-116
[199] *United Dominions Trust Co. v Kirkwood* 1966 1 AllER 968
[200] Ibid 976-7
[201] Ibid 972
[202] Ibid 974
[203] Ibid 974-5
[204] Ibid 979
[205] Ibid 979-80
[206] Ibid 980
[207] Ibid 980
[208] Ibid 981
[209] *Argosam Finance Co. Ltd. v Oxby [Inspector of Taxes]* 1964 3 AllER 561; *Petrotim Securities Ltd v Ayres [Inspector of Taxes]* 1964 1 AllER 269; *Finsbury Securities Ltd. v Bishop [Inspector of Taxes]* 1965 3 AllER 337; *Lupton [Inspector of Taxes] v F.A. and A.B. Ltd.* 1969 3 AllER 1034;
[210] *Petrotim Securities Ltd v Ayres [Inspector of Taxes]* 1964 1 AllER 269 at 271
[211] Ibid 272
[212] *Finsbury Securities Ltd. v Bishop [Inspector of Taxes]* 1965 3 AllER 337
[213] *Finsbury Securities Ltd. v Bishop [Inspector of Taxes]* 1965 3 AllER 337 at 344
[214] *Wilson, Smithett and Cope Ltd v Terruzzi* 1976 1 AllER 817
[215] *Wilson, Smithett and Cope Ltd v Terruzzi* 1976 1 AllER 817 at 820
[216] *Wallersteiner v Moir* 1974 3 AllER 217
[217] Ibid 222
[218] Ibid 223
[219] Ibid 223
[220] Ibid 241
[221] *Bryanston Finance Ltd. v De Vries* 1975 2 AllER 609
[222] Ibid 620
[223] *Rolls Razor Ltd v Cox* 1967 1 AllER 397
[224] Ibid 401
[225] *Re Pergamon Press Ltd* 1970 3 AllER 535
[226] Ibid 540
[227] *Goldsmith v Sperrings Ltd.* 1977 2 AllER 566
[228] Ibid 569
[229] Ibid 569
[230] Ibid 570-1
[231] Ibid 571
[232] *Wallersteiner v Moir* 1974 3 AllER 217
[233] Ibid 575
[234] *Perilly v Tower Hamlets Borough Council* 1972 3 AllER 513; *R v London Borough of Tower Hamlets ex parte Kayne-Levenson* 1975 1 AllER 641
[235] *Perilly v Tower Hamlets Borough Council* 1972 3 AllER 513 at 515-6
[236] *R v London Borough of Tower Hamlets ex parte Kayne-Levenson* 1975 1 AllER

641 at 644
[237] *Dellafiora v Lester* 1962 3 AllER 393
[238] Ibid 394
[239] Ibid 396-7
[240] *Haley v London Electricity Board* 1963 3 AllER 1003 at 1004
[241] *Braham v J. Lyons and Co. Ltd.* 1962 3 AllER 281 at 282-4
[242] *Appleton v Appleton* 1965 1 AllER 44 at 45
[243] *Bennett v Chappell* 1965 3 AllER 130
[244] *Lever [Finance] Ltd. v Westminster Corporation* 1970 3 AllER 496 at 497
[245] *R. and T. Thew Ltd v Reeves* 1981 2 AllER 964
[246] Ibid 968
[247] Ibid 968
[248] Ibid 973
[249] [1917-1998]
[250] *Lane v Holloway* 1967 3 AllER 129
[251] Ibid 130-131
[252] *Maynard v Osmond* 1977 1 AllER 64
[253] Alton is not far from Whitchurch, Lord Denning's home town.
[254] Ibid 76-80
[255] Denning, A *Freedom under the Law* p. 24
[256] *McIlkenny v Chief Constable of West Midlands Police* 1980 2 AllER 227 at 240-1

CHAPTER FOUR

SOMEONE MUST BE TRUSTED. LET IT BE THE JUDGES

Lord Denning's coat of arms was emblazoned with the words *Fiat Justitia*. On either side of the crest of arms of Lord Denning of Whitchurch stood two figures in support adorned with the names 'Coke'[1] and 'Mansfield'[2]. The authority of these two judges was frequently invoked by Lord Denning to support the argument of his judgments. Lord Denning wrote about both of these judges In *What Next in the Law*[3]. He noted that 'as Attorney-General Coke was cruel and unjust' but, quoting Holdsworth, he added that what Shakespeare was to literature, Bacon to philosophy, the Authorized Version to religion, Coke was to the public and private law of England. Lord Denning stressed Coke's great 'courage' in resisting the pretensions of the King in the *Commendams* case and also in refusing to revise any of the 500 cases which he set out in his Reports when commanded to do so by the King; he also noted that he defended the 'liberty of the subject' in Parliament. Lord Denning stressed that although the pleadings in the Reports were in Norman-French or Latin, Coke's commentaries were in English thus making the law available in the vernacular tongue for the first time in a learned and simple style. Lord Denning claimed, invoking the authority of Sir James Fitzjames Stephen, that Coke's Institutes were more important than either Bracton or Blackstone and that they, in effect, remodelled the medieval Common Law[4].

Lord Denning noted that Lord Mansfield 'came from Scotland...no doubt about it'. He was born in Scone, where the Kings of Scotland were once crowned. Although his family was 'Jacobite to the core', he 'became more English than the English' being educated at Westminster, Christ Church and Lincoln's Inn. Lord Denning stressed Lord Mansfield's wide learning in Civil Law, Ethics and History, emphasising that he attended Dr Johnson's literary gatherings and spoke in the tones of Cicero. He also stressed how Lord Mansfield had imported some of the doctrines of

Roman Law into the Common Law, something for which he was criticised in the *Letters of Junius*, in order to reform the law of Insurance and Bills of Exchange, but that he had been supported in this by a panel of special jurymen chosen from leading men of the City of London. Lord Denning stressed that Lord Mansfield, who came from a Catholic family, and was accused of being a Papist or even a Jesuit by Junius, was tolerant in religion and presided with such conspicuous fairness in the trial of Lord George Gordon, who had led the mob which burnt down his house and library in the riots of 1780, that Gordon was acquitted. According to Lord Denning, Lord Mansfield 'extricated' the Common Law from the 'pedantry, technicalities and narrow mindedness' which had weakened its effectiveness in the days since Sir Edward Coke remodelled medieval Common Law, defining the Common Law order which had emerged as a result of the Act of Supremacy[5].

It is clear from these comments that Lord Denning regarded both Coke and Mansfield to be, in rather contrasting ways, authorities of the Common Law. Whereas Coke effectively refounded the Common Law after the 'revolution' of the Act of Supremacy, transforming it from a medieval system based on Latin and Norman-French into a vernacular English legal order, Mansfield enabled that legal order to be reconciled with Scotland in a spirit of religious tolerance which underpinned the fact that, after 1745, the threat posed by Jacobitism to the English legal order had been finally eclipsed with the result that, for the first time since the sixteenth century, there was no dispute about the person of the monarch.

These two moments, one at the beginning of the seventeenth century, the other in the middle of the eighteenth, were identified by Lord Denning as marking decisive stages in the emergence of a stable legal order. The figure of Coke marked the end of the middle ages and the emergence, with the Act of Supremacy, of an independent, sovereign English nation. That of Mansfield marked the final end of the turbulence caused by the Civil Wars of the seventeenth century and the advent of a modern commercial legal order.

The authority of Sir Edward Coke was directly invoked on numerous occasions by Lord Denning in his reported judgments as Master of the Rolls. On each occasion, the authority of Coke provided a crucial underpinning for an innovative piece of judicial reasoning that was intended to develop the law so as to enable justice to be dispensed.

Considering the scope of an exemption clause based on a complex argument in relation the law of bailment[6], Lord Denning referred to *Southcote's Case*[7] in which the bailee was advised to stipulate in advance that he would not be responsible for theft[8]. This authority enabled Lord

Denning to rule that, in the instant case, the exception clause could not be invoked to prevent a customer claiming for the loss of a fur coat that had been stolen by a dishonest employee. In a judgment concerned with the right to work, in this case that of a woman to be a trainer of horses[9], Lord Denning referred to *The Ipswich Taylors Case*[10] in which Sir Edward Coke remarked that the right to work at a trade was recognised by the Common Law and could not be taken away unjustly; to do so would be 'against the liberty and freedom of the subject'[11]. This was one of the first judgments in which Lord Denning invoked the principle of the right to work, 'the true ground of jurisdiction in all cases' which had hitherto been hidden behind a legal fiction which 'we are mature enough, I hope, to do away with'.[12] This principle, here underpinned by the authority of Sir Edward Coke, would play a major part in Lord Denning's approach to trade union law during the 1970s.

Confronted with a problem concerned with the ownership of lambs born of sheep paid for under a hire-purchase scheme,[13] Lord Denning decided the point by using the Roman-Dutch law of leases but, before he could do this, it was necessary to argue that there was no English precedent relevant to the point at issue. Blackstone had argued that with regard to animals the owner of the mother was also the owner of any progeny *partus sequitur ventrem*. However, this was not the case in the human species and in *The Case of Swans*,[14] the owner of the father could claim the cygnets because it was known that swans mated for life. Invoking the Roman law principle *cessante ratione cessat et ipsa lex* deployed by Coke in that case, Lord Denning, invoking the authority of Coke to undermine that of Blackstone, declared that there was no English authority and that he could therefore look to the Roman-Dutch law of leases to decide the case. By using the fact that Coke's authority revealed an exception to Blackstone's general rule, Lord Denning was able to ignore Blackstone, now trumped by Coke's exception, and decide the case as he willed.

In a complex judgment concerning the doctrine of mistake in relation to an elderly woman who had signed a lease when unable to see properly as a result of the fact that her glasses were broken,[15] Lord Denning rejected the argument that, as a result of her poor sight, her signing of the deed could be considered a mistake and that the contract to sell her house was void on the basis that the contract non *est factum*. If the contract were to be set aside then an unjust benefit would accrue to the nephew who was guilty of fraud. Invoking the authority of Coke's decision in *Thoroughgood's Case*[16] in which the signature of 'a layman, unlettered' was set aside because he could neither read nor write', Lord Denning argued, on the basis that Coke was 'the foundation of all learning on the subject', that that case was an exception that proved the general rule, valid in Coke's time, that once it was a reasonable assumption that the plaintiff or defendant could read or write, their signature to a deed could not be set aside because they would be subject to a duty to take care to read the document. Invoking the authority of Coke to provide the exception that proved the general rule, Lord Denning was able to conclude that the deed of sale could not be set aside on the grounds of mistake. The old lady could read and should have had her glasses repaired before signing the deed.

Establishing the principle that the use of the Royal Prerogative by a government minister was subject to judicial review,[17] Lord Denning invoked Sir Edward Coke's judgment in the *Proclamations Case*[18] to support the proposition that the courts had the power to set limits to the discretion exercised by the government, a power which Lord Denning called 'a fundamental principle of our constitution'.[19] In a judgment concerning the obligation to repair by the tenant in circumstances where the landlord had made representations that he would not ask for contributions from the tenant,[20] Lord Denning found that the landlord was estopped from demanding contributions, even though the tenant said that she would have signed the lease anyway. Announcing that 'I prefer to see that justice is done; and let the conveyancers look after themselves',[21] Lord Denning invoked the authority of Coke's Commentaries on Littleton, deploying Coke's statement that 'every estoppel ought to be reciprocal'[22] to underpin his argument.

Deploying the doctrine of 'legitimate expectation',[23] Lord Denning used the authority of Coke to prevent six minicab drivers from touting for business at Heathrow airport. In order to reach his decision, Lord Denning invoked the authority of the *Six Carpenters Case*.[24] In that case the six carpenters had refused to pay for bread and wine which they had consumed in the Queen's Head tavern. Coke found that the fact that they had entered the premises and not paid for the bread and wine meant that they were trespassers and could therefore be excluded from the premises in the future. Lord Denning argued that the misbehaviour of the six minicab drivers was directly analogous to that of the six carpenters and that they could be excluded from the airport without any further consideration of their case. In a judgment concerning legal aid, in which Lord Denning gave priority to the claims of the legal aid fund over those of the solicitors acting for the client,[25] he invoked the authority of Coke who had said in his Institutes that 'a man shall not be allowed to take advantage of a condition that he himself has brought about'.[26] In this case, the solicitors had persisted with the litigation and levied a charge for their costs on the property recovered, knowing that the amount recovered would be less than the accrued cost of the action which had been paid for out of the legal aid fund.

Finally, in a judgment concerned with 'treasure trove',[27] having reviewed all of the authorities from Bracton to Blackstone, including Coke, Lord Denning declared that 'I would leave the old authorities and let them rest in their graves' and then proceeded, using the inherent authority of the court, to declare that 'Bracton and Blackstone were wrong, Coke right'. Free of any authority, Lord Denning aligned himself with the opinion of Coke. This was one of Lord Denning's last judgments; in the course of it he reviewed the whole course of the tradition of the Common Law so as to elucidate the doctrine of 'treasure trove' which dated from 'time immemorial', specifically from the reign of the last Anglo-Saxon King of England, Edward the Confessor. By declaring himself free of authority in relation to the point at issue and then aligning himself with Coke, Lord Denning was making plain his own understanding of his position in the long tradition of the Common Law.

Lord Denning frequently invoked the authority of Lord Mansfield. He described him as 'one of the greatest ornaments of his day'.[28] If Lord Denning's invocations of Coke allowed him to support some of his more innovative judgments by means of an appeal to the authority of the Common Law, his references to Lord Mansfield tended to underline his conception of the Common Law as a legal order which was compatible with London's position as a centre of international commerce. In Lord Denning's view the law should follow the practices of commercial men and be compatible with their outlook. If the law developed in this way then London would retain its position as a leading centre of international trade and commerce, a position which it achieved in the late eighteenth century when Lord Mansfield was Chief Justice of the King's Bench.

During the economic recession of the 1970s, the position of London in the world of international commerce was in some doubt; Lord Denning, following Lord Mansfield, was determined to make sure that the City of London did not lose its position in the international economy as a result of inappropriate decisions by the courts. In his judgments, invoking the authority of Lord Mansfield, he made sure that the law was firmly aligned with the interests and attitudes of the 'commercial men' of the City of London.[29]

Confronted with the problem of establishing the legal definition of a bank,[30] an entity for which there was no statutory definition, Lord Denning invoked the authority of Lord Mansfield to support his argument that the word should be defined according to the meaning which would be understood by 'commercial men'. Lord Denning stated that 'our commercial law has been founded on the opinion of merchants' and referred to Lord Mansfield's practice of sitting with a special jury made up of merchants from the City of London. Lord Denning continued: 'I would follow his example'; if Parliament had offered no guidance on the definition of the word 'bank', he 'would look at the reputation of the concern amongst intelligent men of commerce....when merchants have established a course of business which is running smoothly and well with no inconvenience or injustice, it is not for the judges to put a spoke in the wheel and bring it to a halt'.[31]

Deciding a case which turned on the problem of whether a waiver could be considered to be a form of promissory estoppel,[32] Lord Denning, in the course of a discussion about letters of credit, referred to Lord Mansfield's belief that it was important to 'know the meaning of terms used by commercial men' and to follow the meaning given by such men rather than impose a technical legal meaning.[33] In a judgment concerned with the award of damages in foreign currencies rather than sterling in arbitrations,[34] Lord Denning stated: 'It is always wise for the courts in commercial matters to follow the practice of the City of London. That is what Lord Mansfield did'.[35]

'Discretion, when applied to a court of justice, means sound discretion guided by law. It must be governed by rule not humour; it must not be arbitrary, vague and fanciful, but legal and regular'.[36] Lord Denning quoted this dictum of Lord Mansfield in a judgment which set out guidelines for judges in the award of damages in personal injury cases. Mansfield's remarks were made in 'the celebrated case in 1770 of *R v Wilkes*'[37] in which John Wilkes, remanded in custody as an outlaw, applied to the court for bail. The grant of bail was at the discretion of the court. Lord Mansfield granted bail and so resolved a dangerous political crisis. In a similarly charged political case of the early 1970s involving a trade union, Lord Denning once again invoked the judgment of Lord Mansfield in *R v Wilkes*.

In *Heaton's Transport [St. Helens] Ltd v Transport and General Workers Union*,[38] Lord Denning's judgment overturned that of the National Industrial Relations Court which had imposed a fine of £50,000 on the Transport and General Workers Union for contempt of court. The TGWU had refused to pay the fine. Lord Denning's judgment defused a dangerous political confrontation between the trade unions and the government. Referring to Lord Mansfield's judgment in *R v Wilkes*, Lord Denning emphatically denied that his decision had a political motive: 'The constitution does not allow reasons of state to influence our judgments: God forbid that it should. We must not regard political consequences how formidable soever they might be. If rebellion were the certain consequence, we are bound to say: 'Fiat Justitia, ruat caelum'.[39] Lord Mansfield's judgment, which had led to Wilkes' release, was based on a technical argument based on complex precedents. Lord Denning's argument was also technical and was based on whether the shop stewards in this case could be considered to be 'servants' of the trade union. In deciding that, on the facts, they were not servants, Lord Denning found that the trade union was not responsible for their actions and therefore should not have been fined by the NIRC.

Lord Denning believed that judicial discretion, properly applied in the manner indicated by the example of Lord Mansfield, could be a means of delivering justice. In a series of cases in which he sought to use judicial discretion to deliver justice, Lord Denning invoked the authority of Lord Mansfield to support bold and innovative legal arguments. In a dissenting judgment concerned with an application for *certiorari* based on new evidence in relation to a decision to close a public right of way,[40] Lord Denning argued that the existence of new evidence meant that the original decision should be overturned and that there should be a new hearing to determine the status of the public right of way. To support this argument he invoked the authority of Lord Mansfield who had argued in *Bright v Eynon*[41] that in cases where there could be no appeal from a jury decision on the facts, there should be a new trial if that was the only way in which justice could be done: 'If unjust verdicts, obtained under these and a thousand like circumstances, were to be conclusive for ever, the determination of civil property, in this method of trial, would be very precarious and unsatisfactory. It is absolutely necessary to justice, that there should, upon many occasions, be opportunities of reconsidering the cause by a new trial'.[42]

Lord Denning also invoked the authority of Lord Mansfield to support his argument in a judgment concerned with privity of contract in which he argued a stranger to the contract, who was an intended beneficiary, could sue on the contract despite the rule on privity.[43] Lord Denning, developing his argument, referred to a seventeenth century case, *Dutton v Poole*[44] in which a daughter was able to sue on the contract, despite the rule on privity, because her mother, an executrix of the contract was not legally competent to sue. Lord Mansfield, approving the judgment in that case in *Martyn v Hind* said that 'it is a matter of surprise how doubt could have arisen in this case'.[45] Building on this foundation, Lord Denning then proceeded to make his argument that, in the instant case, a stranger to the contract, who was an intended beneficiary, could sue on the contract. Lord Denning's argument was based on the principles of equity. In another case in which Lord Denning found a way of protecting the interests of a plaintiff who stood to lose out because the trial court had ruled that the contract was not binding because it was a family arrangement,[46] he also invoked the authority of Lord Mansfield to support his legal argument in favour of the plaintiff. Lord Denning claimed that his argument was 'comparable to the legal remedy of money had and received which was, Lord Mansfield said, is very beneficial, and therefore much employed'.[47]

Although Lord Denning quoted Lord Mansfield's dictum that 'no court will lend its aid to a man who founds a cause of action on an illegal or immoral act'[48] in two judgments,[49] he also used the authority of Lord Mansfield to prevent the forfeiture of the lease of a veteran of World War One who had been using the premises as a homosexual brothel, a patently illegal activity.[50] The case involved the point of whether acceptance of rent amounted to a waiver of the right to demand forfeiture of the lease. Drawing a distinction between a new tenancy after a notice to quit had expired, in which the issue was, as Lord Mansfield said, '*quo animo* the rent was received' and the real intention of both parties, and the continuation of an existing lease where the lease 'continues in existence by waiver of forfeiture, then the intention of the parties does not matter',[51] Lord Denning argued that, in the instant case, which concerned a continuing tenancy, the acceptance of rent by the freeholder amounted to a waiver of the right to demand forfeiture for 'immoral user'. By invoking the authority of Lord Mansfield and then making an effective distinction between his authority which related to a new lease and the instant case which related to a continuing lease, Lord Denning was able to find a way of avoiding the clear authority of Lord Mansfield in relation to the foundation of an action on an illegal or immoral act.

It was also the case that although the defendant was guilty of an illegal act, he was not founding an action on an illegal act but, in a manner analogous with *promissory estoppel*, using the law as a defence to possible forfeiture of the lease. Lord Mansfield's authority would have barred him from founding an action, but it could be set to one side with regard to his defence against an action for forfeiture. It was notable that Lord Denning found it necessary to refer to Lord Mansfield at all in this case, given that his authority was not, on the face of it, helpful and that he distinguished the instant case which involved a continuing lease from that for which Lord Mansfield's dictum was authority which concerned the renewal of a lease after the expiry of the term of the previous lease. However, given that Lord Denning was finding in favour of a homosexual, it was significant that Lord Mansfield should be indirectly invoked, and then distinguished, in the course of an argument with which he may well not have been entirely comfortable and for which the dictum of Lord Mansfield in relation to 'illegal or immoral acts' was an unhelpful authority. The ghost of Lord Mansfield's authority, revealed by its double presence in this judgment, plainly haunted Lord Denning as he found in favour of a plaintiff who had abetted the crime which, according to the authority of Coke, *inter Christianos ne nominandum*.

Sir Edward Coke and Lord Mansfield were, for Lord Denning, exemplary judicial figures. Their authority was invoked, at crucial moments, to support the legal reasoning in some of his more controversial and important judgments. Lord Denning made plain, in a number of his judgments, his understanding of the nature of the judicial office in the English constitution. 'It is the judges who are the guardians of justice in this land'[52] stated Lord Denning in a judgment concerned with the doctrine of Crown Privilege. Lord Denning repeated that claim in another judgment concerned with Crown Privilege.[53] In a libel judgment he invoked the authority of Lord Chancellor Bacon, whose words he used to define the nature of the judiciary: 'The principle duty of a judge is to suppress force and fraud, to denounce wrongdoing. He speaks for all lawabiding citizens. His words uphold the opinion of the good and shake the confidence of the wicked. By condemning wrong doing, he reinforces the moral sanction on which law and order so much depend'.[54]

In a dissenting judgment which found that a planning permission for building in the County of Kent, the garden of England close to the Pilgrim's Way was voidable,[55] Lord Denning compared the Common Law, and by implication the judges who administered it, to 'a nursing father'.[56] The judges had an authority to interpret the law which exceeded that of the written word: 'We are not deterred by absence of authority in the books. Our forefathers always held that the law was locked in the breasts of the judges ready to be unlocked whenever the need arose'.[57] To be a judge, for Lord Denning, was to be the law. Lord Denning repeated this proposition in a ground-breaking judgment in which he ruled that a member of the public had *locus standi* to restrain a trade union from breaking the criminal law despite the refusal of consent by the Attorney-General to a relator action: 'The law lies in the breast of the judges....we declare it'.[58] Lord Denning continued: 'We have but one prejudice. That is to uphold the law. And that we will do whatever befall. Nothing shall deter us from doing our duty'.[59] Lord Denning had a very highly developed sense of the importance of the judiciary and of its role in the English constitution. In a dissenting judgment concerned with the scope of the law of contempt of court to inhibit freedom of speech, he declared: 'The stream of justice should be kept pure and clear in all the courts, superior and inferior alike'.[60] It fell to the judiciary to ensure that the clear stream of justice was 'not disturbed by stones or polluted by mud'.[61]

The judiciary should not only ensure the purity of the stream of justice, they should also develop the law. Responding to the argument that the Law Commission should have the leading role in reforming the law, Lord Denning dissented in strong terms: 'I decline to reduce the judges to so sterile a role. They should develop the law, case by case so that cases were decided by the law as it should be and is...not by the law of the past'.[62] In a judgment concerned with the power of the courts to order discovery when documents were protected by Crown Privilege, Lord Denning made plain his enthusiasm for bold judicial law reform: 'This is the very case to throw off the fetters....Crown Privilege is one of the prerogatives of the Crown. As such it extends only so far as the Common Law permits. It is for the judges to define its ambit; and not for any government department however powerful.....thus we shall do our part to keep the Common Law a just system throughout its broad dominion'.[63] In a judgment concerning a claim by a vendor against an estate agent in relation to the return of a deposit, Lord Denning stated: 'I prefer to straighten out the law here and now'.[64] For whatever reason there was a need for law reform, in relation to the most portentous or the most humble of issues, Lord Denning considered that it was the responsibility of the judiciary to take the initiative. He was keen that the judiciary should be bold and courageous: 'To timorous souls I would say in the words of William Cowper: 'Ye fearful saints fresh courage take. The clouds ye so much dread are big with mercy and shall break in blessings on your head'. Instead of 'saints' read judges. Instead of 'mercy' read 'justice'. And you will find a good way to law reform'.[65]

Lord Denning was so convinced of the elevated role of the judiciary in the constitution that he refused to believe that the Rhodesian judiciary, bound by an oath to do justice, would have been affected by the Unilateral Declaration of Independence in November 1965. In a dissenting judgment concerned with the validity of letters of request from the High Court in Rhodesia to the Bankruptcy Division of the English High Court,[66] Lord Denning argued that UDI had not changed the constitutional position of the courts in Rhodesia: 'The white settlers made no complaint against the lawful sovereign, the Queen of England. They pledged their loyalty and allegiance to her. But they rebelled against her ministers in Whitehall....they left the judges undisturbed. They left the judges still pledged under their oath of allegiance to the Queen, and under their judicial oath to well and truly serve her in the office of a judge. They left the courts to carry on with their daily tasks....they left the existing law as it was. After all, they were as much concerned as anyone to see that law and order were maintained'.[67] Lord Denning continued: 'The implication was irresistible that the lawful sovereign authorised the judges to continue in office, and the courts to continue to function'.[68] Lord Denning concluded that 'the judicial branch remained subject to the lawful sovereign the Queen of England' and that UDI had had no impact whatsoever on the authority and nature of the Rhodesian judiciary.

For Lord Denning, the judiciary had a status that made it immune from such things at Unilateral Declarations of Independence by a group of rebellious politicians. The judiciary was also immune from being influenced by the press and the media. On several occasions, Lord Denning insisted that judges could not be influenced by what they read in the newspapers or saw on the television: 'No professionally trained judge would be influenced by anything he had read in the newspapers or seen on the television'.[69] 'No judge is likely to read the newspaper reports, let alone be influenced by them'.[70] 'Judges are not influenced by what they read in newspapers'.[71]

The judiciary possessed an inherent authority, vested in their office, to dispense justice. This meant that the judges could exercise their discretion in order to deliver justice: 'In former times it was thought that the judges should not be given discretionary power. It would lead to too much uncertainty. The law should define with precision the circumstances in which judges should do this or that. Those days are now past'.[72] In this case, which involved a decision as to whether to allow an action to proceed which the period of limitation had passed, Lord Denning said: 'The judges have discretion to override the time limit where it is fair and just to do so'.[73] In a case concerned with the power of a High Court judge to order a blood test to decide the paternity of a child,[74] Lord Denning remarked: 'The judges can be trusted to exercise this discretion wisely. I would set no limit, condition or bounds to the way in which judges exercise their discretion. The object of the court is always to find the truth'.[75]

In order to do justice, the judges had complete control over the procedures of the court: 'We are masters of our own procedure and have authority to adapt it to meet the needs of the time'.[76] The instant case was concerned with the question of whether a broadcasting company could be compelled to exhibit film which they had taken of a pop festival in court. Lord Denning considered that the court possessed an inherent jurisdiction to make such an order in the interests of justice. Lord Denning took this power of the judges to be the masters of the procedures of the court to lengths which some of his brethren may have found excessive. In a libel case, he stated that: 'I have looked into the authorities myself.....I have been rebuked before for doing my own researches......[but] an erroneous proposition should not be accepted as good law simply because counsel have passed it by in silence'.[77]

Lord Denning often emphasised that the courts possessed inherent jurisdiction to do justice as the case demanded. In a case concerned with the status of the child of a stateless couple whose father had taken it to Israel without the mother's consent, Lord Denning remarked: 'The fount of the jurisdiction of the Court of Chancery is the Crown which, as *parens patriae*, takes under its protection every infant child who is ordinarily resident within the realm'.[78] Lord Denning reiterated the point in a case concerned with a dispute between a local authority and the parents of a child, which was with foster parents, over the child's education: 'It seems to me to be very important that the jurisdiction of the Court of Chancery over its wards should be maintained'.[79] The maintenance of the authority of the courts, and the defence of the scope of their inherent jurisdiction, was, for Lord Denning, one of the most important aspects of the role of the judiciary in the English constitution. This was obviously important in relation to the jurisdiction of the courts over children but it extended into many other areas. In a case concerned with nuisance, Lord Denning remarked: 'The High Court has inherent power to secure by injunction obedience to the law by everyone in the land, whenever a person with sufficient interest brings the case before the court'.[80] In this case, under the terms of the Control of Pollution Act 1974 there was a procedure for a summary remedy. Despite the fact that this procedure had not been completed, Lord Denning ruled that an application could be made directly to the High Court for an abatement of the nuisance.

Lord Denning upheld the power of the courts to intervene in the interests of justice, even when there was a statutory remedy which appeared to oust the jurisdiction of the courts. In a case under the Leasehold Reform Act 1967, which provided that a decision of the County Court should be 'final and conclusive',[81] Lord Denning found a way of intervening in the case. The words 'structural alteration' in the Act had been interpreted differently by County Court judges. Although these were 'ordinary English words' and should therefore, following the decision in *Brutus v Couzens*,[82] been left to the tribunal of fact, in this case the County Court, Lord Denning argued that 'however simple the words, their interpretation is a matter of law'.[83] Referring to the case of *Anisminic Ltd v Foreign Compensation Commission*[84] in which, despite apparently clear words ousting the jurisdiction of the courts, the House of Lords had ruled that the courts could still intervene, Lord Denning discussed whether the basis of that decision had been that the Commission had gone wrong by exceeding its jurisdiction or by an error of law: 'So fine is the distinction that in truth the High Court has a choice before it whether to interfere with an inferior court on a point of law. If it chooses to interfere it can formulate its decision in the words: 'The court below had no jurisdiction to decide this point wrongly as it did'. If it does not choose to interfere, it can say: 'The court had jurisdiction to decide wrongly, and it did so'. Softly be it stated, but that is the reason for the difference between the decision of the Court of Appeal in *Anisminic* and that of the House of Lords'. Lord Denning then proceeded to suggest that the distinction should be discarded and that any error of law should take the decision out of jurisdiction and allow the courts to intervene thus preserving, and indeed extending, the power of the courts to intervene in areas where, apparently, they were excluded by statutory provisions. In an earlier case, Lord Denning had made it clear that 'the jurisdiction of the High Court is not to be taken away without express words'[85]; the meaning of those 'express words' would be determined by the judges.

One particular inherent power of the courts which could be exercised by the judiciary was that of fine and imprisonment for contempt of court. In a series of judgments, Lord Denning defined the nature and scope of that power. In a case in which Welsh nationalist students from Aberystwyth disrupted a hearing of the High Court,[86] Lord Denning made plain his views about the importance of the power of the judges to protect the courts by the use of fines and imprisonment for contempt: 'The judge was exercising a jurisdiction which goes back centuries....of all the places where law and order must be maintained, it is here in these courts. The course of justice must not be deflected or interfered with. Those who strike at it strike at the very foundations of our society'.[87] He continued thus: 'If they strike at the course of justice in this land....they strike at the roots of society itself; and they bring down that which protects them'.[88]

Lord Denning's understanding of the jurisdiction of the courts in relation to contempt, and its implications for the place of the judiciary in the constitution was made plain in a judgment concerning the publication of documents which had been used in court proceedings, read out in court, in the press.[89] The documents concerned had been disclosed in discovery and were confidential Home Office papers relating to a prisoner, described by Lord Denning as an 'arch-criminal' and an 'enemy of society'.[90] The seriousness with which Lord Denning viewed the publication of these documents was indicated by the fact that he invoked the authority of Lord

Mansfield quoting words which he used in *R v Wilkes*[91] to describe the role of the judiciary in the English constitution: 'We are to say, what we take the law to be.....if we do not speak our real opinions, we prevaricate with God and our own consciences....once for all, let it be understood, that no endeavour of this kind will influence any who at present sits here'.[92] Having made this categorical statement about the nature of the judiciary, emphasising their independence and integrity, Lord Denning proceeded, using some of the most robust judicial rhetoric that he had ever used, to condemn utterly the publication of the documents, whose discovery had been allowed by the court in the interests of justice: 'They should not be exposed to the ravages of outsiders', to do so would be 'highly detrimental to the good ordering of society'.[93] The documents had been read out in court in the interests of justice; their publication violated the integrity of the court, not least because, while relevant for the purposes of justice, the publication of such material in the press would mean that 'critics of one political colour or another will seize on this confidential information so as to seek changes in government policy....the machinery of government will be hampered, even threatened'.[94]

It is worth noting that this judgment was delivered in February 1981. It was in 1981 that the Supreme Court Act 1981 put into statutory form the procedural rules concerning judicial review of official and ministerial decisions which had been developed since the 1960s and were to provide the Courts with the means of supervising the actions of officials and ministers, not least by being able to order the discovery of confidential documents such as those involved in this case. Lord Denning had played a leading role in this development of the powers of the courts and did not want these new powers to be undermined by the publication of such documents in the press. The decision in this case, very fiercely expressed though it was, could be seen as an attempt to protect the power of the courts to order the discovery of confidential documents, a power which greatly extended the capacity of the courts to control the abuse of power by ministers and officials.

Lord Denning jealously guarded the power of the courts to protect themselves by the use of the contempt jurisdiction. The creation of the Crown Court by the Courts Act 1971 made no provision with regard to the extent of the new court's jurisdiction in relation to contempt of court. Lord Denning ruled that the new courts had full powers in relation to contempt of court at the first opportunity.[95]

Lord Denning took a particularly severe view of any attempt to intimidate witnesses and used the contempt of court jurisdiction to protect witnesses. In a judgment concerning a landlord who had terminated the lease of a tenant who had given evidence against him,[96] Lord Denning did not mince his words; he called the action of the landlord ' a gross affront to the dignity and authority of the court and a grievous wrong to the individual affected'[97] and added 'no system of law can justly compel a witness to give evidence and, on finding him victimised for doing it, refuse to give him redress. It is the duty of the court to protect witnesses by every means at their command. Else the whole process of the law will be set at naught'.[98] In another case concerned with the intimidation of a witness, he remarked: 'The court will always preserve the freedom and integrity of witnesses'.[99] In one of his first judgments as Master of the Rolls, Lord Denning extended that protection to witnesses who gave evidence to the Restrictive Trade Practices Court remarking that 'it may be that there is no authority to be found in the books, but if this is so, all I can say is that the sooner we make one the better'.[100]

Lord Denning believed that the judiciary should, as far as possible, make the law easy to understand. He was intolerant of legal niceties and technicalities, as he put it in one judgment: 'I do not accept counsel's argument. My mind is too simple to follow him in those niceties'.[101] In another judgment, he remarked that 'the merits have become submerged in a sea of technicalities....a game of wits [has been] played out between shipowners and charterers backed up by lawyers and barristers...it may have its fascinations for the players [but] it is very time consuming and expensive' and the outcome was 'as uncertain as the spin of a coin'.[102] Lord Denning presented himself as a judge who could cut through all of the niceties and obscurities of the law to find simple truth which was fair and just; as he put it in one judgment: 'This case, like so many of these cases, looks very complicated at the start, but in the end the essential points become fairly short'.[103] On another occasion, he remarked: 'In dealing with the complicated sections of the Income Tax Acts I always find it beneficial to take a simple illustration of how they work'.[104]

Lord Denning rejected the formalism and technicality which had in the past disfigured the Common Law, remarking in one judgment: 'As I listened to the argument and read the cases, I began to wonder whether we were not in danger of returning to the formalism of earlier days'.[105] Commenting on the practices arising from such formalism which had come to disfigure the Common Law, in this instance with regard to the rules in Tort about 'action on the case', Lord Denning remarked: 'The old Common Lawyers tied themselves in knots over it and we should find ourselves doing the same'.[106] However, the law did not always manage to rise above such things. In a case concerned with whether an originating summons was a nullity,[107] Lord Denning commented that the solicitor had 'overlooked an obscure rule in the 'White Book' for which he might well be excused...it is not even as if it was a serious error'.[108] Invoking the authority of a statement by Bowen LJ in 1887 who had said that honest litigants ought not to be defeated by a technicality, Lord Denning noted, gloomily, that 'in this year 1963, the assertion can no longer be made. We have not followed the handwriting of our predecessors. We have marred our copybook with blots, and more's the pity of it'.[109]

Lord Denning believed that the judiciary had a duty to give judgments in ordinary language that could be understood by the common man, observing that: 'The law is the embodiment of common sense; or, at any rate, it should be'.[110] He sometimes used the metaphor of the law being hidden behind a veil, or a mask, which the judiciary could draw back, making everything plain: 'The courts can and often do draw aside the veil. They can and often do, pull off the mask. They look to see what really lies behind'.[111] On another occasion he remarked: 'If we were at liberty to lift the curtain which conceals the truth, we should see that the sisters each withdrew £40,500...without paying tax on it'.[112] At other times he compared counsel appearing before him as magicians whose tricks attempted to make the law other than it was. The role of the judges was to dissolve the magical spell of these legal arguments: 'In order to avoid estate duty the lawyer turns magician. He advises his client to execute a revocable settlement, and in an instant, before our very eyes, the contingent capital interest is gone. No-one can see it. It is replaced by a continuous life interest. No estate duty is payable. And then, whilst we sit admiring the performance, wondering what is coming next, he can, when he pleases, bring back the capital interest....it makes me rub my eyes. I cannot believe it is true. Those near me acclaim the feat. But I do not. I have a feeling that the contingent capital interest remained there all the time, cloaked by a revocable sub-settlement. Pull the curtain aside and you will see it as it really is'.[113] In one judgment he remarked: 'The lawyers have become magicians who perform conjuring tricks'.[114] In another, he referred to the arguments of counsel as 'having all the indicia of a conjuring trick' and being the result of 'sleight of hand' but as far as he was concerned 'it is too good to be true. So good that I do not believe that it is true'.[115]

On one occasion, Lord Denning had to consider whether a judge could be sued for exceeding his jurisdiction.[116] The case concerned a plaintiff[117] whose appeal against deportation had been dismissed by the judge but who had then, on the judge's order, been detained in the cells of the court. The plaintiff then sued the judge for going beyond his jurisdiction. Lord Denning stated that the role of the judge was 'to do his duty with complete independence and free from fear', and noted that no judge had been sued since the *Marshalsea Case*,[118] in which a judge had exceeded his jurisdiction by giving judgment in a case which concerned the King's Household and had been ordered to pay damages. Lord Denning noted that it 'was a strong decision, you may think, by the superior court to keep the lower court in order' but added that 'the superior courts were never so strict against one of themselves' and that there was 'no case in our books' of any court, other than that of the King's Household, allowing a judge to be sued for going beyond his jurisdiction. The authority for holding that a judge was immune from suit for going out of his jurisdiction was *Hammond v Howell*.[119] Lord Denning noted that 'the root decision arises out of a case famous in our history....it is the trial of the Quakers, William Penn and William Meade, the epic story is told in Howell's State Trials, but the law report is in *Bushell's Case* [1670] Vaugh. 135'.[120] The Recorder of London had imprisoned the jury for refusing to convict the defendants. One of the jurymen had then brought an action against the Recorder of London for false imprisonment. The action was dismissed by the Court of Common Pleas on the grounds that it was a *bona fide* exercise of judicial authority even though it was also a mistake in law. Lord Denning added that, if a judge acted unlawfully then he might be liable because unlike the Pharisee who said 'God, 'I thank thee that I am not as other men are', a judge was not the arbiter of his own jurisdiction but 'his jurisdiction is limited by law'.[121] Judges were therefore 'only liable for acting in bad faith, knowing that they have no jurisdiction to do it'.[122] It was notable that, in finding that the judge was not liable in the instant case, Lord Denning's judgment made it clear that the judges were subject to law but that if they acted in the 'honest belief' that they were within their jurisdiction then they were immune from suit. Lord Denning's argument referred to Coke's Reports, the Bible and one of the most famous cases in the history of English law deploying the most formidable authorities to support the proposition that a judge was immune from suit provided that he acted in 'good faith'.

Notes

[1]Sir Edward Coke [1552-1634] As Speaker of the House of Commons in 1593 Coke supported Elizabeth I's refusal of the House of Commons request to debate changes to the Religious Settlement of 1559. The Puritan MPs wanted to revise the doctrinal settlement of 1559 so as to make the Church of England more Calvinist in doctrine and to weaken the authority of the Bishops. In 1594 he was made Attorney-General and strongly supported the Queen's use of her Prerogative

powers. Coke prosecuted Essex, Southampton, Ralegh and the Gunpowder Plot conspirators for Treason. In 1606 he was appointed Chief Justice of the Court of Common Pleas. In that office he firmly resisted any attempts by the Court of High Commission to take cases away from the jurisdiction of the Common Law courts, declared in *Calvin's Case* [1609] that all Scots born after the Union of the Crowns in 1603 were English subjects and rejected the proposition that the Crown could legislate under the Prerogative in the *Case of Proclamations* [1611]. In 1613, in an attempt to rein in his tendency to challenge the Crown, Coke was appointed Chief Justice of the King's Bench, becoming in effect the first Lord Chief Justice of England. In *Peacham's Case* [1613] he resisted the claim of the King that he could consult judges individually and clashed with Lord Chancellor Ellesmere in 1615 when he rejected his claim that the Court of Chancery could overrule decisions made in the Common Law courts. In 1616, after ignoring an injunction issued by the King that forbade him to hear a case involving the holding of ecclesiastical livings in plurality, the *Commendams Case*[1616], Coke was dismissed from his position as Lord Chief Justice. In 1620, he became, once again, a Member of Parliament and led the attacks made by the Parliamentary opposition on the Spanish Marriage and Monopolies in the Parliament of 1620-22. Coke also brought forward bribery charges against Lord Chancellor Bacon which resulted in his impeachment, the first such action since the fourteenth Century. In 1628, appealing to Magna Carta and medieval precedents contained in the Parliamentary Year Books, Coke drafted the Petition of Right, a document which condemned the abuses of power committed by Charles I. Coke's Reports, a record of, and commentary on, cases decided between 1600 and 1615, asserted the superiority of the Common Law and set out the first printed account of English Law since the momentous changes brought about by the Act of Supremacy in 1534. Coke's Reports, together with the later Institutes, provided an authoritative statement of the Common Law which was contemporaneous with the works of Hooker and Shakespeare and the Authorised Version of the Bible. Taken together these works could be seen as a set of foundational texts which defined the nature of the English constitution as it had developed since the Act of Supremacy. However, in contrast with the published works of Hooker and Shakespeare which, together with the Authorised Version of the Bible were widely circulated in the 1620s and 1630s, Coke's works were considered subversive by the King; all of his papers were seized on his death in 1634 and many of them subsequently lost. Encyclopedia Brittanica 15th Edition. See also 'Sir Edward Coke: Mythmaker' in Hill, C. *Intellectual Origins of the English Civil War* [Oxford 1965]

[2]William Murray, first Earl of Mansfield [1705-1793] represented Edinburgh when the city was threatened by disenfranchisement after the Porteous Riots of 1737. He was appointed Attorney-General and Leader of the House of Commons in 1754 and was Chief Justice of the King's Bench from 1756 to 1788. He presided over the trial of John Wilkes, enabling him to be discharged, defusing a dangerous political crisis, by a subtle use of precedent which showed that the Crown's case was flawed. He supported the coercion of the rebellious American Colonies and

presided over the trial of Lord George Gordon in 1780. Lord Mansfield, developed the Common Law from being primarily a law of land tenure to being a legal order which could accommodate the emerging demands of commerce and capitalism by developing a new jurisprudence in relation to Bills of Exchange, Promissory Notes and Marine Insurance thus enabling the Common Law to adapt to the pressures exerted by the Industrial Revolution and London's emergence as a major centre of international commerce. Although Lord Mansfield pioneered the development of restitution in the Common Law by inventing the doctrine of the fictitious promise to return any money gained unfairly from a transaction, he was overruled by the House of Lords in 1765 when he tried to argue that that a confirmed order of credit was binding in the absence of consideration and in 1772 when he tried to argue that documents should be construed on the basis of the 'plain intention' of the drafter rather than have that intention frustrated by techicalities. Encyclopedia Brittanica 15th Edition. In 1752, Lord Mansfield had tried, but failed, to persuade the Duke of Newcastle to appoint Blackstone as Regius Professor of Civil Law at Oxford. Blackstone's Tory politics made him an unacceptable client for the leader of a Whig administration. [Clarke, J.C.D. *English Society 1660-1832* [2nd Edition 2000 p. 242 n. 26]

[3]Lord Denning, *What Next in the Law* [London 1982]
[4]Ibid pp. 8-12
[5]Ibid pp. 19-25
[6]*Morris v C.W. Martin and Sons Ltd.* 1965 2 AllER 715
[7][1601] 4 Co.Rep. 836
[8]Ibid 733
[9]*Nagle v Fielden* 1966 1 AllER 639
[10][1614] 11 Co. Rep. 55a
[11]Ibid 693
[12]Ibid 694
[13]*Tucker v Farm and General Investment Trust Ltd.* 1966 2 AllER 508
[14][1592] 7 Co. Rep. 156
[15]*Gallie v Lee* 1969 1 AllER 1062
[16][1582] 2 Co. Rep. 9a
[17]*Laker Airways Ltd v Department of Trade* 1977 2 AllER 182
[18][1611] 12 Co. Rep. 74
[19]Ibid 192
[20]*Brikom Investments Ltd v Carr* 1979 2 AllER 753
[21]Ibid 760
[22]Co. Litt. 352a
[23]*Cinnamond v British Airports Authority* 1980 2 AllER 368
[24][1610] 8 Co. Rep. 146a
[25]*Manley v Law Society* 1981 1 AllER 401
[26]Co. Litt. 206b
[27]*Attorney-General of the Duchy of Lancaster v G.F. Overton [Farmers] Ltd.* 1982 1 AllER 524

²⁸*Rothermere v Times Newspapers Ltd* 1973 1 AllER 1013 at 1017. It is notable that, in this judgment, Lord Denning disagreed with Lord Mansfield. The case concerned the right to jury trial in a libel action, a right which Lord Denning upheld. Referring to the behaviour of Wright CJ, 'the lowest wretch that had ever appeared on the bench in England', in the case of the Seven Bishops in 1688, Lord Denning noted that 'at one time there were those who would take away' the right to jury trial, 'there were judges who claimed that it was for them to declare whether a paper was a libel or not'. He continued: 'Nearly one hundred years later - in 1784 - Lord Mansfield, one of the greatest ornaments of his day, repeated the error'. The only other occasion on which Lord Denning disagreed with Lord Mansfield was in *Nagle v Fielden* 1966 1 AllER 689, a case in which Lord Denning found in favour of a woman who wanted to be a racehorse trainer on the basis of the right to work. Having invoked the authority of Coke in the *Ipswich Tailors Case* to support his argument, Lord Denning noted that in *R v Surgeons Co.* [1759] 2 Burr 892 Lord Mansfield had argued that the court would not interfere with a decision that restricted the right to work if that decision were 'reasonable'. In the instant case Lord Mansfield declined to intervene when the Surgeon's Company refused to engage an apprentice because he knew no Latin. By 1966, in Lord Denning's view, lack of knowledge of Latin could no longer be considered a 'reasonable' ground on which to refuse employment. Lord Mansfield's decision in that case would therefore no longer have any weight, though, of course, the principle of 'reasonableness' remained a ground on which the court would decide whether or not to exercise its discretion.

²⁹One implication of this position was that, as regards commercial matters, the law of England should follow the rules of international law. Lord Denning supported this position, invoking the authority of Lord Mansfield: 'The law of nations is part of the law of the land'. *Thakrah v Secretary of State for the Home Department* 1974 2 AllER 261 at 266. Lord Denning repeated Lord Mansfield's authority in *Trendtex Trading Corporation Ltd v Central Bank of Nigeria* 1977 1 AllER 881 to support his argument that a state Bank could not claim sovereign immunity for a commercial transaction. It is interesting to note that in *Thakrah*, the principle that international law should be part of domestic law as regards commercial matters was invoked by Lord Denning to underpin his argument that mass immigration, in particular that of Asians from Uganda into the United Kingdom, was an exception to this principle because, in contrast with commercial matters, 'international law has never had to cope with such a problem. None of the jurists has considered it'. ibid 266. Lord Mansfield was an authority in relation to commercial law, but not in relation to mass immigration, a problem which did not trouble the law in his day. However, although Lord Mansfield had nothing to say about mass immigration, a lacuna which allowed Lord Denning to follow his own counsel on that matter. Lord Denning was able to use his authority to claim that the British Empire had treated the indigenous peoples of Canada well when it extended its authority in Canada after the Seven Years War. In *R v Secretary of State for Commonwealth Affairs ex parte Indian Association of Alberta* 1982 2 AllER 118,

Lord Denning quoted from Lord Mansfield's judgment in *Campbell v Hall* [1774] 1 Comp 204 in which he remarked that the Royal Proclamation of 1763 'was ranked by the Indian Peoples as their Bill of Rights, equivalent to our own Bill of Rights in England 80 years before'. ibid 124. However, Lord Denning's decision was that, despite that relationship between the Royal Proclamation and the Bill of Rights, the Indians of Alberta had no locus standi in the English courts to make the 1763 Proclamation enforceable against the Canadian government. The British government may have given rights to the Indian peoples of Canada in 1763 but they could not enforce them in the English courts in 1982. International law might be relevant to commercial matters but it did not apply in relation to mass immigration, nor to the rights of indigenous peoples as far as Lord Denning was concerned.

[30] *United Dominions Trust Co. v Kirkwood* 1966 1 AllER 968

[31] Ibid 980 Lord Denning supported this line of reasoning, based on the authority of Lord Mansfield's approach to commercial law, by a reference to Coke to reinforce the authority of the position which he was adopting: 'So you will find it said from the time of Lord Coke that the law so favours the public good that it will in some cases permit a common error to pass for right, see the 4th Institute as p. 240'. Lord Denning, supported by the authority of Lord Mansfield, proposed to follow 'the good sense of commercial men', but should that 'good sense' be wrong in law, then he appealed to the authority of Coke who had established the principle that, providing an error favoured the 'public good', the courts would 'permit' it to 'pass for right'.

[32] *W.J. Allen and Co. Ltd v El Nasr Export and Import Co* 1972 2 AllER 127

[33] Ibid 135

[34] *The Folias* 1978 2 AllER 764

[35] Ibid 772 In a dissenting judgment in which he argued that arbitrators should be allowed to award interest on damages, a development which he believed would be beneficial to the City of London, Lord Denning invoked the authority of Lord Mansfield, who had allowed juries to award interest on damages in commercial cases, to support his position. *Techno-Impex v Gebr van Weelde Scheepvartkantoor BV* 1981 2 AllER 669 at 673

[36] *Ward v James* 1965 1 AllER 565 at 571

[37] 1770 4 Burr 2527

[38] 1972 2 AllER 1214

[39] Ibid 1248 It was notable that *Fiat Justitia* was the motto on Lord Denning's coat of arms and that Lord Mansfield was also a figure on the coat of arms. Lord Denning's invocation of this motto at this point in the judgment was, perhaps, an indication of the seriousness with which he regard the legal issues at stake in the case.

[40] *R v West Sussex Quarter Sessions ex parte Albert and Maud Johnson Trust Ltd* 1973 3 AllER 289

[41] [1757] 1 Burr 390 at 393

[42] *R v West Sussex Quarter Sessions ex parte Albert and Maud Johnson Trust Ltd*

1973 3 AllER 289 at 295. Despite this clear statement of principle in a case concerned with a public right of way, Lord Denning did not see fit to order a new trial in the case of the Birmingham Six, *McIlkenny v Chief Constable of the West Midlands Police Force* 1980 2 AllER 227

[43] *Beswick v Beswick* 1966 3 AllER 1
[44] [1678] T. Raym 302
[45] [1779] Cowp 437 at 443
[46] *Hussey v Palmer* 1972 3 AllER 746
[47] Ibid 745
[48] *Holman v Johnson* [1775] 1 Cowp 341 at 343
[49] *Shaw v Shaw* 1 AllER 658 and *Snook v London and West Riding Investments Ltd.* 1967 1 AllER 518
[50] *Central Estates [Belgravia] Ltd. v Woolgar [No 2]* 1972 2 AllER 610
[51] Ibid 614
[52] *Re Grosvenor Hotel, London [No 2]* 1964 3 AllER 354 at 362
[53] *Conway v Rimmer* 1967 2 AllER 1260 at 1262
[54] *Wallersteiner v Moir* 1974 3 AllER 217
[55] *Kingsway Investments [Kent] Ltd v Kent County Council* 1969 1 AllER 601
[56] Ibid 612
[57] *Re P [G.E.] [an infant]* 1964 3 AllER 977
[58] *Gouriet v Union of Post Office Workers* 1977 1 AllER 696
[59] Ibid 719.
[60] *Attorney-General v British Broadcasting Corporation* 1979 3 AllER 45 at 51
[61] Ibid 51
[62] *Liverpool City Council v Irwin* 1975 3 AllER 658 at 666
[63] *Conway v Rimmer* 1967 2 AllER 1260 at 1262
[64] *Barrington v Lee* 1971 3 AllER 1231 at 1238
[65] *The Siskina* 1977 3 AllER 803 at 815. When the BBC made a programme about Lord Denning during his preparation of the Profumo Report in 1963. The music used to accompany images of the judge at work was 'Onward Christian Soldiers'.
[66] *Re James [an insolvent] [Attorney-General intervening]* 1977 1 AllER 364
[67] Ibid 369
[68] Ibid 370
[69] *Attorney-General v British Broadcasting Corporation* 1979 3 AllER 45 at 52
[70] *Wallersteiner v Moir* 1974 3 AllER 217 at 231
[71] *R v Horsham Justices ex parte Farquharson* 1982 2 AllER 269 at 287
[72] *Firman v Ellis* 1978 2 AllER 851 at 859
[73] Ibid 863
[74] *B.R.B v J.B.* 1968 2 AllER 1023
[75] Ibid 1025
[76] *Senior v Holdsworth* 1975 2 AllER 1009 at 1014
[77] *Goldsmith v Sperrings Ltd.* 1977 2 AllER 566 at 571
[78] *Re P [G.E.] [an infant]* 1964 3 AllER 977
[79] *Re S [an infant]* 1965 1 AllER 865 at 868

[80] *London Borough of Hammersmith v Magnum Automated Forecourts Ltd.* 1978 1 AllER 401 at 405
[81] *Pearlman v Keepers and Governors of Harrow School* 1979 1 AllER 365
[82] [1973] A.C. 854
[83] Ibid 369
[84] [1969] 2 A.C. 147
[85] *R v Paddington Valuation Officer ex parte Peachey Property Corporation Ltd.* 1965 2 AllER 836 at 840
[86] *Morris v The Crown Office* 1970 1 AllER 1079
[87] Ibid 1081
[88] Ibid 1083
[89] *Home Office v Harman* 1981 2 AllER 349
[90] Ibid 359. Lord Denning was particularly hostile, to what he saw as criminals trying to use the procedures of the courts to escape the consequences of their crimes. The attempt by one of Peter Rachman's enforcers to sue a barrister for negligence, in part because he claimed that he had not committed 'grievous bodily' harm in that he had torn a man's hand in half with his own hand, not with a knife, a feat which he offered to demonstrate in court, led Lord Denning to reassert the principle that barristers could not be sued for negligence in *Rondel v Worsley* 1966 3 AllER 657. In a series of cases arising from the Great Train Robbery in August 1963, Lord Denning was dismissive of attempts, as he regarded them, by criminals, or those associated with them, to circumvent the consequences of their crimes. In *Goody v Odhams Press Ltd.* 1966 3 AllER 369, Douglas Gordon Goody, one of the Great Train Robbers, tried to sue *The People* for libel, Lord Denning ruled that *The People* could amend their defence to partial justification so that Goody's previous conviction for the crime could be used in evidence to mitigate the damages: 'They [past convictions] are the raw material on which bad reputation is built up'. Ibid 372. Due to the ruling in *Hollington v F. Hewthorn and Co. Ltd.* 1943 2 AllER 35, a previous conviction could not be used as evidence of guilt in a civil action. Lord Denning had acted for the defence in that case against the proposition but had failed to convince the court. *Hollington* remained good law in 1966. In *Barclays Bank v Cole* 1966 3 AllER 946, a convicted bank robber sought to defend himself before a jury in a civil action by the bank for 'money had and received', on the basis that, though convicted of robbery, following *Hollington*, that conviction could not be used as evidence of guilt in a civil case. Dismissing his appeal for a trial by jury, Lord Denning remarked, referring to *Rondel v Worsley* and *Goody v Odhams Press Ltd* that 'there was too much of this sort of thing going on' and ruled that because 'his honour and integrity is no longer at stake....it is gone altogether', the guidelines about jury trial in *Ward v James* 1965 1 AllER 565 at 571 should be followed and Cole should be tried before a judge alone. In *Alloway v Phillips [Inspector of Taxes]* 1980 3 AllER 138 Lord Denning ruled that the wife of one of the Great Train Robbers, now resident in Canada, who had written an article about the crime and her involvement with one of the Train Robbers which was published *in The News of the World* should

pay tax on the fee because the fee was a 'chose in action' which gave its owner the right to demand payment for a sum of money in England and was therefore property in England which was taxable even though the wife of the Train Robber was resident in Canada.

[91] [1770] 4 Burr 2537 at 2562
[92] Ibid 358
[93] Ibid 364
[94] Ibid 364
[95] *Balogh v Crown Court at St. Albans* 1974 3 AllER 283
[96] *Chapman v Honig* 1963 2 AllER 513
[97] Ibid 516
[98] Ibid 517
[99] *Moore v Clerk of Assize, Bristol* 1972 1 AllER 58
[100] *Attorney-General v Butterworth* 1962 3 AllER 326
[101] *Inland Revenue Commissioners v Cleary* 1966 2 AllER 19 at 22
[102] *Mardorf Peach and Co. Ltd v Altica Sea Carriers Corporation of Liberia* 1976 2 AllER 249 at 256-7
[103] *E.Y.L. Trading Co. Ltd v Inland Revenue* 1962 3 AllER 303 at 305
[104] *C.H.W.[Huddersfield] Ltd v Inland Revenue Commissioners* 1962 3 AllER 243 at 246
[105] *Miller-Mead v Minister of Housing and Local Government* 1963 1 AllER 459 at 466
[106] *Letang v Cooper* 1964 2 AllER 929 at 931
[107] *Re Pritchard [deceased]* 1963 1 AllER 873
[108] Ibid 878
[109] Ibid 879
[110] *SCM [United Kingdom] Ltd v W.J. Whitall and Son Ltd* 1970 3 AllER 245 at 250
[111] *Littlewoods Mail Order Stores Ltd v McGregor [Inspector of Taxes]* 1969 3 AllER 855
[112] *Inland Revenue Commissioners v Cleary* 1966 2 AllER 19 at 21
[113] *Morgan v Inland Revenue Commissioners* 1963 1 AllER 481 at 489
[114] *Re Holmden's Settlement Trusts* 1966 2 AllER 661 at 665
[115] *Re Ralli's Settlements* 1964 3 AllER 781 at 784-5
[116] *Sirros v Moore* 1974 3 AllER 776
[117] It is interesting to note that the case was brought on behalf of the plaintiff by the North Kensington Law Centre and that Lord Denning began his judgment with the words 'Michael Sirros is an alien'.
[118] [1612] 10 Co. Rep. 686
[119] [1674] 1 Mod Rep 119, 184
[120] Ibid 782-3
[121] Ibid 784
[122] Ibid 785

Conclusion

Lord Denning, Enoch Powell, Margaret Thatcher and The Constitution

Lord Denning's jurisprudence privileged the role of the judges as the final arbiters of the English constitution. Although he never disputed the primacy of the sovereignty of Parliament, he considered that it was for the judges to interpret Acts of Parliament and that they could interpret those acts in a purposive rather than literal manner, 'filling in the gaps' according to their understanding of the intentions of Parliament. The judges also had the role of controlling abuses of power and of shaping and changing the law when, as in his opinion was usually the case, Parliament was unwilling to act.

In Lord Denning's understanding, the independent judiciary, embodying as they did the identity and values which underpinned the constitution, were its ultimate guardians. However, as many of his own judgments revealed, in particular those which were later overturned by the House of Lords, judicial decisions could also be arbitrary. Furthermore, as the nature of the identity which underpinned the English constitution became increasingly contested and uncertain, the idea that the judiciary could embody that identity and therefore act as the final guardians of the constitution became increasingly difficult to sustain. The circumstances of Lord Denning's resignation in 1982 made this point very clear.

The publication of *What Next in the Law* in May 1982 immediately led to a major controversy as a result of the remarks contained in the book concerning jurors from ethnic minorities. It was important that Lord Denning's remarks, which led to the threat of a libel suit, were premised on the assumption that the English constitution was underpinned and made secure by a homogeneous identity. Lord Denning made the point that jurors from certain ethnic groups, in effect, did not share that identity and therefore could not be considered suitable as jurors. This argument followed from the premise that the English constitution was founded on an homogeneous national identity. The outcry which followed Lord Denning's remarks demonstrated that there was no such homogeneous identity and that any attempt to assert such an identity excluded, in an unacceptable manner, members of the national community. The fact that Lord Denning's remarks about jurors, based as they were on one of the assumptions which underlay his understanding of the constitution, should have played the decisive role in his resignation strongly suggested that his understanding of the constitution was not compatible with the society that had developed by 1982.

The other notorious moment in the final phase of Lord Denning's career, the judgment in *McIlkenny v Chief Constable of the West Midlands* in January 1980 which prevented the Birmingham Six from reopening their trial and thereby securing justice, pointed to the very real danger that an arbitrary decision by the judiciary could threaten the stability of the constitution itself by resulting in a gross miscarriage of justice on an issue connected with the very foundation of the constitution: the Union. The circumstances of Lord Denning's resignation together with his judgment in *McKillkenny v Chief Constable of West Midlands Police* had serious implications for continued relevance of his interpretation of the English constitution, an interpretation which underpinned his conception of the nature and role of the judiciary.

In some respects, in particular in relation to the restriction of trade union power and the importance of individual liberty, Lord Denning's views were congruent with those of the Conservative government which was returned to power in May 1979. However, his emphasis on the decisive importance of the judiciary in the English constitution was not entirely consistent with the approach of the Conservative government, which stressed the importance of sovereignty of Parliament and the use of the power inherent in Parliament to control the abuse of power by trade unions and to enhance the scope of individual liberty. In this task, the judiciary played an ancilliary role, rather than the dominant one which Lord Denning had envisaged. The role of the judiciary, in the understanding of the Conservative government, was simply to enforce 'the rule of law' which enabled market relationships to be conducted effectively and to apply those changes in the law effected by Acts of Parliament, in particular in relation to the trade unions, which were intended to reassert the primacy of market values and reduce the role of the state. It was the legal philosophy of Von Hayek, rather than the jurisprudence of Lord Denning which informed the actions of the Conservative government between 1979 and 1997.

Margaret Thatcher spoke a great deal about the 'rule of law' and believed that her government was re-establishing respect for traditional legal values which had been subverted by 'socialism' with its elevation of special interests, in particular those of the trade unions. Despite her obvious respect for Lord Denning,[1] like herself a member of Lincoln's Inn, it was to Friedrich Von Hayek, rather than to his jurisprudence, that she turned in order to provide a justification for the policies of her government. The political economy of Von Hayek, rather than the jurisprudence of Lord Denning, was, arguably, the most formidable ideological authority for the approach to politics which became known as 'Thatcherism'. Enoch Powell, whose attitude to Margaret Thatcher was initially distinctly sceptical was unimpressed by Von Hayek, with whose work he was familiar. Powell expressed his view of Von Hayek thus:

> I dislike his Teutonic habit of telling the English, whom he does not in the least understand, how to set about governing themselves.....I am content that [his] academic labours should bring [him] laurels; but it is perhaps understandable if those who have reaped the thorns in the same cause in real life are disinclined to add their contribution to those laurels'.[2]

In a contribution to a collection of essays of critical jurisprudence published in 1991,[3] Alan Thompson analysed Von Hayek's approach to law.[4] According to Thompson, Von Hayek, in strong contrast with Lord Denning, who stressed the non-political nature of the judiciary time and again, conceptualised the law as being overtly political and ideological rather than disinterested, autonomous and objective. Even more effectively than Marx, Von Hayek disclosed the ideological nature of law.[5] Unlike Lord Denning, Von Hayek had a vision of 'law without foundations'.[6] Law was simply a system with a 'value orientation'[7] which favoured capitalist economic organisation. Von Hayek abandoned 'the view of jurisprudence as disinterested truth'.[8]

Von Hayek's understanding of 'the rule of law' was distinct from that of Lord Denning, who conceived 'the rule of law 'as embodying the cultural values of English identity. Von Hayek's understanding of 'the rule of law' was that it provided the necessary framework for the effective operation of the market. It followed that law could be used, ideologically, as a weapon against 'socialism'[9] rather than, as Lord Denning conceived it, as the ultimate guarantee of the identity which underpinned the English legal order. For Von Hayek, as for Marx, law was ideology.

As far as Von Hayek was concerned, Law protected individual freedom, without which, a spontaneous, self-regulating market could not come into being. The market was not created by law, rather the fragility of the market was buttressed by law; law was a tool that served the market by enabling it to deal with its enemies who sought to impose reason and order on the market in order to manage it. For Von Hayek, any such intervention would destroy the market and undermine freedom. The role of law was simply to enable the market to function. It was the market, which distributed scarce goods in the most efficient manner, that enabled a free society to exist. The law was not the foundation of that society, rather it was a tool that prevented the market from being distorted and undermined by the power of government.

For Von Hayek, the market, protected by law, was a spontaneous creation of human 'nature'. Law facilitated the market, but had no autonomous value of its own. The relationship between law and the market was instrumental rather than foundational,[10] as Lord Denning would have insisted. The purpose of law was simply to provide the spontaneous market which arose from human nature with rules that facilitated clarity and certainty thereby creating an area in which there could be freedom from coercion by the state. The law insulated the market from the power of government, so that 'natural adaptations to circumstances' could proceed without interference. Judges and lawyers might make marginal improvements to the market but that was all. The market was spontaneous and natural but, like any living thing, it could be damaged. The purpose of law was merely to mitigate that damage. The greatest threat to the market came from attempts to impose 'social justice' or 'reason'. The law was a means whereby the potentially deleterious impact of such attempts could be neutralised. In other words, law was an ideological tool which could be used to defeat socialism.

It was this ideological analysis of law that so appealed to Margaret Thatcher. It was by means of Acts of Parliament rather than judicial decisions that her government sought to use the law to roll back the state, undermine socialism and protect the market. It was the power of sovereignty of Parliament, deployed through a government majority in the House of Commons, which underpinned the approach of the Conservative government rather than the jurisprudence of Lord Denning, for all that some of its principles were congruent with those of 'Thatcherism'.

The increasing irrelevance of Lord Denning's jurisprudence, based as it was on the decisive importance of the judiciary and a stable English identity, can be demonstrated by a comparison between four political speeches, separated by over forty years, in which leading political figures reflected on the nature of the English constitution.

The first two speeches were made by Enoch Powell. Powell was both a scholar and a philosopher as well as a leading Conservative politician. In these speeches, he also addressed himself to a consideration of the basis of the English constitution at a time of gathering crisis. The first speech was delivered in 1961[11], in the immediate aftermath of the decision to join the European Community by the Cabinet of which Powell was a member. The speech should be read in the light of the implications of that decision, implications which Powell was the first to articulate and analyse in relation to the English constitution. The second speech,[12] informed by strong notions of the crucial role played by an homogeneous national identity in the English constitution, responded to the challenges posed by immigration to that identity.

Both of Powell's speeches have points of contact with the jurisprudence of Lord Denning. However, the other two speeches, while having some authority as statements about the nature of the English constitution, reveal the extent to which, in the years following his resignation, Lord Denning's jurisprudence was marginalised by changes in society which undermined the English identity which was intrinsic to his understanding of the constitution and also by the aggressive deployment of Parliamentary sovereignty to restructure the social and political system during the 1980s. These developments led to increasing anxiety about the dangers posed to the English constitution by the power of Parliamentary sovereignty. However, the remedy for the threat posed to the constitution by the sovereignty of Parliament was increasingly seen to be a Bill of Rights and a written constitution[13] rather than, as Lord Denning had maintained, the power of the judges to act as arbiters and guardians of the constitution. In that context, the constitutional theories of the authors of the Federalist Papers would increasingly become more pertinent than the jurisprudence of Lord Denning.

The third speech[14] delivered in 1988 by Margaret Thatcher, was a response to the threat, as she understood it, to the English constitution posed by the move towards European economic and monetary union and the creation of what would soon become the European Union. Margaret Thatcher's speech expressed her understanding of the nature of the English constitution. The final speech,[15] delivered by the Queen in 2002, in Parliament, on the occasion of her Golden Jubilee, could be understood as an oracular pronouncement from the depths of the English constitution by the person who embodied the keystone of its sovereignty - the Crown.

Powell's speech to the Royal Society of St. George in 1961 can be understood as an attempt to set out his understanding of the nature of the English constitution. At the moment of its delivery, it was highly unusual. At that time, the supposed virtues of English constitution were accepted uncritically.[16] The only modestly critical approach was that embodied in H.L.A. Hart's seminal jurisprudential text, *The Concept of Law*,[17] in which the primary rule of recognition was the sovereignty of Parliament, author of constitutional rules which were interpreted by officials, judicial or governmental. Hart's interpretation of the constitution was compatible with a welfare state based on a consensus administered by officials. It provided an attractive, managerialist approach to the constitution which appealed to those who found the traditionalist approach to be outdated. Powell's speech attempted to set out an understanding of the constitution which was very different to that of Hart.

Powell began his text with the following words: 'Introspection for a nation, as for an individual, is an unhealthy attitude'. Although Powell started off in a manner which might have led the unattentive listener to imagine that he was about to hear a self-congratulatory encomium in the traditional mode,[18] the note which he struck was novel for he spoke of England, not Britain, and proceeded to examine the nature of the English nation and its constitution, rather than that of the United Kingdom, a strategy almost unheard of at that time.

Powell was the first politician to understand that the British Empire had come to an end and that the dissolution of that order had implications for England and therefore for the constitution itself. For Powell, the collapse of Empire was an event of fundamental importance rather than a matter of political management and pragmatism, the approach taken by all of his colleagues at that time. Tracing the outline of Imperial history, Powell emphasised that the period of Empire was at an end, and that what now mattered was the English nation that remained.

For Powell, the English nation had remained, unchanged, beneath the carapace of the Empire. Now that the Empire had dissolved, 'leaving not a wrack behind', it was the nation alone that was of consequence. Powell was concerned with the England of Hooker, Coke and Davies, not with the United Kingdom, certainly not the Commonwealth, for which he had unbounded contempt; it was in this sustained attention to the England that the radicalism of his analysis lay. As he put it: 'There was this deep, this providential difference between our empire and those others, that the nationhood of the mother country remained unaltered through it all, almost unconscious of the strange, fantastic structure build around her - in modern parlance 'uninvolved'....so the continuity of her existence was unbroken when the looser connections which had linked her with distant continents and strange races fell away'.

Powell then looked back over what he understood to be the long continuity of English history to its foundation in 'time immemorial', making a rhetorical plea to his ancestors: 'Tell us what it is that binds us together; show us the clue that leads through a thousand years; whisper to us the secret of this charmed life of England, that we in our time may know how to hold it fast'. Powell then emphasised the importance, first of language,[19] then of Parliament,[20] then of the judges of the Common Law[21] and finally the Crown,[22] to the English constitution. Powell maintained that the English constitution was natural, a creation of time and experience: 'Institutions which elsewhere are recent and artificial creations, appear in England almost as works of nature, spontaneous and unquestioned. The deepest instinct of the Englishman - how the word 'instinct' keeps forcing itself again and again! - is for continuity; he never acts more freely nor innovates more boldly than when he is most unconscious of conserving or even of reacting'.

However, Powell, like Lord Denning, identified a threat to this creation of time and nature: the development, since the 1940s, of mass immigration. Immigration weakened and undermined the homogeneous identity which Powell, like Lord Denning, considered intrinsic to the English constitution. As Powell conceived it, the English constitution was founded on a homogeneous national identity, forged out of the language, history and tradition adverted to in his 1961 speech. That identity would be weakened, even subverted, by an influx of immigrants too large to be assimilated and dissolved back into the nation, who did not share the identity of the indigenous poplulation, whose presence could damage that identity, particularly, in Powell's opinion, if the unassimilated immigrant communities were protected by measures such as Race Relations legislation. Such measures, as Powell pointed out, were an unwelcome, and incoherent, innovation. Subjecthood based on a common identity and language, rooted in 'time immemorial' was, according to Powell, radically incompatible with 'citizenship' based on rights such as non-discrimination. Citizenship rights were the basis of the constitutions of revolutionary France and America; regimes which Britain had resisted by force of arms. It was concern about the threat posed to the constitution by the introduction of Race Relations legislation which led to Powell's notorious speech made in Birmingham in April 1968.[23]

Powell's 1968 speech was very different from that of 1961. Whereas that of 1961 was a serene meditation on the traditional English constitution, that of 1968 was a passionate defence against what he now perceived to be a mortal threat: mass immigration. The speech may also have been intended to precipitate a political crisis which would have enabled Powell to seize power on the back of a coalition of Conservative and working class Labour votes, enabling him to form a government which could explicitly defend his conception of the English nation by repealing the Race Relations legislation and removing the threat posed by immigration by encouraging schemes of repatriation.[24] It is possible that, had Powell become Prime Minister, he might have found, in Lord Denning, an important ally. The evidence of the reason and rhetoric of Lord Denning's judgments suggests a certain congruence with the views of Powell.

Much of Powell's speech was devoted to precipitating a mood of crisis by means of emphatic rhetoric, but within this farrago of incitement, directed at the emotions of the Labour voting working classes, there was an insistent reiteration of the themes of the 1961; this time *molto furioso* in contrast with the earlier *sotto voce*. The much quoted final peroration of the Birmingham speech took on a particular resonance in this context. By referring to 'the Roman', Powell was invoking a foundational rhetoric; after all Coke believed that Aeneas, one of the 'Romans' invoked by Powell, had played a part in the creation of the Common Law. His grandson Brutus had become the first king of Britain. The final word of the speech was 'betrayal'; the law of treason was thereby invoked, the existence of a mortal threat to the nation suggested.

The speech made by Margaret Thatcher at Bruges in September 1988 could be read in the light of those two earlier speeches by Powell. By 1988, the British Nationality Act had imposed a concept of identity, based on 'patriality', onto immigration law so as to restrict future immigration. The concept of 'patriality', linked as it was to blood and inheritance, was closer to Powell's conception of the subject than to citizenship on the French or American model. Despite the implications of Race Relations, and later Sex Discrimination, legislation Margaret Thatcher's governments, by categorically rejecting proposals that the European Convention of Human Rights should be incorporated into English law, had resolutely refused to move towards the creation of a law of citizenship. Citizenship remained an empty category in English law. Subjecthood and identity, based on *jus sanguine* rather than *jus sole*, remained, as Powell would have wished, the basis of national identity.

However, in the course of the negotiations which began after the signing of the Single European Act in 1986, the European Community began to move towards the creation of a substantive citizenship based on closer integration under supranational authority. It was not until the Parliamentary debates about the Maastricht treaty in 1992-3 that the full constitutional implications of membership of the European Union, consequent on these changes in the direction of a substantive citizenship under a supranational authority, began to become clear to a significant proportion of the Parliamentary Conservative and Labour parties. Many Conservative and Labour MPs believed that the negotiations for what became the Maastricht treaty involved a decisive shift, imperfectly and confusingly implemented, to create a new European legal order which would decisively compromise the traditional constitution, celebrated by Powell, which remained fundamental to the assumptions of Margaret Thatcher. The Bruges speech[25] was intended to put an end to any prospect of the United Kingdom being absorbed into that European legal order. In the event, as was the case with the Birmingham speech on 1968, it led to the political demise of its author.

Whereas Powell's speeches were eloquent about the virtues of the English nation, it was notable that the Bruges speech was marked by a silence about English identity. The traditional English constitution of Hooker, Coke, Davies and Blackstone, rooted in 'time immemorial', hermetically sealed from the legal order of Europe, was not directly invoked in the Bruges speech. Instead, Thatcher deployed a diffuse and vague rhetoric of historical and cultural allusion. Rather than invoking the authority of Hooker, Coke, Davies or Blackstone she made imprecise references to the British being 'the heirs to the legacy of European culture', to being 'part of the Roman Empire', to the straight lines of the roads the Romans built', to 'our nation being 'restructured' under Norman and Angevin rule', to 'the great Churches and Cathedrals of Britain', to 'the cultural riches which we have drawn from Europe'. Instead of the 'immemorial' nature of a constitution founded on a homogeneous identity, British pragmatism and utilitarianism, the achievements of commerce and science, were invoked. Thatcher stated that 'we have pioneered and developed representative institutions to stand as bastions of freedom' and have made Britain a 'home for people from the rest of Europe who sought sanctuary from tyranny'. The speech was laced with impeccable Benthamite sentiments, couched in a tone of optimism about the benefits of economic growth and the 'open' society, which could have come from the pen of H.L.A. Hart. Ignoring Hooker, Coke and Davies, Thatcher stated the banal proposition that 'from classical and medieval thought we have borrowed that concept of the 'rule of law' which marks out a civilised society from barbarism.......recognition of the unique and spiritual nature of the individual'. Unlike Powell, who turned his back on empire, considering it to be irrelevant to England, Thatcher claimed imperialism as an intrinsic characteristic of Britain, whose subjects 'explored and colonised and - yes, without apology - civilised much of the world'. The echo of the Benthamite reformers of the 1830s who created the Indian legal code and brought the benefits of railways and economic development to the subcontinent[26] could be heard very clearly in Margaret Thatcher's speech.

After this loose and vague set of invocations, Thatcher proceeded to justify the distinctiveness of Britain, not by reference to the importance of an homogeneous identity, but by adversions to her role in the two World Wars in saving Europe from 'falling under the dominance of a single power', the benefits of free trade, economies in the Common Agricultural policy, strong defence and the benefits of the Atlantic alliance with the United States. Although Thatcher was attempting to make a serious justification and defence of Britain against the threat which she perceived in the ambitions of those who desired to create a federal European Union, it was very notable that she was silent about the homogeneous identity which, for both Powell and Lord Denning, was of intrinsic importance. Instead her argument got lost in a series of utilitarian points about economics and defence. The English constitution, as defended by Powell and Lord Denning, was not defended or extolled. The woman who was supposed to be the strongest defender of the national interest since Churchill was unable to mount a defence of the traditional constitution in a speech which purported to be a radical assertion of national resistance against the emergence of a European state. If Margaret Thatcher could not defend the traditional constitution, it was difficult to see who might have been able to do so in the circumstances of the late 1980s.

The Queen's speech to Parliament on the occasion of her Golden Jubilee in 2002[27] was, in formal terms, a moment in which the English constitution could express itself to the nation. The speech was made, in a joint sitting of the Commons and Lords, in Westminster Hall, on April 30th 2002, with the full authority of the Crown in Parliament. In formal terms, the speech was an oracular enunciation of the voice of the Crown, the keystone of the 'sovereignty of Parliament'. In fact, the speech was banal and vacuous, devoid of authority. The natural and 'instinctive' authority of the traditional English constitution, invoked by Powell in 1961, had, by 2002, evaporated into thin air. All that was left was the emptiness of the Queen's enunciation which avoided all forms of authoritative discourse. It was this silence, at the heart of the speech, that was so distinctive and notable.

Speaking of Parliament, the Queen made use of none of Powell's rhetoric saying blandly; "I would like to pay tribute to the work you do in this, the Mother of Parliaments - where you, like so many famous predecessors before you, have assembled to confront the issues of the day, to challenge each other and address differences through debate and discussion, and to play your essential part in guiding this kingdom through the changing times of the past 50 years'. This tone would have been apt in an address to the National Executive of the Labour party, one of 'New' Labour's policy commissions, or even a focus group, but it was decidedly inappropriate in an address by the Monarch to the Commons and Lords sitting under the authority of the Crown in Parliament.

The oracle of the 'sovereignty of Parliament' continued, speaking vacuously of 'change - its breadth and accelerating pace over these years', 'the transformation of the international landscape', 'no less rapid developments at home'. Opining that 'change has become a constant, managing it has become an expanding discipline', the oracle deployed the tonality of bland managerialism, the dialect of a utilitarian Benthamism fundamentally at odds with the doctrines, as understood by Powell or Lord Denning, of the English constitution of whose sovereignty the Queen is the personification. The oracle continued, rhetorically setting herself under the dominion of a utilitarianism which had always been alien to England, as she was understood by Powell and Denning: 'The way we embrace it [change] defines our future'. The 'time immemorial' of the English legal order was expressed, with utter bathos, as 'we in this island have the benefit of a long and proud history'. The oracle of the 'sovereignty of Parliament' continued, with vacuous banality: 'This not only gives us a trusted framework of stability and continuity to ease the process of change, but also tells us what is of lasting value'. If language was intrinsic to English identity then this language was redolent of its death. The mouthpiece of sovereignty continued, with dull inconsequence: 'Only the passage of time can filter out the ephemeral from the enduring and what endures are the characteristics that mark our identity as a nation and the timeless values which guide us'. The oracle of the 'sovereignty of Parliament' concluded on a note of empty assertion: 'I would like to express my pride in our past and my confidence in our future. I would like above all to declare my resolve to continue, with the support of my family, to serve the people of this great nation of ours to the best of my ability through the changing times ahead'. The silence hidden by these pointless words was that of abdication.

In 1962, Lord Denning, newly appointed as Master of the Rolls, was confident that he could defend and sustain the English constitution. By 2002, as the Queen's Golden Jubilee speech demonstrated, the doctrines of the traditional constitution could no longer be voiced. At some point between 1962 and 2002, the foundations of the English constitution crumbled into dust. It is possible that the career of Lord Denning marked the moment at which the old order passed and English tradition became one with those of Nineveh and Tyre. If, as Hegel suggested, the owl of

Minerva flies at twilight, then contemplation of the jurisprudence of Lord Denning offers a means of understanding English identity, tradition and history even though, having understood it, it is revealed revealed to be no more substantial than air, leaving, in the words of Prospero, not a 'wrack behind'. Indeed, the final valediction to Lord Denning's career, the epitaph to his jurisprudence, and perhaps also that of England, could be prounounced in the words of William Shakespeare's Prospero:

> Our revels now are ended. These our actors
> as I foretold you, were all spirits and
> are melted into air, into thin air;
> and like the baseless fabric of this vision,
> the cloud-capped towers, the gorgeous palaces,
> the solemn temples, the great globe itself;
> yea, and all which it inherit, shall dissolve,
> and, like the baseless fabric of this insubstantial pageent faded,
> leave not a wrack behind.[28]

Notes

[1] When Lord Denning died Margaret Thatcher said that 'he was probably the greatest English judge of modern times. He combined a love of liberty with a passion for justice. His life and work will provide inspiration for generations to come'. *Daily Telegraph* 6.3.99

[2] Heffer, S. *Like the Roman: The Life of Enoch Powell* [London 1998] p.645

[3] *Dangerous Supplements: Resistance and Renewal in Jurisprudence*, ed P. Fitzpatrick [London, 1991]

[4] Ibid pp. 68-84

[5] Ibid 68

[6] Ibid 70

[7] Ibid 70

[8] Ibid 70

[9] Ibid 70

[10] Ibid 83-4

[11] Speech to the Royal Society of St. George April 22 1961

[12] Speech at Birmingham April 20 1968

[13] In 1988, the same year as Margaret Thatcher's Bruges speech, Charter 88, a pressure group dedicated to constitutional reform on those lines, was set up.

[14] Speech at Bruges September 20 1988

[15] Speech in Westminster Hall June 10 2002

[16] See above Chapter Three

[17] Hart's text, published in 1961, is exactly contemporaneous with that of Powell. In his own way, Powell was just as authoritative an interpreter of the English legal

order as Hart.

[18] 'From time to time an Englishman among other Englishmen may without harm, and even with advantage, seek to express in spoken words just cause to praise his country'.

[19] 'The tongue made for telling truth in, tuned already to songs that haunt the hearer like the sadness of spring'.

[20] 'A palace near the great city which the Romans built at a ford of the River Thames, a palace with many chambers and one lofty hall, with angel faces carved on the hammer beams, to which men resorted out of all England to speak on behalf of their fellows, a thing called 'Parliament'.

[21] 'And from that hall went out men with fur-trimmed gowns and strange caps on their heads, to judge the same judgments, and dispense the same justice, to all the people of England'.

[22] 'They would point to the kingship of England, and its emblems everywhere visible ...and older still, the crown itself and that sceptred awe, in which Saint Edward the Englishman still seemed to sit in his own chair to claim the allegiance of the English. Symbol, yet source of power; person of flesh and blood, yet incarnation of an idea; the kingship would have seemed to them, as it seems to us, to embrace and express the qualities that are peculiarly England's; the unity of England, effortless and unconstrained, which accepts the unlimited supremacy of Crown in Parliament, so naturally as not to be aware of it; the homogeneity of England, so profound and embracing that the counties and regions make it a hobby to discover their differences and assert their peculiarities; the continuity of England, which has bought this unity and this homogeneity about by the slow alchemy of centuries'.

[23] Powell's Birmingham speech, the so-called 'rivers of blood' speech, was prompted by the third reading of the Race Relations Bill 1968, a measure to which Powell was implacably opposed because he conceived it as posing a direct threat to his conception of a constitution based on subjecthood rather than citizenship rights.

[24] The implications of Race Relations legislation for the traditional constitution, as Powell understood it, were addressed directly in the speech: 'On top of this, they now learn that a one-way privilege is to be established by Act of Parliament: a law, which cannot, and is not intended, to operate to protect them or redress their grievances, is to be enacted to give the stranger, the disgruntled and the agent provocateur the power to pillory them for their private actions....This is why to enact legislation of the kind before Parliament at this moment is to risk throwing a match on to gunpowder....now we are seeing the growth of positive forces acting against integration, of vested interests in the preservation and sharpening of racial and religious differences, with a view to the exercise of actual domination, first over fellow-immigrants and then over the rest of the population'.

[25] http://www.margaretthatcher.org/speeches/displaydocument.asp?docid=107332

[26] Stokes, E. *The English Utilitarians and India* [Cambridge 1959]

[27] http://news.bbc.co.uk/1/hi/uk_politics/1959753.stm

[28] William Shakespeare *The Tempest* IV i

CASES

Agbor v Metropolitan Police Commissioner 1969 2 AllER 707............ 192
Agricultural, Horticultural and Forestry Industry Training Board v Kent 1970 1 AllER 304 196
Allen v Sir Alfred MacAlpine and Sons Ltd 1968 1 AllER 543 140
Allen v Thorn Electrical Industries Ltd. 1967 2 AllER 1137 198
Alloway v Phillips [Inspector of Taxes] 1980 3 AllER 138 224
Allsop v Church of England Newspaper Ltd 1972 2 AllER 26 144
Antco Shipping Ltd. v Seabridge Shipping Ltd. 1979 3 AllER 186 193
Appleton v Appleton 1965 1 AllER 44 200
Argosam Finance Co. Ltd.v Oxby [Inspector of Taxes] 1964 3 AllER 561 199
Argyll v Argyll [1967] Ch 302 60
Ashbridge Investments Ltd. v Ministry of Housing and Local Government 1965 3 AllER 371 195
Associated Leisure Ltd. v Associated Newspapers Ltd. 1970 2 AllER 754 197
Attorney-General [on relation of McWhirter] v Independent Broadcasting Authority 1973 1 AllER 689 .... 67, 198
Attorney-General of the Duchy of Lancaster v G.F. Overton [Farmers] Ltd. 1982 1 AllER 524 220
Attorney-General v British Broadcasting Corporation 1979 3 AllER 45 .... 142, 222, 223
Attorney-General v Butterworth 1962 3 AllER 326 .... 196, 224
Attorney-General v Mullholland; Attorney-General v Foster 1963 1 AllER 767 .... 149, 194
Attorney-General[on relation of McWhirter] v Independent Broadcasting Authority 1973 1 AllER 689 198
Avais v Hartford Shankhouse and District Workingmen's Social Club and Institute Ltd. 1967 3 AllER 987 197
B v B 1978 1 AllER 821 146
B. v B. And E. [B intervening] 1969 3 AllER 1106 145
B.R.B v J.B. 1968 2 AllER 1023 223
Balogh v Crown Court at St. Albans 1974 3 AllER 283 .... 190, 224
Barclays Bank v Cole 1966 3 AllER 948 .... 64, 197
Barker v Bell 1971 2 AllER 867 195

Barrington v Lee 1971 3 AllER 1231.. 222
BBC v Hearn 1978 1 AllER 111 .... 193, 199
Bedson v Bedson 1965 3 AllER 307 141
Belvoir Finance Co. Ltd. v Stapleton 1970 3 AllER 664 195
Bennett v Griffin Finance 1967 1 AllER 515 195
Bentinck Ltd. v Cromwell Engineering Co. 1971 1 AllER 33................ 195
Bernard v Josephs 1982 3 AllER 162.. 146
Bernays v Prosser 1963 2 AllER 321.. 189
Beswick v Beswick 1966 3 AllER 1 222
Bevin v Whimster 1975 3 AllER 706... 192
Bexley Congregational Church Treasurer v London Borough of Bexley 1972 2 AllER 662.. 189
Blow v Norfolk Council 1966 3 AllER 579 195
Blyth v Blyth 1966 1 AllER 524 143
Boal Quay Wharfingers Ltd. v King's Lynn Conservancy Board 1971 3 AllER 597 196
Board of Governors of the Hospital for Sick Children v Walt Disney Productions Inc. 1967 1 AllER 1005 141
Bradbury v London Borough of Enfield 1967 3 AllER 434................... 146
Brady v St Margaret's Trust Ltd. 1963 2 AllER 275 195
Braham v J. Lyons and Co. Ltd. 1962 3 AllER 281 200
Bravery v Bravery 1954 1 WLR 1169.. 145
Brikom Investments Ltd v Carr 1979 2 AllER 753 220
British Airways Board v Customs and Excise Commissioners 1977 2 AllER 873 197
British Railways Board v Glass 1964 3 AllER 418................................. 195
British Steel Corporation v Granada TV Ltd. 1981 1 AllER 417 193
Bryanston Finance Ltd. v De Vries 1975 2 AllER 609 .... 141, 199
Buckoke v Greater London Council 1971 2 AllER 254 139
Burgess v Rawnsley 1975 3 AllER 142................................... 145, 146, 190
Buttes Gas and Oil Co. v Hammer [No 2] 1975 2 AllER 51 .... 148, 193
Buttes Gas and Oil Co. v Hammer [No 3] 1980 3 AllER 475 193
Buttes Gas and Oil Co. v Hammer 1971 3 AllER 1025 193
C. Maurice and Co. Ltd. v Minster of Labour 1968 2 AllER 1030........ 198
C.H.W.[Huddersfield]Ltd v Inland Revenue Commissioners 1962 3 AllER 243 224
Campbell v Inland Revenue Commissioners 1967 2 AllER 625 189
Cantliff v Jenkins 1978 1 AllER 836... 146
Capital Finance Co. Ltd. v Bray 1964 1 AllER 603 195
Car and Universal Finance Co. Ltd. v Caldwell 1963 2 AllER 547...... 195
Central Estates [Belgravia] Ltd. v Woolgar [No 2] 1972 2 AllER 610 144,

222

Central Estates [Belgravia] Ltd. v Woolgar 1971 3 AllER 347 189
Central Property Trust Ltd. v High Trees House Ltd [1947] 1 K.B. 130. 53
Chaplin v Leslie Frewin 1965 3 AllER 764 141
Chapman v Honig 1963 2 AllER 513 224
Chappell v The Times Newspapers Ltd. 1975 2 AllER 233 .... 149, 196
Chief Immigration Officer, Gatwick ex p Kharrazi 1980 3 AllER 373 .. 147
Churchman v Joint Shop Stewards Committee of the Workers of the Port of London 1972 3 AllER 603 199
Cinnamond v British Airports Authority 1980 2 AllER 368 220
Cleveland Petroleum Co. Ltd. v Dartstone Ltd. 1969 1 AllER 201 196
Clifford Davis Management Ltd v WEA Records Ltd. 1975 1 AllER 237 196
Commissioners of Customs and Excise v Top Ten Promotions Ltd. 1969 3 AllER 39 197
Compagnie Tunisienne de Navigation SA v Compagnie d'Armament Maritime SA 1969 3 AllER 589 149
Connel v Motor Insurers Bureau 1969 3 AllER 572 188
Conway v Rimmer 1967 2 AllER 1260 222
Cooke v Head 1972 2 AllER 38 146
Cookson v Knowles 1977 2 AllER 820 148
Cross v British Iron, Steel and Kindred Trades Association 1968 1 AllER 250 188
Daily Mirror Newspapers Ltd. v Gardner 1968 2 AllER 163 196
Danchevsky v Danchevsky 1974 3 AllER 934 190
Davis v Johnson 1978 1 AllER 841 146
Davy v Leeds Corporation 1964 3 AllER 390 195
Dellafiora v Lester 1962 3 AllER 393 .... 189, 200
DHN Food Distributors Ltd. v London Borough of Tower Hamlets 1976 3 AllER 462 189
Dickson v The Pharmaceutical Society of Great Britain 1967 2 AllER 558 139
Dietz v Lennig Chemicals Ltd 1966 2 AllER 962 188
Duke of Buccleuch v Inland Revenue Commissioners 1965 3 AllER 458 147
Dyson Holdings Ltd v Fox 1975 3 AllER 1030 .... 139, 145, 146
E.R. Ives Investments Ltd v High 1967 1 AllER 504 195
E.Y.L. Trading Co. Ltd v Inland Revenue 1962 3 AllER 303 224
Edsell Caravan Parks v Hemel Hempstead RDC 1965 3 AllER 737 195
Eshun v Moorgate Mercantile Co. Ltd. 1971 2 AllER 402 195
Esso Petroleum Co. Ltd v Minister of Labour 1968 3 AllER 425 198

Esso Petroleum Ltd. v Harper's Garage [Stourport] Ltd. 1966 1 AllER 725 196
European Grain and Shipping Ltd. v Johnston 1982 3 AllER 989 189
Eves v Eves 1975 3 AllER 768 .... 145, 146, 190
Ex parte Island Records Ltd. 1978 3 AllER 824 197
Express Newspapers Ltd v McShane 1979 2 AllER 360 196
Feather Supplies Ltd. v Ingham 1971 3 AllER 556 189
Field Place Caravan Park Ltd. v Harding 1966 3 AllER 247 195
Fielding v Variety, Incorporated 1967 2 AllERR 497 141
Financings Ltd v Baldock 1963 1 AllER 443 195
Financings Ltd v Stimson 1962 3 AllER 386 195
Finsbury Securities Ltd. v Bishop [Inspector of Taxes] 1965 3 AllER 337 199
Firman v Ellis 1978 2 AllER 851 223
Fisher v C.H.T. Ltd 1966 1 AllER 88 197
Fisher-Bendix Ltd. v Secretary of State for Employment 1970 2 AllER 286 198
Formosa v Formosa 1962 3 AllER 419 145
Fothergill v Monarch Airlines Ltd 1979 3 AllER 445 150
Fox v Stirk 1970 3 AllER 7 197
Franklin v The Queen 1973 3 AllER 861 192
Fulham v Newcastle Chronicle and Journal Ltd 1977 3 AllER 32 141
Fuller v Fuller 1973 2 AllER 650 190
G[A] v G[T] 1970 3 AllER 546 143
Gallagher Ltd. v Commissioners of Customs and Excise 1968 2 AllER 820 192
Gallie v Lee 1969 1 AllER 1062 219
Garton v Hunter [Valuation Officer] 1969 1 AllER 451 195
George Mitchell [Chesterhall] Ltd v Finney Lock Seeds Ltd 1983 1 AllER 109 141
Gibson v Manchester City Council 1978 2 AllER 583 188
Gilmore [Valuation Officer] v Baker-Carr 1962 3 AllER 12 196
Gohoho v Guinea Press Ltd 1962 3 AllER 785 .... 148, 192
Goldsmith v Sperrings Ltd. 1977 2 AllER 566 .... 199, 223
Goody v Odhams Press Ltd. 1966 3 AllER 369 .... 64, 197, 223
Goulston Discount Co. Ltd. v Clark 1967 1 AllER 61 195
Gouriet v Union of Post Office Workers 1977 1 AllER 696 .... 67, 192, 222
Grapelli v Derek Block [Holdings] Ltd. 1981 2 AllER 272 190
Greater London Council v Connolly 1970 1 AllER 870 147
Greenhalgh v British Railways Board 1969 2 AllER 114 188
Gregson v Cyril Lord Ltd. 1962 3 AllER 907 195

Grunwick Processing Laboratories Ltd v Advisory, Conciliation and Arbitration Service 1978 1 AllER 338 192
Gurasz v Gurasz 1969 3 AllER 822 .... 144, 145
H. Parsons [Livestock] Ltd. v Uttley Ingham and Co. Ltd. 1978 1 AllER 525 188
H.P. Bulmer Ltd v J. Bollinger SA 1974 2 AllER 1226 139
Haley v London Electricity Board 1963 3 AllER 1003 200
Hall v Hall 1971 1 AllER 762 145
Hanlon v Law Society 1980 1 AllER 763 190
Hargrave v Newton [formerly Hargrave] 1971 3 AllER 866 197
Harold Stephen and Co.Ltd v the Post Office 1978 1 AllER 939 .. 139, 193
Hayward v Thompson 1981 3 AllER 450 .... 139, 144, 190
Hector v Hector 1973 3 AllER 1070 190
Henning [Valuation Officer] v Church of Jesus Christ 1962 3 AllER 364 141
Herbert v Byrne 1964 1 AllER 882 139
Hesperides Hotels Ltd. v Aegean Turkish Holdings 1978 1 AllER 277. 192
Hewer v Bryant 1969 3 AllER 578 188
Hodges v Harland and Wolff Ltd 1965 1 AllER 1086 143
Hollington v F. Hewthorn and Co. Ltd. 1943 2 AllER 35 .... 64, 197, 223
Holman v Johnson [1775] 1 Cowp 341 222
Home Office v Harman 1981 2 AllER 349 223
Horwood v Miller's Timber and Trading Co. Ltd. 1916-17 AllER 842 196
Howard Marine and Dredging Co. Ltd. v A. Ogden and Sons [Excavators] Ltd. 1978 2 AllER 1134 188
Howard v Borneman [No 2] 1974 3 AllER 862 141
Hubbard v Pitt 1975 3 AllER 1 195
Hubbard v Vosper 1972 1 AllER 1023 142
Hussey v Palmer 1972 3 AllER 746 .... 141, 222
Imperial Tobacco Ltd. v Attorney-General 1979 2 AllER 592 197
Indyka v Indyka 1966 3 AllER 583 145
Inland Revenue Commissioners v Cleary 1966 2 AllER 19 224
Inland Revenue Commissioners v Educational Grants Association 1967 2 AllER 891 189
Italmare Shipping Co. v Ocean Tanker Co. Inc. 1982 1 AllER 517 189
J. and C. Moores Ltd v Commissioners of Customs and Excise 1963 2 AllER 714 197
J.M. Allan [Merchandising] Ltd v Cloke 1963 2 AllER 258 197
Jackson v Horizon Holidays Ltd. 1975 3 AllER 92 196
Jackson v Jackson 1971 3 AllER 774 145
James Marshall v BBC 1979 3 AllER 80 151

James v Minister of Housing and Local Government 1963 3 AllER 602 195
Jarvis v Swans Tours Ltd. 1973 1 AllER 71 196
Jelbert v Davies 1968 1 AllER 1182 195
Joyce v DPP [1946] AC 347 150
Kelly v London Transport Executive 1981 2 AllER 842 149
Keys v Boulter 1971 1 AllER 289 198
Kingsway Investments [Kent] Ltd v Kent County Council 1969 1 AllER 601 .... 139, 222
Kowalczak v Kowalczak 1973 2 AllER 1042 190
Laker Airways Ltd v Department of Trade 1977 2 AllER 182. 67, 196, 220
Lambert v Ealing Borough Council 1982 2 AllER 394 150
Lane v Holloway 1967 3 AllER 129 200
Langston v AUEW 1974 1 AllER 980 .... 140, 141
Launchbury v Morgans 1971 1 AllER 642 195
Letang v Cooper 1964 2 AllER 929 224
Lever [Finance] Ltd. v Westminster Corporation 1970 3 AllER 496 ... 189, 200
Lewis v Averay 1971 3 AllER 907 150
Littlewoods Mail Order Stores Ltd v McGregor [Inspector of Taxes] 1969 3 AllER 855 224
Liverpool and County Discount Co. Ltd. v A.B. Motors Co. [Kilburn] Ltd 1963 2 AllER 396 195
Liverpool City Council v Irwin 1975 3 AllER 658 222
Liverpool Corporation v Husain 1971 3 AllER 651 189
London Artists Ltd v Littler 1969 2 AllER 193 141
London Borough of Hammersmith v Magnum Automated Forecourts Ltd. 1978 1 AllER 401 223
Lupton [Inspector of Taxes] v F.A. and A.B. Ltd. 1969 3 AllER 1034 .. 199
Macarthys v Smith 1979 3 AllER 325 72
Macsaga Investment Co. Ltd. v Lupton [Inspector of Taxes] 1967 2 AllER 930 190
MacShannon v Rockware Glass Ltd 1977 2 AllER 449 149
Mandla v Dowell Lee 1982 3 AllER 1108 150
Manley v Law Society 1981 1 AllER 401 220
Mardorf Peach and Co. Ltd v Altica Sea Carriers Corporation of Liberia 1976 2 AllER 249 224
Mareva Companionera Naviera SA v International Bulk Carriers SA 1980 1 AllER 213 140
Mason [Inspector of Taxes] v Innes 1967 2 AllER 926 189
Maxwell v Department of Trade and Industry 1972 2 AllER 122 139

Maynard v Osmond 1977 1 AllER 64 200
McIlkenny v Chief Constable of West Midlands Police 1980 2 AllER 227
.... 149, 200
Meade v London Borough of Haringey 1979 2 AllER 1016 139
Midland Bank Trust Co Ltd v Green [no 3] 1981 3 AllR 744 145
Midland Bank Trust Co. Ltd. v Green 1979 3 AllER 29 .... 140, 141, 189
Miliangos v George Frank [Textiles] Ltd 1975 1 AllER 1076 148
Miller-Mead v Minister of Housing and Local Government 1963 1 AllER
    459 224
Mills v Inland Revenue Commissioners 1972 3 AllER 977 141
Ministry of Agriculture, Fisheries and Food v Jenkins 1963 2 AllER 147
.... 189
Ministry of Defence v Jeremiah 1979 3 AllER 833 146
Ministry of Housing and Local Government v Sharp 1970 1 AllER 1009
.... 189
*Monterosso Shipping Co.Ltd v International Transport Workers
    Federation* 1982 2 AllER 841 139
Moore v Clerk of Assize, Bristol 1972 1 AllER 58 224
Morgan v Inland Revenue Commissioners 1963 1 AllER 481 224
Morris v C.W. Martin and Sons Ltd. 1965 2 AllER 715 219
Morris v The Crown Office 1970 1 AllER 1079 .... 149, 223
Munnich v Godstone Rural District Council 1966 1 AllER 930 195
Munson v British Railways Board 1965 3 AllER 441 196
Munton v GLC 1976 2 AllER 815 .... 189, 195
Murray [Inspector of Taxes] v Imperial Chemical Industries Ltd. 1967 2
    AllER 980 .... 190, 196
Myers v Milton Keynes Development Corporation 1974 2 AllER 1096 195
Nagle v Fielden 1966 1 AllER 639 219
Nast and Nast v Walker 1972 1 AllER 1171 146
National Dock Labour Board v John Brand and Co. 1970 2 AllER 577
.... 196
National Provincial Bank Ltd. v Hastings Car Mart 1964 1 AllER 688 145
New Zealand Government Property Corporation v HM and S Ltd 1982 1
    AllER 624 141
Nissan v Attorney-General 1967 2 AllER 1238 .... 150, 192
Nothman v London Borough of Barnet 1978 1 AllER 1243 141
Ocean Tramp Tankers Corp. v v/o Sovfracht 1964 1 AllER 161 ... 189, 192
Oppenheimer v Cattermole 1972 3 AllER 1106 150
Ostreicher v Secretary of State for the Environment 1978 2 AllER 82 .. 141
Panamanian Oriental Steamship Corporation v Wright 1971 2 AllER
    1028 193

Pannett v P. McGuiness and Co Ltd 1972 3 AllER 137 141
Paul Wilson and Co. A/S v Partenreederie Hannah Blumenthal 1982 3 AllER 39 189
Peake v Automotive Products Ltd 1978 1 AllER 106 146
Pearlman v Keepers and Governors of Harrow School 1979 1 AllER 365 223
Peck v Anicar Properties Ltd. 1971 1 AllER 517 189
Perilly v Tower Hamlets Borough Council 1972 3 AllER 513 200
Petrofina [Gt Britain] Ltd v Martin 1966 1 AllER 126 196
Petrotim Securities Ltd v Ayres [Inspector of Taxes] 1964 1 AllER 269 199
Phillips v Minister of Housing and Local Government 1964 2 AllER 824 141
Phonogram Ltd v Lane 1981 3 AllER 182 .... 145, 150
Photo Production Ltd. v Securicor Transport Ltd. 1978 3 AllER 146 .. 188
Plummer v Chapman 1962 3 AllER 823 151
Premor Ltd. v Shaw Brothers 1964 2 AllER 583 195
Prestcold [Central] Ltd. v Minister of Labour 1969 1 AllER 69 198
Public Trustee v Westbrook 1965 3 AllER 398 195
R v Almon [1770] 5 Burr 2686 20, State Tr 803 55
R v Axbridge Rural District Council ex parte Wormald 1964 1 AllER 571 195
R v Barnsley Metropolitan Borough Council 1976 3 AllER 452 139
R v Gaming Board of Great Britain ex parte Benaim 1970 2 AllER 528 197
R v Greater London Council ex parte Blackburn 1976 3 AllER 184 ...... 67, 143, 197
R v Hampden [1637] How. St. Tr. 825 56
R v Herrod ex parte Leeds City District Council 1976 1 AllER 273 197
R v Horsham Justices ex parte Farquharson 1982 2 AllER 269 ... 139, 223
R v Industrial Injuries Commissioner ex parte Cable 1968 1 AllER 9 .. 188
R v Inland Revenue Commissioners ex parte Rossminster 1979 3 AllER 385 70
R v Leicester Gaming Licensing Committee ex parte Shine 1971 3 AllER 1082 197
R v Local Commissioner for Administration for the North and East Area of England ex parte Bradford Metropolitan City Council 1979 2 AllER 881 141
R v London Borough of Hillingdon ex parte Islam 1981 2 AllER 1089 139
R v London Borough of Tower Hamlets ex parte Kayne-Levenson 1975 1 AllER 641 200

R v Metropolitan Police Commissioner ex parte Blackburn [No 3] 1973 1 AllER 324 .... 143, 197, 198
R v Metropolitan Police Commissioner ex parte Blackburn 1968 1 AllER 763 197
R v Paddington Valuation Officer ex parte Peachey Property Corporation Ltd. 1965 2 AllER 836 223
R v Penguin Books Ltd. 1961 Crim. L.R. 176 142
R v Preston Supplementary Benefits Appeal Tribunal ex parte Moore 1975 2 AllER 807 197
R v Registrar General ex parte Segerdal 1970 3 AllER 886 142
R v Secretary of State for Commonwealth Affairs ex p Indian Association of Alberta 1982 2 AllER 118 149
R v Secretary of State for Home Affairs ex parte Soblen 1962 1 QB 829 193
R v Secretary of State for the Environment ex parte Ostler 1976 3 AllER 90 189
R v Secretary of State for the Home Department ex parte Hosenball 1977 3 AllER 452 .... 65, 68, 194
R v Secretary of State for the Home Department ex parte Phansopkar 1975 3 AllER 497 70
R v Selvey 1968 1 AllER 94 144
R v Tottenham District Rent Tribunal ex parte Frazer Bros [Properties] Ltd. 1971 3 AllER 563 189
R v West Sussex Quarter Sessions ex parte Albert and Maud Johnson Trust Ltd 1973 3 AllER 289 222
R. and T. Thew Ltd v Reeves 1981 2 AllER 964 200
Race Relations Board v Associated Newspapers Group Ltd. 1978 3 AllER 419 193
Rank Film Distributors Ltd v Video Information Centre 1980 2 AllER 273 140
Re [F] [a minor][publication of information] 1977 1 AllER 114 143
Re Brocklehurst [deceased] 1978 1 AllER 767 141
Re Grosvenor Hotel, London [No 2] 1964 3 AllER 354 222
Re Gulbenkian's Settlement Trusts 1967 3 AllER 15 141
Re Harmsworth [deceased] 1967 2 AllER 249 189
Re Holmden's Settlement Trusts 1966 2 AllER 661 224
Re James [an insolvent] [Attorney-General intervening] 1977 1 AllER 364 .... 148, 149, 192, 222
Re Jebb [deceased] 1965 3 AllER 358 190
Re Keenan 1971 3 AllER 883 149
Re King [deceased] 1963 1 AllER 781 195

Re L [an Infant] 1962 3 AllER 1 145
Re L 1968 1 AllER 20 145
Re National Federation of Retail Newsagents, Booksellers and Stationers Agreement [Nos 3 and 4] 1971 2 AllER 514 196
Re Newspaper Proprietor's Agreement 1963 1 AllER 36 196
Re P [G.E.] [an infant] 1964 3 AllER 977 .... 150, 222
Re Pergamon Press Ltd 1970 3 AllER 535 199
Re Pritchard [deceased] 1963 1 AllER 873 224
Re Ralli's Settlements 1964 3 AllER 781 225
Re S [an infant] 1965 1 AllER 865 223
Re Stone and Saville's Contract 1963 1 AllER 353 139
Re Trepka Mines Ltd 1962 3 AllER 351 150
Re Tuck's Settlement Trusts 1978 1 AllER 1047 149
Re United Railways of Havana v Regla Warehouses Ltd 1960 2 AllER 333 149
Re Valentine's Settlement 1965 2 AllER 226 .... 145, 146
Re Weston's Settlement Trusts 1968 3 AllER 338 .... 70, 139, 150
Reel v Holder 1980 3 AllER 321 193
Regent Oil Co. Ltd. v Aldon Motors Ltd. 1965 2 AllER 644 195
Registrar of Restrictive Trading Agreements v W.H. Smith 1969 3 AllER 1065 196
Robophone Facilities Ltd. v Blank 1966 3 AllER 128 196
Rolls Razor Ltd v Cox 1967 1 AllER 397 199
Rondel v Worsley 1966 3 AllER 657 .... 197, 223
Rothermere v Times Newspapers Ltd 1973 1 AllER 1013 220
Routhan v Arun District Council 1981 3 AllER 752 145
Royal College of Nursing of the United Kingdom v Department of Health and Social Security 1981 1 AllER 545 144
S v McC [formerly S] and M [intervening] 1970 AllER 1162 145
Sabally v Attorney-General 1964 3 AllER 377 .... 148, 192
Sagnata Investments Ltd. v Norwich Corporation 1971 2 AllER 1441. 197
Schering Chemicals Ltd v Falkman Ltd 1981 2 AllER 321 .... 139, 196
Schmidt v Secretary of State for Home Affairs 1969 1 AllER 904 141
SCM [United Kingdom] Ltd v W.J. Whitall and Son Ltd 1970 3 AllER 245 224
Scott [Inspector of Taxes] v Ricketts 1967 2 AllER 1009 .... 190, 195
Scott v Green 1969 1 AllER 849 188
Secretary of State for Education and Science v Metropolitan Borough of Tameside 1976 3 AllER 665 .... 146, 192
Secretary of State for Employment v Associated Society of Locomotive Engineers and Firemen [No 2] 1972 2 AllER 949 198

Senior [an infant] v Baker and Allen Ltd 1965 1 AllER 818 147
Senior v Holdsworth 1975 2 AllER 1009 .... 193, 223
Shaw v Director of Public Prosecutions [1962] AC 220 HL 59
Shaw v Shaw 1 AllER 658 222
Sheldon v Sheldon 1966 2 AllER 257 .... 143, 144, 146
Shell UK Ltd. v Lostock Garage Ltd. 1977 1 AllER 481 196
Shell-Mex and BP Ltd v Manchester Garages Ltd. 1971 1 AllER 841 .. 189
Shell-Mex and British Petroleum v Langley [Valuation Officer] 1962 3 AllER 433 196
Shepherd v Lomas 1963 2 AllER 902 189
Shields v E. Coombes [Holdings] Ltd. 1979 1 AllER 456 139
Sirros v Moore 1974 3 AllER 776 .... 151, 225
Smith v ILEA 1978 1 AllER 411 141
Smith v Inner London Education Authority 1978 1 AllER 411 147
Snook v London and West Riding Investments Ltd. 1967 1 AllER 518. 195, 222
Somersett v Stewart [1772] Loft 1 19 54
Stafford Borough Council v Elkenford Ltd. 1977 2 AllER 519 196
Staffordshire Area Health Authority v South Staffordshire Waterworks Co 1978 3 AllER 769 .... 148, 188
Stock v Frank Jones [Tipton] Ltd. 1978 1 AllER 58 199
Strick [Inspector of Taxes] v Regent Oil Co. Ltd. 1964 3 AllER 23 ..... 139, 195
Sydall v Castings Ltd 1966 3 AllER 770 145
Tanner v Tanner 1975 3 AllER 776 .... 145, 146, 190
Taylor v British Omnibus Co Ltd 1975 2 AllER 1107 148
Techno-Impex v Gebr van Weelde Scheepvartkantoor BV 1981 2 AllER 669 .... 148, 221
Tehrani v Rostron 1971 3 AllER 790 197
Thakrah v Secretary of State for the Home Department 1974 2 AllER 261 70
The Atlantic Star 1972 3 AllER 705 150
The Case of Swans 1592 7 Co Rep 156 145
The Five Knights Case [1627] 3 How. St. Tr. 1 KB 54
The Folias 1978 2 AllER 764 .... 148, 221
The Maratha Envoy 1977 2 AllER 41 189
The Mihailos Xilas 1979 1 AllER 657 139
The Siskina 1977 3 AllER 803 .... 140, 189, 222
The Teh Hu 1969 3 AllER 1200 .... 139, 148
The Vera Cruz [No 2] 1884 9 PD 9 146
The Weijiang 1982 2 AllER 437 189

The World Beauty 1969 3 AllER 158 192
Third Chandris Shipping Corporation v Unimarine SA 1979 2 AllER 972 140
Thornton v Shoe Lane Parking Ltd 1971 1 AllER 686 141
Total Oil Great Britain Ltd. v Thompson Garages [Biggin Hill] Ltd. 1971 3 AllER 1216 189
Trendtex Trading Corporation Ltd v Central Bank of Nigeria 1977 1 AllER 881 139
Trippas v Trippas 1973 2 AllER 1 190
Tucker v Farm and General Investment Trust Ltd. 1966 2 AllER 508 . 145, 219
United Dominions Trust [Commercial] Ltd. v Ennis 1967 2 AllER 345 195
United Dominions Trust Co. v Kirkwood 1966 1 AllER 968 .... 199, 221
Unity Finance Ltd v Woodcock 1963 2 AllER 270 195
Verrall v Great Yarmouth Borough Council 1980 1 AllER 839 .... 141, 151
Viscount Camrose v Basingstoke Corporation 1966 3 AllER 161 195
W. and J.B. Eastwood Ltd. v Herrod [Valuation Officer] 1968 3 AllER 389 196
W.J. Allen and Co. Ltd v El Nasr Export and Import Co 1972 2 AllER 127 221
Wallersteiner v Moir 1974 3 AllER 217 .... 141, 199, 200, 222, 223
Ward v James 1965 1 AllER 565 .... 143, 221, 224
Warner Brothers Records Inc. v Rollgreen Ltd. 1975 2 AllER 105 197
Warwick University v De Graaf 1975 3 AllER 284 197
Watts v Manning 1964 2 AllER 267 143
Webb v Ministry of Housing and Local Government 1965 2 AllER 193 139
Webber v Minister of Housing and Local Government 1967 3 AllER 981 195
Western Excavating Ltd. v Sharp 1978 1 AllER 713 188
Westminster Bank Executor and Trustee Co. [Channel Isles] Ltd. v National Bank of Greece SA 1969 3 AllER 504 192
Whitehouse v Jordan 1980 1 AllER 650 144
Whitworth Street Estates [Manchester] Ltd v James Millar and Partners Ltd 1969 2 AllER 210 149
Wickham Holdings Ltd. v Brooke House Motors Ltd. 1967 1 AllER 117 195
Williams and Glyn's Bank v Boland 1979 2 AllER 697 189
Wills v Association of Universities of the British Commonwealth 1964 2 AllER 39 197
Wilson, Smithett and Cope Ltd v Terruzzi 1976 1 AllER 817 199
Wiseman v Borneman 1967 3 AllER 1045 190

Wolf v Crutchley 1971 1 AllER 520 189
Woodhouse AC Israel Cocoa Ltd SA v Nigeria Produce Marketing Co Ltd
    1971 1 AllER 665 148
Woodward v Hutchins 1977 2 AllER 751 197
Worcester Works Finance Ltd. v Cooden Engineering Co. Ltd. 1971 3
    AllER 708 195
Wyld v Silver [No2] 1962 2 AllER 809 195
Z Ltd v A 1982 1 AllER 556 140

BIBLIOGRAPHY

Allen, M., Thompson, J. *Cases and Materials on Constitutional Law* Oxford: Clarendon Press, 2002
Allen, T.R.S. *Constitutional Justice: A Liberal Theory of the Rule of Law* Oxford: Clarendon Press, 2001
—. *Law, Liberty and Justice: The Legal Foundations of British Constitutionalism* Oxford: Clarendon Press, 1993
Anderson, B. *Imagined Communities: Reflections on the Origins and Spread of Nationalism* London: Verso, 1983
Annan, N. *Our Age* London: Weidenfeld and Nicolson, 1990
Ashton, R. *The English Civil War: Conservatism and Revolution* London: Weidenfeld and Nicolson, 1989
Austin, J. *The Province of Jurisprudence Determined, and the Uses of the Study of Jurisprudence*, Hart, H.L.A. ed. London: Weidenfeld and Nicolson, 1954
Atiyah, P.S. *Law and Modern Society* Oxford: Clarendon Press, 1995
Bagehot, W. *The English Constitution* London: Collins, 1963
Baker, J.H. *Introduction to Legal History* Cambridge: Cambridge University Press, 1990
Baldwin, S. *On England* London: Harmondsworth, 1937
Ball, S., and Seldon, A. eds. *The Heath Government* London: Longman, 1994
Barker, G. ed. *The Character of England* Oxford: Clarendon Press, 1947
Barrett, M. *The Law Lords* Basingstoke: Macmillan, 2001
Beloff, M., and Peele, G. *The Government of the United Kingdom* Oxford: Clarendon Press, 1980
Benn, T *Arguments for Socialism* London: Cape, 1979
—. *Arguments for Democracy* London: Cape, 1980
—. *Out of the Wilderness: Diaries 1963-1967* London: Hutchinson, 1987
—. *Office without Power: Diaries 1968-1972* London: Hutchinson, 1988
—. *Against the Tide: Diaries 1973-1976* London: Hutchinson, 1989
—. *Conflicts of Interest: Diaries 1977-1980* London: Hutchinson, 1990
—. *The End of an Era: Diaries 1980-1990* London: Hutchinson, 1992
Bennett, G.V. *The Tory Crisis in Church and State* Oxford: Oxford University Press, 1975

Bentham, J. *A Fragment on Government*, Burns, J.H. and Hart, H.L.A. eds. Cambridge: Cambridge University Press, 1988
Blackstone, W. *Commentaries on the Laws of England* ed. Morrison, W. London: Cavendish, 2001
Blake, R. *The Conservative Party from Peel to Thatcher* London: Methuen, 1985
—. *The Decline of Power: Britain 1915-1964* London: Granada, 1985
Bogdanor, V. *Politics and the Constitution: Essays on British Government* Aldershot: Dartmouth, 1996
—. *Devolution in the United Kingdom* Oxford: Clarendon Press, 2001
—. ed. *The British Constitution in the Twentieth Century* London: British Academy, 2003
Bogdanor, V., and Skidelsky, R. *The Age of Affluence 1951-1964* London: Harmondsworth, 1970
Booker, C. *The Neophiliacs* London: Collins, 1969
Bracton *On the Laws and Customs of England Volume* trans. Thorne, S.E. Cambridge: Harvard University Press, 1968
Bradley, A.W., and Ewing, K.D. *Constitutional and Administrative Law* London: Pearson Education Ltd, 2007
Brailsford, H.N. *The Levellers* London: Cresset Press, 1959
Burgess, G. *The Politics of the Ancient Constitution: An Introduction to English Political Thought 1600-1642* Basingstoke: Macmillan, 1992
Butterfield, H. *George III, Lord North and the People* Cambridge: Cambridge University Press, 1948
Campbell, J. *Edward Heath* London: Cape, 1993
Chrimes, S.B. *English Constitutional Ideas in the Fifteenth Century* Cambridge: Cambridge University Press, 1936
Clark, J.C.D. *English Society 1660-1832* Cambridge: Cambridge University Press, 1985
—. *Revolution and Rebellion* Cambridge: Cambridge University Press, 1986
—. *Samuel Johnson* Cambridge: Cambridge University Press, 1995
Coke, Sir E. *The Selected Writings and Speeches of Sir Edward Coke* ed. Sheppard, S. Indianapolis: Liberty Fund 2003
Colley, L. *Britons: Forging the Nation, 1707-1837* London: Yale University Press, 1993
Colls, R. *Identity of England* Oxford: Clarendon Press, 2002
Colls, R. and Dodds, R. *Englishness: Politics and Culture* London: Croom Helm, 1985
Cornish, W.R., and Clark, G. de N. *Law and Society in England 1750-1950* London: Sweet and Maxwell, 1981

Cowling, M. *Religion and Public Doctrine: Vol.1* Cambridge: Cambridge University Press, 1980
—. *Religion and Public Doctrine: Vol.2* Cambridge: Cambridge University Press, 1985
—. *Religion and Public Doctrine: Vol.3* Cambridge: Cambridge University Press, 2004
Cromartie, A. *Sir Matthew Hale 1601-1676* Cambridge: Cambridge University Press, 1991
Crossmann, R.H.S. *Diaries of a Cabinet Minister* London: Mandarin, 1991
Denning, A. *Freedom under the Law* London: Stevens and Sons Ltd, 1949
—. *The Changing Law* London: Stevens and Sons Ltd, 1953
—. *From Precedent to Precedent* Oxford: Clarendon Press, 1959
—. *Report on the Circumstances leading to the Resignation of the Former Secretary of State for War, Mr. J. D. Profumo* London: HMSO, 1963
—. *The Discipline of Law* London: Butterworths, 1979
—. *The Due Process of Law* London: Butterworths, 1980
—. *The Family Story* London: Butterworths, 1981
—. *What Next in the Law* London: Butterworths, 1982
—. *The Closing Chapter* London: Butterworths, 1983
—. *Landmarks in the Law* London: Butterworths, 1984
—. *Leaves from My Library* London: Butterworths, 1986
Devlin, P. *The Enforcement of Morals* London: Clarendon Press, 1965
Dicey, A.V. *The Law of the Constitution* London: Macmillan, 1915
Dworkin, R. *Law's Empire* London: Fontana, 1986
Elton, G.R. *Policy and Police* Cambridge: Cambridge University Press, 1975
—. *Reform and Reformation: England 1509-1558* Cambridge: Cambridge University Press, 1977
—. *The Tudor Constitution* Cambridge: Cambridge University Press, 1982
Fletcher, A. *The Outbreak of the English Civil War* Oxford: Clarendon Press, 1981
Foot, P. *Immigration and Race* London: Harmondsworth, 1968
Fortescue, Sir J. *On the Laws and Governance of England* ed. Lockwood, S. Cambridge: Cambridge University Press, 1997
Fraunce, A. *The Lawiers Logike* Menston: The Scholar Press, 1969
Freeman, I. *Lord Denning* London: Hutchinson, 1993
Gardiner, S.R. *History of England from the Accession of James I to the Outbreak of the Civil War* London: Longman, Green and Co., 1884
Geoffrey of Monmouth *History of the Kings of Britain* London: Harmondsworth, 1966

Goldsworthy, J. *The Sovereignty of Parliament* Oxford: Clarendon Press, 1999
Goodrich, P. *Reading the Law: a Critical Introduction to Legal Method* Oxford: Basil Blackwell, 1986
—. *Legal Discourse* London: Macmillan, 1987
—. *Languages of Law* London: Weidenfeld and Nicolson, 1990
—. *Oedipus Lex* Berkeley: University of California Press, 1995
—. *Law in the Courts of Love* London: Routledge, 1996
—. ed. *Law and the Unconscious: a Legendre Reader* London: Macmillan, 1997
—. 'Poor Illiterate Reason: History, Nationalism and the Common Law' *Social and Legal Studies*
Goulbourne, H. *Race Relations in Britain since 1945* Basingstoke: Macmillan, 1998
Green, J.R. *A Short History of the English People* London: Macmillan, 1888
Griffith, J.A.G. *The Politics of the Judiciary* London: Fontana, 1997
Guy, J. *Tudor England* Oxford: Clarendon Press, 1988
Lord Hailsham *Elective Dictatorship* London: British Broadcasting Corporation, 1976
—. *The Dilemma of Democracy* London: Collins, 1978
—. *A Sparrow's Flight: Memoirs* London: Collins, 1990
—. *On the Constitution* London: Harper Collins, 1992
Hanham, H.J. *The Nineteenth Century Constitution* Cambridge: Cambridge University Press, 1970
Hanafin, P. *Constituting Identity* Aldershot: Ashgate, 1999
Hansen, R. *Citizenship and Immigration in Postwar Britain* Oxford: Clarendon Press, 2000
Hart, H.L.A. *The Concept of Law* Oxford: Clarendon Press, 1961
—. *Law, Liberty and Morality* Oxford: Clarendon Press, 1963
Heffer, S. *Like the Roman: The Life of Enoch Powell* London: Weidenfeld and Nicolson, 1998
—. *Nor Shall My Sword* London: Weidenfeld and Nicolson, 1999

Helgerson, R. *Forms of Nationhood* London: University of Chicago Press, 1992
Hennessy, P. *Whitehall* London: Secker and Warburg, 1989
—. *The Hidden Wiring* London: Gollancz, 1995
Hersey, G. *The Lost Meaning of Classical Architecture* Cambridge: The MIT Press, 1988
Heward, E. *Lord Denning* Chichester: Barry Rose, 1997

Hill, C. *Intellectual Origins of the English Revolution* Oxford: Clarendon Press, 1965
Hobbes, T. *Leviathan*, Macpherson, C.B. ed. London: Harmondsworth, 1968
Horne, A. *Macmillan: Volume One 1894-1956* London: Macmillan, 1987
—. *Macmillan: Volume Two 1957-1986* London: Macmillan
Howard, A. *R.H.S. Crossman* London: Cape, 1989
Jennings, W.I. *The British Constitution* Cambridge: Cambridge University Press, 1950
—. *Law and the Constitution* London: University of London Press, 1959
Jones, E. *The English Nation: The Great Myth* Stroud: Sutton Publishing Ltd, 1998
Jones, J.R. *The First Whigs: The Politics of the Exclusion Crisis* Oxford: Clarendon Press, 1961
—. *The Revolution of 1688 in England* London: Weidenfeld and Nicolson, 1972
Jones, W.J. *Politics and the Bench: The Judges and the Origins of the English Civil War* London: Allen and Unwin, 1971
Jowell, J. and Oliver, D. *The Changing Constitution* Oxford: Clarendon Press, 2004
Kantorowicz, E. *The King's Two Bodies* Princeton: Princeton University Press, 1959
Kavanagh, D. *Thatcherism and British Politics* Oxford: Clarendon Press, 1990
Kenyon, J.P. *Revolution Politics: The Politics of Party 1689-1720* Oxford: Clarendon Press, 1977
—. *The Stuart Constitution* Cambridge: Cambridge University Press, 1986
King, A. *Does the UK still have a Constitution? The Hamlyn Lectures 2001* London: Sweet and Maxwell, 2001
Kishlansky, M. *A Monarchy Transformed: Britain 1603-1714* London: Allen Lane, 1996
Kumar, K. *The Making of English Identity* Cambridge: Cambridge University Press, 2003
Lamb, A. *The Macmillan Years: the Emerging Story* London: John Murray, 1995
Langford, P. *Englishness Identified: Manners and Character* Oxford: Clarendon Press, 2000
LeSeur, A., and Sunkin, M. *Public Law* London: Butterworths, 1998
Letwin, S.R. *The Anatomy of Thatcherism* London: Fontana, 1992
Levin, B. *The Pendulum Years* London: Cape, 1968
Lewis, C.S. *English Literature in the Sixteenth Century* Oxford:

Clarendon Press, 1954
Lewis, G. *Lord Hailsham: a Life* London: Cape, 1997
Loades, D.M. *The Reign of Mary Tudor: Politics, Government and Religion in England 1553-1558* London: Benn, 1979
Loughlin, M. *Public Law and Political Theory* Oxford: Clarendon Press, 1992
—. *Sword and Scales: An Examination of the Relationship between Law and Politics* Oxford: Hart, 2000
Loveland, I. *Constitutional Law: A Critical Introduction* London: Butterworths, 2000
Lyon, A. *A Constitutional History of the United Kingdom* London: Cavendish, 2003
Maitland, F.W. *The Constitutional History of England* Cambridge: Cambridge University Press, 1908
Macaulay, T.B. *A Shortened History of England* London: Harmondsworth, 1959
McAuslan, P. and Jowell, J. *Lord Denning: the Judge and the Law* London: Sweet and Maxwell, 1984
Miller, J. *An English Absolutism? The Later Stuart Monarchy 1660-1688* London: Historical Association, 1992
Milsom, S.F.C. *Historical Foundations of the Common Law* London: Butterworths, 1981
Milton, J *Political Writings* Cambridge: Cambridge University Press, 1991
Morgan, K.O. *The People's Peace* Oxford: Clarendon Press, 1990
—. *Callaghan* Oxford: Clarendon Press, 1997
Mount, F. *The British Constitution Now: Recovery or Decline?* London: Heinemann, 1992
Murphy, W.T. *The Oldest Social Science?* Oxford: Clarendon Press, 1997
Neale, J.E. *Elizabeth I and her Parliaments* London: Cape, 1959
Lord Nolan of Brastead, and Sedley, S. *The Making and Remaking of the British Constitution* London: Blackstone, 1997
Pannick, D. *Judges* London: Clarendon Press, 1986
Parekh, B. *Bentham's Political Thought* London: Croom Helm, 1971
Paterson, A. *The Law Lords* London: Macmillan, 1982
Pimlott, B. *Harold Wilson* London: Harper Collins, 1992
—. *The Queen* London: Harper Collins, 1996
Plumb, J.H. *The Growth of Political Stability in England 1675-1725* Cambridge: Cambridge University Press, 1967
Pocock, J.G.A. *The Feudal Law and the Ancient Constitution* Cambridge: Cambridge University Press, 1957

Posner, R. *Law and Literature* London: Harvard University Press, 1998
Powell, J.E. *The House of Lords in the Middle Ages* London: Weidenfeld and Nicolson, 1968
—. *Freedom and Reality* London: B.T. Batsford, 1969
—. *Joseph Chamberlain* London: Thames and Hudson, 1977
—. ed. Ritchie, R. *Enoch Powell on* London: Anaya, 1992
Raffield, P. *Images and Cultures of Law in Early Modern England: Justice and Political Power 1558-1660* Cambridge: Cambridge University Press, 2004
Richardson, H.G., and Sayles, G.O. *The Governance of Medieval England from the Conquest to Magna Carta* Edinburgh: Edinburgh University Press, 1963
Robertson, D. *Judicial Discretion in the House of Lords* Oxford: Clarendon Press, 1998
Robertson, G. *The Tyrannicide Brief* London: Chatto and Windus, 2005
Robson, P. and Watchman, P. eds. *Justice, Lord Denning and the Constitution* Farnborough: Gower, 1981
Russell, C. *The Origins of the English Civil War* Basingstoke: Macmillan, 1973
—. *Parliaments and English Politics 1621-1629* Oxford: Clarendon Press, 1979
—. *The Causes of the English Civil War* Oxford: Clarendon Press, 1990
—. *The Fall of the British Monarchies 1637-1642* Oxford: Clarendon Press, 1991
Salmon, J.H.M. *The French Religious Wars in English Political Thought* Oxford: Clarendon Press, 1959
Scarisbrick, J.J. *Henry VIII* London: Eyre and Spottiswoode, 1968
Scarman, L. *English Law: The New Dimension* London: Stevens, 1974
Scruton, R. *The Meaning of Conservatism* London: Harmondsworth, 1980
—. *England: an Elegy* London: Chatto and Windus, 2000
Sedley, S. *Freedom, Law and Justice* London: Sweet and Maxwell, 1999
Sharpe, K. *The Personal Rule of Charles I* Oxford: Clarendon Press, 1992
Sked, A., and Cook, C. *Post-War Britain* London: Harmondsworth, 1993
Southern, J. *The Making of the Middle Ages* London: Arrow, 1959
—. *The Church and English Society in the Middle Ages* London: Harmondsworth, 1965
St. Augustine *The City of God* trans. Bettenson, H. London: Harmondsworth, 1972
St. German *Doctor and Student* ed. Plucknett, T.F.T. and Barton, J.L. London: Selden Society, 1974
Stenton, F.M. *Anglo-Saxon England* Oxford: Clarendon Press. 1943

Stevens, R. *Law and Politics: The House of Lords as a Judicial Body* - London: Weidenfeld and Nicolson, 1979
—. *The English Judges: Their Role in the Changing Constitution* Oxford: Hart, 2002
Tanner, J.R. *Constitutional Documents of the Reign of James I* Cambridge: Cambridge University Press, 1930
Tellegen-Couperus, O. *A Short History of Roman Law* London: Routledge, 1993
Thompson, E.P. *The Making of the English Working Class* London: Victor Gollancz, 1963
—. *The Poverty of Theory* London: Merlin Press, 1978
—. *Writing by Candlelight* London: Merlin Press, 1980
—. *Customs in Common* London: Merlin Press, 1991
Tully, J. *Strange Multiplicity: Constitutionalism in an Age of Diversity* Cambridge: Cambridge University Press, 1995
Veall, D. *The Popular Movement for Law Reform 1640-1660* Oxford: Clarendon Press, 1970
Ullmann, W. *Law and Politics in the Middle Ages* Cambridge: Cambridge University Press, 1975
Ward, I. *Law and Literature* Cambridge: Cambridge University Press, 1996
—. *Shakespeare and the Legal Imagination* London: Butterworths, 1999
—. *A State of Mind: The English Constitution and the Popular Imagination* Stroud: Sutton, 2000
—. *The English Constitution: Myths and Realities* Oxford: Hart, 2004
Western, J.R. *Monarchy and Revolution: The English State in the 1680s* London: Macmillan, 1972
Williams, E.N. *The Eighteenth Century Constitution* Cambridge: Cambridge University Press, 1960
Williams, P.H. *The Tudor Regime* Oxford: Clarendon Press, 1979
—. *The Later Tudors* Oxford: Clarendon Press, 1995
Woolrych, A. *Britain in Revolution* Oxford: Clarendon Press, 2002
Wootton, D. ed. *Divine Right and Democracy* London: Harmondsworth, 1980
Wright, P. *The Village that died for England* London: Cape, 1995
Zander, M. *The Law-Making Process* London: Butterworths, 1994

INDEX

Acheson, Dean 153, 190
Acton, Lord 78
Alfred, King 13
Aliens 134
American Civil War 158
Annan, Noel 191
Anti-Nazi League 138
Argyll Divorce 60
Astor, Lord 32
Attlee, Clement 26
Bankers 180
Battery farming 169
Bentham, Jeremy .. 45, 125, 253, 258
Biafra 156
Bill of Rights 257
Binyon, Lawrence 16
Birmingham 6 .... 125, 188, 222, 227
Blackburn, Raymond 38
Blackstone 45, 99, 107, 126, 153, 177, 201, 203, 205, 219, 234
Blackstone, Sir William 253, 258
Blair, Tony 4, 167
Blasphemy Act 23
Bletchley Park 69, 164
Bloom, John 183
Blunt, Anthony 58, 60, 163
Bond, James 33, 36, 65
Boothby, Lord 51
   Homosexual relationship with Ronnie Kray 60
Bootlegging 173
Boulting Brothers 82
Bracton 44, 201, 205, 254
Bradford, John 96, 144
Bradshaw, John 14, 45
Brougham, Lord 45
Buchan, John 14, 51
Burgess, Guy . 58, 69, 145, 146, 163, 190, 254

Callaghan, James 154
Canada 122
Caravans 166
Carroll, Lewis 79, 80
Celebrity culture 173
Champerty 129
Charles I 14, 21, 45, 259
Chatterley Trial 59, 89, 142
Cheap air travel 170
Cheshire, Geoffrey 53
Chitty, Sir Joseph 16
Christiansen, Eric 191
Christie, Agatha 72
Churchill, Winston 52, 143, 198
City of London 180, 182, 205
Clayre, Alasdair 58
Coke, Sir Edward 13, 45, 48, 52, 71, 76, 98, 99, 112, 125, 127, 153, 181, 201, 202, 203, 204, 205, 209, 217, 218, 219, 220, 221, 231, 233, 234, 254
Cook, Peter 154, 190
Cowper, William 77, 78, 210
Cromwell, Oliver 14, 15, 52, 55
Crown, doctrine of unity 123
Cyprus 155
Denning
   Abortion 96, 146
   All Souls 53
   Attitude to the French 127
   Christianity 23, 27
   Church of England 84
   City of London 83
   Conception and Birth 95
   Contraception 97, 146
   Daily Telegraph Obituary 2
   Divorce Law Reform 146

Domicile, doctrine of 102
England as an Island 73
Freedom of the Press 47
Freedom under the Law ...10, 11, 18, 19, 20, 21, 24, 54, 70, 200, 255
Genealogy 13
General Strike 53
Grammar Schools 110
Hippies 91
Homosexuality 93, 94
Illegitimacy 100
Importance of Christmas 103
Importance of Family 12
Importance of Freedom of the Press 26
Importance of Jury Trial ..24, 44, 45, 70, 89
Importance of Marriage 103, 106
Importance of Place 12
Importance of Trial by Jury ... 52
Inflation 114
Literature 74
Magdalen College 16
Male Sexuality 89
Mareva Injunction 77, 78, 79, 80, 140
Marriage as a joint enterprise 105
Marriage as a protection for women 106
On the mystery of the Constitution 17
Paternity 99
Patriotism 73
Pornography 92, 93
President of Birkbeck College 54
Profumo Report 29
Protection of women 104, 107
Race 24
Regulation 18B 55
Resignation 44, 46, 56, 226, 227, 230
Respect for Harold Macmillan 64
Romanes Lecture 27, 56
Scientology 87, 88

Sexual Morality 27
Shakespeare 74
Smith's Leading Cases 16
Sunday Times Obituary 3
The Discipline of Law 11, 37, 40, 67, 255
The Due Process of Law . 11, 37, 40, 63, 67, 255
The Empire 118
The English Character 24
The English Civil War 14, 26
The Falklands War 50
The Family 89
The Misuse of Power . 11, 40, 67
The Second World War 16, 49
The Stage 81
Treaty of Rome 74
Unity, doctrine of 105
Views on Anti-Semitism 22, 132
Views on cars 168
Views on computers 170
Views on Contempt of Court 213
Views on Nazi Germany 132
Views on Rhodesia 121
Views on the Police 187
What Next in the Law 11, 36, 37, 44, 50, 52, 56, 67, 71, 201, 219, 226, 255

Denning Close 186
Denning, Sir Norman 16, 69, 193
Denning, Sir Reginald 16
Devlin, Lord 11, 52, 59, 89, 142, 255
Dicey, Albert Venn 7, 9, 10, 25, 255
Dickens, Charles 15, 77
Dilhorne, Viscount 57
Dividend stripping 181
Donaldson, Lord 4, 41
Dworkin, Ronald 255
Eden, Anthony 51, 65
Edward the Confessor 205
English Civil War 253, 255, 257, 259
Fairbanks, Douglas Jr 67
Fleming, Anne

Affair with Hugh Gaitskell 66
Fleming, Ian 36, 63, 65
Flitton, Pamela 57
Floods of 1953 74
Foot, Michael 50
Fortescue, Sir John 21, 255
Fraunce, Abraham 255
Gaitskell, Hugh 66
Gambia 119, 156
Gambling 153, 176
Garnett, Alf 6
GCHQ 164
Geoffrey of Monmouth 255
George III 254
Ghana 119, 156
Glorious Revolution 257, 258
Goff, Lord 4
Goldfinger, Auric 63
Goldsmith, James 184
Goodrich, Peter 256
Gouriet, John .. 38, 67, 158, 192, 222
Great Train Robbery ...64, 175, 176, 223
Greene, Richard 128
Griffith, J.A.G. 7, 10, 37, 256
Griffith-Jones, Mervyn................ 62
Grunwick 76
Hailsham, Lord 4, 51, 53, 70, 151, 256, 258
Hain, Peter 159
Hale, Sir Matthew 255
Halifax, Lord 57
Hammer, Armand.......................160
Hart, H.L.A. 53, 142, 144, 231, 234, 238
Hayek, Friedrich Von.227, 228, 229
Heath, Edward............ 154, 187, 191
Henry V 15, 53, 76, 139
Henry VIII 259
Hitler, Adolf 138
Hobbes, Thomas 257
Holinshed's Chronicles 75
Hooker, Richard 218, 231, 234
Hope, Anthony 78
Hosenball, Mark 5, 41, 65, 68, 69, 166, 194
Hoxha, Enver 69
India 43
Industrial Relations Act 197110, 39, 178, 179
Ireland 125
Irvine of Lairg, Lord..................... 4
Ivanov, Eugene 32, 58, 166
James II 14, 46, 48
Joyce, William 150
Julius Caesar.75, 76, 117, 139, 155, 191
Keeler, Christine. 29, 32, 58, 59, 62, 166
Kelly, Dr David 63
Kennedy, John Fitzgerald..... 58, 65, 190
Kent 75, 82, 139, 196, 209, 222
Keynes, John Maynard 182
Kilmuir Rules 28
Kilmuir, Viscount 57
King John 50
Larkin, Philip 89
Lester of Herne Hill, Lord 4
Longfellow, Henry Wadsworth . 140
Lucan, Lord 184
Macaulay, Thomas Babington..... 47
Maclean, Donald 58, 69, 163
Macmillan, Harold . 8, 9, 28, 51, 57, 58, 60, 63, 64, 66, 144, 153, 156, 164, 190, 253, 254, 255, 256, 257, 258, 259, 260
Mafia 176
Magna Carta ..14, 47, 100, 218, 259
Manningham-Buller, Eliza 57
Mansfield, Lord 9, 10, 13, 45, 54, 64, 71, 181, 201, 202, 205, 206, 207, 208, 209, 214, 219, 220, 221, 222
Margaret Thatcher
    Bruges Speech 233, 234, 238
Marylebone Grammar School 80, 113
Maxwell, Robert 75, 139, 183
McWhirter, Ross 38, 193

Merchant of Venice 76, 139, 140
Milton, John 258
   Samson Agonistes 40, 68
Mindzenty, Cardinal 21
Morrison, Wayne 253
National Front 80, 136, 137, 138
Nelson, Lord 73
Nixon, Richard 161, 178, 198
Nkrumah, Kwame 148
Noddy 10
Northern Ireland, internment 126
Novotny, Mariella
   Affair with John Kennedy 58
Onward Christian Soldiers 222
Open University 168
Operation Countryman 198
Orpington by-election 153
Orpington, By-election 8
Package holidays 170
Parnell, Charles Stuart 60, 126
Pentonville Three 179
Persian Gulf 120, 148, 160
Petticoat Lane 184
Philby, Kim 33, 58, 69, 163
Phillips, Leslie 58
Pirates of Penzance 140
Popish Plot 31
Pornography 91, 92, 93, 94, 142, 143, 153, 177, 198
Portia 140
Pothier 128
Poulson, John 162, 184
Powell, Anthony 57
Powell, Enoch 50, 114, 115, 116, 117, 118, 147, 149, 151, 228, 230, 231, 232, 233, 234, 235, 236, 237, 238
Prices and Incomes Act 178
Primodos 170
Private Eye 184
Profumo, John ... 6, 8, 11, 29, 30, 31, 32, 33, 34, 35, 36, 58, 59, 61, 63, 64, 65, 66, 69, 144, 154, 155, 163, 164, 165, 166, 175, 222
Rachman, Peter 175, 223

Radcliffe, Lord 11, 35, 164
Raffield, Paul 259
Restrictive Trade Practices 215
Rhodesia 120, 121, 122, 123, 126, 156, 157, 158, 192, 210
Rhodesia, UDI 120, 154
Rice-Davies, Mandy 62
Robertson, Geoffrey 5
Royal Titles Bill 1953 149
Ruritania 79, 140
Salmon, Lord 30
Sandys, Duncan 60, 66, 67
   Relationship with Duchess of Argyll 60
Scarman, Lord 259
Scotland 123
Scott, Sir Walter 52
Sedley, Sir Stephen 2, 5, 6, 7, 10, 70, 258, 259
Selective Employment Tax 178
Seven Bishops, Trial of 14, 46
Sexual Offences Act 1956 ..... 32, 61
Shakespeare, William 15, 31, 45, 50, 52, 53, 56, 74, 75, 76, 77, 79, 81, 83, 117, 191, 201, 218, 237, 239
Simonds, Lord 8, 9, 57, 59
Smith, Adam 182
Soblen, Robert 163, 194
Somme, Battle of 15
South Africa . 24, 123, 157, 158, 159
St. Augustine 259
Stalin, Josef Vissarionovitch 55
Steel Strike, 1980 162
Straight, Michael 33, 65
Students 174
Suez 155
Sunday trading 173
Supreme Court Act 1981 214
Taiwan 161
Tennyson, Lord 138
Terylene 170
Thalidomide 41, 170
Thatcher, Margaret . 4, 7, 10, 37, 58, 69, 116, 118, 153, 154, 156, 190, 191, 228, 229, 230, 233, 234,

235, 237, 238, 254
The Case of Swans......................203
The Man in the Mask 35
The Man without a Head.............. 35
The Tempest 239
Thorpe, Jeremy.................60, 73, 95
Trade Union and Labour Relations
  Act 1974...............................179
Trafalgar................73, 104, 127, 150
Trapnel, X 57
Tree, Sir Herbert Beerbohm......... 81
Trevelyan, G.M. 112, 147
Vassall, John 33, 35, 58, 60, 69, 161, 164
Vietnam......................................160
Wales..125
War time bomb damage 167

Ward, Stephen.... 29, 31, 34, 36, 58, 59, 60, 61, 62, 166
Warhol, Andy............................ 177
Watergate 161, 162, 163
Wells, H.G................................... 82
Whitchurch............ 13, 45, 200, 201
Widmerpool, Kenneth 57
Wilberforce, Lord........................ 53
Wilkes, John.42, 206, 207, 214, 219
Wilson, Harold 32, 58, 154, 156, 184
Wimpole Mews 59
Windsor Park Free Festival 161
Winter of Discontent 75
Wolfenden Report 59, 142
Wordsworth, William.... 56, 80, 113
Young, Hugo................................. 7